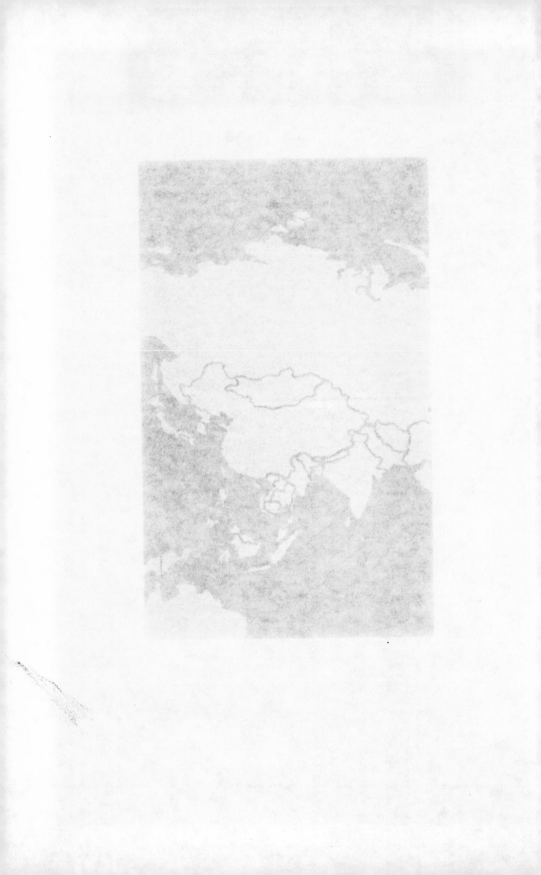

Portugal
a country study

Federal Research Division
Library of Congress
Edited by
Eric Solsten
Research Completed
January 1993

On the cover: The Tower of Belém, on the outskirts of
Lisbon, dates from the early sixteenth century.

Second Edition, First Printing, 1994.

Library of Congress Cataloging-in-Publication Data

Portugal : a country study / Federal Research Division, Library of Congress ; edited by Eric Solsten. — 2d ed.
    p. cm. — (Area handbook series, ISSN 1057-5294)
(DA Pam ; 550-181)
   Rev. ed. of: Area handbook for Portugal / coauthors, Eugene
K. Keefe . . . [et. al.]. 1st ed. 1976.
    "Research completed January 1993."
    Includes bibliographical references (pp. 285–300) and index.
    ISBN 0-8444-0776-3
    1. Portugal. I. Solsten, Eric, 1943- . II. Library of Con-
gress. Federal Research Division. III. Area handbook for Portugal. IV. Series. V. Series: DA Pam ; 550-181.
DP517.P626 1993   93-30722
946.9—dc20   CIP

Headquarters, Department of the Army
DA Pam 550-181

Reprinted without alteration
on acid-free paper

∞ ™

Bernan Press
Lanham, Maryland
April 1994

Foreword

This volume is one in a continuing series of books prepared by the Federal Research Division of the Library of Congress under the Country Studies/Area Handbook Program sponsored by the Department of Army. The last page of this book lists the other published studies.

Most books in the series deal with a particular foreign country, describing and analyzing its political, economic, social, and national security systems and institutions, and examining the interrelationships of those systems and the ways they are shaped by cultural factors. Each study is written by a multidisciplinary team of social scientists. The authors seek to provide a basic understanding of the observed society, striving for a dynamic rather than a static portrayal. Particular attention is devoted to the people who make up the society, their origins, dominant beliefs and values, their common interests and the issues on which they are divided, the nature and extent of their involvement with national institutions, and their attitudes toward each other and toward their social system and political order.

The books represent the analysis of the authors and should not be construed as an expression of an official United States government position, policy, or decision. The authors have sought to adhere to accepted standards of scholarly objectivity. Corrections, additions, and suggestions for changes from readers will be welcomed for use in future editions.

Louis R. Mortimer
Chief
Federal Research Division
Library of Congress
Washington, D.C. 20540

Acknowledgments

This edition supersedes *Portugal: A Country Study,* published in 1976. The authors wish to acknowledge their use of portions of that edition in the preparation of the current book.

Various members of the staff of the Federal Research Division of the Library of Congress assisted in the preparation of the book. Sandra W. Meditz made helpful suggestions during her review of all parts of the book. Timothy L. Merrill assisted in the preparation of some of the maps, checked the content of all the maps, and reviewed the sections on geography and telecommunications. Thanks also go to David P. Cabitto, who provided graphics support; Wayne Horn, who designed the cover and chapter art; Marilyn L. Majeska, who managed editing and production and edited portions of the manuscript; Andrea T. Merrill, who provided invaluable assistance with regard to tables and figures; and Barbara Edgerton, Alberta Jones King, and Izella Watson, who performed word processing.

The authors also are grateful to individuals in various United States government agencies who gave their time and special knowledge to provide information and perspective. These individuals include Ralph K. Benesch, who oversees the Country Studies/Area Handbook Program for the Department of the Army; and Scott B. MacDonald of the Office of the Comptroller of the Currency, who offered advice in the preparation of sections of the manuscript. In addition, the authors wish to thank various members of the staff of the Embassy of the Republic of Portugal in Washington for their assistance.

Others who contributed were Harriett R. Blood and the firm of Greenhorne and O'Mara, who assisted in the preparation of maps and charts; Mimi Cantwell, who edited the chapters; Beverly Wolpert, who performed final prepublication editorial review; Judite Fernandes, who read and commented on portions of the text; and Joan C. Cook, who prepared the index. Linda Peterson of the Library of Congress Composing Unit prepared camera-ready copy, under the direction of Peggy Pixley. The inclusion of photographs was made possible by the generosity of various individuals and public and private agencies.

Contents

Chapter 2. The Society and Its Environment 63
Howard J. Wiarda

List of Figures

xi

Preface

Like its predecessor, this study attempts to review the history and treat in a concise and objective manner the dominant social, political, economic, and military aspects of Portugal. Sources of information included books, scholarly journals, foreign and domestic newspapers, official reports of government and international organizations, and numerous periodicals on Portuguese and international affairs. Chapter bibliographies appear at the end of the book, and brief comments on some of the more valuable sources recommended for further reading appear at the end of each chapter. A Glossary is also included.

Spellings of place-names used in the book are in most cases those approved by the United States Board on Geographic Names. Exceptions are the use of Lisbon rather than Lisboa, the Portguese form of the capital's name, and Azores rather than Açores.

Measurements are given in the metric system. A conversion table is provided to assist those readers who are unfamiliar with metric measures (see table 1, Appendix).

The body of the text reflects information available as of January 1993. Certain other portions of the text, however, have been updated: the Introduction discusses significant events that have occurred since the completion of the research, and the Bibliography includes recently published sources thought to be particularly helpful to the reader.

Country Profile

Country

Formal Name: Portuguese Republic.

Short Form: Portugal.

Term for Citizen(s): Portuguese (singular and plural); adjective—Portuguese.

Capital: Lisbon (Portuguese, Lisboa).

Geography: 92,080 square kilometers; land area: 91,640 square kilometers; includes Azores (Portuguese, Açores), and Madeira islands.

NOTE—The Country Profile contains updated information as available.

Topography: Hills and mountains north of Tagus River (Rio Tejo); rolling plains to south.

Climate: Varied with considerable rainfall and marked seasonal temperatures in north; dryer conditions in south with mild temperatures along coast but sometimes very hot in interior.

Society

Population: Estimated at 10.5 million in 1992; growth rate of 0.4 percent in 1992.

Education and Literacy: Primary education (age six to twelve) and junior high school (age thirteen to fifteen) free and compulsory, but because many children began working at early age, education ended at the primary level for many. Senior high school (age sixteen to seventeen) had academic and vocational components. Twelfth grade (age eighteen) prepared youths for university and technical college. Estimated literacy rate 85 percent for those over age fifteen in 1990.

Health: Uneven provision of health care; health care available ranged from high quality to that prevalent in the Third World. Many Portuguese, especially those living in rural areas, not able to enjoy liberal health benefits provided for in legislation. Infant mortality rate greatly improved in last few decades to estimated rate of 10 per 1,000 in 1992. Life expectancy seventy-one years for males and seventy-eight for females in 1992.

Language: Portuguese.

Ethnic Groups: Homogeneous Mediterranean stock on mainland, Azores, and Madeira Islands. Less than 100,000 citizens of black African descent, who immigrated in 1970s to Portugal from its former colonies in Africa; small number of Gypsies; small Jewish community.

Religion: Nominally Roman Catholic 97 percent; Protestant denominations 1 percent; others 2 percent.

Economy

Gross Domestic Product (GDP—see Glossary): Purchasing power equivalent estimated at US$87.3 billion in 1991 (US$8,400 per capita). Economy stagnant during second half of 1970s and first half of 1980s because of world economic slump and extensive nationalizations during Revolution of 1974. Between 1986 and 1990, GDP grew at 4.6 percent each year.

Agriculture: Made up 6.1 percent of GDP and employed about 17.8 percent of labor force in 1990. Small farms in north, larger farms in south; productivity and mechanization below European Community (EC—see Glossary) levels; imports more than half of food needs. Major crops: grain, corn, rice, potatoes, olives, grapes, cork; important livestock: pigs, cattle, sheep, chickens; dairy farms mostly in northwest. EC membership threatened long-term survival of southern grain-growing and cattle-raising farms; farms producing rice, vegetables, and wine likely to fare well.

Industry: 38.4 percent of GDP in 1990. Concentrated in two regions: Lisbon-Setúbal, much heavy industry (steel, shipbuilding, oil refineries, chemicals); and Porto-Aveiro-Braga, mostly light industry (textiles, footwear, wine, food processing). In 1990 ownership of industries varied: light industry usually privately owned; heavy industry often state owned; high technology manufacturing often foreign owned.

Services: 55.5 percent of GDP in 1990; accounted for 47 percent of work force. Tourism important component of service sector; 19.6 million visitors in 1991.

Imports: In 1990 imports of goods and services accounted for about 47 percent of GDP. Manufactured goods (machinery, transportation equipment, chemicals) accounted for about 75 percent of merchandise imports, food and beverages for about 10 percent, and raw materials (mostly petroleum) for about 16 percent.

Exports: In 1990 exports of goods and services accounted for about 37 percent of GDP. Manufactured goods accounted for 80 percent of merchandise exports in 1989. In 1990 textiles, clothing, and footwear made up 37 percent of total export value; machinery and transport equipment, 20 percent; forest products, 10 percent; and agricultural products, 8 percent.

Major Trade Partners: EC major trading partner, buying nearly 75 percent of Portugal's exports, and supplying nearly 74 percent of its imports in 1992. Germany and Spain the most important trading partners. Only 3.0 percent of Portugal's imports in 1992 came from the United States; Organization of the Petroleum Exporting Countries (OPEC) accounted for less than 4 percent.

Balance of Payments: Despite negative trade balances, large earnings from tourism and remittances from Portuguese living abroad, in addition to direct foreign investment and EC transfers, resulted in generally favorable balances of payments (US$3.5 billion in 1990).

Exchange Rate: In March 1993, 151.04 escudos (Esc—see Glossary) per US$1.

Fiscal Year: Calendar year.

Transportation and Communications

Railroads: Railroad network amounting to about 3,600 kilometers in 1990, of which about 450 kilometers were electrified. Except for several small railroads owned by mining industry and Lisbon's subway system, all of Portugal railroad network operated by the state company, Caminhos de Ferro Portugueses (CP).

Roads: Total road network amounting to about 73,660 kilometers, of which 61,000 surfaced (bituminous, gravel, and crushed stone); 140 kilometers limited-access divided highway.

Inland Waterways: 820 kilometers of navigable inland waterways; relatively unimportant to economy; used by shallow-draft craft limited to 300-metric-ton capacity.

Ports: Lisbon, Leixões, and Sines fully equipped with adequate warehousing facilities. Also important: Viano do Castelo, Aveira, Figueira da Foz, Setúbal, Portimão, Ponta Delgada (Azores), and Velas (Azores).

Civil Airports: 65 total, 62 usable; 36 with permanent surface runways. Lisbon's Portela Airport, major European air terminal and transit point. International flights also scheduled to Porto, Faro, Santa Maria (Azores), São Miguel (Azores), and Funchal (Madeira).

Telecommunications: Generally adequate facilities. Integrated network of coaxial cables and microwave; numerous AM and FM radio stations; International Telecommunication Satellite Corporation (INTELSAT) and European Telecommunication Satellite Corporation (EUTELSAT) service.

Government and Politics

National Government: Constitution of 1976, substantially revised in 1982 and 1989, established system of government, both presidential and parliamentary. Division of executive power between president and the government (prime minister and his cabinet, the Council of Ministers). Division of legislative power between government and parliament (Assembly of the Republic). Government responsible to parliament, from which prime minister and most cabinet members come. President, government, and parliament have varying degrees of power and influence over each other. President elected every five years in nationwide vote; Mário Alberto Nobre Lopes Soares elected in 1986 and 1991. Assembly of the Republic, with 230 to 235 members, elected every four years if legislative period completed. Earlier election possible if parliament dissolved.

Politics: Free and democratic, with variety of parties articulating wide range of political viewpoints. Four main parties consistently in parliament since 1976: Portuguese Communist Party (Partido Comunista Português—PCP); Socialist Party (Partido Socialista—PS); Social Democrat Party (Partido Social Democrata—PSD); Social Democratic Center Party (Partido do Centro Democrático Social—CDS). Political system gradually being dominated by PSD and PS. In 1987 and 1991 national elections, PSD won with slight majorities and formed governments with its leader, Aníbal Cavaco Silva, as prime minister. PS secured 29.3 percent of the vote in 1991; PCP, 8.8 percent; CDS, 4.4 percent.

Legal System: An independent judiciary guaranteed by the constitution. Constitution also provides for Constitutional Court to review constitutionality of legislation, Supreme Court of Justice to oversee regular courts, both civil and criminal, and Supreme Administrative Court to supervise system of administrative courts. In addition, constitution mandates the appointment of ombudsman to protect rights of Portuguese citizens by investigating their complaints about actions of state authorities.

Local Government and Administration: Constitution provides for a number of administrative regions, but not yet realized. In meantime, mainland divided into eighteen districts, each named after its capital. Districts responsible for police, elections, and monitoring local government. Local government managed by 305 municipalities, further divided into about 4,000 parishes. Elections for governing assemblies of municipalities held every four years.

Autonomous Regions and Macau: Archipelagoes of Azores and Madeira enjoyed extensive autonomy since 1976. Each had own assembly; sent members to national parliament; government's representative to each region was minister of the republic. Macau, consisting of peninsula attached to the Chinese mainland and two islands, Portugal's last colony. According to agreement between Lisbon and China, Macau to become part of China in 1999, but to retain its free-market economic system.

Foreign Relations: Historically aloof from European affairs except for 1386 Treaty of Windsor with Britain. Neutral in World War II, but permitted Britain and United States military use of Azores. Since end of World War II, formed many international links. Most notably: founding member of North Atlantic Treaty Organization (NATO) in 1949, joined the United Nations (UN) in 1955, European Free Trade Association (EFTA) in 1959, Organisation for Economic Co-operation and Development (OECD) in 1961, Council of Europe in 1976, European Community (EC) in 1986, and Western European Union (WEU) in 1988.

National Security

Armed Forces (1993): Total personnel on active duty, 50,000 (17,600 conscripts); army 27,200 (15,000 conscripts); navy, 12,500 (800 conscripts); air force, 11,000 (1,800 conscripts). Reserves (all services), 210,000.

Major Units: Army has six territorial commands with one composite brigade, three infantry brigades, and one special forces brigade; navy has three commands (mainland, Azores, and Madeira) and 2,500 marines organized into three battalions (two infantry, one police); air force has one operational command of eighteen squadrons, including three attack squadrons.

Military Equipment (1993): Army has about 200 tanks, 350 armored personnel carriers, variety of other combat vehicles; 300 pieces of towed artillery; fifty-one TOW (tube-launched, optically tracked, wire-guided) missiles, sixty-five Milan wire-guided missiles, and seventeen SAM (surface-to-air) missiles; and 240 recoilless launchers. Navy had three submarines, eleven frigates (including three MEKO 200s), and twenty-nine patrol and coastal boats. Air force had 40 Alpha Jets, about seventy A-7 and A-7P Corsairs, and six Lockheed P-3B Orion maritime reconnaissance aircraft. Major transport aircraft included six C-130H Hercules and forty-four CASA C-212 planes of various types.

Military Budget 1992: US$1.7 billion, 2.0 percent of GDP.

Foreign Military Treaties: Founding member of NATO. Treaty signed in 1951 and periodically renewed permits United States use of Lajes Air Base on Terceira Island in Azores.

Internal Security Forces: National Republican Guard (Guarda Nacional Republicana—GNR), heavily armed paramilitary constabulary, consisted in 1990 of about 19,000 personnel organized into battalions in major cities and companies in district capitals.

Equipped with Commando armored cars and Alouette II helicopters. Available to quell demonstrations and labor unrest. Public Security Police (Polícia de Segurança Pública—PSP), paramilitary force responsible for security in urban areas, consisted of 17,000 personnel in 1990. Subsection, Intervention Police, could be deployed anywhere in the country. Fiscal Guard (Guarda Fiscal), border control force with staff of 8,500 in 1990, also investigated tax evasion and financial fraud.

Figure 1. Administrative Divisions, 1992

Introduction

ON APRIL 25, 1974, scores of junior Portuguese Army officers staged a coup d'état that in a manner of hours toppled the authoritarian regime that had ruled their country for nearly half a century. The virtually bloodless coup was followed by what became known to the world as the Revolution of 1974 as Portugal's archaic and repressive governing system was swept away in a period of political and social turbulence. The young officers, members of the secret Armed Forces Movement (Movimento das Forças Armadas—MFA), wished to end the wars their country had been fighting in its African colonies since the early 1960s. Their modest aim of changing Portugal's political leadership, however, let loose long pent-up social and political energies that soon turned into a veritable revolution and kept Portugal in the headlines of the world's newspapers for the next eighteen months. A nervous Western Europe looked on as Portugal's governing and financial elites fled the country or were exiled, as a variety of forces vied for dominance and the Stalinist Portuguese Communist Party (Partido Comunista Português—PCP) seemed close to seizing power, as leading banks and businesses were nationalized, and as large estates were collectivized by landless peasants.

The revolution eventually played itself out. Many of its feared consequences, such as a communist takeover or a civil war, did not occur. Moreover, many of the actions, for example nationalizations and collectivizations, that were implemented during the revolution, had been reversed to a great extent by 1993, and the serious damage done to the overall economy was gradually being repaired. The economy grew rapidly in the second half of the 1980s and continued to show respectable growth rates in the early 1990s. As another indication of improving economic health, Portugal's currency, the escudo (for value of the escudo—see Glossary), was strong enough to be placed in the exchange rate mechanism of the European Monetary System in April 1992.

The revolution's legacy also had a positive side, however, and nearly two decades after the sequence of events that began in April 1974, some remarkable achievements could be seen. After centuries of isolation and backwardness, Portugal had become an integral part of Western Europe through its membership in the European Community (EC—see Glossary). In the first half of 1992, Portugal assumed the presidency of the EC and fulfilled the obligations of this office in a professional manner. Even more significant, perhaps, were the establishment and consolidation of a system of parliamentary democracy. After a troubled start, this democracy, watched over by a free and vigorous press, had given the country a strong and competent government able to bring about peaceful change.

Portugal has a glorious past. It is the oldest European nation-state, having attained its present extent by about 1200, centuries before neighboring Spain or France became unified states. In the early decades of the fourteenth century, Portugal began a period of exploration that within a hundred years gave it an empire that literally spanned the globe.

The wealth the empire brought mainland Portugal had woeful long-term consequences, however. The country's leaders turned away from Europe and its political and technological advances. Portugal's economy battened on the colonies, rather than developing through competition with other European countries. Because Portugal was too small a country to defend its extensive possessions, much of the empire was soon lost. Even into the second half of the twentieth century, however, enough of the empire remained that Portugal continued to exist somewhat outside the world economy. The colonies provided the mainland with foodstuffs and raw materials and were a captive market for low-quality Portuguese manufactures. A greater threat to the long-term well-being of the Portuguese people than the country's backward economy, however, was perhaps the state of its social and political institutions. Long ruled by a tiny oligarchy supported by the military and a rigid authoritarian church untouched by the Reformation, the mass of the Portuguese population was passive and ignorant. The nation's wealth was reserved for a few, most of whom lived in Lisbon. The small middle class was docile and without experience in government.

The European Enlightenment had a powerful exponent of its ideas in the Marquês de Pombal, who attempted a thorough-going reform of Portugal in the third quarter of the eighteenth century. His reforms were paternalistically enforced from above, however, and after his fall from power were soon reversed. The early nineteenth century saw the fashioning of a constitutional monarchy, but parliamentary politics was soon a cynical rotation of public office among members of a small elite in Lisbon. Most of the population labored neglected and illiterate in the countryside.

A more serious attempt at parliamentary democracy occurred in 1910 when a republic, the so-called First Republic, was proclaimed. Suffrage was restricted, however, and most Portuguese were without the right to vote. The small urban middle class that was active in the republic's affairs formed into numerous personalistic parties that soon showed themselves incapable of governing. The dozens of inefficient governments in the republic's brief life of sixteen years did not win many Portuguese to the cause of parliamentary democracy. Anticlerical laws also alienated many, as did frequent instances of corruption.

When a coup by junior military officers in 1926 put an end to the First Republic, few regretted the death of Portuguese parliamentary democracy. But no member of the military was able to effectively direct Portugal's affairs, and a young economist, António de Oliveira Salazar, gradually came to govern the country. First as minister of finance, then as prime minister beginning in 1932, he brought a new order and stability to the country. In 1933 an authoritarian, traditionalist, statist system, the New State (Estado Novo), was inaugurated to protect Portugal from both Western liberal democracy and communism.

Salazar directed this regime until he was incapacitated by an accident in 1968. He was succeeded by Marcello José das Neves Caetano, who governed until April 1974. The governing system they ruled attempted to shield Portugal from such modern problems as labor strife, rapacious wealth, and departure from traditional concepts of personal morality. Salazar outlawed labor unions, replacing them with organizations that were supposed to bring labor and capital together in such a way that class conflict was avoided. He banned all political parties except one official party, rigorously controlled the press, and carefully supervised the country's few schools. Mindful of the social changes a modernizing economy engenders, he even attempted to arrest commercial change and stop the expansion of the country's small industrial sector. An extensive system of informants and an efficient secret police easily countered the regime's few opponents.

Portugal's authoritarian regime lasted for nearly half a century. It loosened its strictures on the economy somewhat after 1959, and the Portuguese economy grew at a very rapid rate until 1974. It permitted a few elections in which dissenting voices were heard but to no lasting effect. The press was allowed a slightly greater degree of freedom in the early 1970s, but otherwise the regime remained firmly in control.

The sudden collapse of the regime in April 1974 surprised everyone. Also unexpected were the engineers of its collapse, young officers who served in the military, long the regime's chief support. These officers were brought to their extreme action by the regime's stubborn determination to retain Portugal's African colonies. Having served on the front lines and seen the human costs of the wars firsthand, the officers knew that defeating the strong rebel movements in these colonies was beyond Portugal's power. They staged the April coup to stop further futile bloodshed. Their simple coup became a revolution.

The sudden and unexpected collapse of the regime created a political vacuum. Decades of political repression had left the Portuguese people with no practical experience of governing themselves. The widespread hatred of the regime barred its major figures from any active role in politics. A few younger politicians active within the regime were seen as sufficiently untainted to continue to be involved in public affairs. Their experience allowed them to assume leadership positions in several parties located on the moderate right of the political spectrum. Francisco Sá Carneiro took control of the Popular Democratic Party (Partido Popular Democrático—PPD), and Diogo Freitas do Amaral, a law professor, came to head the Party of the Social Democratic Center (Partido do Centro Democrático Social—CDS). Mário Alberto Nobre Lopes Soares, who had long opposed the regime and had endured imprisonment and exile because of his open resistance, returned to Portugal within days of the coup to lead the newly reestablished Socialist Party (Partido Socialista—PS). Communists had been active underground for decades under the leadership of the Stalinist Álvaro Cunhal, who directed the PCP from Eastern Europe. Like Soares, Cunhal also returned to Portugal immediately after the coup and plunged into the turbulent politics that filled the capital's streets and squares. Because the PCP alone among political parties had a sizeable organized infrastructure in place, it occupied a political space greater than its actual strength.

Political power was by no means limited to these parties, which in the first months of the revolution had marginal roles, but was held by a broad variety of groups. Numerous splinter groups to the left of the PCP were soon active and made themselves known through street demonstrations. The PCP-controlled labor union Intersindical emerged from its semi-underground position and worked alongside the often independent Workers' Committees, which quickly began taking control of numerous factories and businesses. The MFA, with its select military force, the Continental Operations Command (Comando Operacional do Continente—COPCON), wielded much power, as well. The most visible politician of the first months of the revolution was General António de Spínola, who became the president of the country's interim government.

Given this array of forces, there was no one center of power. Groups formed temporary alliances, giant street rallies attempted to influence the direction of politics, the PCP placed its people in many key positions in the country's public institutions, and political parties to the right of the PCP attempted to prevent a communist takeover. Given its nature as an organized and disciplined force, the military was the single most important element during the revolution, although most officers were not radicals.

A series of provisional governments was formed that with time became increasingly leftist and dominated by radical military officers. An attempted rightist coup by Spínola in March 1975 caused a leftist countermovement, a wave of nationalizations of banks and other businesses, and the seizure of many large farms in southern Portugal. Attempts to bring the revolution to the north backfired, and that region's smallholders offered the first successful resistance to the revolutionary left's program to turn Portugal into a socialist state.

Another indication that the country as a whole did not wish a revolutionary government was the April 1975 election of the Constituent Assembly, in which parties to the right of the PCP had an overwhelming majority. The assembly had no legislative powers but had as its sole purpose the drafting of a constitution for a democratic government. It began this work against the backdrop of an increasingly radical revolution.

During the summer of 1975, splits appeared within the MFA itself. Moderate elements favoring a political program akin to Scandinavian social democracy gained the upper hand in the organization, deposed the most radical of all the provisional governments in September, and put in place the last of these six governments, one destined to last until the first constitutional government came into existence in July 1976. An attempted coup in November 1975 by extremists was put down by a counterattack led by moderates. The arrest of several hundred radical officers and the dissolution of COPCON ended the radical stage of the Revolution of 1974.

The military remained active in politics, however. Although the African wars ended when the colonies were granted independence in 1975, elements of the military were determined to defend the accomplishments of the revolution. The MFA arranged with the drafters of the constitution that the military would retain guardian rights over the new democracy, ensuring that it remained true to "the spirit of the revolution." The constitution of 1976 provided for a strong president who, with the help of a military-dominated Council of the Revolution, could veto any legislation that reversed such revolutionary actions as the extensive nationalizations of 1975. General António dos Santos Ramalho Eanes, the hero of the November 1975 countercoup, was elected the new democracy's first president in 1976. An austere man of unquestioned integrity, Eanes could be trusted to preserve the revolution's gains.

The first regular parliamentary elections were held in April 1976. The winner was the PS with 35 percent of the vote, far ahead of its competitors, but not enough for an absolute majority in the new unicameral parliament, the Assembly of the Republic. With its leader Soares as prime minister, the PS formed a minority government that governed for eighteen months. When it fell because of a motion of censure, the PS formed a governing coalition with the Christian democrat CDS that lasted another year. Enormous social and economic problems, including the return of an estimated 600,000 Portuguese settlers and demobilized soldiers from Africa, combined with factionalism and personal rivalries, were the undoing of these first two constitutional governments. Eanes then appointed a series of nonpartisan caretaker governments composed of experts and technocrats in the hope that they could better deal with pressing issues and govern until the next parliamentary elections mandated by the constitution for 1980.

Each of the three caretaker governments failed, and Eanes was forced to call for early elections in December 1979, even though parliamentary elections would still have to be held the following year. The Democratic Alliance (Aliança Democrática—AD), a coalition of the PPD—now called the Social Democrat Party (Partido Social Democrata—PSD)—the CDS, and several smaller groups, won the election, but without a majority. The coalition formed a government with the forceful and charismatic PSD leader Sá Carneiro as prime minister. The AD won the October 1980 election, as well, and governed Portugal until 1983. New elections were called that year because the AD, without the leadership of Sá Carneiro, who had died in a December 1980 plane crash, had disintegrated, and no effective government could be formed.

During its time in power, however, the AD coalition had effected some far-reaching constitutional amendments that strengthened the system of parliamentary government. With the support of the PS, which gave the AD the required two-thirds majorities, constitutional amendments were passed in 1982 that weakened the power of the president and strengthened both the prime minister and the legislature. The presidency remained an essential governing institution, but the balance of political power shifted to favor the cabinet and the legislature, as in most other Western democracies. A further amendment ended the military's guardianship over the new democracy. The amendment eliminated the Council of the Revolution, through which the military had frequently vetoed legislation, and replaced it with the Constitutional Court, which functions in the same manner as similar bodies in other parliamentary democracies. President Eanes, easily reelected in late 1980 for a second five-year term, signed the amendments into law, although he opposed them because they reduced the president's powers and returned the military to the barracks.

After the 1983 parliamentary elections, the PS formed a coalition government with the PSD. The huge losses stemming from the many firms nationalized during the revolution, the enormous expansion of the numbers of those employed by the state, the effects of the two oil-price hikes of the 1970s, and the flight of much entrepreneurial talent from Portugal had left the economy in a desperate state. Inflation was as high as 30 percent a year, and many workers had real earnings lower than those of the early 1970s. In addition, many companies were in such financial straits that wages were often months in arrears.

No government had been able to deal with these economic problems in a meaningful way. The AD and PS combination that had effected some vital constitutional changes was not able to amend the constitutional provisions that declared the revolution's nationalizations irreversible. In addition, the country's labor laws in essence guaranteed employees jobs for life and made rational deployment of labor nearly impossible. Given these circumstances, the PS–PSD government had to make some very difficult decisions and became unpopular as the economy worsened. The alliance, troubled also by personal rivalries, collapsed in early 1985.

The PSD began its political ascent in the 1985 parliamentary elections. As the senior partner in the coalition and with its leader Soares as prime minister, the PS was blamed by voters for the failures of the fallen government; it polled only 20.8 percent of the vote, compared with 36.3 percent in 1983. Despite its participation in the government, the PSD won more votes than ever before, 29.9 percent, and for the first time was the party with the most parliamentary seats. Much of the PSD's success was due to its new leader, Aníbal Cavaco Silva, who waged a clever campaign and presented his party in a new light. His personal qualities of austerity, probity, and competence appealed to many Portuguese, who saw in him, an economist and former minister of finance, someone who could deal with the country's serious problems.

Cavaco Silva formed a minority single-party government with himself as prime minister and managed to remain in power for nearly a year and a half. He was fortunate in that painful economic decisions made by the previous government began to bear fruit during his time in office. Portugal's accession to the EC at the beginning of 1986 also benefited the country; the first of the organization's extensive aid packages began to improve Portugal's backward infrastructure almost immediately. When a motion of censure brought down the PSD government in the spring of 1987, Soares, elected president in early 1986, decided to call new elections in July 1987 rather than form another weak single-party or coalition government.

The improving economy and the feeling on the part of many Portuguese that the PSD was taking their country in the right direction allowed the party to win an absolute parliamentary majority in the national elections of 1987. The 50.2 percent of the vote gave the party a solid parliamentary majority, the first in the new democracy, and permitted the formation of a strong single-party government. Cavaco Silva's government also became the first to serve out the entire four-year legislative term. In 1991 Cavaco Silva led his party to a second victory in which it again won more than 50 percent of the vote and 135 seats in the 230-seat parliament.

For many observers, the PSD's electoral successes and the stability of the Cavaco Silva government indicated that Portugal's new democracy, the Second Republic as it is often called, had at last taken root. During the first decade of the new political system, there were numerous weak governments, and four national elections were called because no effective governing coalitions were available. This instability caused some observers to fear that Portugal's second attempt at parliamentary democracy might eventually prove as unsuccessful as was the First Republic.

The Second Republic was more fortunate than the First Republic in several regards, however. Despite its serious problems, Portugal had come to enjoy a much greater prosperity and a higher level of education than in the first decades of the century. As a result, the Portuguese were better able to understand public affairs than in the past. In addition, the new government possessed a greater legitimacy because it was based on universal suffrage and high rates of voter participation. Portugal was also lucky to have a number of capable politicians committed to establishing parliamentary democracy. Also vital was the willingness of the military to abide by the laws of the new republic. All of these factors contributed to the eventual success of the new political system.

However healthy Portuguese democracy was by the 1990s, it still exhibited some shortcomings. Factionalism, whether caused by ideology or personal ambition, was still noticeable. Strict party discipline ensured a degree of party unity, but party ''barons'' sometimes put personal welfare before that of their parties. Small parties centered around an individual were less common than in the past, but in the 1985 elections a big winner was a short-lived group pledged to President Eanes. The parties sometimes overshadowed

the Assembly of the Republic as centers of political power, but internal reforms, increased support staff, and an evolving institutional ethos had increased that body's performance to the benefit of parliamentary democracy.

By the early 1990s, Portuguese democracy appeared to be moving to a two-party system consisting of the PSD and the PS. The two parties together won nearly 80 percent of the vote in the 1991 national elections and between them controlled 90 percent of the seats in parliament. As of early 1993, there was no reason to think this dominance would be upset in the near future.

The PSD, in power since early 1980 through coalitions with parties first to its right, then to its left, and then through both minority and majority single-party governments, gradually came to occupy a large place in the middle of the political spectrum. Generally, the PSD held views similar to those advocated by liberal Republicans in the United States. Aníbal Cavaco Silva, the party's leader since 1985, remained very popular with Portuguese voters, and the government he formed after the October 1991 elections was expected to remain in power for the entire legislative period scheduled to end in late 1995.

Portugal's other leading political party, the PS, had lost its early dominance but far outdistanced its nearest rivals, the PCP and the CDS. The PS had been troubled by leadership problems and inept campaigns since Soares resigned as its head to campaign for the presidency in the mid-1980s. However, it renamed dominant in many areas and won the 1989 local elections. The PS had gradually moved to the center of the political spectrum, having long abandoned the fierce advocacy of socialism that characterized it in the mid-1970s. Indeed, by the early 1990s, its positions on main issues were often hard to distinguish from those of the PSD. To the right of the PSD was the Christian democratic CDS. Long led by its founder Diogo Freitas do Amaral, who nearly won the presidency in 1986, the CDS had seen a steady erosion of support in national elections during the 1980s. The party was last part of a government in early 1983, and only a weakening of the PSD seemed likely to bring it back into power as a coalition partner.

The only major political party not regarded as a wholehearted supporter of liberal democracy was the PCP. Parties to its right never saw the PCP as a suitable coalition partner, however, and after the constitution of 1976 became effective, it was never part of any cabinet. The PCP had many supporters in some southern areas, both rural and industrial, but rival parties were making headway even in these traditional strongholds. The PCP remained resolutely Stalinist even into the 1990s, expelling members who sought to reform it. The PCP's share of votes declined during the 1980s, and by the 1991 election it had lost half its support. This decline and an aging membership suggested that the PCP was condemned to political marginality.

The first decade of the Second Republic was marked by frequent political missteps and failures; the decade was also a very difficult one for Portugal's economy, and in some years there were real declines in both wages and production. This situation was a painful contrast to the accelerated rates of growth between 1960 and 1973 when the Salazar-Caetano regime had allowed partial economic liberalization and increased foreign investment. Growth ended, however, when the revolution's extensive nationalizations and the subsequent mismanagement of the government's large holdings were exacerbated by the global recession caused by the oil price hikes of 1973 and 1979.

Austerity measures undertaken in the mid-1980s and large transfers of financial aid to Portugal by the EC led to a sustained period of growth in the latter half of the 1980s and early 1990s that was among the best achieved by member countries of the Organisation for Economic Co-operation and Development (OECD—see Glossary). Growth was further strengthened by substantial direct foreign investment (US$15 billion in the 1989–92 period) and the government's sales of many companies nationalized during the revolution (nearly US$6 billion in the same period). However favorable these trends were, during the remainder of the 1990s the resourcefulness of Portugal's businesspeople and politicians will be seriously challenged by long-term structural problems in Portugal's economy and its complete opening by 1995 to competition from more efficient rivals in the EC.

Portugal's agricultural sector is only one-half to one-fourth as productive as those of most other EC member states, despite US$2 billion of EC funds that had been invested in modernization efforts between 1986 and the early 1990s. Although nearly one-fifth of the work force was engaged in agriculture in the early 1990s, as much as one-half of the food the country consumed had to be imported. The small fragmented farms of the north are probably too small for efficient farming. Progress has been made in introducing modern methods and equipment to the large estates in the south, many of which were collective farms for a time, but as a whole the sector remains overstaffed and backward.

The industrial sector consists of three components: modern foreign-owned plants that produce a large variety of sophisticated products; a large, generally unprofitable state-owned sector, often concentrated in heavy industry; and privately owned, often quite small and labor-intensive manufacturing firms that have managed to survive international competition because of protective tariffs and low wages. Modern high-technology companies are likely to continue to prosper in the 1990s. The nationalized sector is being privatized by the Cavaco Silva government, and those companies that appear to have a promising future have found buyers. Portugal's privately owned companies, active in textiles, shoe manufacturing, food processing, and similar activities, are likely to find the 1990s difficult. Often too small to purchase or use modern equipment and slow to learn the latest managerial methods, a good number of these firms might well not survive the decade.

Portugal's service sector is also in the throes of meeting the challenges of the European single market (see Glossary). Tourism remains vital to the country and is being upgraded. The financial sector is being transformed by foreign firms that have set up companies in Portugal. The many banks the government nationalized in 1975 were being sold off at a brisk rate in the early 1990s. Portuguese banking as a whole is overstaffed and underautomated, but foreign competition is forcing the sector to strive for greater efficiency.

The government also attempted to deal with legacies of both the Salazar regime and the revolutionary period when it proposed streamlining the state bureaucracy and reforming labor laws. Persistence is needed to deal with the deadening effects of a too large and unresponsive government bureaucracy, which during Salazar's rule had come to regulate much of everyday life and then was expanded in the revolutionary mid-1970s. The bureaucracy takes many of the state's resources and through extensive regulation hinders ordinary citizens in their dealings with state authorities and firms in the conduct of their business. Labor laws passed during the revolution made dismissing employees very difficult. Attempts to reform employment methods have had only moderate success and foundered on union resistance. Companies have circumvented some of these laws by resorting to fixed-term work contracts, but personnel management practices still had not been put on a wholly rational footing as of the early 1990s.

Portugal needs a well-trained work force in order to fare well in an increasingly competitive world economy. More Portuguese are being educated than ever before, even at the university level, which long had been reserved for a tiny elite. It was estimated, however, that in the early 1990s up to 20 percent of Portuguese over the age of fifteen were illiterate. This illiteracy rate represented a striking improvement over the 1930 rate of 68 percent but was still much higher than the European average. Even at the beginning of the 1990s, most Portuguese had had only five or six years of schooling, and the percentage of children attending school beyond the sixth grade was below the EC average by a wide margin. Morale in the teaching profession was also low because teachers, like most state employees, were very poorly paid. EC financial transfers to Portugal to raise the standards of the country's education were significant, but much remained to be done before Portuguese schooling corresponded to that of other West European countries.

The severity of the education system's problems is matched by the serious problems found throughout Portugal's social welfare and health systems. A comprehensive social welfare system had been established by law in the second half of the 1970s but never fully realized, and benefit payments and pensions were set at a very low level. Significant progress had been made in reducing infant mortality and dealing with some other health problems, but public health care is not generally up to West European standards. The country's backwardness when measured against the rest of the EC, with the exception of Greece, is striking and could be seen as a legacy of Portugal's long isolation from Europe and the repression of the Salazar regime.

Given the advances made in the two decades after 1974, however, Portuguese have reasons to rejoice. Poverty remains, especially in rural areas, and housing is frequently inadequate, but the population as a whole lives better than ever before. The traditional necessity to emigrate to find employment that had forced millions of Portuguese to leave their country, especially in the 1960s when Paris, in effect, became the second largest Portuguese city, has lessened greatly. Many Portuguese can now find employment at home, if not in rural regions where emigration is still the rule, then along the coasts where most Portuguese have come to live. The improved economy also gives young Portuguese a greater choice in occupations and a chance for social mobility.

A modernizing society also presents Portuguese with opportunities for a better life. Portuguese society is more varied than during the Salazar period. The free media have brought the outside world to the Portuguese and engendered a greater liberality in how people lived. Divorce was permitted in the old regime, but abortion not legalized until 1984. The change went through despite the opposition of the Roman Catholic Church, which has become less influential. More Portuguese women work outside the home, and if occupational opportunities are not yet as great as those enjoyed by women in Northern Europe, Portuguese women are freer than their mothers. Until 1969, for example, Portuguese women who were not heads of households had to have the permission of their husbands or male relatives to obtain passports. In the new Portugal, in contrast, a government agency existed with the purpose of preventing discrimination against women.

The greatest achievement of the Portuguese people since 1974, however, and the one that has allowed and encouraged other positive developments and permitted confidence about the future, is the consolidation of a system of parliamentary democracy, the first successful such system in the country's history. It is hoped that a modern political system responsive to the people's needs will allow the Portuguese to prepare for the next century in a united Europe.

October 9, 1993   Eric Solsten

Chapter 1. Historical Setting

Ruins of Roman temple in Évora

THE HISTORY OF PORTUGAL can be divided into seven broad periods. The first begins in the Paleolithic period and extends to the formation of Portugal as an independent monarchy. During this period, Lusitania, that portion of the western Iberian Peninsula known today as Portugal, experienced many waves of conquest and settlement by Iberos, Phoenicians, Greeks, Romans, Swabians, Visigoths, and Muslims. Of these successive waves of people, the Romans left the greatest imprint on present Portuguese society.

The second broad period of Portuguese history runs from the founding of the monarchy in 1128 until the disappearance of the House of Burgundy, Portugal's first dynasty, in 1383. During this period, the monarchy was established and expanded by reconquering territory from the Muslims and populating those lands with Christian settlers. Consolidation and economic development were furthered by policies designed to increase agricultural productivity.

The third period begins with the founding of the House of Avis, Portugal's second ruling dynasty. During this period, Portugal experienced a dynastic struggle that brought the House of Avis to the throne, a series of wars with Castile that threatened the independence of the new kingdom, a social revolution, a second dynastic struggle, and the assertion of royal supremacy over the nobility.

The fourth period begins in 1415 when the Portuguese seized Ceuta in Morocco, thus beginning Portugal's maritime expansion. During this period, Portugal explored the west coast of Africa, discovered and colonized Madeira and the Azores, opened the passage to India around Africa, built an empire in Asia, and colonized Brazil.

The fifth period, that of imperial decline, begins with the dynastic crisis of 1580, which saw the demise of the House of Avis. During this period, Portugal was part of the Iberian Union until 1640, when the monarchy was restored and a new dynasty, the House of Bragança, was established. This period includes the advent of absolutism in Portugal and ends with the Napoleonic invasions in the early 1800s.

The sixth period, the period of constitutional monarchy, begins with the liberal revolution of 1820, which established in Portugal for the first time a written constitution. This period includes a civil war in which constitutionalists triumphed over absolutists, the winning of independence by Brazil, and the exploration of Portugal's

3

African possessions. It ends with the collapse of *rotativismo* (see Glossary) in the early twentieth century.

The final period begins in 1910 with the downfall of the monarchy and the establishment of the First Republic. This period includes the corporative republic of António de Oliveira Salazar; the collapse of that regime on April 25, 1974; and the establishment of Portugal's present democratic regime, the Second Republic.

Origins of Portugal

The Iberian Peninsula is a geographic unit encompassing a number of distinct regions distinguished by different climate and geomorphology, such as Andalusia, Castile, Galicia, and Lusitania. Lusitania, which now encompasses the modern nation-state of Portugal, is generally set off from the other regions of the peninsula by areas of higher elevation running parallel to the Atlantic coast, greater rainfall, and a more moderate climate. It was this regional distinctiveness, as well as the internal geography of Lusitania—an area largely open to the south but hemmed in by mountains on the east and the Atlantic Ocean on the west—that gave rise to a culturally and socially distinct people, the Portuguese, and later to an independent nation-state, Portugal.

Early Inhabitants

Lusitania has been inhabited since the Paleolithic period, and implements made by humans have been found at widely scattered sites. The Ice Ages did not touch Lusitania, and it was only after the disappearance of the Paleolithic hunting cultures that a warmer climate gave rise to a river-centered culture. At the end of the Paleolithic period, about 7000 B.C., the valley of the Tagus River (Rio Tejo) was populated by hunting and fishing tribes, who lived at the mouths of the river's tributaries. These people left huge kitchen middens containing the remains of shellfish and crustaceans, as well as the bones of oxen, deer, sheep, horses, pigs, wild dogs, badgers, and cats. Later, perhaps about 3000 B.C., Neolithic peoples constructed crude dwellings and began to practice agriculture. They used polished stone tools, made ceramics, and practiced a cult of the dead, building many funerary monuments called dolmens. By the end of the Neolithic period, about 2000 B.C., regions of cultural differentiation began to appear among the Stone Age inhabitants of the Iberian Peninsula, one of these being the western Megalithic culture. Present-day Portugal is thus rich in Megalithic neocropolises, the best known of which are at Palmela, Alcalar, Reguengos, and Monsaraz.

The Paleolithic and Neolithic periods were followed by the Bronze Age and the Iron Age (probably between 1500 and 1000 B.C.). During this time, the Iberian Peninsula was colonized by various peoples. One of the oldest were the Lígures, about whom little is known. Another were the Iberos, thought to have come from North Africa. The Iberos were a sedentary people who used a primitive plow, wheeled carts, had writing, and made offerings to the dead.

Phoenicians, Greeks, and Carthaginians

In the twelfth century B.C., Phoenicians arrived on the west coast of the Iberian Peninsula in search of metals and founded trading posts at Cádiz, Málaga, and Seville. They traded with the peoples of the interior, taking out silver, copper, and tin and bringing in eastern trade goods. Between the eighth century and sixth century B.C., successive waves of Celtic peoples from central Europe invaded the western part of the peninsula, where the topography and climate were well suited to their herding-farming way of life. They settled there in large numbers and blended in with the indigenous Iberos, giving rise to a new people known as Celtiberians. Their settlements were hilltop forts called *castros,* many vestiges of which remain in northern Portugal.

Later, during the seventh century B.C., Greeks arrived and founded several colonies, including Sargunto on the Mediterranean coast and Alcácer do Sal on the Atlantic coast. During the fifth century B.C., the Carthaginians replaced the Phoenicians and closed the Straits of Gibraltar to the Greeks. The Carthaginians undertook the conquest of the peninsula but were only able to permanently occupy the territory in the south originally controlled by their Phoenician and Greek predecessors. The Carthaginian occupation lasted until the defeat of Carthage by the Romans in the third century B.C.

The Romans made the former Carthaginian territory into a new province of their expanding empire and conquered and occupied the entire peninsula. This invasion was resisted by the indigenous peoples, the stiffest resistance coming from the Lusitanians who lived in the western part of the peninsula. The Lusitanians were led by warrior chieftains, the most powerful of whom was Viriato. Viriato held up the Roman invasion for several decades until he was murdered in his bed by three of his own people who had been bribed by the Romans. His death brought the Lusitanian resistance to an end, and Rome relatively quickly conquered and occupied the entire peninsula. The Portuguese have claimed Viriato as the country's first great national hero.

Romanization

After the conquest was completed, the Romans gathered the indigenous peoples into jurisdictions, each with a Roman center of administration and justice. Olissipo (present-day Lisbon) served as the administrative center of Roman Portugal until the founding of Emerita (present-day Mérida, Spain) in A.D. 25. By the beginning of the first century A.D., Romanization was well underway in southern Portugal. A senate was established at Ebora (present-day Évora); schools of Greek and Latin were opened; industries such as brick making, tile making, and iron smelting were developed; military roads and bridges were built to connect administrative centers; and monuments, such as the Temple of Diana in Évora, were erected. Gradually, Roman civilization was extended to northern Portugal, as well. The Lusitanians were forced out of their hilltop fortifications and settled in bottom lands in Roman towns (*citânias*).

The *citânias* were one of the most important institutions imposed on Lusitania during the Roman occupation. It was in the *citânias* that the Lusitanians acquired Roman civilization: they learned Latin, the lingua franca of the peninsula and the basis of modern Portuguese; they were introduced to Roman administration and religion; and in the third century, when Rome converted to Christianity, so did the Lusitanians. The Roman occupation left a profound cultural, economic, and administrative imprint on the entire Iberian Peninsula that remains to the present day.

Germanic Invasions

In 406 the Iberian Peninsula was invaded by Germanic peoples consisting of Vandals, Swabians, and Alans, a non-Germanic people of Iranian stock who had attached themselves to the Vandals. Within two years, the invaders had spread to the west coast. The Swabians were primarily herders and were drawn to Galicia because the climate was similar to what they had left behind. The Vandals settled to the north of Galicia but soon left with the remnants of the Alans for the east. After the departure of the Vandals, the Swabians moved southward and settled among the Luso-Romans, who put up no resistance and assimilated them easily. The urban life of the *citânias* gave way to the Swabian custom of dispersed houses and smallholdings, a pattern that is reflected today in the land tenure pattern of northern Portugal. Roman administration disappeared. The capital of Swabian hegemony was present-day Braga, but some Swabian kings lived in the Roman city of Cale (present-day Porto) at the mouth of the Rio Douro. The city was a customs post between Galicia and Lusitania. Gradually, the city came to be called Portucale, a compound of *portus* (port) and Cale. This name also referred to the vast territory to the immediate north and south of the banks of the river upstream from the city.

With large parts of the peninsula now outside their control, in 415 the Romans commissioned the Visigoths, the most highly Romanized of the Germanic peoples, to restore Rome's hegemony. The Visigoths forced the Vandals to sail for North Africa and defeated the Swabians. The Swabian kings and their Visigothic overlords held commissions to govern in the name of the emperor; their kingdoms were thus part of the Roman Empire. Latin remained the language of government and commerce. The Visigoths, who had been converted to Christianity in the fifth century, decided to organize themselves into an independent kingdom with their capital at Toledo. The kingdom was based on the principle of absolute monarchy, each sovereign being elected by an assembly of nobles. Visigothic kings convoked great councils made up of bishops and nobles to assist in deciding ecclesiastical and civil matters. Visigoths gradually fused with the Swabians and Hispano-Romans into a single politico-religious entity that lasted until the eighth century, when the Iberian Peninsula fell under Muslim domination.

Muslim Domination

In 711 Iberia was invaded by a Muslim army commanded by Tariq ibn Ziyad. The last Visigothic king, Rodrigo, tried to repel this invasion but was defeated. The Muslims advanced to Córdoba and then to Toledo, the Visigothic capital. The last resistance of the Visigoths was made at Mérida, which fell in June 713 after a long siege. In the spring of 714, a Muslim army commanded by Musa ibn Nusair marched to Saragossa and then to León and Astorga. Évora, Santarém, and Coimbra fell by 716. Thus, within five years, the Muslims had conquered and occupied the entire peninsula. Only a wedge of wet, mountainous territory in the extreme northwest called Astúrias remained under Christian control.

In Lusitania land was divided among Muslim troops. However, bad crops and a dislike for the wet climate put an end to the short-lived Muslim colonization along the Rio Douro. Muslims preferred the dry country below the Tagus River because it was more familiar, especially the Algarve, an area of present-day Portugal where the Muslim imprint remains the strongest. The Muslim aristocracy settled in towns and revived urban life; others fanned out across the countryside as small farmers. The Visigothic peasants readily converted to Islam, having only been

7

superficially Christianized. Some Visigothic nobles continued to practice Christianity, but most converted to Islam and were confirmed by the Muslims as local governors. Jews, who were always an important element in the urban population, continued to exercise a significant role in commerce and scholarship.

Al Andalus, as Islamic Iberia was known, flourished for 250 years, under the Caliphate of Córdoba. Nothing in Europe approached Córdoba's wealth, power, culture, or the brilliance of its court. The caliphs founded schools and libraries; they cultivated the sciences, especially mathematics; they introduced arabesque decoration into local architecture; they explored mines; they developed commerce and industry; and they built irrigation systems, which transformed many arid areas into orchards and gardens. Finally, the Muslim domination introduced more than 600 Arabic words into the Portuguese language.

The Golden Age of Muslim domination ended in the eleventh century when local nobles, who had become rich and powerful, began to carve up the caliphate into independent regional city-states (*taifas*), the most important being the emirates of Badajoz, Mérida, Lisbon, and Évora. These internecine struggles provided an opportunity for small groups of Visigothic Christians, who had taken refuge in the mountainous northwest of the peninsula, to go on the offensive against the Muslims, thus beginning the Christian Reconquest of Iberia.

Christian Reconquest

Although their empire had been defeated by the Muslim onslaught, individual Visigothic nobles resisted, taking refuge in the mountain stronghold of Astúrias. As early as 737, the Visigothic noble Pelayo took the offensive and defeated the Muslims at Covadonga, for which he was proclaimed king of Astúrias, later León. Subsequent kings of Astúrias-León, who claimed succession from Visigothic monarchs, were able to retake Braga, Porto, Viseu, and Guimarães in northern Portugal, where they settled Christians around strongholds. For 200 years, this region was a buffer zone across which the frontier between Christians and Muslims shifted back and forth with the ebb and flow of attack and counterattack.

The creation of Portugal as an independent monarchy is clearly associated with the organization of the military frontier against the Muslims in this area. This buffer zone between Christian and Muslim territory was constantly being reorganized under counts appointed by the kings of León. The territory known as Portucalense was made a province of León and placed under the control of counts, who governed with a substantial degree of autonomy because the province was separated from León by rugged mountains.

In 1096 Alfonso VI, king of León, gave hereditary title to the province of Portucalense and Coimbra as dowry to the crusader-knight Henry, brother of the duke of Burgundy, upon his marriage to the king's illegitimate but favorite daughter, Teresa. Although Henry was to be sovereign in Portucalense, it was recognized by all parties that he held this province as a vassal of the Leonese king. Henry set up his court at Guimarães near Braga. He surrounded himself with local barons, appointed them to the chief provincial offices, and rewarded them with lands. Bound by the usual ties of vassal to suzerain, Henry was expected to be loyal to Alfonso and render him service whenever required. Until Alfonso's death in 1109, Henry dutifully carried out his feudal obligations by attending royal councils and providing military assistance in the king's campaigns against the Muslims. Alfonso's death plunged the kingdom of León into a civil war among Aragonese, Galician, and Castilian barons who desired the crown. Count Henry carefully stayed neutral during this struggle and gradually stopped fulfilling his feudal obligations. When he died in 1112, his wife Teresa inherited the county and initially followed her husband's policy of nonalignment.

The victor in the struggle for the Leonese crown was Alfonso VII, who, when he ascended the throne, decided to assert his suzerainity over Teresa, his aunt, and her consort, a Galician nobleman named Fernando Peres. Teresa refused to do homage and was forced into submission after a six-week war in 1127. Her barons, who saw their fortunes and independence declining, took this opportunity to align themselves with her son and the heir to the province, Afonso Henriques, who had armed himself as a knight. Supported by the barons and lower nobility, Afonso Henriques rebelled against his mother's rule. On July 24, 1128, he defeated Teresa's army at São Mamede near Guimarães and expelled her to Galicia, where she died in exile. Afonso Henriques thus gained control of the province of Portucalense, or Portugal, as it was known in the vernacular.

Formation of the Monarchy

Afonso Henriques was a robust, visionary young man of about twenty years of age when he acquired control of the province of Portugal. He was anxious to free himself from León and establish his own kingdom. Consequently, he invaded Galicia and defeated Fernando Peres and the Galician barons at the Battle of Cerneja. This action brought a response from Alfonso VII, who had in the meantime proclaimed himself emperor. He ordered the Galician barons to make war on Afonso Henriques, who, threatened by Muslims from the south recently reinvigorated by the Almohads from Morocco, made peace with Alfonso VII in 1137 at Tuy.

Afonso Henriques Becomes King

After the peace of Tuy, Afonso Henriques temporarily turned his attention to the Muslim threat in the south. In 1139 he struck deep into the heart of Al Andalus and defeated a Muslim army at Ourique, a place in the Alentejo. After this battle, Afonso Henriques began to be referred to in documents as king. In 1140 he renewed his claim on southern Galicia, which he invaded. This action again sparked a reaction by Alfonso VII who, in return, marched on Portugal. The two armies met at Arcos de Valdevez and engaged in a joust won by the Portuguese knights. Afonso Henriques's self-proclamation as king was finally recognized in 1143 at the Conference of Samora when Alfonso VII recognized him as such, although, because he was an emperor, Alfonso VII still considered Afonso Henriques his vassal.

Territorial Enlargement

Afonso Henriques was a brilliant military commander and during his reign reconquered more Muslim territory than any other of the Christian kings on the peninsula. He established his capital at Coimbra, and as early as 1135 he built a castle at Leiria. In 1147 he took advantage of a series of religious rebellions among the Muslims, and, with the help of a passing fleet of English, Flemish, and German crusaders bound for Palestine, captured Lisbon after a seventeen-week siege. Continued internecine fighting among the Muslims, Lisbon's strategic location, and additional help from passing fleets of crusaders eventually allowed Afonso Henriques to advance across the Tagus and capture and hold large sections of the Alentejo. As a result of this vigorous prosecution of the reconquest, the pope officially recognized Afonso Henriques as king of Portugal in 1179 and granted him all conquered lands over which neighboring kings could not prove rights. At his death in 1185, Afonso Henriques had carved out an officially recognized Christian kingdom that extended well into Muslim Iberia.

Sancho I (r.1185–1211), Afonso Henriques's son and heir, continued to enlarge the realm. In 1189 he captured the Muslim castle

Afonso Henriques, founder and first king of Portugal (r. 1139–85)
Courtesy Embassy of Portugal, Washington

11

at Alvor, the city of Silves, and the castle at Albufeira. These territories however, were retaken by the Muslims and had to be reconquered by his son and heir, Afonso II (r.1211–23). With the help of his brother-in-law, Alfonso VIII of Castile, Afonso retook territory in the Alentejo, fighting major battles at Navas de Tolosa in 1212 and Alcácer do Sal in 1217. Sancho II (r.1223–48) conquered additional territory in the Alentejo and carried the Reconquest into the Algarve, where Muslim armies were defeated at Tavira and Cacela in 1238. The Reconquest was completed by Afonso III (r.1248–79) in 1249 when he attacked and defeated an isolated enclave of Muslims ensconced at Faro in the Algarve. This last battle, which extended Portuguese territory to the sea, established the approximate territorial limits Portugal has had ever since (see fig. 2).

Settlement and Cultivation

The rapid advance of Afonso Henriques from Coimbra to Lisbon created a vast, relatively uninhabited tract of land between north and south. The repopulation of this deserted territory with Christian settlers began immediately. Afonso Henriques invited many of the crusaders to remain after the siege of Lisbon and granted them lands, especially at Atouguia and Lourinhã, as payment for their help. In addition, Sancho I directed most of his time and energy to settling the new monarchy, for which he is known as The Populator (O Povoador). He sent agents abroad, especially to Burgundy, the land of his ancestors, to recruit colonists, who settled at various places, but especially at Vila dos Francos (present-day Azambuja). Such communities spread rapidly throughout the realm thanks to the protection of the king, who saw in them not only a way to populate the kingdom but also a way to diminish the power of the nobility.

The vacant territory between north and south was also filled by various monastic orders, including the Franciscans, Dominicans, and Benedictines. The Roman Catholic Church granted charters to the orders to build monasteries and cultivate the surrounding land. The most successful of these orders were the Benedictines, who built a monastery at Alcobaça and planted the surrounding land in orchards that remain to this day. This monastery grew to over 5,000 monks and occupied a huge territory stretching from Leiria in the north to Óbidos in the south, including the port-town of Pederneira (present-day Nazaré).

In the valley of the Tagus and to the south, settling communities of unarmed colonists was too dangerous; therefore, early

Portuguese kings called upon religious-military orders to fortify, cultivate, and defend this territory. Founded in the early twelfth century to wage war against infidels and protect pilgrims, these religious orders of knights had become powerful in the Holy Land and in many areas of Europe. Several orders of knight-monks were given huge tracts of land in the Tagus Valley and the Alentejo as recompense for their military service to the king at a time when he had no standing army on which to rely. The most successful of these knight-monks was the Order of the Templars, which was granted territory on the Rio Zêzere, a tributary of the Tagus, where they built a fortified monastery in Templar fashion at Tomar. The Templar domain gradually grew to encompass territory from Tomar in the north to Santarém in the south and as far west as the lands of the Benedictines at Alcobaça. As more territory in the Alentejo was reconquered, additional orders were granted tracts of land to defend and cultivate. The Order of the Hospitallers was given land surrounding Crato; the Order of the Calatravans (later Avis) was established at Évora; and the Order of the Knights of Saint James was given lands at Palmela.

Political and Social Organization

Afonso Henriques and subsequent Portuguese kings ruled by divine right until a constitutional monarchy was established in the early nineteenth century. The early kings were assisted by a royal council composed of the king's closest advisers and friends from among the higher nobility and clergy. The royal council was staffed by a number of functionaries, such as the chancellor, who kept the royal seal and was the highest official in the land; the notary, who gave advice on legal matters; the scribe, who wrote the king's letters and documents (many early kings were illiterate); and the majordomo, who commanded the king's household guard.

When questions of exceptional importance arose, the king would convoke the cortes, an expanded royal council that brought together representatives of the three estates of the realm: nobility, clergy, and commoners. The first such cortes was called in 1211 at Coimbra in order to legitimate the succession of Afonso II, Afonso Henriques's grandson, to the throne, as well as to approve certain laws of the realm. After the Cortes of Leiria, which was convoked in 1254 by Afonso III, representatives of the self-governing settler communities began to attend. Cortes were convoked at the king's will and were limited to advising on issues raised by the king and presenting petitions and complaints. Resolutions passed by the cortes did not have the force of law unless they were countersigned

Figure 2. The Reconquest, 1185–1250

by the king. Later, the cortes came to limit the power of the king somewhat, but gradually the monarchy became absolute. The cortes was convoked less and less frequently, and in 1697 it stopped being called altogether.

As to territorial administration, northern Portugal was subdivided into estates (*terras*), each a quasi-autonomous political and economic unit of feudal suzerainity governed by a nobleman (*donatário*) whose title to the land was confirmed by the king. Religious administration

14

was carried out by the Roman Catholic Church, which divided the north into bishoprics and parishes. In the south, administration was the responsibility of the military orders: Templars, Hospitallers, Calatravans, and Knights of Saint James. In the center, administration fell to the monastic orders: Benedictines, Franciscans, and Dominicans. The towns and communities of settlers, as well as a certain amount of land around them, were owned by the king, who was responsible for regulating them.

The settler communities (*concelhos*) were each recognized by a royal franchise, which granted local privileges, set taxes, specified rights of self-government, and controlled the relationship among the crown, the *concelho,* and the *donatário,* if the community was located within a *terra.* Each *concelho* governed itself through an assembly chosen from among its resident "good men" (*homens-bons*); that is, freemen not subject to the jurisdiction of the church, the local *donatário,* or the special statutes governing Muslims and Jews. Each *concelho* was administered by a local magistrate, who was assisted by several assessors selected from among the *homens-bons* of the assembly. The tutelary power of the king was represented by an official (*alcalde*) appointed by the king, who was empowered to intervene in local matters on the king's behalf when necessary to ensure justice and good administration. The degree of self-government of these communities gradually declined as the monarchy became increasingly centralized.

During its formative stages, Portugal had three social classes: clergy, nobility, and commoners. By virtue of the religious fervor of the times, the clergy was the predominant class. It was the most learned, the wealthiest, and occupied the highest office in the realm: the chancellorship. The clergy comprised two categories; the bishops and parish priests of the regular church hierarchy and the abbots and monks of the religious and military orders. These two categories were divided into the higher clergy (bishops and abbots) and low clergy (priests and monks). The clergy enjoyed various privileges and rights, such as judgment in ecclesiastical courts according to canon law, exemption from taxes, and the right to asylum from civil authorities within their churches.

The next social class, the nobility, owed its privileged position above all to its collaboration with the king in the reconquest. The highest level among the nobility was made up of the "rich men" (*homens-ricos*) who owned the largest feudal estates, had private armies, and had jurisdiction over great expanses of territory. Below them were the lesser nobility, who held smaller estates and were entrusted with the defense of castles and towns but did not have private armies or administrative jurisdiction. Below the lesser nobility were the highest class of free commoners, the villein-knights, who maintained their own horses and weaponry, serving the king as required. These knights were often encouraged to settle in or near the colonial communities of the frontier where they were granted special privileges and organized raids against the Muslims for their own profit.

The commoners formed the bottom of the social strata. Among them, the serfs were the lowest group. The most numerous group, they were bound by heredity to the estates of the crown, nobility, and clergy, where they were occupied in agriculture, stockraising, and village crafts. Serfs could become free by serving as colonists in the underpopulated territories in the south. The second lowest group consisted of the clients, that is, freemen who did not own property and received protection from an overlord in exchange for service. Above the clients were the villein-knights, who formed a stratum that merged the commoners with the nobility. Finally, outside the basic social structure were the slaves, usually Muslim captives, who tilled the lands of the military orders in the Alentejo.

Control of the Royal Patrimony

Disputes over land ownership became an increasing source of conflict between the crown and the upper nobility and clergy. Land ownership was important because the crown's main source of revenue was taxes from the great estates and tithes from lands owned directly by the king. But in medieval Portugal, hereditary title to land did not exist in any developed legal form. As the original grants of land were obscured by passing years, many of the upper nobility and clergy of the church came to believe that they held their land by hereditary right. Thus, each time a new king ascended the throne, the crown had to review land grants and titles in order to assert its authority and reclaim land removed from the king's patrimony.

The first king to confront this problem was Afonso II, who discovered when he ascended the throne in 1211 that his father, Sancho I, had willed much of the royal patrimony to the church. In 1216, after a lengthy legal battle between the crown and the Holy See over various provisions of Sancho's will, the pope recognized Afonso II's right to maintain the royal patrimony intact. From 1216 until 1221, the Portuguese crown asserted this general right by requiring those who had received donations from previous kings to apply for letters of confirmation. The crown thus created the power to review grants to nobles and ecclesiastical bodies.

The process of confirmation was carried a step further when the king appointed royal commissions authorized to investigate land ownership, especially in the north where much of the feudal land tenure predated the creation of the monarchy. These inquiries, as they were called, gathered evidence from the oldest, most experienced residents in each locale without consulting local nobles or church officials. They revealed a large number of abuses and improper extensions of boundaries, as well as conspiracies to defraud the crown of income. The first inquiry found that the church was the biggest expropriator of royal property. The archbishop of Braga, angered by the activities of the commissions, excommunicated Afonso II in 1219. The king responded by seizing church property and forcing the archbishop to flee Portugal for Rome. In 1220 the pope confirmed the king's excommunication and relieved him of his oath of fealty to the Holy See. This dispute between church and crown ended temporarily when the excommunicated king died in 1223 and his chancellor arranged an ecclesiastical burial in exchange for the return of the seized church property and the promise that future inquiries would respect canon law.

The conflict between the church and crown concerning property was finally resolved during the reign of King Dinis (r.1279–1325). In 1284 Dinis launched a new round of inquiries and in the following year promulgated deamortization laws, which prohibited the church and religious orders from buying property and required that they sell all property purchased since the beginning of his reign. For this action against the church, Dinis, like his father and grandfather, was excommunicated. This time, however, the king refused to pledge obedience to the pope and established once and for all the power of the Portuguese crown to regulate and control the royal patrimony.

This power allowed Dinis to nationalize the most powerful and wealthy of the military-religious orders. The Calatravans, founded in Castile, had in effect become Portuguese when the town of Avis was bestowed upon them by Afonso and they became known as the Order of Avis. In 1288 the Knights of Saint James, also of Castilian origin, became Portuguese when the order elected its own master. In 1312, as the result of an investigation into the activities of the Templars, Pope Clement V suppressed this order and transferred their vast properties in Portugal to the Hospitallers. Dinis was able to prevail upon the pope to give this wealth to a newly founded Portuguese military-religious order called the Order of Christ, which was initially situated at Castro Marim but was later moved to Tomar. After nationalization, most of these orders became chivalric bodies of quasi-celibate landowners. The Order of Avis, however, remained on a war footing and contributed significantly to Portugal's independence from Castile. The Order of Christ also remained a military-religious order, and its wealth was later used by Prince Henry the Navigator to pay for the voyages of discovery.

Development of the Realm

Having established the boundaries of the national territory, asserted their authority over the church and nobility, and gained control over the resources of the military orders, Portuguese kings began to turn their attention to the economic, cultural, and political development of the realm. This was especially true of King Dinis, who is referred to by the Portuguese as The Farmer (O Lavrador) because of his policies designed to encourage agricultural development. He decreed that nobles would not lose their standing if they drained wetlands, settled colonists, and planted pine forests. The pine forests were to produce timber for the shipbuilding industry, which Dinis also encouraged, the crown having already at that time begun to look toward the sea for future fields of conquest.

Dinis chartered many settlements of colonists on lands conquered from the Muslims and authorized the holding of fairs and markets in each of these, thereby creating a national economy. He laid the basis for Portugal's naval tradition by bringing the Genoese, Emmanuele Pessagno (Manuel Peçanha in Portuguese) to Portugal in 1317 to be the hereditary admiral of the Portuguese navy. Maritime commerce was encouraged when Dinis negotiated an agreement with Edward II of England in 1303 that permitted Portuguese ships to enter English ports and guaranteed security and trading privileges for Portuguese merchants. Dinis provided the impetus for the development of Portuguese as a national language when he decreed that all official documents of the realm were to be written in the vernacular. Finally, Dinis stimulated learning when, in 1290, he founded an academic center similar to the ''General Studies'' centers that had been created in León and Aragon. In 1308 this center was moved to Coimbra where it remained, except for a brief time between from 1521 to 1537, and became the University of Coimbra, Portugal's premier institution of higher learning.

Afonso IV (r.1325–57) continued his father's development policies. He also improved the administration of justice by dismissing corrupt local judges and replacing them with judges he appointed. When a large Muslim army landed on the peninsula in 1340,

Afonso IV allied himself with the king of Castile, Alfonso XI, and the king of Aragon in order to do battle against this threat to the Christian kingdoms. Afonso sent a fleet commanded by Manuel Peçanha to Cádiz and marched overland himself to meet the Muslim army, which was destroyed at the Battle of Salado.

When Afonso's grandson and heir, Fernando I (r.1367–83), ascended the throne, the economic productivity of the country had been so greatly disrupted by a plague that had ravaged the country in 1348 and 1349 that he found it necessary to take measures to stimulate food production. In 1375 he promulgated a decree, called the Law of the Sesmarias, which obliged all landowners to cultivate unused land or sell or rent it to someone who would. The law also obligated all who had no useful occupation to work the land. This decree had its intended effect and led to the rebuilding of the country's wealth. Fernando also stimulated the development of the Portuguese merchant fleet by allowing all shipbuilders who constructed ships of more than 100 tons to cut timber from the royal forests and by exempting the owners of these ships from the full tax on the exports and imports of their first voyage. He also established a maritime insurance company into which owners of merchant ships of more than fifty tons paid 2 percent of their profits and from which they received compensation for shipwrecks.

The House of Avis

When Fernando died in 1383, he left no male heir to the throne. His only daughter, Beatriz, was married to Juan I, king of Castile. The marriage writ stipulated that their offspring would inherit the Portuguese crown if Fernando left no male heir and that, until any children were born, Portugal would be ruled by a regency of Fernando's widow, Leonor Teles. When Fernando died, Leonor assumed the regency in accordance with the marriage writ. The assumption of the regency by the queen was badly received in many Portuguese cities because Leonor was a Castilian and considered an interloper who intended to usurp the Portuguese crown for Castile and end Portugal's independence. Leonor's principal rival for control of the throne was João, the master of the Order of Avis and illegitimate son of Fernando's father, Pedro I (r.1357–67). On December 6, 1383, João broke into the royal palace and murdered Count Andeiro, a Galician who had been Fernando's chancellor. Leonor Teles fled to the town of Alenquer, the property of the queens of Portugal. She appealed to Juan I for help, and he invaded Portugal in January 1384. Leonor abdicated as regent. In Lisbon the people proclaimed João governor and defender of the realm. João immediately began to prepare an army and sent a mission to England to recruit soldiers for his cause.

Wars with Castile

The bourgeoisie of Lisbon, enriched by commerce, decided to support João and donated substantial sums for war expenses. Money also arrived from the bourgeoisie in Porto, Coimbra, and Évora. The majority of the nobility, among whom national sentiment was not well developed and feudal customs based on oaths of vassalage were still obeyed, took the side of Juan of Castile, which gave him the support of fifty castles. A few nobles, however, including Álvaro Pais, João Afonso, and Nun'Álvares Pereira, were more attuned to national sentiment and sided with João.

In March 1384, Juan marched on Lisbon, which he besieged by land and sea. In April, in the Alentejo, Nun'Álvares Pereira defeated the Castilians at the Battle of Atoleiros, a victory that resulted from the new military tactic of forming defensive squares from dismounted cavalry because the Portuguese had far fewer troops than the enemy. The siege of Lisbon was broken after seven months by an outbreak of the plague in the Castilian camp, and Juan retreated to Seville to prepare another invasion the following year.

The retreat of the Castilians gave João an opportunity to legitimate his claim to the throne. In March 1385, a cortes was summoned to resolve the succession. João's case was argued by João das Regras, who attacked the claims of the various pretenders to the throne. On April 6, the opposition ended and João was proclaimed king as João I (r. 1385–1433). The new king named Nun'Álvares Pereira constable of Portugal. At the same time, a contingent of English longbowmen began to arrive. Nun'Álvares Pereira marched north in order to obtain the submission of Braga, Guimarães, and other places loyal to Juan, who responded by sending an army to attack Viseu. The Portuguese routed this Castilian force at Rancoso using the same new military tactic that had brought them victory at Atoleiros. Juan, nonetheless, was still intent on besieging Lisbon and led his army southward. João I and Nun'Álvares Pereira decided to engage Juan's army before it arrived in the capital. The two armies met on the plain of Aljubarrota about sixty kilometers north of Lisbon on August 14, 1385. Using the same tactic of defensive squares of dismounted cavalry that had brought them success in previous battles, a force of 7,000 Portuguese annihilated and scattered a Castilian army of 32,000 in little more than thirty minutes of combat. Although additional battles were fought and final peace was not made with Castile until October 1411, the Battle of Aljubarrota secured the independence of Portugal for almost two centuries.

Anglo-Portuguese Alliance

English aid to the House of Avis set the stage for the cooperation with England that would be the cornerstone of Portuguese foreign policy for more than 500 years. In May 1386, the Treaty of Windsor confirmed the alliance that was born at Aljubarrota with a pact of perpetual friendship between the two countries. The next year, John of Gaunt, duke of Lancaster, son of Edward III, and father of Henry IV, landed in Galicia with an expeditionary force to press his claim to the Castilian throne with Portuguese aid. He failed to win the support of the Castilian nobility and returned to England with a cash compensation from the rival claimant.

John of Gaunt left behind his daughter, Philippa of Lancaster, to marry João I in order to seal the Anglo-Portuguese alliance. By this marriage, celebrated in 1387, João became the father of a generation of princes called by poet Luís de Camões the "marvelous generation," who led Portugal into its golden age. Philippa brought to the court the Anglo-Norman tradition of an aristocratic education and gave her children good educations. Her personal qualities were of the highest, and she reformed the court and imposed rigid standards of moral behavior. Philippa provided royal patronage for English commercial interests that sought to meet the Portuguese desire for cod and cloth in return for wine, cork, salt, and oil shipped through the English warehouses at Porto. Philippa's sons were accomplished. Her eldest son, Duarte, authored moral works and became king in 1433; Pedro, who traveled widely and had an interest in history, became regent when Duarte died of the plague in 1438; Fernando, who became a crusader, participated in the attack on Tangiers in 1437; and Henrique—Prince Henry the Navigator—became the master of the Order of Avis and the instigator and organizer of the early voyages of discovery.

Social Revolution

The crisis of 1383–85 that brought João I to the throne was not only a dynastic revolution but also a social one. João I distrusted the old aristocracy that had opposed his rise to power and promoted the growth of a new generation of nobility by confiscating the titles and properties of the old and distributing them to the new. He thus formed a new nobility based on service to the king.

João rewarded members of the urban bourgeoisie that had supported his cause by giving them positions and influence and by allowing them to send representatives to the king's royal council.

21

Artisans grouped themselves according to professions into guilds and were permitted to send delegates to the governing chamber of Lisbon, where they were actively involved in the administration of the capital and other cities. The king also surrounded himself with skilled legalists who professionalized royal administration and extended royal jurisdiction at the expense of the old aristocracy. This new class of bureaucrats, having studied Roman law at the university, defended the Caesarist principle that the will of the king had the force of law. This belief encouraged the later development of absolutism in Portugal and pitted the king against the landed nobility, especially the old aristocracy that wished to regain its lost power and privilege.

Intradynastic Struggle

The future of the House of Avis seemed assured by the presence of João's five legitimate sons, but the king also provided for his illegitimate children as he had been provided for by his father. João conferred on his bastard son Afonso the hereditary title of duke of Bragança and endowed him with lands and properties that amounted to the creation of a state within a state supported by a huge reserve of armed retainers. The House of Bragança accumulated wealth to rival that of the crown and eventually assumed the leadership of the old aristocracy in opposition to Avis.

When João I died in 1433, the crown was assumed by his eldest son, Duarte, who died five years later of the plague. Before his death, Duarte convoked a cortes in order to legitimate the compilation of Portuguese royal law, but the work was not completed until the reign of his son, Afonso, and is, therefore, named the Afonsine Ordinances. He also declared that the grants of land so lavishly awarded by his father to his supporters would have to be confirmed, as was the custom at the start of each reign.

Afonso was six years old when his father died and his mother, Queen Leonor of Aragon, assumed the regency. There was opposition to the assumption of all authority by a woman, and Leonor agreed that Duarte's brother, Pedro, should become regent. This was opposed by Afonso, duke of Bragança, the eldest illegitimate son of João I. Both men aspired to gain influence over the young king by marrying him to their daughters. The populace of Lisbon strongly favored Pedro and acknowledged him as regent. Pedro received confirmation for his regency by summoning the cortes at Évora and paved the way for his continuance in power by arranging the marriage of his daughter Isabel to the young king, who, when he reached his majority in 1446, agreed to the match and asked his uncle to continue the regency.

The duke of Bragança reasserted his ambitions and was able to influence the young king to dismiss Pedro by convincing him that his uncle was plotting to seize the throne. Pedro was banished to his estates. When rumors of a plot against him surfaced, he decided to resist and marched on Lisbon, where he had the support of the populace. Pedro was met by the troops of the king and the duke of Bragança at the Battle of Alfarrobeira on May 24, 1449, where he was killed and his army defeated. This battle resulted in the enlargement of the property and wealth of the illegitimate line of the House of Avis, which allowed it to enjoy enormous influence over the pliable Afonso V until his death in 1481.

Assertion of Royal Supremacy

When Afonso's son and heir, João II (r.1481–95), assumed the throne, the power of the Braganças and their supporters had reached its height. The new king, who was more resolute than his father, convoked a cortes at Évora, where he imposed a new written oath by which nobles swore upon their knees to give up to the king any castle or town they held from the crown. At Évora commoners complained about the abuses of the nobility and asked for the abolition of private justice and the correction of abuses in the collection of taxes. The king ordered that all nobles present their titles of privilege and that his constables be admitted to their estates in order to investigate complaints concerning administration.

These measures provoked a reaction by the nobility led by the powerful Fernando, duke of Bragança, who conspired against the king with the help of the king of Castile. Upon learning of the intrigues of Fernando, the king accused the duke of treason and tried him at a special court in Évora. He was sentenced to death and beheaded in the main square on June 29, 1484. The king confiscated his properties and those of his accomplices, some of whom were also killed, while others fled Portugal. A second conspiracy was hatched by the duke of Viseu, but it, too, was discovered, and the duke was killed, perhaps by the king himself, in Setúbal. These events established the supremacy of the crown over the nobility once and for all.

Maritime Expansion

The maritime expansion of Portugal was the result of the threat to Mediterranean commerce, especially the trade in spices, that had developed very rapidly after the crusades. Spices traveled by various overland routes from Asia to the Levant, where they were loaded aboard Genoese and Venetian ships and brought to Europe. Gradually, this trade became threatened by pirates and the

Turks, who closed off most of the overland routes and subjected the spices to heavy taxes. Europeans sought alternative routes to Asia in order to circumvent these difficulties.

The Portuguese led the way in this quest for a number of reasons. First, Portugal's location on the southwesternmost edge of the European landmass placed the country at the maritime crossroads between the Atlantic and the Mediterranean. Second, Portugal was by the fifteenth century a compact, unified kingdom led by an energetic, military aristocracy, which, having no more territory on the peninsula to conquer, sought new fields of action overseas. Third, Portuguese kings were motivated by a deeply held belief that their role in history was as the standard-bearers of Christianity against the Muslims. Fourth, Portugal's kings had, since the founding of the monarchy, encouraged maritime activities. Dinis founded the Portuguese navy, and Fernando encouraged the construction of larger ships and founded a system of maritime insurance. Finally, Portugal led the world in nautical science, having perfected the astrolabe and quadrant and developed the lantine-rigged caravel, all of which made navigating and sailing the high seas possible.

Early Voyages

Portugal's maritime expansion began in 1415 when João I seized Ceuta in Morocco, the western depot for the spice trade. The military campaign against Ceuta was launched for several reasons. First, war in Morocco was seen as a new crusade against the Muslims that would stand Portugal well with the church. Second, there was a need to suppress Moroccan pirates who were threatening Portuguese ships. Third, the Portuguese wanted the economic benefit that controlling Ceuta's vast market would bring to the crown. Finally, the campaign against Ceuta was seen as preparatory to an attack on Muslims still holding Granada. The possession of Ceuta allowed the Portuguese to dominate the Straits of Gibraltar.

After the conquest of Ceuta, Prince Henry the Navigator, who had participated in the campaign as an armed knight, settled at Sagres on the extreme end of Cape St. Vincent, where in 1418 he founded a naval school. He continued to direct Portugal's early maritime activity. As the master of the Order of Christ, Prince Henry was able to draw on the vast resources of this group to equip ships and pay the expenses of the early maritime expeditions. Prince Henry was motivated by scientific curiosity and religious fervor, seeing the voyages as a continuation of the crusades against the Muslims and the conversion of new peoples to Christianity, as well as by the desire to open a sea route to India.

Monument to the Discoveries, Lisbon Courtesy Embassy of Portugal, Washington

Shortly after the school was established, two of Prince Henry's captains discovered the island of Porto Santo, and the following year the Madeira Islands were discovered. In 1427 Diogo de Silves, sailing west, discovered the Azores archipelago, also uninhabited. Both Madeira and Porto Santo were colonized immediately and divided into captaincies. These were distributed to Prince Henry's captains, who in turn had the power to distribute land to settlers according to the Law of the Sesmarias.

Prince Henry's plan required the circumnavigation of Africa. His early voyages stayed close to the African coast. After repeated attempts, Gil Eanes finally rounded Cape Bojador on the west coast of Africa in present-day Western Sahara in 1434, a psychological, as well as physical, barrier that was thought to be the outer boundary of the knowable world. After passing Cape Bojador, the exploration of the coast southward proceeded very rapidly. In 1436 Gil Eanes and Afonso Baldaia arrived at the Senegal River, which they called the River of Gold because two Africans they had captured were ransomed with gold dust. In 1443 Nuno Tristão arrived at the Bay of Arguin off the coast of present-day Mauritania. These voyages returned African slaves to Portugal, which sparked an interest in the commercial value of the explorations, and a factory was established at Arguin as an entrepôt for human cargo. In 1444 Dinis Dias discovered the Cape Verde Islands, then heavily forested, and Nuno Tristão explored the mouth of the Senegal River. In

25

1445 Cape Verde was rounded, and in 1456 Portuguese arrived at the coast of present-day Guinea. The following year, they reached present-day Sierra Leone. Thus, when Prince Henry died in 1460, the Portuguese had explored the coast of Africa down to Sierra Leone and discovered the archipelagoes of Madeira, the Azores, and the Cape Verde Islands.

Sea Route to India

After the death of Prince Henry, the Portuguese continued to explore the coast of Africa, but without their earlier singleness of purpose. A dispute had arisen among the military aristocracy over whether Portugal could best achieve its strategic objectives by conquering Morocco or by seeking a sea route to India. Duarte had continued his father's Moroccan policy and undertook a military campaign against Tangiers but was unsuccessful. Afonso V ordered several expeditionary forces to Morocco. In 1458 he conquered Alcázarquivir; in 1471 he took Arzila, followed by Tangiers and Larache. Afonso's successors continued this policy of expansion in Morocco, especially Manuel I (r.1495–1521), who conquered Safim and Azamor. The Moroccan empire was expensive because it kept Portugal in a constant state of war; therefore, it was abandoned by João III (r.1521–57), except for Ceuta and Tangiers.

In 1469 Afonso V granted to Fernão Gomes a monopoly of trade with Guinea for five years if he agreed to explore 100 leagues (about 500 kilometers) of coast each year. A number of expeditions were carried out under this contract. In 1471 Portuguese sailors reached Mina de Ouro on the Gold Coast (present-day Ghana) and explored Cape St. Catherine, two degrees south of the equator. Mina de Ouro became the chief center for the gold trade and a major source of revenue for the crown. The islands of São Tomé and Príncipe were also discovered in 1471, and Fernão do Pó discovered the island that now bears his name in 1474.

During the reign of João II, the crown once again took an active role in the search for a sea route to India. In 1481 the king ordered a fort constructed at Mina de Ouro to protect this potential source of wealth. Diogo Cão sailed farther down the African coast in the period 1482–84. In 1487 a new expedition led by Bartolomeu Dias sailed south beyond the tip of Africa and, after having lost sight of land for a month, turned north and made landfall on a northeast-running coastline, which was named Terra dos Vaqueiros after the native herders and cows that were seen on shore. Dias had rounded the Cape of Good Hope without seeing it and had proven that the Atlantic connected to the Indian Ocean.

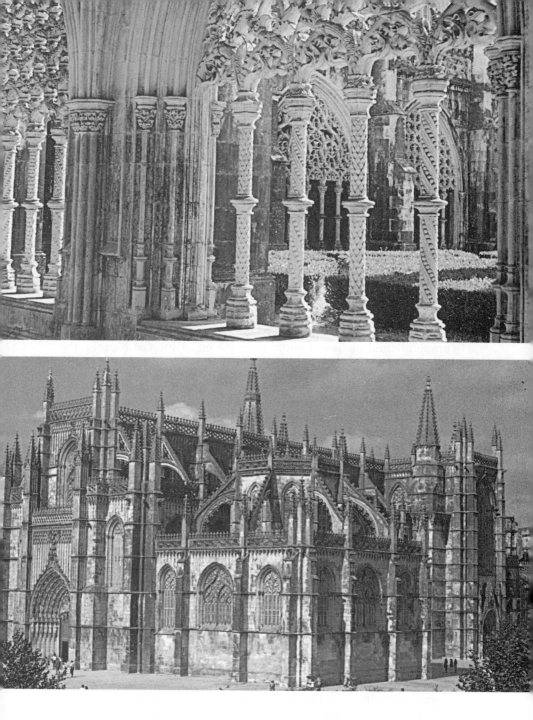

Arches of the Royal Cloister at the Monastery of Santa Maria da Vitória, Batalha
Courtesy Danièle Köhler
Monastery of Santa Maria da Vitória, Batalha
Courtesy Walter Opello

In the meantime, João sent Pêro da Covilhã and Afonso de Paiva, who were versed in warfare, diplomacy, and Arabic, on a mission in search of the mythical Christian kingdom of Prester John. Departing from Santarém, they traveled to Barcelona, Naples, and the island of Rhodes, and, disguised as merchants, entered Alexandria. Passing through Cairo, they made their way to Aden, where they separated and agreed to meet later in Cairo at a certain date. Afonso de Paiva went to Ethiopia, and Pêro da Covilhã headed for Calicut and Goa in India by way of Ormuz, returning to Cairo via Sofala in Mozambique on the east coast of Africa. In Cairo he learned from two emissaries sent by João II that Afonso de Paiva had died. One of the emissaries returned to Portugal with a letter containing the information Pêro da Covilhã had collected on his travels. Da Covilhã then left for Ethiopia where he was received by the emperor but not allowed to leave. He settled in Ethiopia, married, and raised a family. The information provided in his letter complemented the information from the expedition of Bartolomeu Dias and convinced João II that it was possible to reach India by sailing around the southern end of Africa. He died during preparations for this voyage in 1494.

Manuel I assumed the throne in 1495 and completed the preparations for the voyage to India. On July 8, 1497, a fleet of four ships commanded by Vasco da Gama set sail from Belém on the outskirts of Lisbon. The expedition was very carefully organized, each ship having the best captains and pilots, as well as handpicked crews. They carried the most up-to-date nautical charts and navigational instruments. Vasco da Gama's fleet rounded the Cape of Good Hope on November 27, 1497, and made landfall at Natal in present-day South Africa on December 25. The fleet then proceeded along the east coast of Africa and landed at Quelimane in present-day Mozambique in January 1498, followed by Mombasa in present-day Kenya. An Arab pilot directed the fleet to India. After sailing for a month, the fleet reached Calicut on the Malabar coast in southwest India. In August, after sailing to Goa, the fleet left for Portugal, arriving in September 1499, two years and two days after the departure.

In 1500 Manuel organized a large fleet of thirteen ships for a second voyage to India. This fleet was commanded by Pedro Álvares Cabral and included Bartolomeu Dias, various nobles, priests, and some 1,200 men. The fleet sailed southwest for a month, and on April 22 sighted land, the coast of present-day Brazil. Cabral sent a ship back to Lisbon to report to Manuel his discovery, which he called Vera Cruz. The fleet recrossed the Atlantic and sailed to India around Africa where it arrived on September 13, 1500.

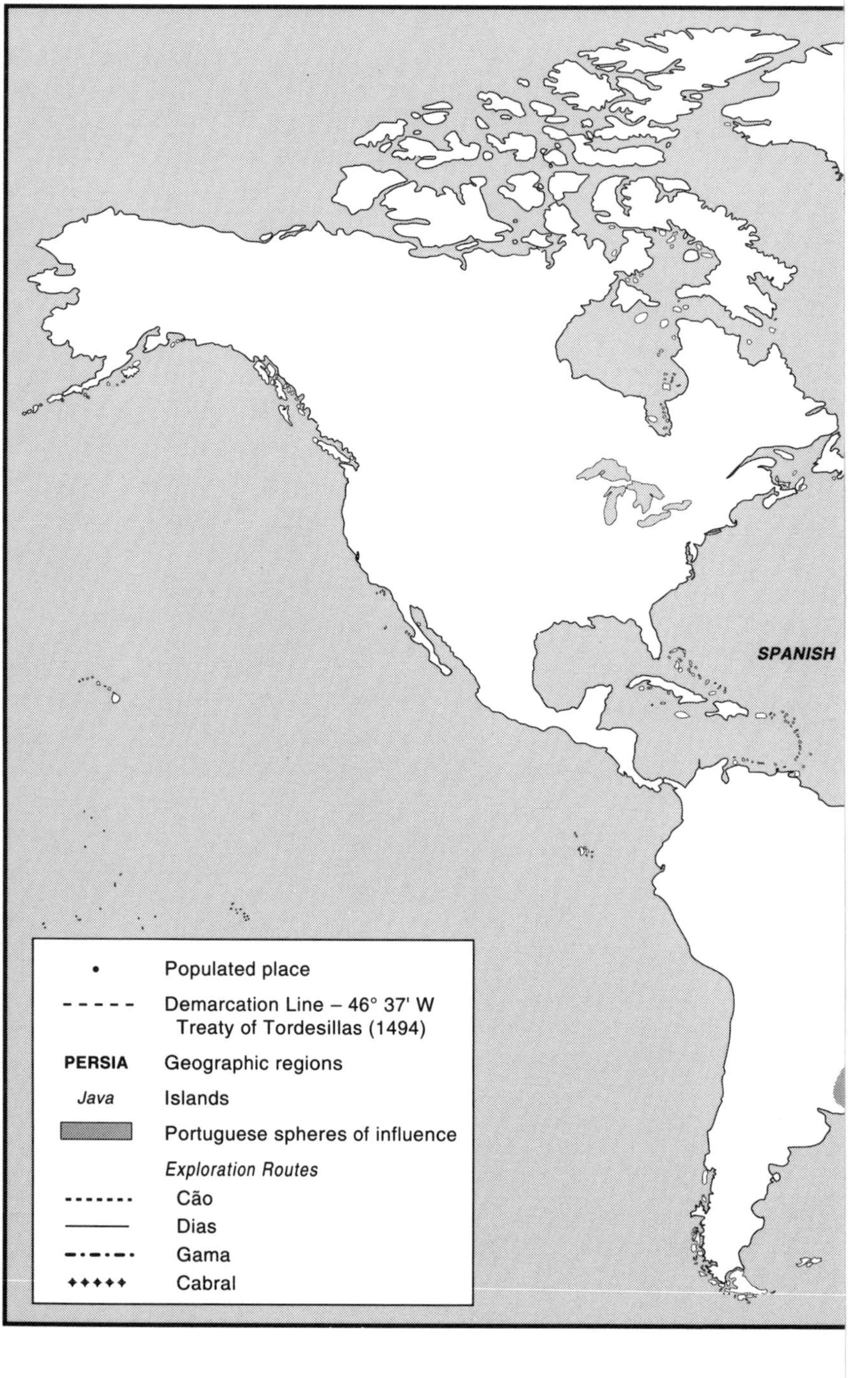

Legend:

•	Populated place
- - - - -	Demarcation Line – 46° 37' W Treaty of Tordesillas (1494)
PERSIA	Geographic regions
Java	Islands
▓▓▓	Portuguese spheres of influence
Exploration Routes	
• • • • • •	Cão
———	Dias
— · — · — ·	Gama
✦✦✦✦✦	Cabral

Figure 3. The Portuguese Empire and Routes of Exploration, Fifteenth and S

After four months in India, Cabral sailed for Lisbon in January 1501, having left a contingent of Portuguese to maintain a factory at Cochin on the Malabar coast (see fig. 3).

Empire in Asia

Having discovered the sea route to India, Manuel organized successive fleets to that region in order to establish Portuguese commercial hegemony. In 1505 Francisco de Almeida left Lisbon with a fleet of 22 ships and 2,500 men, 1,500 of whom were soldiers. Invested with the title of viceroy of India, Almeida was instructed to conclude alliances with Indian rulers, set up factories, and build forts on the east coast of Africa, which he did at Mombasa and at Kilwa in present-day Tanzania before arriving in India. After his arrival, he fortified the island of Angediva and Cochin. He imposed a system of licenses on trading vessels that threatened to ruin the Muslim traders, who reacted by seeking spices in Malacca in present-day Malaysia and the Sunda Islands in the Malay Archipelago and sailing directly to the Persian Gulf, bypassing India.

Almeida sought to suppress this trade and secure Portuguese commercial hegemony. He was joined in this effort by two more fleets sent from Lisbon, one under the command of Tristão da Cunha and the other under Afonso de Albuquerque, who had been appointed Almeida's successor as viceroy. Cunha explored Madagascar and the coast of east Africa, occupied the island of Socotra (now part of Yemen), and built a fort at the mouth of the Red Sea, before sailing to India. Albuquerque ravaged the Oman coast and attacked Ormuz, the great entrepôt at the mouth of the Persian Gulf, where he began constructing a fort.

The activities of the Portuguese motivated the Muslims to take military action. The sultan of Egypt, allied with the Venetians and Turks, organized a large armada that crossed the Indian Ocean to Diu, where it was engaged by a Portuguese fleet. On February 2, 1509, a great sea battle was fought and the sultan's armada destroyed. This victory assured Portuguese commercial and military hegemony over India and allowed Portugal to extend its empire to the Far East.

Albuquerque established his capital at Goa, which he attacked and occupied in 1510. In 1511 he departed for the conquest of Malacca, the emporium for the spice trade and trade with China, which he accomplished in August of that year. After returning to Goa, Albuquerque made plans to occupy strategic positions in the Persian Gulf and Red Sea. On his first expedition, he failed to take Aden and returned to Goa. His second expedition, which was to be his last, attempted to conquer Ormuz and Aden, as well as seize

Mecca. During this expedition, Albuquerque fell ill and returned to Goa, where he died in 1515.

When Manuel I died in 1521, his son and heir, João III, sent expeditions to the islands of Celebes, Borneo, Java, and Timor, all part of the Malay Archipelago. Relations were established with Japan after the visits of Francisco Xavier and Fernão Mendes Pinto in 1549. Portuguese captains founded factories in China and took possession of Macau in 1557.

Colonization of Brazil

The growth of Portuguese interests in the Americas was slow, the king being absorbed with establishing Portuguese hegemony in Asia. In addition, the Treaty of Tordesillas of 1494, arranged by Pope Alexander VI, divided the unexplored world between Spain and Portugal and forbade Portugal from exploring beyond a meridian drawn 1,600 kilometers miles west of the Cape Verde Islands. In 1502 Fernão Noronha was given a three-year commercial monopoly on dyewood in return for exploring 300 leagues (about 1,500 kilometers) of the Brazilian coast each year. During the last years of Manuel I's reign, the first colonists were sent to Brazil to establish a sugar industry. Additional colonists were sent during the reign of João III, and, in 1530, Martim Afonso de Sousa was named major captain of Brazil and invested with the power to distribute land among captains or *donatários,* much as had been done in Madeira when it was colonized a century before. These captaincies were large strips of land that extended from the coast into the interior. The captains settled colonists in their respective captaincies and were required to provide them protection and justice.

Because captaincies were independent of one another and hence weak, they were unable to defend themselves from foreign pirates. Consequently, João III appointed a governor general with authority over the captaincies. The first governor general, Tomé de Sousa, was appointed in 1549 and established his capital at São Salvador da Baía. He defeated French pirates in a naval engagement in the bay of Rio de Janeiro. Intensified colonization under de Sousa began in the form of coastal settlements and spread to the interior. The colonists cultivated indigenous crops, especially manioc, and introduced new ones such as wheat, rice, grapes, oranges, and sugarcane from Madeira and São Tomé. Sugar soon became Brazil's most important export.

Counter-Reformation and Overseas Evangelization

The eruption of the Protestant Reformation in the first decades of the sixteenth century brought forth a Roman Catholic response, the Counter-Reformation, a determined campaign to strengthen the Roman Catholic Church and restore religious unity to Europe. One of Rome's key instruments to purify doctrine and root out heresy was the Inquisition. The Counter-Reformation soon reached Portugal, and João III was granted permission to establish the Court of Inquisition in 1536. The court did not began its work until 1539 when the first inquisitor general was replaced by a religious zealot, the archbishop of Évora, who stood for public confession and immediate execution. As elsewhere, the Inquisition in Portugal dealt with all forms of heresy, corruption, and disbelief, but its main victims were the so-called New Christians, Jews who had converted to Christianity after Manuel I had ordered in 1497 the expulsion from Portugal of all Jews who refused to accept the Christian faith. Many Portuguese believed that the New Christians secretly practiced Judaism at home, and the Inquisition was used to stop such an "abomination." Courts of the Inquisition functioned in larger settlements around Portugal. The first auto-da-fé, or public burning of a heretic, took place in 1540 in Lisbon. In the next 150 years, an estimated 1,400 people perished in this manner in Portugal.

Another of Rome's strongest weapons in the Counter-Reformation was the Society of Jesus, a religious order founded by Ignatius de Loyola in 1539. The order was dedicated to furthering the cause of Catholicism and propagating its teachings in missions among nonbelievers. In 1540 three of Loyola's followers—Simão Rodrigues, who was Portuguese; Paulo Camerte, who was Italian; and Francisco Xavier, who was Spanish—arrived in Portugal. Simão Rodrigues became the tutor of the king's son and later founded Jesuit schools at Coimbra and Évora. By 1555 the Jesuits had control of all secondary education in the realm and by 1558 had established a university in Évora.

João III invited the Jesuits to carry out their apostolic mission in the lands of Portugal's overseas empire. Francisco Xavier left Portugal in 1541 for India as a result of the king's request. He arrived in Goa in 1542 and immediately began proselytizing among the indigenous inhabitants, converting many thousands. From Goa he went to Cochin and Ceylon; in 1545 he traveled to Malacca, and in 1549, to Japan, where he stayed for two years. After returning to Goa, in 1552 he went to China, where he died.

Evangelization began in Brazil in 1549 with the arrival of six Jesuits led by Father Manuel de Nóbrega, who accompanied Tomé de Sousa, the first governor general. They built a church at São Salvador da Baía, as well as schools at Rio de Janeiro and São Paulo. They also evangelized northern and southern Brazil. In the south,

Father José Anchieta opened a school for Indians and authored the first grammar in a native language, Tupí-Guaraní. The Jesuits built churches, schools, and seminaries. They settled the indigenous inhabitants in villages and defended them against attempts to enslave them.

Imperial Decline

Portugal's empire in Asia made its monarchy the richest in Europe and made Lisbon the commercial capital of the world. This prosperity was more apparent than real, however, because the newfound wealth did not transform the social structure, nor was it used to lay the basis for further economic development. The country's industry was weakened because the profits from Asian monopolies were used to import manufactured goods. As the empire in Asia was a state-run enterprise, no middle class or commercial sector independent of the crown of any consequence emerged as it had in other parts of Europe. Moreover, the persecution of the Jews, who possessed vital technical skills, robbed the country of an important force for modernity and reinforced feudal elements. Adding to the drain on the economy was the large amount of money spent on sumptuous palaces and churches.

Because the wealth from the discoveries did not produce a middle class of competent, trained individuals to whom the affairs of state gradually fell, leadership in Portugal remained in the hands of the king and the military aristocracy. Moreover, the imperial system had intensified the already centralized system of government, which meant that the quality of national policy was closely tied to the abilities of the top leadership, especially the king himself. Unfortunately, the House of Avis did not produce a king of great merit after João II, and Portugal entered a long period of imperial decline.

Dynastic Crisis

When João III died in 1557, the only surviving heir to the throne was his three-year-old son, Sebastião, who took over the government at the age of fourteen. Sickly and poorly educated, Sebastião proved to be mentally unstable, and as he grew to young manhood he developed a fanatical obsession with launching a great crusade against the Muslims in North Africa, thus reviving the Moroccan policy of Afonso V. In 1578, when he was twenty-four years old, Sebastião organized an army of 24,000 and assembled a large fleet that left Portugal on August 4 for Alcázarquivir. Sebastião's army, poorly equipped and incompetently led, was defeated, and the king, presumed killed in battle, was never seen again. A large number of the nobility were captured and held for ransom. This defeat, the most disastrous in Portuguese military history, swept away the flower of the aristocratic leadership and drained the coffers of the treasury in order to pay ransoms. Worse, it resulted in the death of a king who had no descendants, plunging Portugal into a period of confusion and intrigue over the succession.

With Sebastião's death, the crown fell to his uncle, Henrique, the last surviving son of Manuel I. Henrique's crowning solved the succession crisis only temporarily because Henrique was an infirm and aged cardinal who was unable to obtain dispensation from the pope to marry. There were several pretenders to the throne, one of whom was Philip II of Spain, nephew of João III.

When Henrique died in 1580, a powerful Spanish army commanded by the duke of Alba invaded Portugal and marched on Lisbon. This force routed the army of rival contender, António, prior of Crato and the illegitimate son of João III's son Luís. Portugal was annexed by Spain, and Philip II was declared Filipe I of Portugal.

Iberian Union

After Philip was declared king of Portugal, he decreed that his new realm would be governed by a six-member Portuguese council; that the Portuguese cortes would meet only in Portugal; that all civil, military, and ecclesiastical appointments would remain Portuguese; and that the language, judicial system, coinage, and military would remain autonomous. Philip supported the two institutions in Portugal that he believed might unite the two countries: the Jesuits and the Inquisition. One result was that New Christians were persecuted even more severely.

The incorporation of Portugal into the Iberian Union was accepted by the Portuguese nobility without much difficulty. The royal court had used the language and etiquette of Castile since the fifteenth century, and much serious work had been done in Castile by Portuguese writers, who were conscious of belonging to a common Iberian culture. In the countryside, however, there developed a current of resistance that took the form of a messianic cult of the "hidden prince," Sebastião. Members of this cult believed that Sebastião did not actually die at Alcázarquivir but would return to deliver Portugal from Spanish domination. This cult became deeply rooted, and over the years a number of impostors appeared and sparked rebellions, all of which were easily put down. To this day, Sebastianism (Sebastianismo), or the nostalgic longing for the unattainable, is a continuing feature of Portuguese life.

During the reign of Philip II, the terms of the proclamation of the union of the two crowns were generally upheld. With Philip's death in 1598 and the ascension to the Spanish throne of his son, Philip III, much less respect began to be paid to the provision that preserved Portugal's autonomy. Philip III did not visit Portugal until 1619, very near the end of his reign, and he began to appoint Spaniards to the six-member governing council as well as to lesser posts. His son and heir, Philip IV, had no interest in government and consequently turned over the administration of Portugal to the duke of Olivares. The duke alienated Portuguese of all classes, including the hispanophile elite. In order to prop up the waning power of the Spanish monarchy, he levied excessive taxes and troop requisitions on Portugal to support Spanish military activities, especially against France. Moreover, he sought to unify Portugal with Spain.

In 1637 a rebellion broke out in Évora when the Spanish attempted to collect these taxes by force. Portuguese nobles were summoned to Madrid and ordered to recruit soldiers for war against France. The Portuguese nobility, encouraged by Cardinal Richelieu of France, who promised to support a Portuguese pretender with soldiers and ships, began to conspire against the Spanish. During the 1637 rebellion, the populace acclaimed João, duke of Bragança, as king. The duke, who was the nearest noble to the House of Avis, was Portugal's leading aristocrat and largest landowner. The choice of the populace was supported by the nobility, which conspired to make João king. The duke, who was cautious, initially resisted accepting the Portuguese crown, but eventually began to equip a private army. In 1640 the Catalans rebelled against Philip IV, and, thus encouraged, João's supporters went into action on December 1. They entered the royal palace and arrested Portugal's Spanish governor, the duchess of Mantua, a cousin of the king of Spain. Five days later, the duke of Bragança arrived in Lisbon and was crowned as João IV (r.1641–56), thus restoring the Portuguese monarchy and founding a new ruling dynasty, the House of Bragança.

Although Portugal's seaborne empire had begun to decline before the sixty years of incorporation in the Iberian Union, the "Spanish captivity," as this period is called by the Portuguese, hastened this process. The Portuguese, who were dragged into Spain's wars with England and Holland, began to see those two countries attack their holdings in Asia, as well as in Brazil. By the time independence was regained, Portugal's empire was greatly reduced, having lost its commercial monopoly in the Far East to the Dutch and in India to the English. Only the resolute action

of Portuguese settlers had saved Brazil from the Dutch, who had attacked Rio de Janeiro and Baía, and occupied Pernambuco.

Restoration

João IV was proclaimed king by a cortes convoked in 1641. Faced with the general ruin of the realm and threats to his crown from Spain, his first act was to defend the kingdom. He immediately created a council of war, appointed military governors in the provinces, recruited soldiers, rebuilt forts, and constructed an arms foundry. At the same time, he vigorously sought diplomatic recognition of his monarchy and Portugal's independence from Spain. On June 1, 1641, João IV signed an alliance with Louis XIII of France and soon made peace with Holland and England. By the time of his death in 1656, João IV had consolidated and restored the monarchy by making peace with former enemies, recouped some lost colonial possessions, and defeated Spanish attempts to reincorporate Portugal into the Iberian Union.

When João died, his queen, Luísa de Gusmão, became regent because the royal couple's oldest son, Teodósio, had died three years before his father and their youngest son, Afonso, was only ten years old. Although a disease in infancy had left Afonso partially paralyzed and had impaired his intelligence, his mother succeeded in having him proclaimed king. Afonso VI (r.1662–67) grew into a degenerate who preferred riding, coursing bulls, and watching cockfights. His marriage to Marie-Françoise Isabelle of Savoy was annulled, and, in 1667, aware of the need for a successor, Afonso consented to his own abdication in favor of his brother, Pedro. During this period, the Portuguese managed to fight off the last attempt by Spain to reincorporate them into the Iberian Union by defeating the Spanish invaders at Ameixial near Estremós. In 1666, three years after this victory, Spain at last made peace and recognized Portugal's independence.

When Afonso abdicated, he was banished to Terceira Island in the Azores and his brother, who had married Marie-Françoise, assumed the regency of the throne until Afonso's death in 1683, after which he ruled in his own right as Pedro II until 1706. During his regency, Pedro had given the task of producing a coherent economic policy to Luís de Menenses, count of Ericeira, who was appointed head of the treasury. Known as the "Portuguese Colbert," Ericeira implemented mercantilist policies in Portugal similar to those of France. These policies sought to protect Portuguese industries against foreign competition. He published laws to enforce sobriety and criticized luxury. Ericeira organized the textile industry and imported looms from England. He stimulated the national production of wool and silk by decreeing that only Portuguese woolens and silks could be worn.

Development of Brazil

Having lost the empire in Asia, Portugal's policy makers turned their attention to Brazil, where they intensified the cultivation of sugar, cotton, and spices. This expansion of agriculture required a great deal of labor, which led to the importation of slaves from Angola and Guinea. Amerindians were saved from this fate by the Jesuits, who protected them from enslavement.

The southern part of Brazil was occupied first and the north, later, owing to resistance put up by Amerindians allied with French pirates. In 1580 the Portuguese conquered Paraíba and, later, Sergipe. In 1603 they penetrated to Ceará and, later, to Pará, where they founded the city of Belém. In 1637 Pedro Teixeira launched a daring expedition into the Amazon Basin, following the river to its headwaters near the Pacific coast. During the sixteenth and seventeenth centuries, various expeditions were sent into the interior, especially at the end of the seventeenth century when gold was discovered.

These expeditions were made up of adventurers known as *bandeirantes* (after the Portuguese word for flag) because they traveled under the flag of their leader, who took with him kin, friends, slaves, and friendly Amerindians. These expeditions, which followed rivers into the interior, lasted years. The most notable *bandeirantes* were Pais Leme, who traveled for seven years throughout present-day Minas Gerais, and his son-in-law, Manuel Borba Gato, who discovered several sources of gold on the Rio das Velhas. In addition to gold, diamonds were also found in abundance. The discovery of gold and diamonds sparked a gold rush from all over the world to Brazil and from the central zones to the interior, which devastated Brazilian agriculture. The gold and diamonds enriched the Portuguese crown and allowed it to spend lavishly on imported goods and baroque palaces, thus destroying once again the initiatives previously taken for indigenous economic development.

Brazilian gold also encouraged England to update its commercial relations with Portugal. The Methuen Treaty of 1703 allowed the Portuguese a preferential duty on wine exported to England, in return for which Portugal removed restrictions on the importation of English-made goods. The Portuguese market was soon absorbing 10 percent of the English export trade, which represented an increase of 120 percent above the quantity of goods imported to Portugal before the treaty. Portuguese exports to England, mainly wine, rose by less than 40 percent. Gold from Brazil was used to pay for this trade imbalance.

Absolutism

Pedro II was succeeded by João V (r.1706–50), a youth of seventeen. He was an energetic king who introduced absolutist rule into Portugal, copying the style of the royal court of Louis XIV of France. Brazilian gold allowed João V to spend lavishly on major architectural works, the greatest being the royal palace at Mafra, begun in 1717, which sought to rival the Escorial in Spain. He also endowed the University of Coimbra with an elegantly decorated library, and built the Aqueduct of Free Waters (Aqueduto das Águas Livres) that brought water to Lisbon. João encouraged the development of decorative arts such as furniture design, clockmaking, and tapestry weaving. He pursued mercantilist policies to protect indigenous industries, including papermaking at Lousã, glassmaking at Marinha Grande, and textile weaving at Covilhã. He subsidized the publication of notable works such as Caetano de Sousa's *História Genealógica da Casa Real*. In general, João V animated what has been called Portugal's second renaissance.

João V died in 1750 and was succeeded by his son José I (r.1750–77), who was indolent and placed the reins of government into the hands of Sebastião José de Carvalho e Melo, later the Marquês de Pombal. A petty noble who managed to surmount Portugal's rigid class system by a combination of energy, intelligence, good looks, and a shrewd marriage, Pombal became the veritable dictator of Portugal. Once Portugal's ambassador to Britain and Austria, Pombal had been influenced by the ideas of the Enlightenment. Realizing how backward Portugal was, he sought through a ruthless despotism to reform it and create a middle class.

On the morning of November 1, 1755, a violent earthquake shook Lisbon and demolished most of the city. Thousands were killed in the subsequent fire and tidal wave. Pombal, who was at Belém at the time, energetically took appropriate measures. He improvised hospitals for the injured, controlled prices for various services, requisitioned food from the countryside, and organized public security. He decided to rebuild the city after a survey of the ruins. Under the direction of the architect Eugénio dos Santos and the engineer Manuel da Maia, a master plan for a new city was drawn up. The old city center was cleared of rubble and divided into squares of long avenues and cross streets. New buildings conforming to a standard architectural style were quickly erected using the latest construction techniques. Lisbon thus emerged from the earthquake as Europe's first planned city. Flanked by the Praça do Rossio at one end and the Praça do Comércio at the other, this quarter of the city is known today as the Baixa Pombalina.

For his prompt and efficient action, Pombal was elevated to chief minister, which allowed him to consolidate his power. Desiring to destroy all forces within the society that could oppose his plans for modernizing Portugal, he began systematically to annihilate them, beginning with the nobility. An attempt on the life of the king on September 3, 1758, provided Pombal with a pretext to take action against the nobility. He accused many nobles of responsibility for the attempt and arrested about 1,000 individuals. Many confessed under brutal torture and were executed.

Pombal also attempted to rid Portugal of the Jesuits, whom he accused of taking part in the attempt on the king's life. He searched the houses belonging to the Jesuits, confiscated their belongings, closed their schools, and, in 1759, expelled them from the kingdom and its overseas possessions. In an effort to restrain the church, Pombal broke diplomatic relations with the Holy See in 1760 and imprisoned the bishop of Coimbra.

Pombal's economic policies were inspired by the protectionist doctrines of Colbert, which gave royal companies monopolies in certain fields. Following the initiatives in this regard established by the count of Ericeira, Pombal prohibited the export of gold and silver. In order to increase cereal cultivation, he prohibited the growing of grape vines in certain areas of the country. He protected the winemaking industry by founding, in 1756, a company with a monopoly on exporting port wine. Pombal created other companies with exclusive rights to commercial activities in various regions of Brazil, as well as a fishing and processing company for sardines and tuna in Portuguese waters. He transformed the silk industry into a textile industry and turned over the operation of the glassmaking factory at Marinha Grande to a British manager, who introduced new manufacturing techniques.

Pombal also made notable changes in the area of education. After expelling the Jesuits and confiscating their schools, he took the first steps toward establishing a system of public instruction. He founded a commercial school and established schools, paid for with a special tax, in the major cities. In addition, Pombal instituted numerous reforms of the university, whose decline he blamed on the Jesuits. He created two new departments—mathematics and philosophy—and increased the number of professors in the already existing departments. He put forward new methods of instruction based on the writings of Luís António Verney and António Nunes that stressed observation and experience, and set up laboratories, a natural history museum, a botanical garden, and an observatory.

José I died in 1777 and was succeeded on the throne by his daughter Maria I (r.1777–92), who dismissed Pombal and banished him to the village of Pombal. She immediately freed hundreds of prisoners, restored the old nobility to its former status, reestablished relations with the Holy See, revoked laws against the clergy, abolished many of the state companies, and generally dismantled Pombal's dictatorship. The strong, secular society that Pombal hoped to create did not materialize, and the old social and economic order quickly restored itself.

Peninsular Wars

The events of the French Revolution, especially the regicide of Louis XVI and the Terror, made the rest of Europe's monarchs fear for their lives. The Portuguese monarchy, like others, took measures to prevent the infiltration of revolutionary propaganda into the kingdom. Maria I, who suffered nightmares and fits of melancholy, imagined that she was damned. In 1792 she turned the reigns of government over to her second son, João, who was prince of Brazil. As the situation in France deteriorated, Portugal signed treaties of mutual assistance with Britain and Spain in 1793. In the same year, the Spanish army, reinforced by 6,000 Portuguese troops, attacked France across the Basque frontier. In 1794 the French launched a major counterattack, which forced the combined Spanish-Portuguese army to retreat from French territory. The French army reached the Ebro River and threatened Madrid.

In 1795 Spain made peace at Basel with France without consulting the Portuguese. Despite having fought with the Portuguese against France, the Spanish now allied themselves with the French and signed a secret treaty at San Idelfonso in 1800. In 1801 France and Spain sent the Portuguese an ultimatum threatening to invade Portugal unless it abandoned its alliance with Britain, closed its ports to the British and opened them to French and Spanish ships, and handed over one-quarter of its territory as a guarantee for Spanish territories held by Britain. The Portuguese refused to comply, and the Spanish marched into the Alentejo in May. After two weeks of fighting, the "War of the Oranges," as it is known, was concluded in 1801 at Badajoz. According to the terms of the peace treaty, Portugal agreed to close its ports to British shipping, granted commercial concessions to the French, paid an indemnity, and ceded Olivença to Spain.

When Napoleon became emperor in 1804, he renewed his struggle with Britain. The British declared a naval blockade of France, and, in retaliation, Napoleon decreed that all nations of Europe should break relations with Britain. Portugal declared itself neutral in the struggle. Napoleon ordered the Portuguese to close their ports to the British, which they were prepared to do if they could do so without breaking relations with their old ally. In October 1807, Napoleon signed a treaty with Spain at Fontainebleau, according to which France and Spain agreed to invade Portugal and partition the country, one-third going to France, one-third to Spain, and one-third to Spain's chief minister, Manuel de Godoy.

On November 17, 1807, an army of French and Spanish soldiers under the command of the French general Andoche Junot entered Portugal and marched on Lisbon. The British were in no position to defend their ally; consequently, the prince regent and the royal family left for Brazil. On November 27, Junot's army took control of Lisbon.

French occupation eventually sparked rebellions among the populace, and provisional juntas were organized in several cities. The junta in Porto, to which other local juntas finally pledged obedience, organized an army and, with British help, was able to defeat a strong French force at Lourinhã on August 21, 1808. After this defeat, the French opened negotiations with the Portuguese and signed the Convention of Sintra, which provided for the evacuation of Junot's forces. The government was placed in the hands of the juntas. In January 1809, the prince regent designated a British officer, William Carr Beresford, to reorganize the Portuguese army, granting him the rank of marshall and commander in chief.

In March 1809, French troops under the command of General Nicholas Soult invaded Portugal once again. Entering the country from Galicia, they occupied Chaves and marched on Porto. A combined Portuguese-British army, commanded by Sir Arthur Wellesley, pushed Soult back to Galicia and defeated another French army at Tavera in Spain, after which Wellesley was made the duke of Wellington.

The expulsion of Soult's forces gave the Anglo-Portuguese army time to prepare for Napoleon's third invasion, which was ordered in 1810. The third French army under the command of General André Masséna entered Portugal at Guarda and marched to Viseu. Because Wellington's forces held the main roads, Masséna took his army across the Buçaco Mountains and marched on Coimbra, which he sacked. Wellington withdrew his army southward, luring Masséna into positions he had prepared at Tôrres Vedras. Finding the positions impenetrable, Masséna, far from his source of supply and short of food, withdrew his forces. Wellington pursued

Masséna and overtook him at Sabugal where his army was defeated. Masséna retreated from Portugal.

Constitutionalism

Although the ideology of liberalism was known in Portugal in the late 1700s by way of the American and French revolutions, it was not until after the Peninsular Wars that it became a force with which the monarchy had to contend. Freemasonry introduced by foreign merchants played an important role in spreading liberal doctrines in Portugal. In 1801 there were five Masonic temples in Lisbon, and the first Portuguese grand master was elected in 1804. The three French invasions encouraged the spread of liberal ideas. In 1812 Freemasons founded the Sinédrio, a secret society that propagated revolutionary ideas. Radical ideas were also discussed by Portuguese who lived in London or Paris where they had observed and been influenced by the functioning of the British and French systems. Newspapers and pamphlets, despite the vigilance of the crown's censors and police, were smuggled into Portugal and widely read by a small and increasingly important educated elite, called the *afrancesados,* who wanted to reconstruct Portugal on the French model. After the Peninsular Wars, the exiles themselves returned to Portugal and began to agitate for a constitutional monarchy. One of these was General Gomes Freire Andrade, the grand master of Portuguese Masons, who became the leader of liberals in Portugal. The liberals were eventually to be successful because of a crisis of royal leadership.

Revolution of 1820

In 1816 Maria I, after twenty-four years of insanity, died, and the prince regent was proclaimed João VI (r.1816–26). The new king, who had acquired a court and government in Brazil and a following among the Brazilians, did not immediately return to Portugal, and liberals continued to agitate against the monarchy. In May 1817, General Gomes Freire Andrade was arrested on treason charges and hanged, as were eleven alleged accomplices. Beresford, who was still commander in chief of the Portuguese army, was popularly blamed for the harshness of the sentences, which aggravated unrest in the country. The most active center of Portuguese liberalism was Porto, where the Sinédrio was situated and quickly gaining adherents. In March 1820, Beresford went to Brazil to persuade the king to return to the throne. His departure allowed the influence of the liberals to grow within the army, which had emerged from the Peninsular Wars as Portugal's strongest institution. On August 24, 1820, regiments in Porto revolted and established a provisional junta that assumed the government of Portugal until a cortes could be convoked to write a constitution. The regency was bypassed because it was unable to cope with Portugal's financial crisis, and Beresford was not allowed to enter the country when he returned from Brazil.

In December 1820, indirect elections were held for a constitutional cortes, which convened in January 1821. The deputies were mostly constitutional monarchists. They elected a regency to replace the provisional junta, abolished seignorial rights and the Inquisition, and, on September 23, approved a constitution. At the same time, João VI decided to return to Portugal, leaving his son Pedro in Brazil. Upon his arrival in Lisbon, João swore an oath to uphold the new constitution. After his departure from Brazil, Brazilian liberals, inspired by the independence of the United States and the independence struggles in the neighboring Spanish colonies, began to agitate for freedom from Portugal. Brazilian independence was proclaimed on October 12, 1822, with Pedro as constitutional emperor.

The constitution of 1822 installed a constitutional monarchy in Portugal. It declared that sovereignty rested with the nation and established three branches of government in classical liberal fashion. Legislative power was exercised by a directly elected, unicameral Chamber of Deputies; executive power was vested in the king and his secretaries of state; and judicial power was in the hands of the courts. The king and his secretaries of state had no representation in the chamber and no power to dissolve it.

Two broad divisions emerged in Portuguese society over the issue of the constitution. On the one hand were the liberals who defended it and, on the other, the royalists who favored absolutism. The first reaction to the new liberal regime surfaced in February 1823 in Trás-os-Montes where the count of Amarante, a leading absolutist, led an insurrection. Later, in May, Amarante once again sounded the call to arms, and an infantry regiment rose at Vila Franca de Xira, just north of Lisbon. Some of the Lisbon garrison joined the absolutists, as did the king's younger brother, Miguel, who had refused to swear to uphold the constitution. After the Vilafrancada, as the uprising is known, Miguel was made generalissimo of the army. In April 1824, Miguel led a new revolt—the Abrilada—which sought to restore absolutism. João, supported by Beresford, who had been allowed to return to Portugal, dismissed Miguel from his post as generalissimo and exiled him to France. The constitution of 1822 was suspended, and Portugal was governed under João's moderate absolutism until he died in 1826.

War of the Two Brothers

João's death created a problem of royal succession. The rightful heir to the throne was his eldest son, Pedro, emperor of Brazil. Neither the Portuguese nor the Brazilians wanted a unified monarchy; consequently, Pedro abdicated the Portuguese crown in favor of his daughter, Maria da Glória, a child of seven, on the condition that when of age she marry his brother, Miguel. In April 1826, as part of the succession settlement, Pedro granted a new constitution to Portugal, known as the Constitutional Charter. Pedro returned to Brazil leaving the throne to Maria, with Miguel as regent.

The Constitutional Charter attempted to reconcile absolutists and liberals by allowing both factions a role in government. Unlike the constitution of 1822, this document established four branches of government. The legislature was divided into two chambers. The upper chamber, the Chamber of Peers, was composed of life and hereditary peers and clergy appointed by the king. The lower chamber, the Chamber of Deputies, was composed of 111 deputies elected to four-year terms by the indirect vote of local assemblies, which in turn were elected by persons meeting certain tax-paying and property-owning requirements. Judicial power was exercised by the courts; executive power by the ministers of the government; and moderative power by the king, who held an absolute veto over all legislation.

The absolutists, however, were not satisfied with this compromise, and they continued to regard Miguel as the legitimate successor to the throne because he was Portuguese whereas Pedro was Brazilian. In February 1828, Miguel returned to Portugal to take the oath of allegiance to the charter and assume the regency. He was immediately proclaimed king by his supporters. Although it initially appeared that Miguel would abide by the charter, pressure mounted for a return to absolutism. A month after his return, Miguel dissolved the Chamber of Deputies and the Chamber of Peers and, in May, summoned the traditional cortes of the three estates of the realm to proclaim his accession to absolute power. The Cortes of 1828 assented to Miguel's wish, proclaiming him king as Miguel I and nullifying the Constitutional Charter.

This usurpation did not go unchallenged by the liberals. On May 18, the garrison in Porto declared its loyalty to Pedro, Maria da Glória, and the Constitutional Charter. The rebellion against the absolutists spread to other cities. Miguel suppressed these rebellions, and many thousands of liberals were either arrested or fled to Spain and Britain. There followed five years of repression.

In Brazil, meanwhile, relations between Pedro and Brazil's political leaders had become strained. In 1831 Pedro abdicated in favor of his son, Pedro II, and sailed for Britain. He organized a military expedition there and then went to the Azores, which were in the hands of the liberals, to set up a government in exile in March 1831. In July 1832, Pedro occupied Porto, which was subsequently besieged by the absolutists. In June 1833, the liberals, still encircled at Porto, sent a force commanded by the duke of Terceira to the Algarve. At the same time, a liberal squadron defeated the absolutists' fleet near Cabo São Vincente. Terceira landed at Faro and marched north through the Alentejo to capture Lisbon on July 24. A stalemate of nine months ensued. The absolutists controlled the rural areas, where they were supported by the aristocracy and the peasantry. The liberals occupied Portugal's major cities, Lisbon and Porto, where they commanded a sizeable following among the middle classes. Finally, the Miguelists lifted their siege of Porto and marched on Lisbon, but they were defeated at Évora-Monte. Peace was declared in May 1834, and Miguel, guaranteed an annual pension, was banished from Portugal, never to return. Pedro restored the Constitutional Charter.

Moderate vs. Radical Liberals

Pedro survived his victory by less than three months. After his death, fifteen-year-old Maria da Glória was proclaimed queen as Maria II (r. 1834–53). Despite their victory over the absolutists, the liberals were themselves divided between moderates, who supported the principles of the charter, and radicals, who wanted a return to the constitution of 1822. Maria's first government was made up of moderates headed by the duke of Palmela, whose government collapsed in May 1835. He was succeeded by the duke of Saldanha, whose government fell in May 1836. In July 1836, radicals were elected from Porto by advocating a return to the constitution of 1822 as a way of resolving Portugal's economic crisis. When these deputies arrived in Lisbon, they were met by demonstrations supporting their cause. The following day, the moderate liberal government collapsed, and, in September, the radicals, led by Manuel da Silva Passos, formed a new government. The radicals nullified the Constitutional Charter and reestablished the constitution of 1822 until it could be revised by a constituent cortes to make it more compatible with changed social and economic circumstances.

The actions of the radicals resulted in a violent reaction from the moderates, who saw their power threatened and considered the charter the symbol of the liberal victory in the War of Two Brothers.

As a compromise, the Constituent Assembly, convoked in March 1838, attempted to reconcile the constitution of 1822 and the Constitutional Charter. In April 1838, Portugal's third constitution was approved. The document abolished the royal moderative power and returned to liberalism's classical tripartite division of government into legislative, executive, and judicial branches. It reaffirmed, as did the 1822 constitution, that sovereignty rested with the nation. It abolished the Chamber of Peers and substituted a Chamber of Senators, and it established direct election of the Chamber of Deputies, although only selected citizens were allowed to vote. The monarch's role was enhanced, and the Chamber of Senators was restricted to leading citizens, or notables.

The radicals, now called Septemberists after the September 1836 revolution, held office until June 1841. On that date, they were replaced in a bloodless coup d'état by moderates, who abolished the 1838 constitution and restored the charter. António Bernardo da Costa Cabral, who organized and led the revolt, took various measures designed to reform Portugal's political, economic, and social systems. Some of these measures, especially new sanitary regulations that prohibited burials in churchyards, stirred the rural countryside, still Miguelist, into active resistance against the liberal government in Lisbon.

The women of the Minho region, who had traditionally played an important role in churchyard burials, began to demonstrate against the authorities. Supported by the rural nobility and clergy, the Maria da Fontes, as this movement was called, spread throughout the rural north. Unable to suppress it by force, the government of Costa Cabral fell on May 20, 1846. The new government, a confusing hodgepodge of radicals and moderates, rescinded the cemetery regulations. The government divided when the duke of Palmela, who was its prime minister, called for new elections in October, hoping to unite the moderates, themselves divided into two factions. This development sparked a reaction by the Septemberists, who were particularly strong in Porto, where they rebelled and set up a provisional junta. The duke of Saldanha, Palmela's replacement, attempted without success to suppress the Septemberist rebellion, which by now had spread beyond Porto to other areas. With the country on the brink of a second civil war, Queen Maria sought help from the Quadruple Alliance, consisting of Britain and France, as well as Spanish and Portuguese liberal elements. After the alliance imposed a naval blockade and sent troops, the Septemberists capitulated, Saldanha resigned, and a peace agreement was signed on June 29, 1847. Costa Cabral returned to power.

Rotativismo

In 1851 Saldanha staged a revolt and, supported by the garrison in Porto, gained control of the government and sent Costa Cabral into exile. Saldanha and his followers were called Regenerators because they recognized the need to modify the charter to make it more compatible with the social and political situation. These modifications appeared as amendments, the first of which was a new electoral law that made the franchise more acceptable to the Septemberists. Gradually, government became stabilized. The Septemberists began to be referred to as Historicals and, later, Progressives.

The Regenerators and Progressives were not political parties in today's sense of the term. The electorate comprised less than 1 percent of the population; therefore, the Regenerators and Progressives were essentially loose coalitions of notables, or leading citizens, based on personal loyalties and local interests. Elections were held after a change in governing factions to provide the new faction with a majority in the legislature. By tacit agreement, one faction would govern as long as it was able and then turn over power to the other. After 1856 this practice of alternating factions at regular intervals, called *rotativismo,* was all but institutionalized and produced relatively stable government until the end of the nineteenth century.

Portuguese Africa

With the advent of *rotativismo* and subsequent political stability, the attention of Portugal turned toward its colonial possessions in Africa. In East Africa, the chief settlement was Mozambique Island, but there was little control over the estates of the mainland where Portuguese of mixed ancestry ruled as feudal potentates. In West Africa, the most important settlements were Luanda and Benguela on the Angolan coast, linked to Brazil by the slave trade conducted through the African island of São Tomé. It was during this period that the Portuguese began to send expeditions into the interior.

In 1852 António Francisco Silva Porto explored the interior of Angola. In 1877 a scientific expedition led by Hermenegildo Capelo and Roberto Ivens, two naval officers, and Alexandre Serpa Pinto, an army major, departed from Luanda and traveled to the Bié region in central Angola, where they separated. Serpa Pinto explored the headwaters of the Cuanza River in Angola and followed the course of the Zambezi River to Victoria Falls in present-day Zimbabwe. Exploring areas now part of South Africa, he crossed the Transvaal and arrived in Natal in 1879. In 1884 Capelo and

Ivens departed from Moçamades on the coast of Angola and crossed
the continent through entirely unexplored territory, arriving at Que-
limane on the east coast of Mozambique in 1885. In the same year,
Serpa Pinto and Augusto Cardoso explored the territory around
Lake Nyassa. Various Portuguese, such as Paiva de Andrade and
António Maria Cardoso, explored the interior of Mozambique.

Despite Portugal's historical claim to the Congo region, the
colonial ambitions of the great powers of the day—Britain, France,
and Germany—gave rise to disputes about its ownership. Portugal therefore proposed an international conference to resolve the
disputed claim to the Congo. This conference, which met in Berlin in 1884–85, awarded the Congo to the king of Belgium and
established the principle that in order for a claim to African territory to be valid, the claimant had to demonstrate "effective occupation," not historical rights. The Berlin Conference, as it is known,
resulted in the partition of Africa among the European powers,
and awarded Mozambique, Angola, and Guinea to Portugal.

In 1886 Portugal signed two treaties that delimited the boundaries between Portuguese territories and those of France and Germany. France and Germany recognized Portugal's right to exercise
sovereignty in the interior territory between Mozambique and Angola. This claim was represented on a map, annexed to the treaty
with France, on which the claimed territory was colored red. In
order to validate this claim, the Portuguese published the "rose-
colored map" and organized successive expeditions into the interior
between Mozambique and Angola. Meanwhile, the British were
also exploring the territory from south to north under the auspices
of Cecil Rhodes, who had designs on the territory for the construction of a railroad that would run from Cape Town through central
Africa to Cairo.

Portugal protested against the activities of the British in what
they considered to be their territory. The British, having signed
a number of treaties with African chiefs, claimed that the territory
was under their protection and refused to recognize the rose-colored
map. Moreover, they said the territory was not Portuguese because
Portugal had not effectively occupied it as required by the terms
of the Berlin Conference. Portugal proposed that the conflicting
claims be resolved through arbitration. Britain refused and sent
the Portuguese an ultimatum, on January 11, 1890, demanding
the withdrawal of all Portuguese forces from the disputed territory.
Portugal, faced with the armed might of the British, complied.

Republicanism

The ultimatum of 1890 caused astonishment and indignation in

Lisbon. As a result, the Progressive government fell and a non-party government came to power. The ultimatum was strongly denounced by Portugal's growing band of republicans, who had organized themselves into a formal party in 1878. The republicans based their appeals on crude nationalism and played on the fears of many that a continuation of the inept government of the liberals would make Portugal either a British colony or a province of Spain. Teachers, journalists, small-business persons, clerks, and artisans were drawn to republicanism, with its appeals to nationalism, universal suffrage, separation of church and state, and the abolition of the monarchy and nobility, which were seen as irrational institutions that sapped the strength of Portugal.

The appeal of republicanism was also enhanced by the collapse of *rotativismo*. After 1890 the system ceased to function smoothly. Conflicts between the Regenerators and Historicals, formerly settled in secret, were brought into the open in an effort to generate public support for the system. But open debate proved to be unsettling in Portugal's depoliticized society. By 1906 neither faction could attain a parliamentary majority. In that year, the republicans managed to elect from Lisbon four deputies who proceeded to create tumultuous scenes in parliament. In May 1907, the situation came to a standstill. The king, Carlos I (r.1889–1908), dissolved parliament and gave to João Franco, a conservative reformist who had bolted from the Regenerators to form his own party, the power to govern by decree. João Franco's dictatorship was condemned by all political parties, and the republicans attempted an unsuccessful coup d'état. A crackdown on the republican movement followed. On February 1, 1908, the king and the royal family were attacked by two disgruntled republicans as they crossed the Praça do Comércio by open landau. The king and his youngest son were killed, and his oldest son, Manuel, survived a bullet wound in the arm. Manuel, who was eighteen at the time, became king as Manuel II (r.1908–10).

In an effort to salvage the monarchy, João Franco stepped down as prime minister and went into exile. New elections were held, but factionalism among the Regenerators and Historicals prevented the formation of a stable government even after six attempts. On October 1, 1910, the appearance in Portugal of the president of the Brazilian republic after a visit to Germany provided a pretext for extensive republican demonstrations. On October 3, the army refused to put down a mutiny on Portuguese warships anchored in the estuary of the Tagus and took up positions around Lisbon. On October 4, when two of the warships began to shell the royal palace, Manuel II and the royal family fled to Britain. On October

Manuel II, Portugal's last king (r.1908–10)
Courtesy Embassy of Portugal, Washington

5, a provisional republican government was organized with the writer Teófilo Braga as president.

The First Republic

In May 1911, the provisional government held elections for the Constituent Assembly, which undertook to write a new constitution. This document, which appeared on August 21, abolished the monarchy and inaugurated Portugal's first republican government. The constitution secularized the state by disestablishing the church, forbidding religious instruction in the public schools, and prohibiting the military from taking part in religious observances. It granted workers the right to strike and opened the civil service to merit appointments. The blue and white flag of the monarchy was replaced with one of red and green, embellished with an armillary sphere in gold.

The constitution vested legislative power in a bicameral Congress of the Republic. The upper house, called the Senate, was indirectly elected from local governments for six-year terms; the lower house, or Chamber of Deputies, was directly elected for three-year terms. Executive power was vested in a cabinet and prime minister responsible to the Congress, which also chose the president of the republic, the nominal head of state. The Constituent Assembly became the first Congress by electing one-third of its members to the Senate; the remaining two-thirds constituted the Chamber of Deputies.

The Portuguese Republican Party (Partido Repúblicano Português—PRP) was Portugal's first political party in the modern sense of the term. Although its base of support was primarily urban, the PRP had a nationwide organization that extended into the rural areas. It did not remain unified, however. In 1911 moderate and radical republican deputies divided over the election by the Constituent Assembly of the new president of the republic. The candidate of the radical republicans, led by Afonso Costa, was defeated by the candidate of the moderates, led by Manuel Brito Camacho and António José de Almeida, who opposed Costa's intransigent republicanism and feared that he would gain control of the new government. The split widened at the PRP Congress in October 1911 when the moderates where hooted down and left in disgust. The moderates then formed the Republican National Union (União Nacional Repúblicana—UNR), the directorate consisting of Camacho, Almeida, and Aresta Branco. The UNR was essentially a personal clique of several moderate leaders whose purpose was to get through parliament a program that would mitigate the impact of the more radical republican government. After this breakup, the PRP became known as the Democratic Party (Partido Democrático—PD).

In February 1912, the UNR leadership itself split into two republican splinter parties. The immediate cause of the rift was disagreement over the UNR program and rivalry between Camacho and Almeida. The rump, led by Camacho, was renamed the Republican Union (União Repúblicana—UR), and its members became known as Unionists. The other group, led by Almeida, was called the Republican Evolutionist Party (Partido Repúblicano Evolucionista—PRE), and its followers became known as Evolutionists. The program of the PRE was quite similar to that of the UR, but it urged a policy of moderation and conciliation and advocated proportional representation and revision of intolerant laws.

The splintering of the original PRP, personalism, and petty squabbles produced acute governmental instability during the First Republic. In its fifteen years and eight months of existence, there were seven elections for the Congress, eight for the presidency, and forty-five governments. Instability was also encouraged by the government's total dependency upon the Congress, where no stable majority could be organized. This political turmoil led to several periods of military rule during the First Republic and eventually to its overthrow.

In January 1915, senior military officers, who were becoming increasingly alienated from the republic, imposed a period of military rule at President Manuel de Arriaga's request. In May of the same year, however, prorepublican junior officers and sergeants returned the government to civilians and held new elections. The PD, led by Afonso Costa, won the day.

In 1916 Prime Minister Costa, who feared that a German victory in World War I would mean the loss of Portugal's African colonies of Mozambique and Angola, sent an expeditionary force of 40,000 men to fight on the side of the Allies. Poorly trained and equipped, the force suffered horrendous casualties in Flanders. This debacle, as well as severe food shortages caused by the war mobilization, paved the way for a second military intervention in December 1917, led by Major Sidónio Pais. Pais, who had held a diplomatic post in Prussia some years before, was sympathetic to Germany and antiliberal. He was an energetic, charismatic individual who sought to build a broadly based popular following. Gradually, however, he came to rely on upper-class youths, young army officers, students, and sons of big landowners, who were antiliberal and traditionalist. In December 1918, Pais was assassinated by a radical republican corporal recently returned from the front. Portugal's government was returned to civilians.

Political instability continued under civilian government. A small-scale civil war erupted in northern Portugal as monarchists led by Henrique Paiva Couciero attempted to restore the monarchy. A wave of violence swept the country, and leading republican figures, including the prime minister, were murdered. Political instability and violence brought economic life to a standstill. The middle class, which had initially supported the republic, began to turn toward traditional values as liberal and republican ideals were increasingly discredited.

By 1925 the republic had become the butt of ridicule and cynicism. It never satisfactorily resolved its dispute with the church, against which some of its first legislation had been directed. Official anticlericism made it impossible for many to accept the republic and stimulated the development of a politically involved Catholic intelligentsia in opposition to the parliamentary regime. The apparitions at Fátima in 1917 occurred at the height of Prime Minister Costa's anticlerical campaign. Those dissatisfied with the republic viewed the authoritarian governments established in Italy (in 1922) and Spain (in 1923) as attractive alternatives.

Many military officers, despite their previous negative experiences in government, thought that only they could save Portugal from disintegration. Their inclination to intervene once again was heightened by grievances over low pay and poor equipment. During the last thirteen months of the republic, there were three attempts to overturn the regime. The last of these was successful.

On May 26, 1926, General Manuel Gomes da Costa, the coup d'état's leader selected by the young officers who had organized it, announced from Braga his intention to march on Lisbon and take power. This announcement was followed by a massive military uprising that met little resistance. On May 28, General Gomes da Costa symbolically entered Lisbon, a dramatic gesture emulating Benito Mussolini's march on Rome in 1922. Prime Minister António Maria da Silva resigned on May 29, and the First Republic was ended.

Military Dictatorship

The coup d'état was bloodless because no military units came to the aid of the government. On May 30, the president of the republic, Bernardino Machado, turned the reins of power over to Commander José Mendes Cabeçadas, a naval officer and staunch republican, not to General Gomes da Costa, the titular leader of the military uprising. This action resulted in two months of behind-the-scenes infighting among various factions of the military. The promonarchist tendency within the May 28 Movement, as the coup was called, allied itself with right-wing but not necessarily monarchist junior officers who wanted some form of authoritarian state. In the hope of preventing the rise of a monarchist or authoritarian regime, Mendes Cabeçadas formed a joint government with Gomes da Costa on June 1. On June 17, Gomes da Costa ousted Mendes Cabeçadas and his followers from the provisional government. General da Costa's supremacy was temporary; he too was ousted on July 9. On the same day, General Óscar Fragoso Carmona was named head of the military government.

The military government was now in the hands of monarchists and authoritarian officers, and it seemed as if a restoration of the monarchy would follow. This was not to be, however, because of the reaction that such an outcome could have provoked among a substantial number of republicans within the officer corps. Carmona, who was both a republican and a devout Catholic, was acceptable to a broad range of views. He carefully preserved a balance between pro- and antimonarchists and pro- and anticlerical officers in order to ensure that the military regime would survive. On March 25, 1928, General Carmona was elected to the presidency of the republic and appointed Colonel José Vicente de Freitas, a staunch republican, as prime minister, which virtually assured that the monarchy was not going to be restored, at least not during the military dictatorship.

Carmona named António de Oliveira Salazar, a professor of political economy at the University of Coimbra, as minister of finance.

Salazar accepted the post on April 27, 1928, only after he had demanded and had been granted complete control over the expenditures of all government ministries. In his first year at the Ministry of Finance, he not only balanced the budget but achieved a surplus, the first since 1913. He accomplished this feat by centralizing financial control, improving revenue collection, and cutting public expenditures. Salazar remained minister of finance as military prime ministers came and went. From his first successful year as minister of finance, Salazar gradually came to embody the financial and political solution to the turmoil of the military dictatorship, which had not produced a clear leader. Salazar easily overshadowed military prime ministers and gradually gained the allegiance of Portugal's young intellectuals and military officers, who identified with his authoritarian, antiliberal, anticommunist view of the world. Moreover, Salazar's ascendancy was welcomed by the church, which saw in him a savior from the anticlericalism of the republicans. It was also welcomed by the upper classes of landowners, businessmen, and bankers, who were grateful for his success in stabilizing the economy after the financial crisis of the First Republic.

The New State

As Salazar came to be seen as the civilian mainstay of the military dictatorship, he increasingly took it upon himself to lay out the country's political future. He set forth his plans in two key speeches, one on May 28, 1930, and the other on July 30 of the same year. In the first, he spoke of the need for a new constitution that would create a strong authoritarian political order, which he dubbed the New State (Estado Novo). In the second, he announced his intention to establish such a state. The military approved of Salazar's speeches, and on July 5, 1932, after the collective resignation of the government of General Júlio Domingos de Oliveira, which had come to power two years earlier, he was appointed prime minister.

Salazar came from a peasant background. He had studied for the priesthood before turning to economics at the University of Coimbra, where he received his doctorate in 1918 and afterward taught. While a faculty member, he earned a reputation as a scholar and a writer, as well as a leader in Catholic intellectual and political movements. After taking up the reins of government, he retained his professorial style, lecturing the cabinet, his political followers, and the nation. Salazar never married and lived ascetically. A skillful political manipulator with a capacity for ruthlessness, he was a respected rather than a popular figure.

55

The period of transition to the authoritarian republic promised after the military takeover in 1926 ended in 1933 with the adoption of a new constitution. The 1933 constitution, dictated by Salazar, created the New State, in theory a corporate state representing interest groups rather than individuals. The constitution provided for a president directly elected for a seven-year term and a prime minister appointed by and responsible to the president. The relationship of the office of prime minister to the presidency was an ambiguous one. Salazar, continuing as prime minister, was head of government. He exercised executive and legislative functions, controlled local administration, police, and patronage, and was leader of the National Union (União Nacional—UN), an umbrella group for supporters of the regime and the only legal political organization.

The legislature, called the National Assembly, was restricted to members of the UN. It could initiate legislation but only concerning matters that did not require government expenditures. The parallel Corporative Chamber included representatives of cultural and professional groups and of the official workers' syndicates that replaced free trade unions.

Women were given the vote for the first time, but literacy and property qualifications limited the enfranchised segment of the population to about 20 percent, somewhat higher than under the parliamentary regime. Elections were held regularly, without opposition.

In 1945 Salazar introduced so-called democratic measures, including an amnesty for political prisoners and a loosening of censorship, that were believed by liberals to represent a move toward democratic government. In the parliamentary election that year, the opposition formed the broadly based Movement of Democratic Unity (Movimento de Unidade Democrática—MUD), which brought democrats together with fascists and communists. The opposition withdrew before the election, however, charging that the government intended to manipulate votes. General Norton de Matos, a candidate who opposed Carmona in the 1949 presidential election, pulled out on the same grounds. In 1958 the eccentric General Humberto Delgado ran against the official candidate, Admiral Américo Tomás, representing the UN. Delgado pointedly campaigned on the issue of replacing Salazar and won 25 percent of the vote. After the election, the rules were altered to provide for the legislature to choose the president.

Salazar's was a low-keyed personalist rule. The New State was his and not a forum for a party or ideology. Although intensely patriotic, he was cynical about the Portuguese national character

António de Oliveira Salazar, founder of the New State Courtesy Embassy of Portugal, Washington

that in his mind made the people easy prey for demagogues. He avoided opportunities to politicize public life and appeared uncomfortable with the political groups that were eventually introduced to mobilize opinion on the side of the regime's policies. Politics in Salazar's Portugal consisted of balancing power blocs within the country—the military, business and commerce, landholders, colonial interests, and the church. All political parties were banned. The UN, officially a civic association, encouraged public apathy rather than political involvement. Its leadership was composed of a small political and commercial elite, and contacts within ruling circles were usually made on an informal, personal basis, rather than through official channels. Within the circle, it was possible to discuss and criticize policy, but no channels for expression existed outside the circle.

The UN had no guiding philosophy apart from support for Salazar. The tenets of the regime were said to be authoritarian government, patriotic unity, Christian morality, and the work ethic. Despite a great deal of deference paid to the theory of the corporate state, these tenets were essentially the extent of the regime's ideological content. Although the regime indulged in rallies and youth movements with the trappings of fascist salutes and paraphernalia, it was satisfied to direct public enthusiasm into "fado, Fátima, and football"—music, religion, and sports.

A devout Roman Catholic, Salazar sought a rapprochement with the church in Portugal. A concordat with the Vatican in 1940 reintroduced state aid to Roman Catholic education, but Salazar resisted involving the church—which he called "the great source of our national life"—in political questions. His policies were aimed essentially at healing the divisions caused within Portuguese society by generations of anticlericalism. Although the church had consistently supported Salazar, the regime came under increasing criticism by progressive elements in the clergy in the 1960s. One such incident led to the expulsion of the bishop of Porto.

Whatever may be said of his political methods, Salazar had an exceptional grasp of the techniques of fiscal management and, within the limits that he had set for the regime, his program of economic recovery succeeded. Portugal's overriding problem in 1926 had been its enormous public debt. Salazar's solution was to achieve financial solvency by balancing the national budget and reducing external debt. This solution required a strong government capable of cutting public expenditures and reducing domestic consumption by raising taxes and controlling credit and trade. In a few years Salazar singlemindedly achieved a solvent currency, a favorable balance of trade, and surpluses both in foreign reserves and in the national budget.

The bulk of the Portuguese remained among the poorest people in Europe, however. The austerity that Salazar's fiscal and economic policies demanded weighed most heavily on the working class and the rural poor, forestalling the development that would raise their standards of living. Outside the cities, traditional patterns of life persisted, especially in the conservative north, which had been stabilized by evenly distributed poverty and was a stronghold of support for the regime. To create an atmosphere of rising expectations without having the means to satisfy them, Salazar argued, would return the country to the chaotic conditions Portugal had known earlier in the century.

Stable government and a solvent economy would eventually attract foreign investment regardless of the attitude abroad to the nature of Salazar's regime. Cheap labor and the promise of competitive prices for Portuguese-made goods provided an incentive for investment, particularly in labor-intensive production, which was becoming uneconomic in Northern Europe. Priority was given, however, to colonial development. Salazar insisted that the overseas territories be made to pay for themselves and also to provide the trade surpluses required by Portugal to import the essentials that it could not produce itself. In essence, he updated Portuguese mercantilist policy: colonial goods were sold abroad to create a surplus at home.

In the years before World War II, Salazar cultivated good relations with all major powers except the Soviet Union. Intent on preserving Portuguese neutrality, he had entered into a nonintervention convention with the European powers during the Spanish Civil War (1936–39); however, Soviet activity in Spain and the leftward course of the Spanish Republic persuaded him to support Francisco Franco's nationalists, with whom more than 20,000 Portuguese volunteers served. The war in Spain also prompted Salazar to mobilize a political militia, the Portuguese Legion, as a counterweight to the army.

Although he admired Benito Mussolini for his equitable settlement of Italy's church-state conflict, Salazar found the "pagan" elements in German Nazism repugnant. He opposed appeasement, protested the German invasion of Poland in 1939, and would appear to have been among the first, with Winston Churchill, to express confidence in ultimate Allied victory as early as 1940. Portugal remained neutral during World War II, but the Anglo-Portuguese alliance was kept intact, Britain pledging to protect Portuguese neutrality. The United States and Britain were granted bases in the Azores after 1943, and Portuguese colonial products—copper and chromium—were funneled into Allied war production. Macau and Timor were occupied by Japan from 1941 to 1945.

Portugal became a charter member of the North Atlantic Treaty Organization (NATO) in 1949, and in 1971 Lisbon became headquarters for NATO's Iberian Atlantic Command (IBERLANT). Portugal also maintained a defensive military alliance (the Iberian Pact, also known as the Treaty of Friendship and Nonaggression) with Spain that dated from 1939. Admission to the United Nations (UN) was blocked by the Soviet Union until 1955. In 1961 Indian armed forces invaded and seized Goa, which had been Portuguese since 1510.

Into the early twentieth century, the European settler communities in Portuguese Africa had virtual autonomy, and colonial administrations were perpetually bankrupt. Lisbon's concern in Angola and Mozambique was to make good the Portuguese claim to those territories, and pacification of the interior was still underway in the 1930s. Control over the colonies was tightened under Salazar.

The Colonial Act of 1930 stated that Portugal and its colonies were interdependent entities. The New State insisted on increased production and better marketing of colonial goods to make the overseas territories self-supporting and to halt the drain on the

Portuguese treasury for their defense and maintenance. New land was opened for settlement, and emigration to the colonies was encouraged.

Portugal ignored the UN declaration on colonialism in 1960, which called on the colonial powers to relinquish control of dependent territories. Angola, Mozambique, and Guinea were made provinces with the same status as those in metropolitan Portugal by constitutional amendment in 1951. Armed resistance to the Portuguese colonial administration broke out in Angola in 1961 and had spread by 1964 to Mozambique and Guinea. By 1974 Portugal had committed approximately 140,000 troops, or 80 percent of its available military forces, to Africa; some 60 percent of these were African. Portuguese combat casualties were relatively light, and fighting consisted of small-unit action in border areas far from population centers. Only in Guinea did rebel troops control substantial territory. Portuguese forces appeared to have contained the insurgencies, and although large numbers of troops were required to hold the territory, Portugal seemed to some observers capable of sustaining military activity in Africa indefinitely. These same observers considered that, from a military standpoint, the wars had been won.

The wars did not interrupt the colonial production on which Portuguese economic stability depended. Indeed, they had provided a windfall to economic development in Angola and Mozambique, both with large settler communities. A large rural development project was underway in the Cahora Bassa region of Mozambique, as was the exploitation of oil in Cabinda enclave near Angola. More colonial income was being diverted into social services for Africans and Europeans, and in areas of medicine and education better facilities were thought to be available in Luanda and Lourenço Marques (now Maputo) than in Lisbon. However, forced native labor remained a factor in the economic development of Portuguese Africa into the 1960s. Foreign investment capital often came to the colonies from countries whose governments had officially condemned Portuguese colonialism.

No one except Pombal left so broad a mark on modern Portuguese history as Salazar. For nearly forty years, he completely dominated Portuguese government and politics. He died on July 27, 1970, more than two years after suffering an incapacitating stroke brought on by a freak accident.

The Social State

President Tomás appointed Marcello José das Neves Caetano to succeed Salazar as prime minister, although the regime did not admit for some time that Salazar would not be returning to power. Caetano was a teacher, jurist, and scholar of international reputation who had been one of the drafters of the 1933 constitution. Considered a moderate within the regime, he had taken unpopular stands in opposition to Salazar. He had resigned as rector of Lisbon University in 1960 in protest over police repression of student demonstrations. Unlike Salazar he came from the upper middle class, was ebullient and personable, and sought contact with the people.

It was clear from the start that Caetano was a different sort of leader. He spoke of "evolution within continuity," change fast enough to keep up with expectations but not so fast as to antagonize conservatives. He brought technocrats into the government and eased police repression. The elections held in 1969 were the freest in decades. He even altered the nomenclature of the regime; the New State became the Social State, but it remained essentially an authoritarian regime.

In contrast to Salazar, Caetano advocated an expansionist economic policy and promoted rapid development and increasing consumption without, however, supplementing the means of production. The consequence of liberalization was the first perceptible inflation in years, reaching 15 percent on such working-class staples as codfish and rice in the early 1970s.

Prime Minister Caetano had inherited Salazar's office but not his power nor, apparently, his skill as a politician and economist. President Tomás, meanwhile, had emerged with greater authority, as Salazar's death put him in a position to exercise the constitutional authority of the presidency to the fullest. Deeply conservative and supported by an entrenched right wing within the official political movement, Tomás employed threats of an army coup to oppose Caetano's policy of liberalization. Caetano took a harder line on Africa in an effort to head off opposition by the president and the officers close to him.

As the events of spring 1974 were to demonstrate, the regimes of Salazar's New State and Caetano's Social State had depended on personalities. In existence for nearly fifty years, the institutions of the corporate state had never put down roots in Portuguese political soil. Apathy had not implied support. On April 25, 1974, the officers and men of the Armed Forces Movement (Movimento das Forças Armadas—MFA) ousted Caetano and Tomás, paving the way for a junta under General António de Spínola to take command of the Portuguese Republic.

* * *

A comprehensive introduction to the history of the Iberian Peninsula is a two-volume study by Stanley G. Payne, *A History of Spain and Portugal*. The best history of Portugal in the English language up to the First Republic is H.V. Livermore's *A New History of Portugal*. A succinct survey of Portugal's overseas empire is C.R. Boxer's *Four Centuries of Portuguese Expansion, 1415–1825*. Douglas L. Wheeler provides a thorough treatment of the First Republic in *Republican Portugal*. A sympathetic portrait of António de Oliveira Salazar can be found in Hugh Kay's *Salazar and Modern Portugal*. Salazar's New State is analyzed by Howard J. Wiarda in *Corporatism and Development* and by Tom Gallagher in *Portugal: A Twentieth-Century Interpretation*. The standard history of Portugal in Africa is James Duffy's *Portuguese Africa*. Walter C. Opello, Jr. covers recent history in his book, *Portugal: From Monarchy to Pluralist Democracy*. (For further information and complete citations, see Bibliography.)

Chapter 2. The Society and Its Environment

Monsaraz, a medieval village near the Spanish frontier

As a RESULT OF CHANGES wrought by the Revolution of 1974, Portugal in the 1990s would be almost unrecognizable to persons who knew the country twenty or thirty years ago. The Revolution of 1974 set loose social and political forces that the country had not seen before on such a large scale and which could not be entirely controlled. The revolution, in turn, had occurred and had such a profound impact because of other, gradual social pressures that had been building for decades and even centuries. In the mid-1970s, these changes exploded to the surface. In the aftermath of the revolution, as Portuguese society continued to modernize and the country was admitted as a full member of the European Community (EC—see Glossary), social change continued, but not so frenetically and dramatically as during the revolutionary mid-1970s.

Before 1974 Portugal was a highly traditional society. It resembled what historian Barbara Tuchman has called the "Proud Tower" of pre-World War I European society. Class and social divisions were tightly drawn and defined, society was organized on a rigidly hierarchical and authoritarian basis, and social relations were often stiff and formal. One was born into a certain station in life and was expected to stay there and to accept that fact; social mobility was limited. Class standing and class relations were clearly delineated by criteria of birth, dress, speech, and manner of behavior. Visitors often remarked that in Portugal one could still find a nineteenth-century society existing within a twentieth-century context.

Even within this rigid, very conservative, and traditionalist society, however, considerable change was beginning to occur, particularly during the 1960s as economic development accelerated. The trade unions had grown in size and assertiveness. The middle class was emerging as a numerically larger and sociologically more important element than before. A new business-industrial class had grown up alongside, and frequently overlapped with, the more traditional landed and noble class. In addition, Portugal experienced urbanization; at the same time, many Portuguese left the country in search of better opportunities abroad. Literacy was also rising, though slowly. As modernization and social change began to accelerate in the 1960s and early 1970s, discontent with the closed and authoritarian regime of António de Oliveira Salazar (1928–68) and his successor Marcello José das Neves Caetano

(1968–74) also began to mount. These and other pressures culminated in the Revolution of 1974.

Following the revolution, which led to the establishment of democracy in Portugal, societal pressures continued. Pressures for education, land, jobs, better health care, housing, social equality, and solutions to Portugal's pressing social problems mounted. Portugal remained, even with the economic growth of the 1980s and early 1990s, a poor country compared to West European standards. Moreover, rising expectations were threatening to overwhelm the democratic regime's capacities for resolving the problems. Portugal's full economic participation in the EC at the end of 1992, at which time it would no longer have the protection of high tariff barriers, added to social tensions and uncertainties. Thus, as Portugal began the 1990s, the promise of a new, stable, democratic era of development coexisted with a fear of what the future might bring.

The Physical Environment

Portugal shares the Iberian Peninsula with Spain, although it is only about one-sixth as large as its neighbor. Including the Azores (Açores) and Madeira, the country has a total area of 92,080 square kilometers. Portugal lies on the westernmost promontory of continental Europe. The rugged Pyrenees Mountains separate Iberia from the heart of the European continent, and Portugal is even farther distant across the vastness of Spain. Distance and isolation have created in Portugal a sense that it is a part of Europe geographically but apart from it culturally, socially, economically, politically, and even psychologically. Even in the early 1990s, Lisbon (Lisboa) was a two-to-three-day drive from Paris.

Portugal is bounded on the west and south by the Atlantic Ocean and on the north and east by Spain. The country's shape is roughly that of a rectangle, with its short sides on the north and south and its long sides on the east and west. Portugal's Atlantic coastline is 837 kilometers long; its northern and eastern frontiers with Spain are 336 and 839 kilometers long, respectively.

Historically, Portugal emerged as a separate country during centuries of struggle with the Spanish provinces of León and Castile. Even hundreds of years after Portugal broke away from Spain for the last time in 1640, fears remained in the country that it might one day be swallowed up by larger and more powerful Spain, perhaps not militarily, but culturally and economically. That sentiment is expressed by the Portuguese proverb that "neither a good wind nor a good marriage ever come from Spain." Meanwhile, Portugal's long coast had given it an "Atlantic vocation" and propelled its historic ventures of global exploration and colonization.

Portugal is not a homogeneous country geographically. The physical environment varies enormously, creating several distinct geographic regions that, in turn, have shaped the culture of the people and their economy and society. Northern Portugal is a mountainous, rainy region, characterized by many small farms and vineyards. The Portuguese nation began in this region, fending off León and Castile while simultaneously driving the Moors south and eventually out of the peninsula. It is a desolate area of rocky hillsides where smallholders have eked out a meager existence for hundreds of years. This region is also said to be the origin of the strongest Portuguese national values of hard work, thrift, traditionalism, Roman Catholicism, and practicality. It is also an area, however, that has lost many of its inhabitants through emigration.

Central Portugal, between the Rio Douro in the north and the Tagus River (Rio Tejo), including the capital city of Lisbon and its environs, is less homogeneous. The central coastal region consists of dunes and pine forests, and many residents of the area earn their livelihood from fishing. The central eastern areas, known as the Beira, consist mainly of small and medium-sized farms, with some mining and light industry. The greater Lisbon area, including both the city and its suburbs, accounts for most of the nation's commerce and much of its industry.

Southern Portugal, known as the Alentejo (literally, ''beyond the Tagus'') is an area of gently rolling hills and plains dominated by extensive estates with large-scale agriculture and grazing. It was traditionally also a land of often embittered tenant farmers and peasants. In contrast to the conservative north, the Alentejo was an area of radical political movements; for a long time, the Portuguese Communist Party (Partido Comunista Português—PCP) was the strongest party in the region.

The extreme south of Portugal is known as the Algarve. It is a dry region of smallholdings, grazing, and fishing, and coastal towns. This is the area of Portugal most strongly influenced by the Moors; even today Moorish influence is present in the region's dialect and architecture. With its warm climate and Mediterranean sky, the Algarve has also become a center for tourism and a home to many foreign retirees.

Historically, Portugal was divided administratively into six provinces that corresponded closely to these natural geographic divisions (see fig. 4). The north consisted of two provinces, the coastal Minho and the interior Trás-os-Montes. The center was made up of Beira and Estremadura, and the south consisted of the Alentejo

Figure 4. Historical Regions

and the Algarve. Later these historical provinces were further subdivided for administrative purposes, but the historical names have
been retained in popular usage (see fig. 1).

Even though it is a small country, Portugal has a wide variety
of landforms, climatic conditions, and soils. The major difference
is between the mountainous regions of the north and, across the
Tagus River, the great rolling plains of the south. Within these
two major regions are further subdivisions that reflect the country's

vast differences. The Minho and Trás-os-Montes are both mountainous, but whereas the former is green with abundant rainfall,
the latter is dry and parched. The Beira Litoral and Estremadura
are younger geologically and contain sandstone, limestone, and vol-
canic rock. Beira Alta (Upper Beira) is mountainous and forms
a barrier across the center of Portugal, but Beira Baixa (Lower
Beira) is dry and windswept, an extension of the Spanish plateau.
The Alentejo consists of gentle hills and plains. Because it is one
of the driest areas in the country, it is not suitable for intensive
agriculture. The area does support cattle raising, as well as cork
oak and some grains. It is separated from the Algarve by two mountain ranges, the Serra de Monchique and the Serra do Caldeirao.

Geography and topography are also reflected in the climate. The
mountainous regions of the north are considerably colder than the
south. Winter snows in the Serra da Estrêla (which contains Portugal's highest peak at 1,986 meters) and the Serra do Gerês near
the northern Spanish border may block roads for a time. The
weather along the northern coasts and in the center of the country
is milder; Lisbon has an average high temperature of 14°C in January and 27°C in August. Southern Portugal is warmer. The ocean
moderates coastal temperatures, but the interior of the Alentejo
can be quite warm, with temperatures sometimes above 40°C during the summer months. Because of its Mediterranean climate, most
of Portugal's rainfall occurs in the winter, the north receiving much
more rain than the south.

Portugal has ten major rivers, five of which have their origins
in Spain. The Rio Minho begins in Spanish Galicia and for a distance of seventy-four kilometers forms the northern Portuguese
frontier with Spain. The Rio Douro is of great importance to the
commerce of northern Portugal. It also originates in Spain and flows
the entire width of Portugal before emptying into the Atlantic at
Porto, the country's second largest city. The Rio Douro is navigable
by small craft for its full distance of 198 kilometers in Portugal;
historically the river was used to transport casks of port wine to
Porto. Its steep banks are terraced with vineyards, and the valley
of the Rio Douro is one of the most picturesque in all Portugal.

The Tagus River is the country's longest river, has the largest
drainage basin, and is the most important economically. It is navigable only eighty kilometers upstream, but that includes the vast estuary on which Lisbon is located. The Tagus estuary is the best
natural port on the European continent and able to handle large
ocean-going vessels. It also contains the Cacilhas drydocks, the
largest in the world.

The most important river in the south is the Rio Guadiana, which, flowing north to south, forms part of the border with Spain. Other important rivers in Portugal include the Rio Lima and the Rio Tâmega in the north, the Rio Mondego in the center, and the Rio Sado and Rio Chança in the south.

The soil systems of Portugal are usually sandy, arid, and acid, reflecting the soils of the Iberian Peninsula generally. Soil in the north can be rocky. Northern Portugal is better suited for agriculture than the south because of abundant rainfall, but with proper irrigation the south could support more intensive agriculture.

About one-fourth of Portugal is covered by forests (mainly pine and deciduous oak); if such cultivated tree crops as olives, cork oak, almonds, chestnuts, and citrus are counted, about one-third of the country's area is tree covered. In the northern mountains, pine, oak, poplar, and elm trees are prevalent. Vegetation is more varied in the central region and includes citrus trees and cork oak. The warm, dry south contains many areas of rough pasture, as well as abundant cork oak.

In addition to continental Portugal, the country's territory also includes the Azores and Madeira islands. The Azores consist of nine inhabited islands and several uninhabited rock outcroppings 1,280 kilometers west of the mainland in the Atlantic Ocean. The archipelago has an area of 2,278 square kilometers and a population of about 250,000. The Azores produce sufficient foodstuffs for internal consumption and some exports, but they remain even poorer than the mainland. The Madeira archipelago, located about 560 kilometers miles west of North Africa, consists of two inhabited and several uninhabited islands. With a total area of 788 square kilometers and a population of about 270,000 people, the archipelago is severely overpopulated (see fig. 5).

Demography

By the early 1990s, Portugal's population was just over 10 million, a little more than triple the 3.1 million estimated to live in the country in 1801. The main causes for this slow growth were a high infant mortality rate for much of these two centuries and an emigration rate so extreme that in one decade, the 1960s, the country's population actually fell. These trends have reversed in recent decades. The country's infant mortality rate at the beginning of the 1990s—10 per 1,000 in 1992—remained somewhat higher than the European average but was one-fifth of that registered two decades earlier. Emigration also slowed markedly as prosperity appeared in Portugal in the second half of the 1980s. Moreover, in the second half of the 1970s a massive influx of

Figure 5. Topography and Drainage

refugees from former Portuguese colonies in Africa caused a population surge.

Population Size and Structure

Although population estimates are available for earlier years, the first official Portuguese census was taken in 1864. It showed a population of approximately 4.3 million (see table 2, Appendix). Thereafter, the population increased slowly at rates often well under 1 percent per year. Only during the 1930s and 1940s did the population increase at over 1 percent per year. During the 1960s, the population actually fell by over 300,000 and in 1970 amounted to about 8.5 million. During the early 1970s, population continued to fall or was stagnant. This demographic trend was the result of widespread emigration. Many Portuguese left their country in these years to find employment abroad or to avoid military service in the wars Portugal was fighting in its colonies in Africa.

In 1974 the country's population showed its first sizeable increase and by 1981 reached nearly 9.8 million, 1.2 million more than it had been ten years earlier. The settling in Portugal of an estimated 500,000 to 800,000 refugees from the country's African colonies accounted for most of this increase. During the first half of the 1980s, the population grew at a rate of about 0.8 percent a year, then declined. As of the early 1990s, population growth was estimated at 0.4 percent a year. By the beginning of 1992, the population of Portugal, including the Azores and Madeira, was estimated at nearly 10.5 million. Population specialists projected that if existing trends continued, the country's population would peak at 10.8 million in 2010 and fall to 10.5 in 2025.

This population is not evenly distributed. As of the late 1980s, continental Portugal had an average population density of 109.6 persons per square kilometer, but some districts were much more crowded than others. The eastern districts bordering Spain, with the exception of Faro, had the lowest population density, ranging between 17.0 per square kilometer in Beja and 35.6 per square kilometer in Guarda. Coastal districts from the northern border down to and including Setúbal registered the highest concentrations of people. The districts of Lisbon and Porto, with 770.2 and 697.5 persons per square kilometer, respectively, were as densely populated as many urban regions of Northern Europe (see table 3, Appendix).

Some of these differences in population density result from topography. Mountainous regions typically contain fewer people than flat coastal regions. But some differences result from migration from one area to another within Portugal or from migration abroad. During the period 1911–89, five districts, all of them bordering Spain in the east, lost population: Guarda lost about one-fourth of its population, Beja and Castelo Branco lost about one-tenth, and Bragança and Portalegre each lost about one-twentieth. The only eastern district posting a gain in this period was Évora, which grew by about one-sixth. Two inland districts, Vila Real and Viseu, showed almost no growth; another inland district, Santarém, with significant industrial employment, grew by one-half. All coastal districts gained in population during this period. Coimbra and Faro grew by one-fourth, Aveiro and Braga doubled their populations, the districts of Lisbon and Porto increased by two-and-one-half times, and Setúbal increased more than three times. The Azores showed almost no gain in population, but that of Madeira grew by two-thirds.

The main areas of population growth were urban centers and the district capitals. The urban-industrial centers along the coast—Lisbon, Porto, and Setúbal—took in the largest numbers of new immigrants. However, only the cities of Lisbon and Porto had significant populations, approximately 830,000 and 350,000, respectively, at the end of the 1980s. They were followed by Amadora with 96,000 (part of greater Lisbon), Setúbal with 78,000, and Coimbra with 75,000. At the beginning of the 1990s, therefore, some two-thirds of all Portuguese still lived in what were classified as rural areas despite the significant growth of some urban areas.

The Lisbon area was the region of greatest population growth in absolute terms, in part because it was the seat of much of the country's governmental apparatus, as well as its manufacturing and service-sector jobs. Until the 1960s, the area's population increases were mainly inside the city of Lisbon, but since then the suburbs have grown most rapidly. The central city's population remained largely stagnant or even declined in some years, whereas that of the suburbs surged. High city rents, crowding, the decline of old neighborhoods, pollution, and the squeezing out of housing by commercial enterprises were among the causes of this new suburbanization of Lisbon's outlying districts.

Government population estimates showed that in the late 1980s women outnumbered men by a wide margin and that the number of old persons in Portugal was unusually high. The 1864 census and every census since has shown that women outnumber men. In 1988 this was the case in all but two of the districts of continental Portugal, Beja and Bragança. The greatest disproportions were found in northern and central areas where male emigration was most intense. However, during the 1980s, men formed the majority in twenty-two of the country's 305 municipalities. Eighteen of these statistically unusual municipalities were in southern Portugal.

Portugal has long had an aging population. The percentage of the population under age thirty has been decreasing since 1900. Moreover, the rate at which the country's population has aged accelerated as ever more young Portuguese males in their physical prime left the country. Between 1960 and 1990, the percentage of those under fifteen fell from 29.0 to 20.9, whereas the percentage of those sixty-five and older rose from 8.1 to 13.1. The north had a disproportionate number of old and very young people, mainly those still too young to migrate. In some areas of Portugal where employment has been available, this preponderance was not the case. Lisbon and the growth areas of Santarém and Setúbal had a disproportionate share of those of working age, between twenty and sixty-five (see fig. 6).

Emigration

Portugal has long been a nation whose people emigrated. Socially significant emigration first occurred in the fifteenth century and sixteenth century during the great explorations. Although the Portuguese established trading posts at many places in Africa and Asia, Brazil was the main colony of settlement. Later, numbers of Portuguese settled in the African colonies of Angola and Mozambique.

Emigration on a massive scale began in the second half of the nineteenth century and continued into the 1980s. Between 1886 and 1966, Portugal lost an estimated 2.6 million people to emigration, more than any West European country except Ireland. Emigration remained high until 1973 and the first oil shock that slowed the economies of West European nations and reduced employment opportunities for Portuguese workers. Since then, emigration has been moderate, ranging between 12,000 and 17,000 a year in the 1980s, a fraction of the emigration that occurred during the 1960s and early 1970s.

The main motive for emigration, at least in modern times, was economic. Portugal had long been one of the poorest countries in Europe. With the countryside able to support only a portion of farmers' offspring and few opportunities in the manufacturing sector, many Portuguese had to go abroad to find work. In northern Portugal, for example, many young men emigrated because the land was divided into "handkerchief-sized" plots. In some periods, Portuguese emigrated to avoid military service. Thus, emigration increased during World War I and during the 1960s and early 1970s, when Portugal waged a series of wars in an attempt to retain its African colonies.

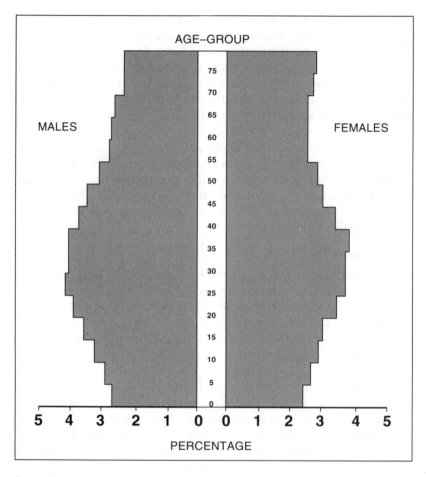

Source: Based on information from *Grande Enciclopédia Portuguesa e Brasileira*, 9, Lisbon, 1987, 408.

Figure 6. Estimated Population Distribution by Age and Sex, 2000

For centuries the majority of emigrants were men. Around the turn of the century, about 80 percent of emigrants were male. Even in the 1980s, male emigrants outnumbered female emigrants two to one. Portuguese males traditionally emigrated for several years while women and children remained behind. For several decades after World War II, however, women made up about 40 percent of emigrants.

The social effects resulting from this extensive and generally male emigration included an aging population, a disproportionate number of women, and a slower rate of population growth. Childbearing was postponed, and many women were obliged to remain single or to spend many years separated from their husbands. In some areas where emigration was particularly intense, especially in the north, villages resembled ghost towns, and visitors noted that only women appeared to be working in the fields.

Although emigration brought with it untold human suffering, it had positive effects, as well. The women who stayed behind became more independent as they managed the family farm and fended for themselves. Emigrants abroad absorbed the more open and pluralistic mores of more advanced countries; they also learned about independent labor unions and extensive social welfare programs. The money that emigrants sent back to Portugal from their job earnings abroad became crucial for the functioning of the Portuguese economy. Quite a number of the Portuguese who had done well abroad eventually returned and built houses that were considerably better than the ones they had left behind years earlier.

During the latter half of the nineteenth century and during much of the twentieth century, the greatest number of emigrants went to the Western Hemisphere. The Americas were seen as a New World offering hope, jobs, land, and a chance to start fresh. Between 1864 and 1974, the Americas received approximately 50 percent of all Portuguese emigration.

Brazil was the destination of choice. In addition to the climate, ties of history, culture, and language attracted the Portuguese to Brazil and enabled them to assimilate easily. Despite occasional tensions between them and the Brazilians, the Portuguese saw Brazil as a land of the future with abundant land and jobs. Hence, about 30 percent of Portugal's emigrants settled there between 1864 and 1973. A final surge of Portuguese emigrants was caused by the Revolution of 1974, when an estimated 20,000 to 30,000 Portuguese associated with the former regime fled or were exiled to Brazil. According to government estimates, more than 1 million Portuguese were living in Brazil in the 1980s.

Among the other Latin American countries, Venezuela has ranked second to Brazil in terms of Portuguese emigration and Argentina third. Other Latin American countries have received only a few Portuguese immigrants, for the Portuguese, like other peoples, preferred to go to countries where their fellow countrypeople could help them get settled.

Emigration to North America was also heavy. By the late 1980s, it was estimated that more than 1 million Portuguese and persons of Portuguese descent lived in the United States and 400,000 lived in Canada, most notably in Toronto and Montreal. Significant Portuguese migration to the United States began in the nineteenth century. Early in the twentieth century, substantial Portuguese communities were established in California, New Jersey, and Massachusetts. Since the 1950s, the most intense migration has been to the northeast—Rhode Island and Connecticut—and to cities in southeastern Massachusetts.

Portuguese emigration to the United States often involved whole families, rather than just the men. For this reason, emigrants to the United States settled permanently, unlike Portuguese emigrants to Northern Europe, who were mostly men who set out alone with the intention of returning home after a few years. Another characteristic of the Portuguese migration to the United States was that many migrants were fishermen from the Azores who came to work in areas offshore of New England. Others migrated from Madeira and São Tomé.

Portugal was never as successful at stimulating emigration to its African territories as it wanted to be. For centuries the number of Europeans in these territories was small. Faced with competition from other European imperialist powers in the nineteenth century, Portugal sought to fill up its vast African spaces with people. The state allowed prisoners to work off their sentences by settling in Africa, offered land grants and stipends to prospective settlers, encouraged its soldiers assigned there to stay, and tried to lure other Europeans to settle there to augment the thin Portuguese population. These efforts were not notably successful, however, and Portuguese emigration to Africa never amounted to more than 4 percent of total emigration.

With mounting opposition in the 1960s to its efforts to retain its African territories, Portugal's settlement efforts again reflected political, as well as economic, motives. The government tried to persuade the unemployed, especially those in the north, to settle in Africa rather than emigrate illegally to Europe, but in the long run was unsuccessful in these efforts. Even the construction of major dams and other infrastructure projects in the territories failed to lure significant numbers of settlers. By the mid-1970s, the African colonies were lost, and Portugal was flooded with refugees from these areas instead of providing emigrants to them.

Upwards of 1 million Portuguese or persons of Portuguese descent were living in the country's African colonies in 1974 when these colonies gained independence. Most of these settlers left the former colonies rather than live under the rule of the Marxist-Leninist groups that came to power. Sizeable numbers went to South Africa and to Brazil, but an estimated 800,000 returned to Portugal, where they increased the already high unemployment rate and added to the social and political tensions of the late 1970s.

Eventually, however, most of these returnees were assimilated into Portuguese society, and some of them achieved notable political or financial success.

During the first half of the twentieth century, most Portuguese emigrating from their country went to Portugal's colonies or to the Western Hemisphere. This pattern changed dramatically in the 1950s when Western Europe began to experience an economic boom that lasted at least up to the first oil crisis of 1973. The boom created millions of jobs, and Portuguese migrants traveled north to fill them. Alongside Italians, Spaniards, Turks, North Africans, and others, Portuguese worked in restaurants, in construction, in factories, and in many other areas. Although much of the work was menial and poorly paid, such employment provided significant economic advancement for many Portuguese. By the late 1960s, an estimated 80 percent of Portuguese emigrants went to Europe. Many of these emigrants did so illegally, without the required documents, because the lure of Europe's prosperity was too strong to be resisted.

France was the most popular destination. By the early 1970s, it was estimated that 8 percent of Portugal's population lived there. The Federal Republic of Germany (West Germany) had the next largest contingent. There were also sizeable Portuguese communities in Switzerland, Belgium, Britain, and the Netherlands. Chaotic economic and social conditions resulting from the Revolution of 1974 caused a slight surge of emigration in the later 1970s, but it never again reached the levels of the 1960s and early 1970s.

During the 1980s, the rate of emigration slowed as revolutionary turmoil subsided and the economy began to grow. Greater governmental efficiency and membership in the EC attracted much foreign investment and created jobs. Portuguese no longer had to go abroad to find economic opportunity.

Family and Kinship Relations

The deep-reaching political, economic, and social changes that Portugal has experienced in the last few decades have left their mark on the family, women's place within society, and the role of kinship relations. Women were the most affected, for a modernizing economy offered them a greater range of choices than they had in previous times, and the radical reforms enacted after the Revolution of 1974 gave them much greater rights. Kinship relations, whether based on biology or social relationships, were perhaps the least affected, for they remained vitally important in how Portuguese lived and worked with one another.

Family

The patriarchal and nuclear family traditionally has served as the norm and the ideal in Portugal. Until the constitution of 1976 was promulgated, the father was seen as the head of the family, and his wife and children were obliged to recognize his authority. He, in turn, was obliged by law to support and protect his family. The men worked outside the home, and women were expected to care for the children and manage household affairs. Marriage was considered permanent; divorce was virtually unknown. During the period of Salazar's rule from 1928 to 1968, the family was even seen as the primary institution of politics. Voting was organized under the regime, the New State (Estado Novo), on a family basis—only ''heads of households'' (usually men but sometimes women) could vote.

Although the nuclear and patriarchal family was the ideal, the cultural patterns varied considerably depending on class status and region. Upper- and middle-class families corresponded most closely to the ideal. Women remained at home tending the children and rarely ventured out unaccompanied, and husbands managed their businesses or followed their professions. Peasant and working-class families were marked by greater variation. In northern Portugal, for example, names and property were often passed on through the mother because of the absence abroad of male heads of households for long periods. The fact that women could inherit land in Portugal gave women in rural areas some independence, and many of them managed their own farms, took their produce to market, and did much heavy work elsewhere seen as suitable for men. The absence of men because of emigration meant that many women never married and also resulted in a higher rate of illegitimacy than in other Mediterranean countries.

The slow modernization of the Portuguese economy, the increasing employment of women outside the home, and the emigration of many women, as well as the spread of new ideas about the place of women and the nature of marriage, gradually changed the nature of the Portuguese family, despite the attempts of Salazar's Estado Novo to preserve the male-dominated nuclear family. The Revolution of 1974 responded to these long pent-up social pressures.

The reforms enacted after the revolution established in the civil code that men and women are equals in marriage, with the same rights to make family decisions. Divorce became much easier, and the number of divorces increased from 1,552 in 1975 to 5,874 in 1980 and 9,657 in 1989. The number of separations, formerly the main method of ending a marriage, fell from 670 in 1975 to 70

View of central Lisbon
Courtesy General Directorate of Mass Communication, Lisbon

out climbed to 195 in 1989. Illegitimacy was no longer mentioned in official documents because such mention was ed as discriminatory; the frequency of births out of wedlock rose from 7.2 percent to 14.5 percent between 1975 and 1989. Abortion under certain conditions became legal in 1984. Maternal leave with full pay for ninety days was established for working mothers in 1976. A small family allowance program was also instituted that made payments at the birth of a child and all through his or her childhood. Family planning also became an integral part of Portugal's social welfare program; the number of children born per woman fell from 2.2 in 1980 to 1.7 in 1985 and 1.5 in 1988.

Relations within the family came to resemble more closely those of the rest of Western Europe. Children were less respectful to their parents, dating without chaperones was the rule, and outings in mixed gender groups or as couples were taken for granted—all things that would not have happened during much of the Salazar era.

Still, some characteristics of Portuguese family life have remained constant. Marriage and kinship networks in Portugal are often based on social and political criteria as much as on love or natural attraction. To a degree that often surprises outsiders, many Portuguese marriages are arranged, even in the early 1990s. For the peasant class, considerations of land are often most important in determining marriage candidates. Marriages might be arranged to consolidate property holdings or to tie two families together rather than as a result of the affection two people might feel for one another. Middle-class families often have status and prestige considerations in mind when they marry. Among the upper classes, marriage might be for the purposes of joining two businesses, two landholdings, or two political clans.

Women

The constitution of 1976 guaranteed Portuguese women full equality for the first time in Portuguese history. Until the reforms made possible by the Revolution of 1974, Portuguese women had notably fewer political, economic, or personal rights than the women of other European countries. In family matters, they were subordinate to their husbands, having to defer to male decisions about how the children should be reared and educated. It was only in 1969 that all married women obtained the right to obtain a passport or leave Portugal without their husbands' consent.

Equality for women was not attained through steady progress, but rather after reverses and defeats. For centuries, Portuguese women were obliged by law and custom to be subservient to men. Women had few rights of either a legal or a financial nature and were forced to rely on the benevolence of their male relatives. Late in the nineteenth century and early in the twentieth century, some educated persons saw the need for women's equality and emancipation. A small Portuguese suffragette movement formed, and some young women began to receive higher educations. Shortly after the proclamation of the First Republic in the fall of 1910, laws were enacted establishing legal equality in marriage, requiring civil marriages, freeing women of the obligation to remain with their husbands, and permitting divorce. However, women were still not allowed to manage property or to vote.

Salazar's New State meant the end to these advances. The constitution of 1933 proclaimed everyone equal before the law "except for women, the differences resulting from their nature and for the good of the family." Although the regime allowed women with a secondary education to vote (men needed only to read and write), it once again obliged women to remain with their husbands. The Concordat of 1940 between the Portuguese government and the Roman Catholic Church gave legal validity to marriages within the church and forbade divorce in such marriages. Later amendments to the civil code, even in the 1960s, cemented the husband's dominance in marriage.

The constitution of 1976 brought Portuguese women full legal equality. Anyone eighteen or over was granted the right to vote, and full equality in marriage was guaranteed. A state entity, the Commission on the Status of Women, was established and from 1977 on was attached to the prime minister's office. Its task was to improve the position of women in Portugal and to oversee the protection of their rights. This entity was renamed the Commission for Equality and Women's Rights (Comissão para a Igualdade e Direitos das Mulheres) in 1991.

The position of women improved as a result of these legal reforms. By the early 1990s, women were prominent in many professions. Thirty-seven percent of all physicians were women, as were many lawyers. Slightly more than half of those enrolled in higher education were women. Working-class women also made gains. A modernizing economy meant that many women could find employment in offices and factories and that they had a better standard of living than their mothers.

Despite these significant gains, however, Portuguese women still have not achieved full social and economic equality. They remain underrepresented in most upper-level positions, whether public or private. Women usually hold less than 10 percent of the seats in the country's parliament. Women are also rarely cabinet members or judges. In the main trade unions, women's occupancy of

ıip positions is proportionally only half their total union
ʝrship, and, on the whole, working-class women earned less
heir male counterparts.

The Extended Family and Kinship Relations

The extended family and kinship relations, including ritual kinship, are also important. The role of the godparent, for example, has an importance in Portugal that it lacks in the United States. Being a godparent implied certain lifetime obligations, such as helping a godchild in trouble, arranging admission to a school, finding employment, or furthering a professional or political career. The godchild, in turn, owes loyalty and service to the godparent. The system is one of patronage based on mutual obligation.

Political kinship networks can consist of several hundred persons. Such extended networks are especially prevalent among the elite. Members of the elite are bound not only by marriage and family, but also by business partnerships, friendships, political ties, university or military academy bonds, and common loyalties. It has long been the practice to have such family connections in the government so as to be able to extract favors and contracts. The elite and middle-class families also try to have a ''cousin,'' real or ritual, in all political parties so that their interests are protected no matter which party is in power. Sometimes the parties or interest groups are just ''fronts'' for these family groupings. These extended families also try to have members in different sectors of the economy, both to enhance profits and to enable each sector to support and reinforce the others. Although these extended family networks are difficult for outsiders to penetrate, some observers regard them as the country's most important political and economic institutions, of greater real consequence than political parties, interest organizations, or government institutions.

The poor and working class lack the extended family networks of the middle class and the wealthy. Kin relations outside the nuclear family are weak. Little premium is placed on building economic alliances through an extended family network because there is little wealth to be shared or gained. Similarly, there is no reason to build strong political connections because the poor lack political power. However, a poor person might succeed in persuading a local landowner or village notable to serve as godfather to his children. In that way, the individual becomes part of a larger network, expecting favors in return for loyalty and service. If that network becomes wealthy or achieved political prominence, then the poor person attached to it might also expect to benefit—perhaps by obtaining a low-level government job. But if it falls, the individual also falls. The entire Portuguese local and national system is based on these extended family and patronage ties, which are often as important as formal institutions.

Social Structure and Social Classes

For centuries the most distinctive feature of Portugal's social structure was its remarkable stability. Portuguese society was long cast in an almost premodern, quasifeudal mold. It was based on strong considerations of rank, place, and class. The system consisted of a small elite at the top, a huge mass of peasants at the bottom, and almost no one in between. Because Portugal's industrialization arrived late, the country did not experience until late in the nineteenth century some of the class changes associated with rapid economic development in other nations. When industrialization finally did come, Salazar's dictatorship held its sociopolitical effects in check almost to the very end. Then these pent-up changes exploded in the Revolution of 1974.

Historically, Portuguese society consisted of two main classes: nobility and peasants. Social prestige, political power, and economic prosperity were based on the ownership of land. The land was concentrated in large estates owned by a small elite that had obtained lands and titles during the reconquest of the peninsula from the Moors. As the Portuguese armies drove the Moors farther and farther south, their leaders acquired rights to the use and eventually ownership of the lands they had conquered. These titles were confirmed by the king in return for the landowners' loyalty and service. It was, in its origins, a classical feudal contract but derived in the Portuguese case from warfare and territorial conquest. The Roman Catholic Church also held vast lands. From the very birth of Portugal, then, landed, governmental, military, and religious authority were closely bound.

The rest of the population counted for very little in this social order. The small traditional middle class, consisting of soldiers, merchants, artisans, and low-level bureaucrats, lacked any solidarity as a class or sufficient numbers to give it political power. The remaining 90 percent of the population eked out meager existences as tenant farmers, serfs, and peasants. Little social mobility existed. Instead, one accepted one's station in life and did not rebel against it; rebelling was not only forbidden but also seen as an affront to God's immutable laws. Generation after generation, down through the centuries, this rigid, unyielding, hierarchical social structure persisted.

It was not unusual that from the twelfth century through the fourteenth century, Portugal's formative years as a nation, the country was organized in this two-class system and on a feudal basis; such organization was the norm in Europe. What was surprising was that this class system and all its rigidities lasted through the seventeenth century, when the system became even more consolidated, and beyond. During the eighteenth and nineteenth centuries, a "new rich" class emerged that was based on commerce and investment, but members of this class bought land, intermarried with the old elite, and thus perpetuated the two-class system.

Even in the twentieth century, despite the onset of modernization, this structure persisted. With economic stimulus, a new middle class began to emerge. But it largely imitated upper-class ways—disdaining manual labor, cultivating genteel virtues, and distancing itself from the lower classes—and was coopted into the elite's way of thinking and behaving. In addition, an industrial work force began to grow up alongside the traditional peasantry. However, under Salazar its labor unions were kept under control, and the workers had no independent bargaining power. Just as the emerging middle class joined the elite, the emerging working class was kept down as a sort of urban "peasantry." In this way, the essentially conservative and two-class system of Portugal was perpetuated even into the era of industrialization.

Under Salazar the regime did little to ameliorate the social inequalities that had long existed in Portugal. Salazar recognized that his strength lay with the conservative, traditional elements, especially the strongly Catholic peasantry of the north, so he did little to increase literacy or improve the road system that would lead to increased mobility, urbanization, and the eventual undermining of his power. He also tried consciously to keep Portugal isolated from the modernizing and culture-changing currents of the rest of Europe. His corporative system brought some benefits to the workers, but it also kept them under the strict control of the regime. Moreover, during Salazar's rule, Portugal lagged even further behind other nations in terms of housing, education, and health care.

Several sociological studies carried out in the 1960s confirmed that Portugal's ossified, hierarchical social structure continued even into modern times. One study found four social categories: an upper class of industrialists, proprietors, and high government officials accounting for 3.8 percent of the population; a middle stratum of rural proprietors, military officers, teachers, and small-scale entrepreneurs constituting 6.9 percent; a lower-middle stratum of clerks, low-level civil servants, military enlisted men, and rural shopkeepers adding up to 27.2 percent; and a majority—62.1 percent—consisting of workers, both rural and urban. Another study located

*Óbidos, a small town in the region of Estremadura
Street scene in Alfama, the oldest quarter of Lisbon
Courtesy Danièle Köhler*

87

1 to 2 percent of the population in the upper class, 15 to 20 percent in the middle class, and 75 percent in the lower class. Both studies, carried out independently, arrived at strikingly similar conclusions.

Yet, even with all this rigidity, class change was beginning to occur as a result of the slow modernization of the economy. Some groups were losing their traditional status and social power and were being displaced by groups better able to function in the evolving economy. These changes can be shown through a closer examination of the various groups that made up the country's elite, middle, and lower classes.

The Elite

Before the Revolution of 1974, Portugal's elite could be divided into five groups; the nobility, the large landowners, the heads of large businesses, the members of learned professions, and high-ranking military officers. These elites were closely connected and intertwined in numerous complex ways.

The oldest group historically was the nobility. It generally traced its origins to the formative period of Portuguese history. The monarchy had frequently granted noble titles to the elite in return for loyalty and service. In modern times, this nobility continued frequently to use the titles of duke, count, or marquis. A title was a symbol of status and was often eagerly sought, although the younger, more liberal generation frequently scoffed at such titles. Some of the titled nobility went into the learned professions or high government service. In the modern age, a titled nobility seemed anachronistic, but in Portugal this elite lingered on.

A second group, often overlapping with the first, consisted of large landowners, or *latifundiários*. They were chiefly concentrated in the Alentejo, but other areas of Portugal, such as the Beira and Ribatejo, also contained large estates. Increasingly, this landholding element had become absentee landlords, settling in Lisbon and leaving their estates in the hands of managers. In Lisbon, the landed elites frequently diversified into business and industry but kept their estates, sometimes as profit-making enterprises, but most often as symbols of status. This elite was also in the process of being eclipsed when the Revolution of 1974 occurred.

More important than either of these first two groups were business people and industrialists. These elements had come to prominence in Portugal in the 1960s and early 1970s as Portuguese economic growth accelerated and the country industrialized. The business elite was often well educated and had emerged from the middle class. It filled the ranks of managers, administrators, and company presidents. Quite a number married, or their children married, into the nobility or the landed class. As Portugal continued to develop economically, the business groups gained in influence, particularly as the survival of the regime came to depend on a prosperous economy.

A fourth group among the elite consisted of the learned professions, including university professors. Medicine as a profession had traditionally enjoyed particular prestige in Portugal. Lawyers similarly enjoyed prestige; many of them went into government service or became managers of banks and major companies. University professors were also valued: Salazar and Caetano were both university dons, and their cabinets often included several professors. The high prestige stemmed in part from the fact that university education was so rare in Portugal and a professor far rarer still; it also stemmed from the need for technical expertise in the government. Because of the large number of university professors, Salazar's regime was often referred to as a *catedratocracia,* a term derived from the Portuguese word for university chair, *cátedra.*

The fifth elite was the military officer corps. These were men, often from middle- or lower middle-class ranks, who had made it to the top in a very important institution: the armed forces. Education and the military, in fact, were among the few means open to ambitious middle-class youth to rise in the social scale in highly class-conscious Portugal. The military officers did not always mingle well with the upper-class civilians, but the power and importance of the armed forces meant they had to be paid serious attention. In addition, many of the banks, large businesses, and elite family groups, as a way of protecting their interests, placed military officers on their payrolls.

These elites were closely interrelated. A landowner living in the city might go into business or banking; a wealthy business person or industrialist might buy land. They themselves or their children would acquire an education and enter the learned professions. Business elites formed groups in which they owned diverse holdings: typically, insurance, hotels, construction, banking, real estate, and newspapers. They hired university professors and military officers to help administer these holdings—or as an ''insurance policy.'' Some members of the group held government positions—often carrying out private and public activities simultaneously. These groups were tightly inbred and often overlapping, with powerful political-economic-military connections.

The Revolution of 1974 largely destroyed this oligarchic system. Many of the old political elites associated with the regime were forced into exile, and others had their businesses confiscated. Almost all lost their positions and many of their holdings as a result of the revolution. Many members of the old elite eventually found their way back to Portugal and some began again to prosper in the late 1980s. But the strength of the elite was nowhere near so great as it was before 1974 and may have been ended permanently.

The Middle Class

The middle class in Portugal had long been growing in size but grew more rapidly beginning in the early 1960s as economic growth quickened. Depending on the criteria used, at the beginning of the 1990s Portugal's middle class could account for 25 to 30 percent of the population.

The traditional principle of political science states that the growth of a middle class brings greater social stability and better chances for the flourishing of democracy. However, the correlation of middle-class stability and democracy does not necessarily hold in Portugal. The reason for this lack of correlation stems from the fact that "middle class" in Portugal has two definitions. One definition is based on social and cultural criteria and the other on economics. The definition using economic criteria is the easiest to state: everyone above a certain income level but below another income level is middle class. This criterion includes some less wealthy professionals, business people, soldiers, government workers, small farmers who own their own lands, clerks, and better-off industrial workers. This list includes a large variety of persons of diverse occupations with little connecting them in terms of education, family background, or political values.

According to the socio-cultural definition of middle class, persons belonging to the middle class do not engage in manual labor, disdain it, and tend to feel a sense of superiority to those below them in the social hierarchy. The social-cultural definition regards professionals, business and commercial elements, military officers, and government workers as middle class, but not enlisted members of the military, farmers, or industrial workers, no matter what their earnings. This latter definition of middle class results in a smaller group, more homogeneous in outlook than that resulting from purely economic criteria.

If the older, more traditional variety of middle class with its essentially aristocratic values (disdain for manual labor, for example) proved to be the prevailing model even in the 1990s, Portugal would remain essentially a two-class society divided between those who work with their hands and those who do not. A two-class society increases chances for division, class conflict, and even civil war. By contrast, the emergence of a large and independent middle class defined by economic categories rather than socio-cultural traits favors the growth of social pluralism and political stability. As both definitions of the middle class are employed in Portugal, predicting the country's future is more difficult than elsewhere in Western Europe.

An indication that economic criteria have greater validity than in the past is that Portugal's middle class, traditionally deeply divided on a host of social and political issues, increasingly votes for the moderate, centrist Social Democrat Party (Partido Social Democrata—PSD). The PSD has come to be seen by its foes, as well as its supporters, as a "bourgeois" party. The Portuguese working class, in contrast, has voted increasingly for the Socialist Party (Partido Socialista—PS), although the Portuguese Communist Party (Partido Comunista Português—PCP) also has won some of its votes.

The Lower Class

Portuguese have long used the all-encompassing term *o povo* to describe the lower class. *O povo* means "the people," but the term has a class connotation, as well. Analysts of Portuguese society have postulated that *o povo* encompasses perhaps four main groups, including agricultural workers who either own or do not own land and organized and unorganized labor in urban areas.

Ownership of land is the main criterion for subdividing the poor in rural areas. There is a strong regional difference in ownership. Portugal's north is noted for its small farms and self-employed small farmers. Farmers who own land tend to be independent, rather conservative, and strongly Catholic in their beliefs. They tend to vote for the center and center-right political parties. Within this class of smallholders, some are better off than others. Some are obliged to work part-time on other farms. Many offspring of smallholders migrate to the cities or emigrate abroad. Their female relatives often remain behind to till the land.

The rural poor of the south in the Alentejo, like those of the north, are often referred to as "peasants," but that catchall term obscures important regional differences between these two groups. Relatively few of the *o povo* in the Alentejo own their own land. Instead, they work on the region's large estates, some full-time, others perhaps only two days a week. Their politics are often radical, and, in contrast to the smallholders of the north, they tend to vote for socialist and communist parties. The Alentejo was the area most strongly affected by the Revolution of 1974, and many of the large estates were nationalized and designated for agrarian reform or were taken over in a land seizure by their workers.

Urban areas also have two major groups of the working class, mainly defined in terms of whether or not they are politically organized. The unorganized lumpen proletariat, usually recent arrivals from the countryside, are often unemployed or under-employed. Members of the urban working class who belong to labor unions are considerably better off and could be regarded as the "elite" of Portugal's lower classes.

The lumpen proletariat live in urban slums, the most extensive of which are in Lisbon. Migrants from the countryside, they are often illiterate and not members of a labor union. Many can find no regular work but are employed in menial jobs on a part-time basis. The slums they live in are often partly hidden from view behind walls or fences and even in the early 1990s frequently lacked electricity, water, and sewerage systems. The housing in these slums is often fabricated from any available materials, including fiber glass, cardboard, and tin; hence, these areas are called in Portuguese *bairros de lata*—neighborhoods of tin. In addition to physical hardships, slum dwellers have to contend with violence and crime. Portugal's increasing prosperity since the second half of the 1980s has not yet been sufficient to efface these districts, which look as if they are part of the Third World.

Portugal's organized working class has a better standard of living than does the unskilled and unorganized poor. Their salaries are relatively high, and they are strongly entrenched in Portugal's key industries. Portugal has a long history of urban trade unions. Under Salazar's corporative system, they were strictly controlled, but after the Revolution of 1974 they became major actors in the political system and managed to secure decent wages for their membership.

A New Portugal?

Portugal was long a closed, hierarchical, elitist, rigidly structured society whose social institutions seemed to be more nineteenth century than twentieth. Portugal was called a "society of uniforms" because people could be identified and their class rank determined by the clothes they wore, their manner of speech, and how they walked and carried themselves. Social structure was seen as immutable, and persons were expected to accept their station in life. Other than a few slots in the university or the military officer corps, few opportunities existed for upward mobility.

The Revolution of 1974 destroyed, undermined, or at least precipitated the toppling of many of these hierarchical institutions. In the years since then, Portuguese society has become more flexible. More opportunities for social mobility have appeared, and old

A fishing boat at Aveiro in Northern Portugal
A fisherman uses cattle to draw in fishing boats at Aveiro.
Courtesy Danièle Köhler

categories of place and position have became blurred. Portuguese society has become more egalitarian, pluralist, and democratic, and there was more of what the Portuguese liked to call *movimento* (change, dynamism, or movement).

In the years following the mid-1970s, the country's middle class grew in size and solidarity, the working class enjoyed a rising standard of living, and the number of entrepreneurs and technicians increased markedly. The most significant of these changes was the growth of a sizeable and more stable middle class that offered the hope for a more stable and democratic country. The middle class largely replaced the old elite and came to dominate most Portuguese social and political institutions: the political parties, the church, business, the military officer corps, government and bureaucracy, and even union leadership. Thus, a major class shift occurred. It has begun earlier in the century, continued through the Salazar era, and by the early 1990s appeared to have been consolidated. This shift from upper- to middle-class leadership could give Portugal the basis for stable, democratic rule that it lacked before.

Ethnicity and Ethnic Groups

Portugal's population is remarkably homogeneous and has been so for all of its history. This lack of ethnic variety helped it become the first unified nation-state in Western Europe. For centuries Portugal had virtually no ethnic, tribal, racial, religious, or cultural minorities. Almost all Portuguese speak the national language, almost all are Roman Catholic, and almost all identify with Portuguese culture and the nation of Portugal. Whereas neighboring Spain was deeply divided along ethnic, linguistic, and regional lines all through its history, Portugal, which historically represented but one of the Iberian Peninsula's many regional entities, was united. In Portugal, ethnic unity and homogeneity were the rule, rather than the exception.

Although Portugal lacks socially significant ethnic differences, some regional differences exist. The north is generally more conservative and Catholic than the south and is said to be less "tainted" by Moorish or Islamic influences. Regional dances, dress, festivals, and customs were once very distinctive, but modern communications and transportation have opened up and connected formerly closed regions and produced a greater homogeneity. The Portuguese language still exhibits regional differences, and linguists can often pinpoint a person's geographic origin from his speech, but these differences are not extreme enough to impede understanding among Portuguese.

Protestants live in Portugal, but they are largely confined to the communities of foreigners residing in the country. The small but growing Muslim population from North Africa, mainly guest workers attracted by Portugal's new prosperity, is concentrated in the Algarve and in Lisbon. The Jewish population in Portugal is very small (from 500 to 1,000) and, like the Protestant population, mainly limited to foreign residents.

Portugal has a sizeable Gypsy population, perhaps as many as 100,000, most of whom live in the Algarve. Despite government efforts to integrate them into the larger society, Gypsies remain a group apart, seminomadic, earning their living by begging, fortune-telling, handicrafts, and trading.

Portugal's foreign community numbered about 90,000 in 1987. It consists mainly of Africans (about 40 percent), Spaniards, British, Americans, French, and Germans, most of whom live in Porto, Lisbon, the area around Cascais, the Algarve, and the Azores and Madeira. These communities are not large and generally do not become involved in Portuguese life.

Portugal's long colonial history, more than half a millennium, has left some traces of ethnic diversity. In the early 1990s, the indigenous residents of the former colonies were found mainly in Lisbon, particularly after the colonies were granted independence in the mid-1970s. Groups of Angolans, Mozambicans, São Tomans, Timorese, Goans, and Macaoans have settled in the capital city, and, along with Brazilian immigrants, ended Portugal's traditional ethnic homogeneity.

The Goans come from the Indian subcontinent and are usually educated, Roman Catholic, and Portuguese speaking. They are better assimilated than most other groups. The Macaoans are generally of Chinese descent, and many had opened businesses. Another group from Asia, the Timorese, are not as well educated as the other eastern groups. A population of varying size of black immigrants from Portugal's African colonies often lives together in small ghettos in Lisbon and does not generally assimilate. Many of these minorities use Portugal as a stopping-off point en route to more prosperous countries in Western Europe, but as the Portuguese economy began to improve in the second half of the 1980s, more chose to stay permanently. These ethnic minorities from the former colonies are not fully assimilated and often face, to a varying degree, racial and cultural prejudice. The small size of these diverse ethnic groups, however, prevents their apartness from being a serious social problem.

The only group from the former colonies that is fully assimilated, despite some cultural and adjustment problems, is the group coming from the former colonies in Africa who are of Portuguese descent. They have much the same racial and cultural background as the Portuguese themselves. Some of them, like some of the Brazilians, did very well in their cultural homeland and even became wealthy.

Religion and the Role of the Roman Catholic Church

Portugal is profoundly Roman Catholic. According to a common saying, "To be Portuguese is to be Catholic"; in the early 1990s, approximately 97 percent of the population considered itself Roman Catholic—the highest percentage in Western Europe. Only about one-third of the population attends mass and takes the sacraments regularly, but nearly all Portuguese wish to be baptized and married in the church and to receive its last rites.

Portugal is Roman Catholic not only in a religious sense, but also socially and culturally. Although church and state were formally separated during the First Republic (1910–26), a separation reiterated in the constitution of 1976, the two still form a seamless web in many areas of life. Catholic precepts historically undergird the society as well as the polity. The traditional notions of authority, hierarchy, and accepting one's station in life all stem from Roman Catholic teachings. Many Portuguese holidays and festivals have religious origins, and the country's moral and legal codes derive from Roman Catholic precepts. The educational and health care systems have long been the church's preserve, and whenever a building, bridge, or highway is opened, it receives the blessing of the clergy. Hence, although church and state are formally separated, absolute separation is not possible in practice.

History

Portugal was first Christianized while part of the Roman Empire. Christianity was solidified when the Visigoths, a Germanic tribe already Christianized, came into the Iberian Peninsula in the fifth century (see Germanic Invasions, ch. 1). Christianity was nearly extinguished in southern Portugal during Moorish rule, but in the north it provided the cultural and religious cement that helped hold Portugal together as a distinctive entity (see Muslim Domination, ch. 1). By the same token, Christianity was the rallying cry of those who rose up against the Moors and sought to drive them out (see Christian Reconquest, ch. 1). Hence, Christianity and the Roman Catholic Church predated the establishment of the Portuguese nation, a point that shaped relations between the two.

Under Afonso Henriques (r.1139–85), the first king of Portugal and the founder of the Portuguese state, church and state were unified into a lasting and mutually beneficial partnership (see Formation of the Monarchy, ch. 1). To secure papal recognition of his country, Afonso declared Portugal a vassal state of the pope. The king found the church to be a useful ally as he drove the Moors toward the south and out of Portuguese territory. For its support of his policies, Afonso richly rewarded the church by granting it vast lands and privileges in the territories conquered from the Moors. The church became the country's largest landowner, and its power came to be equal to that of the nobility, the military orders, and even, for a time, the crown. But Afonso also asserted his supremacy over the church, a supremacy that—with various ups and downs—was maintained.

Although relations between the Portuguese state and the Roman Catholic Church were generally amiable and stable, their relative power fluctuated. In the thirteenth century and fourteenth century, the church enjoyed both riches and power stemming from its role in the reconquest and its close identification with early Portuguese nationalism. For a time the church's position vis-à-vis the state diminished until the growth of the Portuguese overseas empire made its missionaries important agents of colonization.

In 1497, reflecting events that had occurred five years earlier in Spain, Portugal expelled the Jews and the remaining Moors— or forced them to convert. In 1536 the pope gave King João III (r.1521–57) permission to establish the Inquisition in Portugal to enforce the purity of the faith (see Counter-Reformation and Overseas Evangelization, ch. 1). Earlier the country had been rather tolerant, but now orthodoxy and intolerance reigned. The Jesuit order was placed in charge of all education.

In the eighteenth century, antichurch sentiment became strong. The Marquês de Pombal (r.1750–77) expelled the Jesuits in 1759, broke relations with Rome, and brought education under the state's control (see Absolutism, ch. 1). Pombal was eventually removed from his office, and many of his reforms were undone, but anticlericalism remained a force in Portuguese society. In 1821 the Inquisition was abolished, religious orders were banned, and the church lost much of its property. Relations between church and state improved in the second half of the nineteenth century, but a new wave of anticlericalism emerged with the establishment of the First Republic in 1910 (see The First Republic, ch. 1). Not only were church properties seized and education secularized, but the republic went so far as to ban the ringing of church bells, the wearing of clerical garb on the streets, and the holding of many popular, religious festivals. These radical steps antagonized many deeply religious Portuguese, cost the republic popular support, and paved the way for its overthrow and the establishment of a conservative right-wing regime.

The Salazar Regime

Under the dictatorship of António de Oliveira Salazar (r. 1928–68), the church experienced a revival (see The New State, ch. 1). Salazar was himself deeply religious and infused with Roman Catholic precepts. Before studying law he had been a seminarian; his roommate at the University of Coimbra, Manuel Gonçalves Cerejeira, later became cardinal patriarch of Lisbon. In addition, Salazar's corporative principles and his constitution and labor statute of 1933 were infused with Roman Catholic precepts from the papal encyclicals *Rerum Novarum* (1891) and *Quadragesimo Anno* (1931).

Salazar's state was established on the principles of traditional Roman Catholicism, with an emphasis on order, discipline, and authority. Class relations were supposed to be based on harmony rather than the Marxist concept of conflict. The family, the parish, and Christianity were said to be the foundations of the state. Salazar went considerably beyond these principles, however, and established a full-fledged dictatorship. His corporative state continued about equal blends of Roman Catholic principles and Mussolini-like fascism.

In 1940 a concordat governing church-state relations was signed between Portugal and the Vatican. The church was to be "separate" from the state but to enjoy a special position. The Concordat of 1940 reversed many of the anticlerical policies undertaken during the republic, and the Roman Catholic Church was given exclusive control over religious instruction in the public schools. Only Catholic clergy could serve as chaplains in the armed forces. Divorce, which had been legalized by the republic, was again made illegal for those married in a church service. The church was given formal "juridical personality," enabling it to incorporate and hold property.

Under Salazar, church and state in Portugal maintained a comfortable and mutually reinforcing relationship. While assisting the church in many ways, however, Salazar insisted that it stay out of politics—unless it praised his regime. Dissent and criticism were forbidden; those clergy who stepped out of line—an occasional parish priest and once the bishop of Porto—were silenced or forced to leave the country.

Changes after the Revolution of 1974

In the Portuguese constitution of 1976, church and state were again formally separated. The church continues to have a special place in Portugal, but for the most part it has been disestablished. Other religions are now free to organize and practice their beliefs.

In addition to undergoing constitutional changes, Portugal became a more secular society. Traditional Roman Catholicism flourished while Portugal was overwhelmingly poor, rural, and illiterate, but as the country became more urban, literate, and secular the practice of religion declined. The number of men becoming priests fell, as did charitable offerings and attendance at mass. By the early 1990s, most Portuguese still considered themselves Roman Catholic in a vaguely cultural and religious sense, but only about one-third of them attended mass regularly. Indifference to religion was most likely among men and young people. Regular churchgoers were most often women and young children.

The church no longer has its former social influence. During the nineteenth century and on into the Salazar regime, the church was one of the most powerful institutions in the country—along with the army and the economic elite. In fact, military, economic, governmental, and religious influences in Portugal were closely intertwined and interrelated, often literally so. Traditionally, the first son of elite families inherited land, the second went into the army, and the third became a bishop. By the early 1990s, however, the Roman Catholic Church no longer enjoyed this preeminence and had fallen to seventh or eighth place in power among Portuguese interest groups.

During the height of the revolutionary turmoil in the mid-1970s, the church had urged its communicants to vote for centrist and conservative candidates and to repudiate communists, especially in northern Portugal, but after that period the church refrained from such an overt political role. The church was not able to prevent the enactment of the constitution of 1976, which separated church and state, nor could it block legislation liberalizing divorce and abortion, issues it regarded as moral issues within the realm of its responsibility. By the 1980s, the church seldom tried to influence how Portuguese voted, knowing such attempts would probably backfire.

Religious Practices

The practice of religion in Portugal shows striking regional differences. Even in the early 1990s, 60 to 70 percent of the population in the traditionally Roman Catholic north regularly attended religious services, compared with 10 to 15 percent in the historically anticlerical south. In the greater Lisbon area, about 30 percent were regular churchgoers.

99

The traditional importance of Roman Catholicism in the lives of the Portuguese is evident in the physical organization of almost every village in Portugal. The village churches are usually in prominent locations, either on the main square or on a hilltop overlooking the villages. Many of the churches and chapels were built in the sixteenth century at the height of Portugal's colonial expansion and might and were often decorated with wood and gold leaf from the conquests. In recent decades, however, they have often been in disrepair, for there are not enough priests to tend them. Many are used only rarely to honor the patron saints of the villages.

Much of the country's religious life has traditionally taken place outside the formal structure and official domain of the Roman Catholic Church. This is especially true in rural areas where the celebration of saints' days and religious festivals are popular. The most famous of Portuguese religious events is the supposed apparition of the Virgin Mary to three children in 1917 in the village of Fátima in the province of Santarém. Hundreds of thousands of pilgrims have visited the shrine at Fátima in the belief that the pilgrimage could bring about healing.

Rural Portuguese often seek to establish a close and personal relationship with their saints. Believing God to be a remote and inaccessible figure, they petition patron saints to act as intermediaries. This system of patronage resembles that operating in the secular realm. To win their saint's goodwill, believers present the saint with gifts, gave alms to the poor, and demonstrate upright behavior, hoping that the saint might intercede on their behalf with God.

Women tend to practice their religion more than men do, as evidenced by church attendance. In addition, the Virgin Mary, who is the most popular of the spiritual mediators, is often revered more than Jesus and serves as the patron of religious processions. The image of the Virgin, as well as that of Christ, is commonly displayed, even in labor union offices or on signs in demonstrations.

The Roman Catholic Church sometimes criticizes religious folk practices for dividing people from their God. The church cannot monitor all folk customs, however, and such practices continue even in the 1990s. Moreover, the church recognizes that many Portuguese feel at least as much loyalty to their saints and customary religious practices as they do to the more formal church. For these reasons, it is not unusual that the church tolerates and sometimes even encourages these practices as a way of maintaining popular adherence to Roman Catholicism.

Streetcar in Lisbon
Children playing in a Lisbon courtyard
Courtesy Danièle Köhler

101

Other aspects of Portuguese folk religion, including witchcraft, magic, and sorcery, are not approved by the official church. Formal religion, folk beliefs, and superstition are frequently jumbled together, and in the popular mind all are part of being Roman Catholic. Particularly in the isolated villages of northern Portugal, belief in witches, witchcraft, and evil spirits is widespread. Some persons believe in the concept of the ''evil eye'' and fear those who supposedly possess it. Again, women are the main practitioners. Almost every village has its ''seers,'' practitioners of magic, and ''healers.'' Evil spirits and even werewolves are thought to inhabit the mountains and byways, and it is believed that people must be protected from them. Children and young women are thought to be particularly vulnerable to the ''evil eye.''

As people became better educated and moved to the city, they lost some of these folk beliefs. But in the city and among educated persons alike, superstition can still be found, even in the early 1990s. Sorcerers, palm readers, and readers of cards have shops, particularly in poorer neighborhoods, but not exclusively so. In short, a strong undercurrent of superstition still remains in Portugal. The formal church disapproves of superstitious practices but is powerless to do much about them.

In contrast to the Catholicism found in Spain, Portuguese Catholicism is softer and less intense. The widespread use of folk practices and the humanization of religion made for a loving though remote God, in contrast to the harshness of the Spanish vision. In Portugal, unlike in Spain, God and his saints are imagined as forgiving and serene. In Spain the expressions depicted on the faces of saints and martyrs are painful and anguished; in Portugal they are complacent, calm, and pleasant.

Non-Catholic Religious Groups

For most of Portugal's history, few non-Catholics lived in the country; those who did could not practice their religion freely. Until the constitution of 1976 was enacted, laws restricted the activities of non-Catholics. By the early 1990s, only some 50,000 to 60,000 Protestants lived in Portugal, about 1 percent of the total population. They had been kept out of the country for three centuries by the Inquisition. However, the British who began settling in Portugal in the nineteenth century brought their religions with them. Most belonged to the Church of England, but others were Methodists, Congregationalists, Baptists, and Presbyterians. Protestantism remained largely confined to the foreign communities. The 1950s and 1960s saw the arrival of Pentecostals, Mormons, and Jehovah's Witnesses, all of whom increased in numbers more rapidly than the earlier arrivals did. All groups, however, were hampered by prohibitions and restrictions against the free exercise of their religions, especially missionary activities.

These restrictions were lifted after the Revolution of 1974. The constitution of 1976 guarantees all religions the right to practice their faith. Protestant groups have been recognized as legal entities with the right to assemble. In addition, Portuguese who are both Protestant and conscientious objectors have the right to apply for alternative military service. The Roman Catholic Church, however, still seeks to place barriers in the way of Protestant missionary activities.

The Jewish community in Portugal numbered between 500 and 1,000 as of the early 1990s. The community is concentrated in Lisbon, and many of its members are foreigners. The persecution of Portuguese Jewry had been so intense that until recent decades Portugal had no synagogue or even regular Jewish religious services. The few Jewish Portuguese were hence isolated from the main currents of Judaism. Their community began to revive when larger numbers of foreign Jews (embassy personnel, business people, and technicians) began coming to Portugal in the 1960s and 1970s. In northern Portugal, there are a few villages of Marranos, descendants of Jews who converted to Christianity to avoid persecution and whose religion is a mixture of Judaism and Christianity. Portugal's Muslim community consists of a small number of immigrants from Portugal's former colonies in Southern Africa and larger numbers of recent immigrant workers from Northern Africa, mainly Morocco.

Education

Even before Portugal emerged as an independent country in the twelfth century, it had monastic, cathedral, and parish schools. The education provided by these schools was based on the teachings of the Roman Catholic Church, rote memorization, and a deductive system of reasoning. The educational system expanded through the founding of primary and secondary schools in larger settlements and the establishment in 1290 of the University of Coimbra, one of the oldest universities in the world. The system was infused with the principles of authority, hierarchy, and discipline. Although local authorities, both municipal and ecclesiastical, had some say about the management of local schools, officials in Lisbon, most of them clerics, determined the curriculum and selected textbooks and instructors. Education was thus firmly under the control of the church and civil authorities. The introduction of the Inquisition in the 1530s served to further "purify" teaching; in 1555 the Jesuits were given much control over education.

A reaction against church- and Jesuit-dominated education set in during the eighteenth century. Reformers such as Luís António Verney sought to infuse Portuguese education with the ideals of the Enlightenment. The reforms were carried out by the Marquês de Pombal, prime minister from 1750 to 1777, who expelled the Jesuits in 1759, created the basis for public and secular primary and secondary schools, introduced vocational training, created hundreds of new teaching posts, added departments of mathematics and natural sciences to the University of Coimbra, and introduced new taxes to pay for these reforms.

During the nineteenth century, educational reform was slow and halting. Reforms initiated in 1822, 1835, and 1844 were left uncompleted and largely unimplemented. However, at the beginning of the century, the first schools for girls were opened in Lisbon. Other new schools included the Agricultural Institute, polytechnical schools in Lisbon and Porto, new medical schools in the same two cities, and a new department of liberal arts in Lisbon. The educational system remained highly elitist, however, with illiteracy rates of over 80 percent and higher education reserved for a small percentage of the population. When the First Republic was established in 1910, efforts were made to overcome these problems. New universities were created in Lisbon and Porto, new teacher training colleges were opened, and a separate Ministry of Public Instruction was established. The republican government sought to reduce illiteracy, reintroduce (as with Pombal) a more secular content to education, and to bring more scientific and empirical methods into the curriculum. But these reforms largely stopped when the republic was overthrown in 1926 and the military and Salazar came to power.

Salazar authorized the creation of a new technical university in Lisbon in 1930. But for the next three decades, educational innovation lagged, illiteracy remained high, vocational training was almost nonexistent, and Portugal reverted to a situation of quasi-feudalism characterized by the most backward economy and education in Western Europe. Only in the mid-1960s did the country make public education available for all children between the ages of six and twelve. The government enacted laws to equalize educational opportunities, but implementation lagged behind. However, more elementary and preparatory schools were opened, and universities were established in Lisbon and other regional centers.

The Revolution of 1974 and the overthrow of the Salazar regime disrupted the education system. Students challenged teachers, and all groups challenged administrators. For a time after the revolution, faculty and curriculum were highly politicized as socialist, communist, and other groups vied for control of the schools and the school system. During the 1980s, however, as Portuguese politics quieted and returned to the center, the education system also became less frenetic, greater emphasis was placed on learning, and efforts were made to raise the level of the country's schools closer to that of the rest of Europe.

The Portuguese educational system is governed by the constitution of 1976. The constitution guarantees the right to create private schools. It proposes to eliminate illiteracy, to provide special education to those children who need it, and to preserve the autonomy of the universities. It guarantees the rights of teachers and students to take part in the democratic administration of the schools. In addition to the overall guidance provided by the constitution, Portuguese education is governed by decree-laws promulgated by the executive branch, some of which date from the eighteenth century.

As of the early 1990s, preschool education in Portugal was limited. Most preschools were private, but government regulation and involvement in preschool education was increasing. Primary education consisted of four years in the primary cycle and two years in the preparatory, or second, cycle (see fig. 7). Most primary schools were public. Many Portuguese living in rural areas received only the primary cycle of schooling. The preparatory cycle (fifth and sixth grades) was intended mainly for children going on to secondary education. Provision was also made for attendance by older students who might already be working.

Secondary education was roughly equivalent to junior and senior high schools in the United States. It consisted of three years of a unified course curriculum, followed by a two-year complementary course (tenth and eleventh grades). A twelfth-grade course prepared students to take the university and technical college entrance examinations.

Portuguese primary school enrollments were close to 100 percent in the early 1990s, and immense strides had been made in eliminating illiteracy, especially among the young; an estimated literacy rate of 85 percent was achieved among those over age fifteen in 1990. After primary school, however, school enrollments dropped off sharply. Only 30 percent of children attended secondary schools, and only 20 percent were enrolled in the twelfth grade.

A new vocational education program was introduced in 1983. By the late 1980s, it was training 10,000 to 12,000 young people a year, about 6 to 7 percent of an age-group. The program was

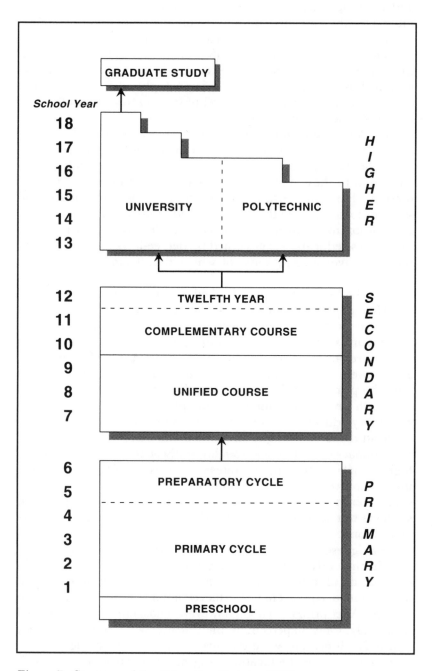

Figure 7. Structure of the Education System, 1992

conceived as a three-year course that would permit students to enter the work force with a set of skills after the eleventh grade.

In the early 1990s, higher education included four older universities (Lisbon, Coimbra, Porto, and the Technical University of Lisbon), as well as six newer universities (Nova University in Lisbon and others in Minho, Aveiro, Évora, in the Algarve, and in the Azores). The university sector also included the private Catholic University and the Free University, both in Lisbon. In addition, there were special postsecondary institutes, schools, and academies such as the Institute of Applied Psychology, the social welfare institutes of Lisbon and Porto, the engineering institutes of Lisbon, Porto, and Coimbra, an agricultural college at Coimbra, technical colleges in Santarém and in the Algarve, and a school of education at Viseu.

Admission to the university is a highly competitive process, although it can be waived if a student obtains a high score in the final examinations from secondary school. Only about 10 percent of college-age students attend one of the country's universities or postsecondary institutes, compared with 50 percent in the United States. Thus, higher education is by no means universal but rather oriented toward a small elite. This elite, in turn, tends to dominate government, big business, and the professions.

The average length of study at the university level is five years and leads to the awarding of a licentiate, although some schools have two-year programs and others offer a bachelor's degree. Doctorates are awarded in some departments after further advanced studies, an oral examination, and the defense of a thesis.

The faculties had four ranks as of the early 1990s: full professors, associate professors, lecturers, and assistants. Full professors could be appointed directly, or their appointments might come through competitive examinations. Full professors receive life appointments; persons of other ranks are under contract. University staffs, including faculty, are part of the civil service and receive pay and pensions like other civil servants.

The Portuguese educational system is highly centralized. Despite some efforts at decentralization in the constitution of 1976, the Ministry of Education and Culture in Lisbon sets education policy for the entire nation. Local or regional districts have little independent authority to tax, with the result that funds, curriculum, policy, and other matters are set at the national level.

As of the early 1990s, Portugal still had an illiteracy rate that ranged between 14 and 20 percent according to various studies and estimates, although many of those who could not read were older people. Another serious problem was low school enrollment after the primary cycle, especially in rural areas, where many children begin work at an early age. As of 1987, 87.4 percent of Portuguese completed less than the upper level of secondary school, a rate that had improved only slightly in recent decades and was much inferior to the EC average of 54 percent. Facilities and equipment at all levels are often outdated and in short supply. Although the number of school teachers has increased greatly in recent years, teachers are poorly paid, and their overall morale is poor. Many specialists hold that the curriculum at the secondary level needs to be revised to make it more relevant in preparing young people for their working lives. In addition to more modern facilities, the universities need to increase their enrollments and support research more strongly.

Social Welfare

On most indices of social modernization, Portugal ranks at or near the bottom for all of Western Europe. Even in the early 1990s, despite some significant economic growth in the second half of the 1980s, Portugal remains relatively poor by West European standards. Although its range of public welfare programs is extensive, it lacks the funds to fully implement them and to pay substantial benefits.

Charity and alms-giving were traditionally thought to be the responsibility of the church. It provided welfare to the poor and took care of the sick, widows, and orphans. In addition, landowners and employers fulfilled their obligations of Christian charity by aiding the less fortunate through gifts, assistance, patronage, and benefits. The charitable institution established by Queen Leonor in the late fifteen century, Santa Casa de Misericórdia, had, even in the early 1990s, offices all through Portugal. Its charitable operations were financed by the national lottery. This system of charity provided by the church and the elite probably worked tolerably well through the 1920s, as long as Portugal remained a rural and Roman Catholic society. But urbanization, secularism, and large-scale impersonal organizations rendered the old system inadequate.

Salazar's corporative system attempted to fill the void but did so poorly. Only in the 1960s, far later than in other countries, were the first steps taken toward a modern state-run welfare system. As could be expected, the services this system provided were incomplete, irregular, and woefully underfunded. Urban centers received some benefits, but almost none went to the countryside. During the revolutionary 1970s, numerous health and social welfare programs were established, but only in the 1980s did Portugal have the stability and the resources to begin their implementation.

Social Welfare Programs

As of the early 1990s, Portugal had a fairly elaborate social welfare system, including programs that provided benefits for the elderly and the seriously ill or disabled. However, the benefits paid by these programs were still quite low, and an estimated 3 million Portuguese lived below the EC poverty line.

The programs' benefits were financed by employee and employer contributions (roughly 10 and 25 percent, respectively). Most of the programs were the responsibility of the Ministry of Employment and Social Security and were administered by regional social security centers. The Ministry of Health was involved in programs concerned with medical care.

As of the early 1990s, men and women could retire at sixty-five and sixty-two years of age, respectively, and be eligible for old-age pensions. Miners were eligible for retirement at fifty and merchant sailors at fifty-five years of age. Benefits ranged from 30 to 80 percent of recent average wages. Permanent disability and survivor benefits were also paid. Unemployment benefits could be paid over a period of from ten to thirty months and amounted to 65 percent of earnings, with a maximum of three times the national minimum wage of about US$300 a month.

As of 1991, maternity benefits amounted to 100 percent of the mother's pay for a period of three months, one month before and two months after the birth. Sickness benefits amounted to 65 percent of wages for up to 1,095 days; after this period, the benefit was converted to a permanent disability benefit. Accidents at work were covered by private insurance carried by employers; payments could amount to two-thirds of basic earnings. Small family allowances were paid to help rear children until they reached the age of fifteen or the age of twenty-five if they were students.

Health Care

Health conditions in Portugal have long been among the poorest in Western Europe. Although recent decades have seen substantial improvements, Portugal still lags behind most of the continent in some categories of health care. Portuguese life expectancy at birth rose from sixty-two years for men and sixty-seven for women in 1960 to seventy-one and seventy-eight, respectively, in 1992. The country's infant mortality rate in 1970 was 58 deaths per 1,000—one of the highest in Europe and close to Third World levels—but by 1992 it had dropped to 10 per 1,000. However, the chief causes of death among the young are infectious and parasitic diseases and diseases of the respiratory system, a Third World pattern found in rural areas and in city slums. Malnutrition and related diseases are also widespread. The chief cause of deaths among adults is thrombosis, followed by cancer. About 400 Portuguese die each year from tuberculosis.

The number of doctors, dentists, and nurses increased greatly between 1960 and the early 1990s. At 26,400 in 1987, the number of physicians actively practicing medicine in Portugal represented a fourfold increase over the total in 1960. The number of dentists expanded even more dramatically, from 120 in 1960 to 5,700 in 1986. As of 1987, the number of medical personnel per occupied hospital bed was 1.7, compared with 0.24 in 1960. By 1990 there were 2.9 doctors per 1,000 Portuguese, a ratio higher than that found in most West European countries. However, most medical personnel are concentrated in urban centers, to the detriment of those needing health care in rural areas. In the latter areas, folk health practitioners are not uncommon, even in the early 1990s. Their medical practices are often fused with magical, religious, and superstitious elements.

Portuguese are able to take advantage of a national health system that, since the second half of the 1970s, had paid 100 percent of most medical and pharmaceutical expenses. The system, managed by the Ministry of Health, offers care at large urban hospitals, several dozen regional hospitals, and numerous health centers. The health centers specialize in providing primary care. Care provided by the national system ranges from the most sophisticated to basic preventive medicine.

The national health system's overriding problems are the long waits, frequently months in duration, for medical care, that result from shortages of financial resources, lack of personnel, and inadequate facilities. Medical facilities in Portugal range from those of centuries past to the ultramodern. Partly as a result of these inadequacies, there is a substantial private medical sector that offers better care. Many doctors and other medical personnel work in both the public and private system, often because of the low salaries paid by the national system.

Housing

Much Portuguese housing is substandard, both in rural and in urban areas. Many rural villages were not electrified even by the early 1990s, and villagers often had to carry water from a common source. The influx of rural migrants to urban centers in recent decades intensified demand on an already inadequate housing supply. Although 60 percent of Portuguese rent their houses (80 percent in Lisbon and Porto), rigid rent control laws in effect between 1948 and 1985 had discouraged the construction of apartments, as did a sluggish bureaucracy. As a result, in the late 1980s an estimated 700,000 illegally constructed dwellings existed in Portugal, 200,000 of which were located in the Lisbon area. Some were built on public or unused private lands. The resulting urban shantytowns (*bairros da lata*) often lacked electricity, running water, or sewage systems.

In Lisbon's suburbs, gigantic apartment houses were built for the more affluent new city-dwellers, but the supply of decent, affordable housing lagged far behind the demand, estimated at 800,000 dwellings for the entire country. A succession of Portuguese governments recognized this severe housing problem and sought to do something about it. For example, the National Housing Institute planned to build 70,000 dwellings a year during the 1990s, and various programs to help people become homeowners had been put into practice.

* * *

Portugal was long the most understudied country in Western Europe. The authoritarian nature of the Salazar regime made social science research on contemporary issues all but impossible to carry out; Portuguese social sciences also lagged behind. Despite these obstacles, some very good studies were done. Among them were works by Joyce Firstenberg Riegelhaupt in anthropology, João Baptista Nunes Pereira Neto and Aderito Sedas Nunes in sociology, and José Cutileiro's pioneering *A Portuguese Rural Society*. Harry M. Makler broke new ground in his investigations of Portugal's business elite, as did Massimo Livi Bacci in his demographic study, *A Century of Portuguese Fertility*.

Social science scholarship has flourished in Portugal since the Revolution of 1974, as specialists there have looked into many unexplored aspects of their society. Readers needing sociological analyses in English will profit from the survey edited by Lawrence S. Graham and Douglas L. Wheeler, *In Search of Modern Portugal,* and the study edited by Lawrence S. Graham and Harry M. Makler, *Contemporary Portugal.* Economic and social data are also found in the historical surveys *Contemporary Portugal* by Richard Alan Hodgson Robinson and *Portugal: A Twentieth Century Interpretation* by Tom Gallagher.

Among the best political-sociological studies are Nancy Bermeo's *The Revolution Within the Revolution,* which deals with revolution in the countryside, and Caroline Brettel's *Men Who Migrate, Women Who Wait,* an excellent study of Portuguese emigration. Thomas

C. Bruneau, Victor M.P. Da Rosa, and Alex Macleod provide much useful information in their *Portugal in Development.* Rainer Eisfeld's "Portugal and Western Europe," in *Portugal in the 1980s,* edited by Kenneth Maxwell, is also helpful. Finally, Marion Kaplan's 1991 book, *The Portuguese: The Land and Its People,* although not aimed at a scholarly audience, is often highly informative about contemporary Portuguese society. (For further information and complete citations, see Bibliography.)

Chapter 3. The Economy

. Tending wine casks

PORTUGAL'S POLITICAL ECONOMY holds our interest for a number of reasons. First, Portugal, a founding member both of the North Atlantic Treaty Organization (NATO) and the European Free Trade Association (EFTA—see Glossary), is one of the newest members (along with Spain) of the European Community (EC—see Glossary). Second, scholars interested in revolutionary change and the associated economic consequences can compare the Portuguese experience with that of other nations that have undergone rapid systemic transformation. Third, Portugal's recent experiment with nationalization of the means of production is of particular interest to students of industrial organization and public enterprise economics.

As a fledgling member of the EC, Portugal was required to adopt the EC's Common External Tariff on imports from nonmember countries and the Common Agricultural Policy (CAP). Portugal also was required to eliminate all barriers to the movement of goods, services, and capital between itself and the other members of the European Economic Community (EEC—see Glossary), as well as to phase out fiscal subsidies that distort competition. During a transition period ending in 1993, Portugal was a net recipient of EC funds to assist in the restructuring of its relatively backward economy.

At the beginning of the 1990s, Portugal's economy was classified by the World Bank (see Glossary) as an upper-middle-income economy. Its 1990 gross domestic product (GDP—see Glossary) on a purchasing power parity basis was US$82 billion, and its per capita GDP was estimated at US$8,364. With a per capita GDP growth rate of 5.4 percent in 1989, Portugal moved ahead of Greece to eleventh place among the twelve members of the EC.

Several distinctive features characterized Portugal's economy at the time of its accession to the EC. One of the most striking was its dependence on foreign "invisible" income. This income, consisting of tourism receipts and emigrant worker remittances, financed the country's large merchandise trade deficit. The growth and magnitude of tourism together with the explosive rise of government services largely explain the expansion of the services sector to nearly 56 percent of GDP in 1990 from 39 percent of GDP in 1973. One of every three Portuguese workers in the active labor force was engaged in temporary work in high-income countries, mainly France. These emigrant workers, numbering about 2 million, contributed significantly to Portugal's foreign exchange income, as well as to the country's household savings. Although less educated and technically less proficient than their EC counterparts, Portuguese workers are recognized for their strong work ethic and frugality.

Another distinguishing feature is Portugal's anachronistic agricultural sector, whose overall performance is unfavorable when considered in the context of the country's natural resources and climatic conditions. In the mid-1980s, agricultural productivity was half that of the levels in Greece and Spain and a quarter of the EC average. The land tenure system was polarized between two extremes: small and fragmented family farms in the north and large collective farms in the south that proved incapable of modernizing. The decollectivization of agriculture, which began in modest form in the late 1970s and accelerated in the late 1980s, promised to increase the efficiency of human and land resources in the south during the 1990s.

A third economic distinction is the scale and sectoral spread of Portugal's public enterprises. Before the Revolution of 1974, private enterprise ownership dominated the Portuguese economy to a degree unmatched in other West European countries; in 1982 the relative size of Portugal's public enterprise sector (based on an average of value added, employment, and gross capital formation) substantially exceeded that of the other West European economies.

The dispossession of the family-based financial-industrial groups, together with the "antifascist" purges of the mid-1970s, inflicted a serious "brain drain" on Portugal through the exile of entrepreneurs and professional managers. Recent Portuguese governments have recognized the highly politicized public enterprise sector as a major obstacle to the resolution of macroeconomic problems, such as large fiscal deficits, inflation, and burdensome external debt.

Portugal's commodity trade increasingly has become dominated by the EC, and since the accession of both Iberian countries to the organization in 1986, Spain has suddenly emerged as a significant trading partner for Portugal. The latter's major commodity exports at the beginning of the 1990s included textiles, clothing and footwear, machinery and transport equipment, forest products (including pulp and paper and cork products), and agricultural products (mainly wine). With the rising participation of multinational firms, Portugal also is gaining competitive strength in the export of higher technology automotive and electronic components and parts.

Privatization, economic deregulation, debt reduction, and supply-side tax reform became the salient concerns of government as

Portugal prepared itself for the challenges and opportunities of full participation in the EC's single market in the 1990s. These market-driven policies deserved much of the credit for Portugal's economic resurgence. Led by expanding exports and robust capital formation, Portugal's GDP grew by an annual rate of 4.6 percent from 1986 to 1990. During this five-year period, only Japan among the Organisation for Economic Co-operation and Development (OECD—see Glossary) countries exceeded Portugal's economic performance.

Economic Growth and Structural Change

Portugal's First Republic (1910–26) became, in the words of historian Douglas L. Wheeler, "midwife to Europe's longest surviving authoritarian system." Under the sixteen-year parliamentary regime of the republic with its forty-five governments, growing fiscal deficits financed by money creation and foreign borrowing climaxed in hyper-inflation and a moratorium on Portugal's external debt service. The cost of living around 1926 was thirty times what it had been in 1914. Fiscal imprudence and accelerating inflation gave way to massive capital flight, crippling domestic investment. Burgeoning public-sector employment during the First Republic was accompanied by a perverse shrinkage in the share of the industrial labor force in total employment. Although some headway was made toward increasing the level of literacy under the parliamentary regime, 68.1 percent of Portugal's population was still classified as illiterate by the 1930 census.

The Economy of the Salazar Regime

The First Republic was ended by a military coup in May 1926, but the newly installed government failed to solve the nation's precarious financial situation. Instead, President Óscar Fragoso Carmona invited António de Oliveira Salazar to head the Ministry of Finance, and the latter agreed to accept the position provided he would have veto power over all fiscal expenditures. At the time of his appointment as minister of finance in 1928, Salazar held the Chair of Economics at the University of Coimbra and was considered by his peers to be Portugal's most distinguished authority on inflation. For forty years, first as minister of finance (1928–32) and then as prime minister (1932–68), Salazar's political and economic doctrines were to shape the Portuguese destiny (see The New State, ch. 1).

From the perspective of the financial chaos of the republican period, it was not surprising that Salazar considered the principles of a balanced budget and monetary stability as categorical imperatives. By restoring equilibrium both in the fiscal budget and in the balance of international payments, Salazar succeeded in restoring Portugal's credit worthiness at home and abroad. Because Portugal's fiscal accounts from the 1930s until the early 1960s almost always had a surplus in the current account, the state had the wherewithal to finance public infrastructure projects without resorting either to inflationary financing or to borrowing abroad.

At the height of the Great Depression, Premier Salazar laid the foundations for his Estado Novo, the "New State." Neither capitalist nor communist, Portugal's economy was cast into a quasi-traditional mold. The corporative framework within which the Portuguese economy evolved combined two salient characteristics: extensive state regulation and predominantly private ownership of the means of production. Leading financiers and industrialists accepted extensive bureaucratic controls in return for assurances of minimal public ownership of economic enterprises and certain monopolistic (or restricted-competition) privileges.

Within this framework, the state exercised extensive de facto authority regarding private investment decisions and the level of wages. A system of industrial licensing (*condicionamento industrial*), introduced by law in 1931, required prior authorization from the state for setting up or relocating an industrial plant. Investment in machinery and equipment designed to increase the capacity of an existing firm also required government approval. Although the political system was ostensibly corporatist, as political scientist Howard J. Wiarda makes clear, "In reality both labor and capital—and indeed the entire corporate institutional network— were subordinate to the central state apparatus."

Under the old regime, Portugal's private sector was dominated by some forty great families. These industrial dynasties were allied by marriage with the large, traditional landowning families of the nobility, who held most of the arable land in the southern part of the country in great estates. Many of these dynasties had business interests in Portuguese Africa. Within this elite group, the top ten families owned all the important commercial banks, which in turn controlled a disproportionate share of the national economy. Because bank officials were often members of the boards of directors of borrowing firms in whose stock the banks participated, the influence of the large banks extended to a host of commercial, industrial, and service enterprises.

Portugal's shift toward a moderately outward-looking trade and financial strategy, initiated in the late 1950s, gained momentum during the early 1960s. A growing number of industrialists, as well as government technocrats, favored greater Portuguese integration with the industrial countries to the north as a badly needed stimulus to Portugal's economy. The rising influence of the Europe-oriented technocrats within Salazar's cabinet was confirmed by the substantial increase in the foreign investment component in projected capital formation between the first (1953–58) and second (1959–64) economic development plans. The first plan called for a foreign investment component of less than 6 percent, but the plan for the 1959–64 period envisioned a 25-percent contribution. The newly influential Europe-oriented industrial and technical groups persuaded Salazar that Portugal should become a charter member of the European Free Trade Association (EFTA) when it was organized in 1959. In the following year, Portugal also added its membership in the General Agreement on Tariffs and Trade (GATT), the International Monetary Fund (IMF—see Glossary), and the World Bank.

In 1958 when the Portuguese government announced the 1959–64 Six-Year Plan for National Development, a decision had been reached to accelerate the country's rate of economic growth—a decision whose urgency grew with the outbreak of guerrilla warfare in Angola in 1961 and in Portugal's other African territories thereafter. Salazar and his policy advisers recognized that additional claims by the state on national output for military expenditures, as well as for increased transfers of official investment to the "overseas provinces," could only be met by a sharp rise in the country's productive capacity. Salazar's commitment to preserving Portugal's "multiracial, pluricontinental" state led him reluctantly to seek external credits beginning in 1962, an action from which the Portuguese treasury had abstained for several decades.

Beyond military measures, the official Portuguese response to the "winds of change" in the African colonies was to integrate them administratively and economically more closely with Portugal through population and capital transfers, trade liberalization, and the creation of a common currency—the so-called Escudo Area. The integration program established in 1961 provided for the removal of Portugal's duties on imports from its overseas territories by January 1964. The latter, on the other hand, were permitted to continue to levy duties on goods imported from Portugal but at a preferential rate, in most cases 50 percent of the normal duties levied by the territories on goods originating outside the Escudo Area. The effect of this two-tier tariff system was to give Portugal's exports preferential access to its colonial markets.

Despite the opposition of protectionist interests, the Portuguese government succeeded in bringing about some liberalization of the industrial licensing system, as well as in reducing trade barriers to conform with EFTA and GATT agreements. The last years of

the Salazar era witnessed the creation of important privately organized ventures, including an integrated iron and steel mill, a
modern ship repair and shipbuilding complex, vehicle assembly
plants, oil refineries, petrochemical plants, pulp and paper mills,
and electronic plants. As economist Valentina Xavier Pintado observed, "Behind the facade of an aged Salazar, Portugal knew deep
and lasting changes during the 1960s."

The liberalization of the Portuguese economy continued under
Salazar's successor, Prime Minister Marcello José das Neves
Caetano (1968–74), whose administration abolished industrial
licensing requirements for firms in most sectors and in 1972 signed
a free-trade agreement with the newly enlarged EC. Under the
agreement, which took effect at the beginning of 1973, Portugal
was given until 1980 to abolish its restrictions on most community
goods and until 1985 on certain sensitive products amounting to
some 10 percent of the EC's total exports to Portugal. EFTA membership and a growing foreign investor presence contributed to Portugal's industrial modernization and export diversification between
1960 and 1973.

Notwithstanding the concentration of the means of production
in the hands of a small number of family based financial-industrial
groups, Portuguese business culture permitted a surprising upward
mobility of university-educated individuals with middle-class backgrounds into professional management careers. Before the revolution, the largest, most technologically advanced (and most recently
organized) firms offered the greatest opportunity for management
careers based on merit rather than on accident of birth.

Changing Structure of the Economy

The Portuguese economy had changed significantly by 1973,
compared with its position in 1961. Total output (GDP at factor
cost) grew by 120 percent in real terms. The industrial sector was
three times greater, and the size of the services sector doubled; but
agriculture, forestry, and fishing advanced by only 16 percent.
Manufacturing, the major component of the secondary sector, was
three times as large at the end of the period. Industrial expansion
was concentrated in large-scale enterprises using modern technology.

The composition of GDP also changed markedly from 1961 to
1973. The share of the primary sector (agriculture, forestry, and
fishing) in GDP shrank from 23 percent in 1961 to 16.8 percent
in 1973, and the contribution of the secondary (or industrial) sector (manufacturing, construction, mining, and electricity, gas and
water) increased from 37 percent to 44 percent during the period.

The services sector's share in GDP remained constant at 39.4 percent between 1961 and 1973. Within the industrial sector, the contribution of manufacturing advanced from 30 percent to 35 percent and that of construction from 4.6 percent to 6.4 percent.

The progressive ''opening'' of Portugal to the world economy was reflected in the growing shares of exports and imports (both visible and invisible) in national output and income. Further, the composition of Portugal's balance of international payments altered substantially. From 1960 to 1973, the merchandise trade deficit widened, but owing to a growing surplus on invisibles—including tourist receipts and emigrant worker remittances—the deficit in the current account gave way to a surplus from 1965 onward. Beginning with that year, the long-term capital account typically registered a deficit, the counterpart of the current account surplus. Even though the nation attracted a rising level of capital from abroad (both direct investments and loans), official and private Portuguese investments in the ''overseas territories'' were greater still—hence the net outflow on the long-term capital account.

The growth rate of Portuguese merchandise exports during the period 1959 to 1973 was 11 percent per annum. In 1960 the bulk of exports was accounted for by a few products—canned fish, raw and manufactured cork, cotton textiles, and wine. By contrast, in the early 1970s, Portugal's export list reflected significant product diversification, including both consumer and capital goods. Several branches of Portuguese industry became export-oriented, and in 1973 over one-fifth of Portuguese manufactured output was exported.

The radical nationalization-expropriation measures in the mid-1970s were initially accompanied by a policy-induced redistribution of national income from property owners, entrepreneurs, and private managers and professionals to industrial and agricultural workers. This wage explosion favoring workers with a high propensity to consume had a dramatic impact on the nation's economic growth and pattern of expenditures. Private and public consumption combined rose from 81 percent of domestic expenditure in 1973 to nearly 102 percent in 1975. The counterpart of overconsumption in the face of declining national output was a contraction in both savings and fixed capital formation, depletion of stocks, and a huge balance-of-payments deficit. The rapid increase in production costs associated with the surge in unit labor costs between 1973 and 1975 contributed significantly to the decline in Portugal's ability to compete in foreign markets. Real exports fell between 1973 and 1976, and their share in total expenditures declined from nearly 26 percent to 16.5 percent.

The economic dislocations of metropolitan Portugal associated with the income leveling and nationalization-expropriation measures were exacerbated by the sudden loss of the nation's African colonies in 1974 and 1975 and the reabsorption of overseas settlers (the so-called *retornados*), the global recession, and, as well, the international energy crisis.

Over the longer period, 1973–90, the composition of Portugal's GDP at factor cost changed significantly. The contribution of agriculture, forestry, and fishing as a share of total production continued its inexorable decline, to 6.1 percent in 1990 from 12.2 percent in 1973. In contrast to the prerevolutionary period, 1961–73, when the industrial sector grew by 9 percent annually and its contribution to GDP expanded, industry's share narrowed to 38.4 percent of GDP in 1990 from 44 percent in 1973. Manufacturing, the major component of the industrial sector, contributed relatively less to GDP in 1990 (28 percent) than in 1973 (35 percent). Most striking was the 16-percentage-point increase in the participation of the services sector from 39 percent of GDP in 1973 to 55.5 percent in 1990. Most of this growth reflected the proliferation of civil service employment and the associated cost of public administration, together with the dynamic contribution of tourism services during the 1980s.

Economic Growth, 1960–73 and 1981–90

There was a striking contrast between the economic growth and levels of capital formation in the 1960–73 period and in the 1980s decade (see table 4, Appendix). Clearly, the pre-revolutionary period was characterized by robust annual growth rates for GDP (6.9 percent), industrial production (9 percent), private consumption (6.5 percent), and gross fixed capital formation (7.8 percent). By way of contrast, the 1980s exhibited a pattern of slow-to-moderate annual growth rates for GDP (2.7 percent), industrial production (4.8 percent), private consumption (2.7 percent), and fixed capital formation (3.1 percent). As a result of worker emigration and the military draft, employment declined during the earlier period by a half percent annually, but increased by 1.4 percent annually during the 1980s. Significantly, labor productivity (GDP growth/employment growth) grew by a sluggish rate of 1.3 percent annually in the recent period compared with the extremely rapid annual growth rate of 7.4 percent earlier. Inflation, as measured by the GDP deflator, averaged a modest 4 percent a year before the revolution compared with nearly 18 percent annually during the 1980s.

Although the investment coefficients were roughly similar (24 percent of GDP allocated to fixed capital formation in the earlier

The Bridge of April 25, Lisbon
Courtesy General Directorate of Mass Communication, Lisbon

period; 26.7 percent during the 1980s), the overall investment productivity or efficiency (GDP growth rate/investment coefficient) was nearly three times greater (28.6 percent) before the revolution than in the 1980s (10.1 percent).

How did Portugal's per capita GDP compare with the average of the twelve members of the EC, the European Twelve (EC–12), during the past three decades? In 1960, at the initiation of Salazar's more outward-looking economic policy, Portugal's per capita GDP was only 38 percent of the EC–12 average; by the end of the Salazar period, in 1968, it had risen to 48 percent; and in 1973, on the eve of the revolution, Portugal's per capita GDP had reached 56.4 percent of the EC–12 average. In 1975, the year of maximum revolutionary turmoil, Portugal's per capita GDP declined to 52.3 percent of the EC–12 average.

Convergence of real GDP growth toward the EC average occurred as a result of Portugal's economic resurgence since 1985. In 1991 Portugal's per capita GDP climbed to 54.9 percent of the EC average, gradually approaching the level attained just before the Revolution of 1974.

Revolutionary Change

The military coup of April 1974, which ousted the long-lived authoritarian Salazar-Caetano regime, was rapidly transformed into a social revolution that profoundly recast Portugal's political and economic systems (see Spínola and Revolution, ch. 4). The revolutionary leadership undercut the old elite's economic base by nationalizing the banks and most of the country's heavy and medium-sized industries; expropriating landed estates in the central and southern regions; and giving independence to Angola, Mozambique, and other colonies. The last action dismantled the web of economic relationships, known as the Escudo Area, through which metropolitan Portugal was linked to its "overseas provinces."

In the brief period between the collapse of the old regime in April 1974 and the abortive leftist coup of November 1975, a variety of economic models were proposed for Portugal by the provisional Armed Forces Movement (Movimento das Forças Armadas—MFA) governments, including the West European, Yugoslav, and Albanian models. In the early months following the military coup, the new Portuguese government's economic orientation could be described as moderate-reformist. The regime's Economic and Social Program published on May 15, 1974, made no provision for large-scale nationalization of industry or agriculture. The program simply provided for the "adoption of new measures of government intervention in the basic sectors of the economy and particularly in the sectors of national interest, without prejudice to the legitimate interest of private enterprise"; argued for "reform of the tax system so as to rationalize it and ease the tax burden on less well-off groups, with a view of a fairer distribution of income"; recommended measures "to stimulate agriculture and gradually reform the land tenure system"; and, within the sphere of social policy, favored introduction of "a minimum wage to be progressively extended to all sectors of activity."

The initial moderate-reformist policies reflected the views of General António de Spínola, who was chosen by the MFA to lead the coup and to serve as the country's president. Spínola, the celebrated war hero, favored the establishment of civil liberties and the creation of democratic institutions. He also advocated rapid improvement of living standards, a modernized financial structure, and eventual Portuguese participation in the EC—objectives laid down in an economic plan he commissioned from Erik Lundberg of the World Bank. Spínola's view on the economy and the pace of decolonization diverged from those of the Coordinating Committee of the MFA, most of whose members were prepared to end completely the Portuguese presence in Africa and to expand substantially the scope of the public sector. By the early autumn of 1974, events both within and outside Portugal favored the course chosen by the MFA coordinating committee. Unable to stop the leftward drift of the country, Spínola resigned in September 1974.

Nationalization

The reorganization of the MFA coordinating committee in March 1975 brought into prominence a group of Marxist-oriented officers who, in league with the General Confederation of Portuguese Workers-National Intersindical (Confederação Geral dos Trabalhadores Portugueses-Intersindical Nacional—CGTP-IN), the communist-dominated trade union confederation known as Intersindical prior to 1977, sought the radical transformation of the nation's social system and political economy. Abandoning its moderate-reformist posture, the MFA leadership set out on a course of sweeping nationalizations and land expropriations. During the balance of that year, the government nationalized all Portuguese-owned capital in the banking, insurance, petrochemical, fertilizer, tobacco, cement, and wood pulp sectors of the economy, as well as the Portuguese iron and steel company, the major breweries, the large shipping lines, most public transport, two of the three principal shipyards, core companies of the Companhia União Fabril (CUF) conglomerate, the radio and TV networks (except that of the Roman Catholic Church), and important companies in the glass, mining, fishing, and agricultural sectors. Because of the key role of the domestic banks as holders of stock, the government indirectly acquired equity positions in hundreds of other firms. An Institute for State Participation was created to deal with the many disparate (often tiny) enterprises in which the state had thus obtained a majority shareholding. Another 300 small to medium enterprises came under public management as the government "intervened" to rescue them from bankruptcy following their takeover by workers or abandonment by management.

Although foreign direct investment was statutorily exempted from nationalization, many foreign-controlled enterprises curtailed or ceased operation because of costly forced labor settlements or worker takeovers. The combination of revolutionary policies and negative business climate brought about a sharp reversal in the trend of direct investment inflows from abroad.

A study by the economists Maria Belmira Martins and José Chaves Rosa showed that a total of 244 private enterprises were directly nationalized during the sixteen-month interval from March 14, 1975 to July 29, 1976. Nationalization was followed by the consolidation of the several private firms in each industry into state monopolies. As an example, Quimigal, the chemical and fertilizer entity, represented a merger of five firms. Four large companies were integrated to form the national oil company, Petroleos de Portugal (Petrogal). Portucel brought together five pulp and paper companies. The fourteen private electric power enterprises were joined into a single power generation and transmission monopoly, Electricidade de Portugal (EDP). With the nationalization and amalgamation of the three tobacco firms under Tabaqueira, the state gained complete control of this industry. The several breweries and beer distribution companies were integrated into two state firms, Central de Cervejas (Centralcer) and Unicer; and a single state enterprise, Rodoviaria, was created by joining the ninety-three nationalized trucking and bus lines. The forty-seven cement plants, formerly controlled by the Champalimaud interests, were integrated into Cimentos de Portugal (Cimpor). The government also acquired a dominant position in the export-oriented shipbuilding and ship repair industry. Former private monopolies retained their company designations following nationalization. Included among these were the iron and steel company, Siderurgia Nacional; the railway, Caminhos de Ferro Portugueses (CP); and the national airline, Transportes Aéreos Portugueses (TAP).

Unlike other sectors, where existing private firms were typically consolidated into state monopolies, the commercial banking system and insurance industry were left with a degree of competition. By 1979 the number of domestic commercial banks was reduced from fifteen to nine. Notwithstanding their public status, the remaining banks competed with each other and retained their individual identities and certain differences in their activities.

Before the revolution, private enterprise ownership dominated the Portuguese economy to a degree unmatched in other West European countries. Only a handful of wholly owned or majority owned state entities existed; these included the post office, the armaments industry, and the ports, as well as the National Development Bank and Caixa Geral de Depósitos, the largest savings bank. The Portuguese government held minority interests in TAP, the national airline; in Siderurgia Nacional, the integrated steel mill; and in oil refining and oil marketing firms. The railroads, two colonial banks, and the Bank of Portugal were majority privately owned but publicly administered. Finally, although privately owned, the tobacco companies and Radio Marconi were operated under government concessions.

Two years after the military coup, the enlarged public sector accounted for 47 percent of the country's gross fixed capital formation (GFCF), 30 percent of total value added (VA), and 24 percent of employment. These shares should be compared with 10 percent of GFCF, 9 percent of VA, and 13 percent of employment for the traditional public sector of 1973. Expansion of the public sector since the revolution was particularly noteworthy in heavy manufacturing; in public services, including electricity, gas, transport and communications; and in banking and insurance. Further, according to the Institute for State Participation, these figures did not include private enterprises under temporary state intervention, private enterprises with minority state participation (less than 50 percent of the common stock), or worker-managed firms and agricultural collectives.

The Brain Drain

Compounding the problem of massive nationalizations was the heavy drain of managerial and technical expertise away from the public enterprises. The income-leveling measures of the MFA revolutionary regime, together with the "antifascist" purges in factories, offices, and large agricultural estates, induced an exodus of human capital, mainly to Brazil. This loss of managers, technicians, and business people inspired a popular Lisbon saying, "Portugal used to send its legs to Brazil, but now we are sending our heads."

Notwithstanding the concentration of the means of production in the hands of a small number of family-based financial-industrial groups, Portuguese business culture permitted a surprising upward mobility of educated individuals with middle-class backgrounds into professional management careers. Before the Revolution of 1974, the largest, most technologically advanced (and most recently organized) firms offered the greatest opportunity for management careers based on merit.

A detailed analysis of Portugal's loss of managerial resources is contained in Harry M. Makler's follow-up surveys of 306 enterprises, conducted in July 1976, and again in June 1977. His study makes clear that nationalization was greater in the modern, large, technically advanced industries than in the traditional industries such as textiles, apparel, and construction. In small enterprises (fifty to ninety-nine employees), only 15 percent of the industrialists had quit as compared with 43 percent in the larger. In the giant firms (1,000 or more employees), more than half had quit. Makler's calculations show that the higher the socioeconomic class origin, the greater the likelihood that the industrialist had left the firm. He also notes that "the more upwardly mobile also were more likely to have quit than those who were downwardly socially mobile." Significantly, a much larger percentage of professional managers (52 percent) compared with owners of production (i.e.,

127

founders—18 percent, heirs—21 percent, and owner-managers—32 percent) had left their enterprises.

The constitution of 1976 confirmed the large and interventionist role of the state in the economy. Its Marxist character before the 1989 revisions was revealed in a number of its articles, which pointed to a "classless society" and the "socialization of the means of production" and proclaimed all nationalizations made after April 25, 1974, as "irreversible conquests of the working classes." The constitution also defined new power relationships between labor and management, with a strong bias in labor's favor. All regulations with reference to layoffs, including collective redundancy, were circumscribed by Article 53.

Role of the Consolidated Public Sector

After the revolution, the Portuguese economy experienced a rapid, and often uncontrollable, expansion of public expenditures—both in the general government and in public enterprises. The lag in public-sector receipts resulted in large public enterprise and general government deficits. In 1982 the borrowing requirement of the consolidated public sector reached 24 percent of GDP, its peak level; it was subsequently reduced to 9 percent of GDP in 1990.

To rein in domestic demand growth, the Portuguese government was obliged to pursue IMF-monitored stabilization programs in 1977–78 and 1983–85. The large negative savings of the public sector (including the state-owned enterprises) became a structural feature of Portugal's political economy after the revolution. Other official impediments to rapid economic growth after 1974 included all-pervasive price regulation, as well as heavy-handed intervention in factor markets and the distribution of income.

In 1989 Prime Minister Aníbal Cavaco Silva succeeded in mobilizing the required two-thirds vote in the Assembly of the Republic to amend the constitution, thereby permitting the denationalization of the state-owned banks and other public enterprises. Privatization, economic deregulation, and tax reform became the salient concerns of public policy as Portugal prepared itself for the challenges and opportunities of membership in the EC's single market in the 1990s.

The Nonfinancial Public Enterprises

Following the sweeping nationalizations of the mid-1970s, public enterprises became a major component of Portugal's consolidated public sector. Portugal's nationalized sector in 1980 included a core of fifty nonfinancial enterprises, entirely government owned. This so-called public nonfinancial enterprise group included the

Institute of State Participation, a holding company with investments in some seventy subsidiary enterprises; a number of state-owned entities manufacturing or selling goods and services grouped with nationalized enterprises for national accounts purposes (arms, agriculture, and public infrastructure, such as ports); and a large number of over 50-percent state-owned subsidiaries operating under private law. Altogether these public enterprises accounted for 25 percent of VA in GDP, 52 percent of GFCF, and 12 percent of Portugal's total employment. In terms of VA and GFCF, the relative scale of Portugal's public entities exceeded that of the other West European economies, including the EC member countries.

Although the nationalizations broke up the concentration of economic power in the hands of the financial-industrial groups, the subsequent merger of several private firms into single publicly owned enterprises left domestic markets even more subject to monopoly. Apart from special cases, as in iron and steel, where the economies of scale are optimal for very large firms, there was some question as to the desirability of establishing national monopolies. The elimination of competition following the official takeover of such industries as cement, chemicals, and trucking probably reduced managerial incentives for cost reduction and technical advance.

As hybrid institutions, public enterprises find it difficult to separate market choices from political considerations. Their poorer economic performance may partially be explained by public management's frustration at attempting to reconcile impossible goals: on the one side, a concern for the "bottom line"; on the other, coping with the distributional struggles of interest groups. Special interest groups that shape the policies of state-owned firms include "elite" public enterprise unions aspiring to guarantee employment and above-market wages; consumer groups desiring goods and services at below user cost or market price; oversight ministries intent upon expanding their authority; and politicians, including chiefs of state, seeking to expand patronage opportunities. As a vehicle for redistribution, public enterprise often becomes the servant of special interest groups—those who are politically connected—rather than a guardian of the public or general interest.

It was not surprising that numerous nationalized enterprises experienced severe operating and financial difficulties. State operations faced considerable uncertainty as to the goals of public enterprises, with negative implications for decision making, often at odds with market criteria. In many instances, managers of public firms were less able than their private-sector counterparts to resist strong wage demands from militant unions. Further, public firm managers were required for reasons of political expediency to maintain a redundant labor force and freeze prices or utility rates for long periods in the face of rising costs. Overstaffing was particularly flagrant at Petrogal, the national petroleum monopoly, and Estaleiros Navais de Setúbal (Setenave), the wholly state-owned shipbuilding and repairing enterprise. The failure of the public transportation firms to raise fares during a time of accelerating inflation resulted in substantial operating losses and even obsolescence of the sector's capital stock.

As a group, the public enterprises performed poorly financially and relied excessively on debt financing from both domestic and foreign commercial banks. The operating and financial problems of the public enterprise sector were revealed in a study by the Bank of Portugal covering the years 1978–80. Based upon a survey of fifty-one enterprises, which represented 92 percent of the sector's VA, the analysis confirmed the debilitated financial condition of the public enterprises, i.e., their inadequate equity and liquidity ratios. The consolidated losses of the firms included in the survey increased from 18.3 million contos (for value of the conto—see Glossary) in 1978 to 40.3 million contos in 1980, or 4.6 percent to 6.1 percent of net worth, respectively. Losses were concentrated in transportation and to a lesser extent in transport equipment and materials (principally shipbuilding and ship repair). The budgetary burden of the public enterprises as a result of their overall weak performance was substantial: enterprise transfers to the Portuguese government (mainly taxes) fell short of government receipts in the forms of subsidies and capital transfers. The largest nonfinancial state enterprises recorded (inflation-discounted) losses in the seven-year period from 1977 to 1983 equivalent to 11 percent on capital employed. Notwithstanding their substantial operating losses and weak capital structure, these large enterprises financed 86 percent of their capital investments from 1977 to 1983 through increases in debt, of which two-thirds was foreign. The rapid buildup of Portugal's external debt from 1978 to 1985 was largely associated with the public enterprises.

The General Government

The share of general government expenditure (including capital outlays) in GDP rose from 23 percent in 1973 to 46 percent in 1990 (see table 5, Appendix). On the revenue side, the upward trend was less pronounced: the share increased from nearly 23 percent in 1973 to 39.2 percent in 1990. From a modest surplus before the revolution in 1973, the government balance swung to a wide deficit of 12 percent of GDP in 1984, declining thereafter to around 5.4 percent of GDP in 1990. Significantly, both current expenditures and capital expenditures roughly doubled their shares of GDP between 1973 and 1990: government current outlays rose from 19.5 percent to 40.2 percent, capital outlays from 3.2 percent to 5.7 percent.

Apart from the growing investment effort, which included capital transfers to the public enterprises, government expenditure patterns since the revolution reflected rapid expansion in the number of civil servants and pressure to redistribute income, mainly through current transfers and subsidies, as well as burgeoning interest obligations. The category "current transfers" nearly tripled its share of GDP between 1973 and 1990, from under 5 percent to 13.4 percent, reflecting the explosive growth of the social security system, both with respect to the number of persons covered and the upgrading of benefits. Escalating interest payments on the public debt from less than half a percent of GDP in 1973 to 8.2 percent of GDP in 1990 were the result of both a rise in the debt itself and higher real effective interest rates.

The narrowing of the government deficit since the mid-1980s and the associated easing of the borrowing requirement was caused both by a small increase in the share of receipts (by two percentage points) and by the relatively sharper contraction of current subsidies, from 7.6 percent of GDP in 1984 to 1.5 percent of GDP in 1990. This reduction was a direct consequence of the gradual abandonment by the government of its policy of curbs on rises in public utility rates and food prices, against which it paid subsidies to public enterprises.

Tax reform—comprising both direct and indirect taxation—was a major element in a more comprehensive effort to modernize the economy in the late 1980s. The key objective of these reforms was to promote more efficient and market-oriented economic performance. Beyond considerations of efficiency, a good tax system also should be simple (i.e., easy to administer), fair, and transparent.

Prior to the reform, about 90 percent of the personal tax base consisted of labor income. Statutory marginal tax rates on labor income were very high, even at relatively low income levels, especially after the revolution. The large number of tax exemptions and fiscal benefits, together with high marginal tax rates, entailed the progressive erosion of the tax base through tax avoidance and evasion. Furthermore, Portuguese membership in the EC created the imperative for a number of changes in the tax system, especially the introduction of the value-added tax (VAT—see Glossary).

Reform proceeded in two major installments: the VAT was introduced in 1986; the income tax reform, for both personal and corporate income, became effective in 1989. The VAT, whose normal rate was 17 percent, replaced all indirect taxes, such as the transactions tax, railroad tax, and tourism tax. Marginal tax rates on both personal and corporate income were substantially cut, and in the case of individual taxes, the number of brackets was reduced to five. The basic rate of corporate tax was 36.5 percent, and the top marginal tax rate on personal income was cut from 80 percent to 40 percent. A 25 percent capital gains tax was levied on direct and portfolio investment. Business proceeds invested in development projects were exempt from capital gains tax if the assets were retained for at least two years.

Preliminary estimates indicated that part of the observed increase in direct tax revenue in 1989–90 was of a permanent nature, the consequence of a redefinition of taxable income, a reduction in allowed deductions, and the termination of most fiscal benefits for corporations. The resulting broadening of the income tax base permitted a lowering of marginal tax rates, greatly reducing the disincentive effects to labor and saving.

Macroeconomic Disequilibria and Public Debt

Between 1973 and 1988, the general government debt/GDP ratio quadrupled, reaching a peak of 74 percent in 1988. This growth in the absolute and relative debt was only partially attributable to the accumulation of government deficits. It also reflected the reorganization of various public funds and enterprises, the separation of their accounts from those of the government, and their fiscal consolidation. The rising trend of the general government debt/GDP ratio was reversed in 1989, as a surge in tax revenues linked to the tax reform and the shrinking public enterprise deficits reduced the public-sector borrowing requirement (PSBR) relative to GDP. After falling to 67 percent in 1990, the general government debt/GDP ratio is expected to continue to decline, reflecting fiscal restraint and increased proceeds from privatization.

The financing structure of the public deficits has changed since the mid-1980s under the effect of two factors. First, the easing of the PSBR and the government's determination to reduce the foreign debt/GDP ratio led to a sharp reduction in borrowing abroad. Second, since 1985 the share of nonmonetary financing has increased steeply, not only in the form of public issues of Treasury bills but also, since 1987–88, in the form of medium-term Treasury bonds.

The magnitude of the public-sector deficit (including that of the public enterprises) had a crowding-out effect on private investment. The nationalized banks were obliged by law to increase their holding of government paper bearing negative real interest rates. This massive absorption of funds by the public sector was largely at the expense of private enterprises whose financing was often constrained by quantitative credit controls.

Portugal's membership in the EC resulted in substantial net transfers averaging 1.5 percent of annual GDP during 1987–90. The bulk of these transfers was "structural" funds that were used for infrastructure developments and professional training. Additional EC funds, also allocated through the public sector, were designed for the development of Portugal's agricultural and industrial sectors.

After 1985 the PSBR began to show a substantial decline, largely as a result of the improved financial position of public enterprises. Favorable exogenous factors (lower oil prices, lower interest rates, and depreciation of the dollar) helped to moderate operating costs. More important, however, was the shift in government policy. Public enterprise managers were given greater autonomy with respect to investment, labor, and product pricing. Significantly, the combined deficit of the nonfinancial public enterprises fell to below 2 percent of GDP on average in 1987–88 from 8 percent of GDP in 1985–86. In 1989 the borrowing requirements of those enterprises fell further to 1 percent of GDP.

In April 1990, legislation concerning privatization was enacted following an amendment to the constitution in June 1989 that provided the basis for complete (100 percent) divestiture of nationalized enterprises. Among the stated objectives of privatization were to modernize economic units, increase their competitiveness, and contribute to sectoral restructuring; to reduce the role of the state in the economy; to contribute to the development of capital markets; and to widen the participation of Portuguese citizens in the ownership of enterprises, giving particular attention to the workers of the enterprises and to small shareholders.

The Portuguese government is concerned about the strength of foreign investment in privatizations and wants to reserve the right to veto some transactions. But as a member of the EC, Portugal eventually will have to accept investment from other member countries on an equal footing with investment of its nationals. Significantly, government proceeds from privatization of nationalized enterprises will primarily be used to reduce public debt; and to the extent that profits will rise after privatization, tax revenues will expand. In 1991 proceeds from privatization were expected to amount to 2.5 percent of GDP.

Human Resources and Income Distribution

One of the striking characteristics of the Portuguese people is their propensity to emigrate (see Emigration, ch.2). In the late 1980s, an estimated 3.5 to 4.0 million Portuguese passport holders were living in foreign lands, equal to over a third of the population residing in Portugal. Emigration, which was once a reflection of Portugal's international importance as a maritime and colonial power, became in the twentieth century, according to Thomas G. Sanders, ''a reflection of its poverty and economic weakness.'' As a consequence of this population diaspora, large numbers of Portuguese migrants lived in Latin America (mainly Brazil and Venezuela), industrial Western Europe (mainly France and Germany), Africa (predominantly the Republic of South Africa), and North America (the United States and Canada). The Portuguese emigrants to the EC countries, numbering over 1 million, differed in several ways from those who went overseas: most of them were temporary workers who planned to return to their homeland, and most originated from the mainland rather than Madeira and the Azores (Açores).

Portugal's comparative poverty within the EC is closely associated with lower per capita investment in human and physical capital. On the other hand, Portuguese workers are recognized for their strong work ethic, adaptability, and frugality. Among middle-income countries, few can match Portugal for its high family savings rate. Real wage rates over extended time periods closely reflect labor productivity, which in turn is correlated with the factors mentioned above. Although government intervention can temporarily alter the distribution of income in favor of labor through the manipulation of wage rates and consumer prices—as indeed happened in the mid-1970s—labor productivity eventually determines labor's earnings.

Employment and Sectoral Composition of the Labor Force

From 1960 to 1973, Portuguese policy measures supported a shift of resources, including labor, from low-productivity toward high-productivity uses, especially export-oriented industries. Rapid and accelerated economic growth was reflected in the profound alteration of the sectoral composition of the work force. Between 1960 (the year after Portugal became a charter member of EFTA) and 1973, the share of the civilian labor force engaged in agriculture, forestry, and fishing fell from nearly 44 percent to just under 28 percent, whereas the share of labor engaged in industry (including construction) increased from slightly less than 29 percent to

Fruit vendor, Porto
Courtesy Andrea Matles Savada
Portuguese fishermen unload their catch.
Courtesy Portuguese National Tourist Office, New York

almost 36 percent, and in the services sector (including transport and communications) from nearly 28 percent to slightly more than 36 percent. The shift of labor out of agriculture involved a reduction of the number engaged in that sector (a decline of about 550,000 workers between 1960 and 1973), as well as in the proportion of farmers in the total labor force.

Because of heavy emigration, the working population of continental Portugal shrank from more than 3.1 million in 1960 to just 2.9 million in 1973, and employment fell by an annual rate averaging 0.5 percent. The rapid shrinkage in the number of workers in agriculture was not accompanied by an equal or greater rise in the industrial and services sectors. Nearly two out of every three Portuguese taking up nonagricultural employment during this period did so in another West European country. France was, even at the beginning of the 1990s, host to about 80 percent of the emigrant workers, most of whom worked at unskilled or semi-skilled jobs. The 110,000 Portuguese in Germany, by contrast, had found higher-skilled work, with some two-thirds employed in industry in 1977. Consequently, net emigration between 1960 and 1973 exceeded 1 million, a number greater than the natural increase in the Portuguese population. In the thirteen years of war, from 1961 to 1974, 1.5 million Portuguese had seen military service in Africa, and during 1974 one in every four adult males was in the armed forces. During this period, unemployment was kept down to about 4 percent (and to less than 3 percent in the early 1970s), largely because of massive labor emigration to industrialized Western Europe and the military draft.

After the revolution, the demobilization of the military draftees and the return of Portuguese nationals from Africa produced important additions to the mainland population and labor force. From a combined strength of 220,000 at the beginning of 1974, the armed forces demobilized some 95,000 persons in that year and 60,000 in 1975. Furthermore, an estimated 500,000 returnees (*retornados*) were repatriated, mainly from Angola and Mozambique, and most of them were totally without resources, having had to leave the former colonies with only the barest essentials. Initially, their former occupations made them difficult to integrate into the metropolitan economy: 67 percent had held service jobs (as public employees or office workers), whereas only 20 percent had been engaged in industry and 4 percent in agriculture. Consequently, the Portuguese government had to shoulder an extremely heavy burden in the form of the various benefits granted to the returnees, including cash subsidies, provision of hotel accommodations, and assistance with purchases of essential goods. The sum of these benefits was estimated at 14 billion escudos (for value of the escudo—see Glossary) in 1976, or about 11 percent of total government spending. In all, the increase in the civilian population from 1974 to 1976 was probably about 900,000, i.e., 10 percent of the total population in 1973.

Following this brief population burst in the number of mainland residents, Portugal's population and labor force resumed their natural rates of growth; for example, in the 1980–89 decade, the annual percentage increases were 0.5 percent and 1.4 percent, respectively. Between 1973 and 1990, Portugal's labor force grew by more than 1.8 million (see table 6, Appendix), of which more than half was absorbed in the services sector and over a third in the industrial sector. Although the share of the work force in agriculture, forestry, and fishing resumed its historical relative decline (from nearly 28 percent of the total in 1973 to almost 18 percent in 1990), the absolute number of workers in that sector increased slightly. Industry's share in the labor force remained virtually unchanged between 1973 and 1990 (at about 35 percent), but the services sector added nearly 1.2 million employees, its share in the total rising from over 36 percent in 1973 to 47.4 percent in 1990. A major explanation for this growth of almost 11 percent was the explosive increase of civil service employment after the Revolution of 1974.

Wages and the Distribution of Income

Two approaches are used to determine how income is divided among citizens of a country. The first approach, involving the size of distribution of income, compares the household income shares received by the richest 20 percent of the population, the poorest 20 percent, and the three quintiles between these extremes. This approach yields an income concentration, or Gini ratio: the higher the ratio, the greater the degree of inequality. Gini ratios can be useful in comparing the degree of income inequality within a country over time or among countries during the same time frame. The International Labour Organisation estimates for Portugal indicate that the Gini ratio changed little between 1967–68 (0.423) and 1973–74 (0.431), corresponding to the end of the Salazar and Caetano administrations, respectively. By comparison, in the early 1970s, France's Gini ratio was 0.416, Germany's 0.376, and Sweden's 0.346. It may also be useful to compare the household income share received by the poorest 40 percent of the population with the share received by the richest 20 percent. According to this indicator (richest 20 percent and poorest 40 percent), Portugal's income distribution profile at the end of the Caetano period (3.5) reveals by comparison relatively greater equality in Spain (2.4) and

Italy (3.0) but greater relative inequality in Costa Rica (4.6), Mexico (5.3), and Brazil (9.5). Portugal's income concentration profile, on the other hand, was similar to that of France (3.3) and Argentina (3.6) during the early 1970s.

The second, or functional, approach to income distribution measures the shares going to the various productive factors—entrepreneurship, land, capital, and labor. Wages and salaries or compensation of employees are concepts that normally show the proportion of national income or national product going to labor. In the aftermath of the 1974 military coup, from mid-1974 to November 1975, the newly formed labor unions within the General Confederation of Portuguese Workers-National Intersindical (Confederação Geral dos Trabalhadores Portugueses-Intersindical Nacional—CGTP-IN) greatly increased their strength. The unions focused on expansion of the public sector, employment guarantees, and income redistribution. In response to labor's demands, the government instituted income-leveling policies that included a large increase in the minimum wage for a substantial proportion of the work force, a freeze on rents, a highly graduated income tax, and a ceiling on salaries. As a consequence of official measures affecting wages and salaries (including the US$800 a month ceiling on the maximum salary), the average pay gap between unskilled workers and managers shrank from 1:7 in 1973 to 1:4 in 1975. To protect increases in nominal wages, prices of essential commodities, particularly food, were fixed at below market levels. Real wages increased 25 percent between 1973 and 1975, and the share of the wage bill in national income rose explosively from 52 percent in 1973 to 69 percent in 1975. At the same time, the proportion of national income flowing to capital and entrepreneurship (including income of artisans and other self-employed workers) was sharply eroded.

Official policies were also reflected in the distribution of income. Average wage income of the lowest quintile almost doubled in real terms between 1972 and 1976; the second and third quintiles obtained an increase of 59 percent and 45 percent, respectively; but the real remuneration of the top 5 percent declined by 19 percent from 1972 to 1976.

In January 1979, the General Union of Workers (União Geral dos Trabalhadores—UGT) was organized. The UGT was viewed as a viable, democratic alternative to the CGTP-IN, which, as of the beginning of the 1990s, continued to be communist dominated, as it had been since its formation. By 1990 these two union confederations were roughly equal in size, and 30 percent of the labor force was unionized.

How has the working class fared since the revolution? Following the short-lived, government-induced wage explosion in 1975–76, the share of employee compensation in national income (52.9 percent in 1979) was again much the same as in 1973 (51.6 percent), and from 1979 to 1989 that share was on a downward trend. Real wages per capita increased only 10 percent between 1973 and 1989, a reflection both of slow labor productivity growth (20 percent) during this sixteen-year postrevolutionary period and the widening "tax wedge," i.e., the higher social security taxes contributed by both the employer and the employee. Real wages per capita moved on a downward trend from their peak level in 1976 to their lowest point (below their level in 1973) in 1984. From 1984 to 1990, real wages rose each year in response to the brisk demand for labor associated with Portugal's economic recovery. The rate of unemployment fell to 4.7 percent in 1990, the lowest level since the mid-1970s. This rate brought the cumulative decline since the unemployment peak of 1985 (8.5 percent) to 3.8 percentage points. An estimated 250,000 new jobs were added between 1985 and 1990.

The Portuguese government submitted legislation in 1988 to abolish the restrictive individual and collective dismissal regulations that had been in effect since 1976. Although approved by parliament, the law was declared unconstitutional by the courts. In the following year, however, the government gained court approval of less sweeping labor reforms: dismissal procedures were simplified and the conditions eased regarding both the termination of individual contracts and collective layoffs. Under this law, older unemployed workers were permitted reduction of the early retirement age from sixty-two to sixty. Until the 1989 labor reform, unemployment rigidity was coupled with a high degree of real wage flexibility. Consequently, adjustment to external shocks, such as the sudden price explosion of imported oil between 1979 and 1980, was effected by reducing real wages rather than the numbers of employed.

As a result of its EC membership, Portugal received transfers from the European Social Fund in support of training programs managed by private firms. The fund's contribution to the Portuguese labor market amounted to 1 percent of GDP in both 1987 and 1988, of which two-thirds was invested in training an estimated 160,000 young persons.

Agriculture, Forestry, and Fishing

Agriculture, forestry, and fishing employed 17.8 percent of Portugal's labor force but accounted for only 6.2 percent of GDP in 1990. With the principal exception of the alluvial soils of the

Tagus River (Rio Tejo) valley and the irrigated sections of the Alentejo, crop yields and animal productivity remained well below those of the other EC members. Portugal's agro-food deficit (attributable mainly to grain, oilseed, and meat imports) represented about 2.5 percent of GDP, but its surplus on forestry products (wood, cork, and paper pulp) offset its food deficit.

Portugal's overall agricultural performance is unfavorable when viewed in the context of the country's natural resources and climatic conditions. Agricultural productivity (gross farm output per person employed) was well below that of the other West European countries in 1985, at half of the levels in Greece and Spain and a quarter of the EC average.

A number of factors contribute to Portugal's poor agricultural performance. First, the level of investment in agriculture was traditionally very low. The number of tractors and the quantity of fertilizer used per hectare were one-third the EC average in the mid-1980s. Second, farms in the north are small and fragmented; half of them are less than one hectare in size and 86 percent, less than five hectares. Third, the collective farms set up in the south after the 1974–75 expropriations proved incapable of modernizing, and their efficiency declined. Fourth, poor productivity is associated with the low level of education of farmers. Finally, distribution channels and economic infrastructure are inadequate in parts of the country.

Agricultural Zones

Portugal is made up of the mainland and the Azores and Madeira islands, which altogether amount to a land area of 91,640 square kilometers, about the size of Indiana. The mainland's land area of slightly more than 9.2 million hectares is classified as follows (in thousands of hectares): 2,755 arable land and permanent crops (including 710 in permanent crops), 530 permanent pasture, 3,640 forest and woodland, and 2,270 other land.

A useful categorization divides the mainland into three distinct topographical and climatic zones: the south (the Alentejo and the Algarve), the center (the Tagus River Valley and coastal areas), and the north (the area between the Rio Douro and the Rio Minho, Trás-os-Montes, and the Beira region).

The north is mountainous, with a rainy, moderately cool climate. This zone contains about 2 million hectares of cultivated land and is dominated by small-scale, intensive agriculture. High population density, particularly in the northwest, has contributed to a pattern of tiny, fragmented farms that produce mainly for family consumption interspersed with larger and often mechanized farms that specialize in commercial production of a variety of crops. On the average, northern levels of technology and labor productivity are among the lowest in Western Europe. Extreme underemployment of agricultural workers accounts for the north being the principal and enduring source of Portuguese emigrant labor.

The center is a diverse zone of about 75,000 hectares that includes rolling hills suitable primarily for tree crops, poor dryland soils, and the fertile alluvial soils of the banks of the Tagus River. A variety of crops are grown on the productive areas under irrigation: grains, mainly wheat and corn, oilseeds (including sunflowers), and irrigated rice. Farms located in the Tagus Valley typically are 100 hectares in size.

The south is dominated by the Alentejo, a vast, rolling plain with a hot, arid climate. The Alentejo occupies an area of approximately 2.6 million hectares, about 30 percent of the total area of mainland Portugal, and produces about 75 percent of the country's wheat. Although much of the area is classified as arable land, poor soils dominate most of the area, and consequently yields of dryland crops and pasture are low by West European standards. The Alentejo is also known for its large stands of cork oak and its olive groves. The Algarve, less than a third the area of the Alentejo, occupies the extreme southern part of Portugal. This dryland area is characterized by smallholdings where animal grazing and fishing are the principal occupations of the inhabitants.

Crops and Livestock

In 1990 wheat was the leading Portuguese grain crop, followed by corn, which was grown mainly on the small farms of the north. Rice, although occupying less than one-tenth of the area of either wheat or corn, was a significant grain crop. Potatoes and corn silage were found throughout the north.

Portugal's leading edible tree crop in the early 1990s was olive oil. In spite of the importance of olive oil for the economy and the increasing production of other edible oilseeds, such as safflower and sunflower, Portugal was a net importer of vegetable fats and oils. The country produced a variety of horticultural crops, some of which were exported. As an example, Portugal was a leading world exporter of tomato paste.

In the mid-1980s, over 300,000 hectares were in vineyards. Portugal is one of Western Europe's major producers and exporters of wines. The most important vineyards are located in the northern valleys of the Rio Douro, Rio Mondego, and Rio Lima, but vineyards are also found in the Algarve and the Setúbal Peninsula. Portugal's dessert wines—port and muscatel—and rosé wines, notably Mateus, are well known abroad. Portuguese red and white table wines are less well known outside of the country, but their export and reputation are gradually increasing.

Crop yields, as noted above, and animal productivity remained well below those of Portugal's European counterparts as of the early 1990s. Yields of dryland crops and pastures are low by EC standards, but yields on irrigated land and in the alluvial soil areas of the Ribatejo are comparable with EC member countries. Portuguese grain-crop yields (kilograms per hectare) are less than a third of those in Germany and France and about 60 percent of those in Greece (see table 7, Appendix). Portugal's wheat, corn, and barley yields compare unfavorably with its European counterparts. Portuguese rice, grown on irrigated land, shows yields only about 14 percent below those of France and about 25 percent below those of Spain and Greece.

Although pastureland is scarce, livestock constitutes a significant share of total agricultural production. Because of growing domestic demand for animal products and low livestock productivity, Portugal has to import about 10 percent of its meat requirements. Three-fourths of the mainland's milk is produced in the northwest's coastal areas.

The mainland's livestock numbers in 1990 included over 1.3 million head of cattle, over 5 million sheep, about 2.5 million pigs, and 860,000 goats. About 18 million chickens supplied the country's poultry industry that year.

Forestry and Fishing

As of the early 1990s, over a third of the mainland was forest and woodlands, and commercially valuable timber stands included pine, cork oak, and eucalyptus. Pine is used not only for timber but also for resin, pitch, and turpentine. Eucalyptus, a fast growing import from Australia, has become a major source of pulp and paper. Cork oak, found mostly in the Alentejo, is the source of processed cork, a traditional Portuguese export commodity accounting for about 60 percent of world sales.

The country's long coastline and seafaring tradition make fishing a significant, but declining, source of income and jobs. Lisbon, Setúbal, Matosinhos, and Portimão are Portugal's main fishing ports and centers of commercial fish processing. Of the more than 200 edible species caught in Portuguese coastal waters and off West Africa, the most valuable is the sardine, an important source of domestic food supply and, in canned form, a traditional manufactured export product.

Notwithstanding Portugal's maritime tradition, the country's fishing industry in terms of fish catches in 1990 (322,000 tons) compared unfavorably with those of other small European countries, notably Norway (1,747,000 tons), and Denmark (1,517,000 tons).

Land Tenure and Agrarian Reform

The system of land tenure on the eve of the revolution was anachronistic. Very large estates in the south-central region coexisted with peasant farming in minute, fragmented plots in the north. The small farms typically were owner-operated, with the proprietors' families clustering in villages. Absentee landownership characterized the latifundio system with day-to-day operations in the hands of estate managers. Because of the high concentration of ownership in the south-central provinces, nearly half of the country's agricultural labor force in 1973 consisted of landless wage-earning rural workers whose standard of living was extremely low.

Holdings of over 200 hectares (about 0.3 percent of the total number) accounted for 39 percent of all farm land, whereas at the other end of the scale holdings of less than one hectare (about 39 percent of the total) represented no more than 2.5 percent of total Portuguese farm land.

The Agrarian Reform Law of July 29, 1975, which laid down the principles for the expropriation of land, validated de facto land seizures by rural workers that actually had begun five months earlier. The law provided that expropriation should apply to rural estates in the "intervention zone" south of the Tagus River. Lands that could have been expropriated under the provisions of the Agrarian Reform Law amounted to 1,640,000 hectares, but the area occupied by the rural workers reached only 1,140,800 hectares, or about one-fifth of the country's total farm land. On the occupied land, 449 "collective production units" were set up, bringing various estates of the former owners under a single peasant directorate. Major expropriations took place in the districts of Évora, Beja, Portalegre, Setúbal, and Santarém (see table 8, Appendix). Very large collective farms were formed in Portalegre and Beja (averaging between about 3,500 and 4,200 hectares); smaller units were created in Santarém and Setúbal (averaging between about 860 and 1,180 hectares).

As Portugal shifted toward moderation and the political center, collectivized agriculture increasingly was perceived as a counterproductive approach to the problems of the rural south. By the middle of 1990, only one-tenth (104,000 hectares) of the more than 1,080,000 hectares taken from the original landowners was still in possession of the remaining 30 collective farms. The gradual decollectivization of agriculture, which began in modest form in the late 1970s, culminated in a reformed agrarian law enacted by parliament in late 1988. Under its provisions, the maximum size of properties eligible for reprivatization was increased, and land could be divided among the heirs to an estate. Many collective farm members agreed to accept cash payments from the original owners in order to facilitate change of ownership or received individual titles to small shares of the former collective production units.

Agricultural Policy and the European Community

Portuguese agricultural markets, both inputs and outputs, were subjected to substantial policy intervention, particularly after the revolution. Under the old regime, agricultural pricing policy was largely oriented toward the provision of low-priced foodstuffs to urban areas, which required extensive controls over imports and marketing. Three state marketing enterprises were organized after 1974, primarily to manage trade in their respective commodity groups—cereals, oilseeds, and sugar and alcohol—in pursuit of price control objectives. Public assistance to farmers and ranchers involved subsidizing intermediate inputs, primarily fuels, fertilizers, and mixed feeds. These subsidies, however, were largely removed in June 1983. After the revolution, de facto credit subsidies for farmers (often associated with negative real interest rates) entailed very high transaction costs. As a result, only large farmers had access to the formal credit system.

As a condition of EC membership, Portugal adopted the Common Agricultural Policy (CAP), a basic instrument of the community's integration since 1962. The CAP is based on the principles of common pricing, EC preference, and joint financing. As Portugal adopted the transitional arrangements leading to full compliance with the CAP, both the locus of agricultural decision making and the level of incentives given by the system of price supports shifted from the nation to the EC. Portuguese prices of some commodities at the time of entry into the community were well above the EC levels. Cereal and dairy sectors will experience the most serious declines in real prices because they benefited most from price increases in the early 1980s and because they produce the commodities in chronic surplus in the EC. The Alentejo wheat and livestock systems, both based on poor soils, will likely become unprofitable during the transition to EC price levels. On the other hand, the prospects for rice, tomatoes, sunflowers, and potatoes, as well as Portugal's higher quality wine systems, appear to be favorable under the CAP regime.

Lisnave docks near Lisbon
Courtesy General Directorate of Mass Communication, Lisbon

The Industrial Sector

The growth of Portugal's industrial sector since the revolution was less dynamic than in the 1960–73 period. In this later period, growth was strongly affected by a number of major events, both domestic and external: the two oil price hikes, the nationalizations of 1975–76, and the country's accession to the EC. Nevertheless, Portugal's industrial production grew at a respectable 4.8 percent annual rate during the 1980–89 decade, leading GDP growth (2.7 percent annually). The overall industrial index advanced 43 percent between 1980 and 1989, with significant divergence in the growth rates among the subsectors of manufacturing (39 percent); electricity, gas, and water (74 percent); and mining (74 percent). Mining output was stagnant from 1980 to 1988, but in the following year it surged by 74 percent as the Neves Corvo copper mine went into operation. Manufacturing, the largest component of the industrial sector, also showed marked growth differences among the several branches. Lumber and cork products, a traditional rural-based industry, declined by 26 percent during the decade; on the other hand, paper (75 percent), chemicals and plastics products (97 percent), and nonmetallic mineral products (65 percent) led the advance in manufacturing.

Industrial Regions

Manufacturing is concentrated in two major industrial regions: Lisbon-Setúbal in the south-central region and Porto-Aveiro-Braga in the north. Together they account for about three-fourths of Portugal's net industrial output. The Lisbon area includes such major industries as iron and steel; shipbuilding and repair; oil refining, machinery, chemicals, cement, and electronics; and food and beverages. Setúbal, about eighty kilometers to the southeast of Lisbon, also has a large shipyard and automobile assembly and machine industry plants, as well as cement, woodpulp, cork, and fish processing. Sines, located about 140 kilometers south of Lisbon, is the site of a major deepwater port and heavy industrial complex. Begun during the Caetano administration, Sines includes an oil refinery, petrochemical plants, and a 1,200-megawatt coal-fired power plant.

Porto is primarily a center of light industry, including textiles, footwear, furniture, wine, and food processing. Porto is also the location of the nation's largest petroleum refinery; the other is located at Lisbon. Portimão is a center for fishing. Aveiro specializes in woodpulp and other wood products but also produces footwear and machinery. Braga specializes in textiles and clothing, cutlery, furniture, and electronics. Covilha is also an active textiles area.

The two premier industrial regions offer the greatest concentrations of population, thereby stimulating market-oriented manufacturing operations. Furthermore, because of the dependence of modern industry on imports of raw materials, machinery, and fuel, the location of processing plants near the two major ports minimizes their operating costs (see fig. 8).

Industrial Organization

Industrial organization in Portugal reflects three major ownership patterns: private domestic firms are concentrated in traditional, light industries and in construction; public enterprises dominate mining and major heavy industries, mainly iron and steel, petrochemicals, shipbuilding, petroleum refining, and electricity; and subsidiaries of multinational corporations dominate the technically more advanced electronics, automotive, pharmaceutical, and electrical machinery industries. The foreign investor presence is also important in the pulp and paper, chemical, food products, and clothing industries.

In general, the traditional light industries—textiles, clothing and footwear, food and beverages, cork products, and furniture—are labor intensive and technologically backward. Within this group, however, the medium-sized establishments (between 100 and 200 employees) enjoy superior management capabilities and higher levels of productivity.

The Portuguese construction industry, which was largely unaffected by the 1975 nationalizations, emerged in the late 1980s from several years of recession. Since the mid-1980s, EC and local counterpart funds have financed a variety of infrastructure projects, including roads, bridges, and sewage and water treatment plants. Commercial building and house construction was also on an upward trend after that time.

According to the Economist Intelligence Unit, of the twenty-five largest industrial firms ranked by sales in 1986, ten were public enterprises (including nine of the largest ten), and nine were subsidiaries of foreign-owned firms. Significantly, by the mid-1980s, over one-fifth of Portuguese manufacturing sales were by subsidiaries of multinational firms, with their export share even higher. Seven of the ten largest manufacturing export-oriented firms were controlled by foreign investors.

By the mid-1980s, the large industrial public enterprises faced extremely difficult financial problems associated with earlier errors in investment and pricing policies. After the second oil shock, many of these enterprises borrowed heavily abroad to finance investment projects, which often were poorly conceived and poorly managed. In 1986 operating losses of Quimigal (chemicals), Siderurgia Nacional (steel), and the shipbuilding company Estaleiros Navais de Setúbal (Setenave) totaled 29 billion escudos, or 30 percent of total public enterprise losses.

As a result of their excessive dependence on debt financing, Quimigal and Setenave, as well as Companhia Nacional de Petroquímica (CNP), a state-owned petrochemical enterprise, had a negative equity or net worth position (i.e., their debts exceeded their assets). Many of these firms in the mid-1980s were overstaffed and had concluded wage settlements that were generally higher than in the private sector.

The major state-owned industrial enterprises are candidates for ultimate privatization. In anticipation of their divestiture, they underwent financial and managerial restructuring in the late 1980s. As an example, loss-making enterprises such as CNP and Setenave had been operating under private management contracts to make them viable for privatization. Two major privatizations were announced at the end of 1990: Siderurgia Nacional and Petrogal (the largest state-owned petrochemical firm). To assure that the national steel company can operate successfully within the EC's single

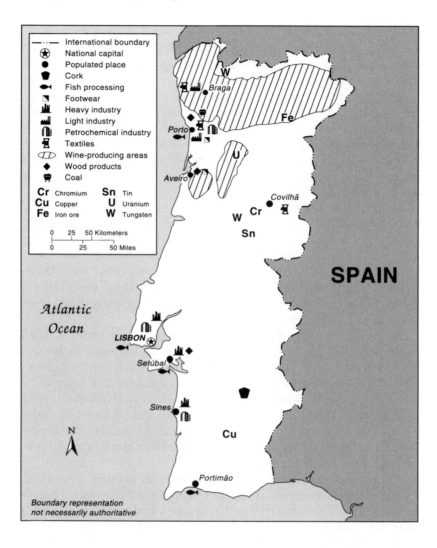

Figure 8. Economic Activity, 1992

market, the Portuguese government was considering selling Siderurgia Nacional to a leading European steelmaker, preferably linked to a Portuguese minority partner.

Energy and Mineral Resources

Portugal produces less than a quarter of its primary energy requirements and depends heavily on imported hydrocarbon fuels, mainly petroleum. Although efforts were made to locate domestic petroleum deposits in the early 1970s, none were found. Coal accounts for less than 5 percent of Portugal's primary energy use. Apparent consumption in 1988 is around 2.9 million tons, of which 240,000 tons were mined domestically. Portugal's low-grade anthracite coal, the production of which has stagnated since the mid-1970s, is mined near Porto. The United States has emerged as Portugal's main supplier of metallurgical and steam coal. A 5-million-ton-per-year capacity coal terminal, capable of handling 150,000 deadweight-ton vessels, was scheduled to be completed at Sines early in the 1990s. Because Portugal has no known natural gas reserves, the government has plans to build a liquified natural gas terminal at Setúbal and a gas distribution network. Portugal's hydroelectric potential is well developed and provides nearly half of the economy's electricity requirements.

As a result of Portugal's accession to the EC, the country's energy sector is rapidly being deregulated and diversified. The state electric power company, Electricidade de Portugal (EDP), planned to invest US$700 million between 1990 and 1995 on dams and hydroelectric equipment. In 1990 EDP completed its second coal-burning power plant station to reduce its dependency on imported oil. In addition, coal consumption in the cement industry was forecast to grow as more facilities converted to coal from fuel oil.

Portugal's metallic mineral resources are more impressive for their variety than for their contribution to GDP. The most important mines are in the north, in the mountains of Beira, where tungsten, tin, chromium, and other alloy minerals are mined in commercial quantities. Iron ore is mined in Moncorvo in the upper Douro Valley; formerly exported in its entirety, the Moncorvo mine production came to supply the government's integrated iron and steel works at Seixal near Lisbon and its Maia electric steel plant near Porto. Portugal is a significant world source of tungsten concentrate, most of which is exported. The mine has an annual production capacity of 1,400 tons of tungsten concentrate.

Portugal's metallic mineral production was greatly enhanced upon the completion of the US$200 million Neves Corvo copper mine near Castro Verde in southern Portugal—the largest non-coal mining development project in Western Europe. An estimated 33 million tons of 7.8 percent copper were proven at the site as of 1986. The concentrator initially will process one million tons of ore annually, yielding 400,000 tons of concentrate containing nearly 150,000 tons of copper. The Neves Corvo operating company is owned 51 percent by the government and 49 percent by RTZ Metals Group of Britain.

Services

Portugal's services sector dwarfs agriculture and industry, both as a contributor to GDP and as a source of employment. In 1973 services accounted for 39 percent of GDP; by 1990, that share had risen to nearly 56 percent. In 1973 services employed slightly over 36 percent of the total labor force, and in 1990 that share reached more than 47 percent. In the latter year, government employed 14.5 percent of the Portuguese labor force, followed by commerce (11.7 percent), transportation (4.3 percent), financial services (3.2 percent), and other services (12.3 percent).

Commerce and Tourism

Portuguese domestic commerce is dominated by numerous small, family-owned firms concentrated in the major urban areas. Retail outlets, around 80,000 in the late 1980s, are declining in numbers as supermarkets increase their market share. At the same time, upscale but smaller sales outlets are growing in number, replacing traditional retail shops. In both retailing and wholesaling, foreign investor participation is helping to accelerate the modernization of Portugal's domestic trade.

Foreign tourism is an important component of Portugal's services sector. Foreign exchange receipts from tourism income amounted to US$3.58 billion in 1990, compared with US$0.55 billion in 1973 and US$1.15 billion in 1980. This service industry directly employed an estimated 150,000 persons, equivalent to nearly 4 percent of the active labor force that year, but indirectly had strong secondary impacts, particularly on construction. From 1973 to 1990, tourism income as a share of GDP was roughly stable, fluctuating between 5 and 6 percent. The mid-1970s proved to be an exception: the brief period of radical politics combined with the global recession led to a halving of foreign arrivals to 2 million in 1975 from over 4 million in 1973 and to a sharp reduction in the receipts/GDP ratio to 2 percent from 5 percent in the earlier year. There were 7.3 million foreign arrivals in 1981, 16.5 million in 1989, and 19.6 million in 1991.

Of the 16.5 million recorded foreign visitors in 1989, 93 percent were from Western Europe. Spaniards, not surprisingly, constituted three-fourths of all visitors, although most of them were excursionists, that is, visitors staying for a period of less than twenty-four hours. Visitors from Britain, although only 7 percent of the total, contributed about 30 percent of tourism earnings.

Portugal offers many attractions to vacationers from northern

Petroleum refinery near Lisbon
Cement factory in the Estremadura region
Courtesy General Directorate of Mass Communication, Lisbon

Europe and the United States: medieval castles and other architectural landmarks, a number of which serve as government-operated inns; more than 100 beaches along the southern coast of the Algarve; and a resort area stretching westward from Lisbon at the mouth of the Tagus River, notably the famed resorts of Cascais and Estoril. Other attractions include Portugal's mild climate and its relatively low cost.

The major goals of the Portuguese government for this significant export industry are to improve the quality of tourism services, to attract visitors to northern locations, to safeguard the environment, and to encourage investment in tourism facilities.

Transportation and Communications

Portugal's transportation system in the late 1980s comprised 73,660 kilometers of roads, of which 61,000 kilometers were paved; a railroad network of 3,630 kilometers; and 820 kilometers of navigable inland waterways. Lisbon, on the Tagus estuary, and the two other major ports at Leixões, near Porto, and Sines are fully equipped and have adequate warehousing facilities. Lisbon's Portela Airport is a major European air terminal and transit point for some eighteen airlines. Porto and the Algarve, as well as the Azores and Madeira islands, are also served by international airports. Transportes Aéreos Portugueses (TAP), the national airline, operates flights within the country and also serves major European cities and several large cities in the United States, South America, and Africa (see fig. 9).

Much of Portugal's transportation infrastructure—the nationalized railroad, airline, merchant fleet, and trucking and bus lines—is to be restructured and/or privatized in the early 1990s. For example, Caminhos de Ferro Portuguese (CP), the national railroad, approved a 1988 plan that called for a US$1.5 billion investment to modernize the rail system by 1994. The plan includes high-speed "super trains" to connect Portugal's major cities and Lisbon to Madrid. In addition, in the second half of the 1980s the EC began to give substantial assistance for improving the transportation infrastructure.

Portugal is following an ambitious program to modernize its communications system. The Assembly of the Republic approved in July 1989 the deregulation/liberalization of some telecommunications activities, which will allow private firms to operate complementary services, such as cellular phones, videotex, and highly value-added services such as fax, audiotex, and voicemail. Radio and television are also opening to private participation, and reception of satellite television is expanding rapidly.

Banking and Finance

The importance of the financial system to the economy dwarfs its direct impact on employment and income. A well-functioning financial system serves not only to increase the mobilization of saving but also, more importantly, to direct capital resources toward their most productive uses. Since the mid-1980s, when commercial banking and insurance were reopened to private initiative, the Portuguese financial system has evolved toward greater liberalization, diversification, and internationalization.

Although the private financial sector has grown rapidly, the eleven nationalized banks and eight public insurance companies still accounted for 80 percent and 60 percent of their respective markets in 1989. Notwithstanding their improved operating conditions and higher solvency ratios, the profitability of most nationalized banks is depressed by their large holdings of low-interest-bearing public debt. Bad and doubtful loans continue to burden several state-owned banks. The nationalized banks are also plagued by undercapitalization, overstaffing, and an excessive branching structure. Many of these banks have large pension liabilities, which, being unfunded, are not reflected in their balance sheets. The continuing structural problems of the state banks date back to the late 1970s and early 1980s when the Portuguese government followed a "soft budget" policy that emphasized social or political objectives over market criteria. Banks were required by law to extend preferential credit, usually at negative real interest rates, to the large nonfinancial public enterprises, as well as to the general government. Relaxation of the normal banking sanctions against troubled or failing public enterprises threatened the capital of the banks and their own financial viability. The Bank of Portugal's quantitative credit controls served mainly to facilitate commercial bank financing of the large deficits of the consolidated public sector. The administrative control of credit penalized private small and medium-sized enterprises, in particular.

Portuguese financial markets experienced accelerated change after the country joined the EC in 1986. Deposit and lending rates were freed, new money market instruments were introduced, and in 1990, the Bank of Portugal removed credit ceilings on commercial banks. The Lisbon Stock Exchange was modernized with more stringent rules governing the disclosure of financial information; precautions were also taken against insider trading.

Enabling legislation in 1984 allowed private banks and insurance firms to be organized. By the late 1980s, six new foreign bank branches had been established: Manufacturers Hanover Trust,

Figure 9. Transportation System, 1992

Chase Manhattan, Barclays, Banque Nationale de Paris, Citicorp, and Générale de Banque of Belgium. Four majority Portuguese private banks were also set up: Banco de Comércio e Indústria (BCI), Banco Internacional de Crédito (BIC), Banco Português de Investimento (BPI), and Banco Comercial Português (BCP). By December 1990, BCP had become Portugal's leading and fastest growing private commercial bank with total assets of nearly US$6 billion. A number of private investment (para-banking) institutions and venture capital funds have also become part of the financial picture since the mid-1980s.

During the first phase of "partial" privatization—in 1988 before the 1989 constitutional amendment—the government selected a medium-sized bank (Banco Totta e Açores) and two public insurance companies (Aliança Seguradora and Companhia de Seguros Tranquilidade) as the first to be privatized. Share issues for 49 percent of these companies were substantially oversubscribed in 1989. After passage of the Reprivatization Law in April 1990, the sale of the remaining 51 percent of both Tranquilidade and Aliança shares took place later that year, and an additional 31 percent of Banco Totta e Açores shares were also sold. Other 100 percent privatizations of financial firms envisaged for 1991 included the Banco Português do Atlântico, the country's largest commercial bank.

Significantly, the late 1980s saw the reemergence of some of the prerevolutionary family groups in Portugal's economic landscape, particularly in the financial sector. As an example, the Espíritu Santo family became the majority shareholder in BIC and in the Espíritu Santo Sociedade de Investimento and was reported to be attempting to retake control of the Tranquilidade insurance company. The return of some of these dispossessed family groups to Portugal reflects a turnaround in confidence in Portugal's future, as well as the prospect for reinvestment of large sums of flight capital.

Notwithstanding the privatization trend, the Portuguese government intends to maintain an important position in the financial system in addition to its control over central banking through the Bank of Portugal. The two major financial groups reserved for the state include, first, the Caixa Geral de Depositos, the largest savings bank; the Banco Nacional Ultramarino (a commercial bank); and Fidelidade (an insurance company). The second group deals with international trade and export promotion and consists of Banco de Fomento e Exterior (an investment bank); Banco Borges e Irmão (a commercial bank); and an external credit insurance company, Companhia de Seguros de Créditos (Cosec). Together, these two financial groups accounted for about 40 percent of Portugal's banking transactions in 1990.

Foreign Economic Relations

After becoming a charter member of EFTA in 1959, Portugal became increasingly open to the rest of the world through international trade and other payment flows. In 1990 exports of goods and services accounted for about 37 percent of Portugal's GDP, and imports of goods and services represented about 47 percent of GDP. The accession of Portugal to the EC on January 1, 1986, required fundamental changes in the country's commercial and foreign investment policies. A seven-year transition period ending in 1993 would eliminate most barriers to trade, capital flows, and labor mobility among the twelve EC member countries. During this period, Portugal was a net recipient of EC financial transfers to help modernize its agricultural and industrial sectors for competition in the single market.

To rein in domestic demand growth—mainly the result of the public sector deficits after 1973—the Portuguese government was obliged to pursue IMF-monitored stabilization programs in 1977–78 and 1983–84 to help achieve a return to current account equilibrium in the balance of international payments. Building on the 1983–85 stabilization program and in the context of Portugal's accession to the EC, the Council of Ministers introduced in March 1987 the Program for the Structural Adjustment of the Foreign Deficit and Unemployment (Plano de Correcção Estrutural do Déficit Externo e Desemprêgo—PCEDED), a medium-term program aimed at a lasting correction of structural imbalances— inflation, fiscal deficit, external deficit, and unemployment. The program's macroeconomic approach included a set of articulated measures involving fiscal, monetary, exchange, and incomes policy. As an instrument of the government's "controlled development strategy," this program was to be implemented in two stages covering the periods 1987–90 and 1991–94 and is designed to reduce Portugal's susceptibility to external shocks by strengthening especially the energy and agricultural sectors.

Composition and Direction of Trade

Portugal's rising share of manufactured goods in total merchandise exports, which reached 80 percent in 1989, is indicative of the country's newly industrialized status. Between 1980 and 1988, exports of manufactured goods increased by 10 percent per year by volume, which was double the rate of its European neighbors, and Portugal gained market share. The country's major commodity exports in 1990 included textiles, clothing, and footwear (accounting for 37 percent of total export value); machinery and transport equipment (20 percent); forest products (10 percent, including pulp and paper and cork products); agricultural products (8 percent, mainly wine and tomato paste); chemicals and plastic products (5 percent); and energy products (about 4 percent). Portugal's comparative advantage appears to lie with high forestry resources content (wood and cork products, including pulp and paper) and labor-intensive products (textiles, clothing, and footwear). With the participation of multinational firms, Portugal is also gaining competitive strength in the export of automobiles and automotive components and electrical and electronic machinery.

When compared with the other EC member countries and the United States, Portugal has a strong competitive advantage because of its low wage scale. As an example, 1989 hourly labor costs in Portuguese manufacturing (in United States dollars) averaged approximately half those of Greece (a country with a similar per capita GDP), a third those of Spain, and about a fifth of most other West European countries and the United States.

Manufactured goods (notably machinery, transportation equipment, and chemicals) accounted for about 75 percent of merchandise imports in 1989, food and beverages for about 10 percent, and raw materials (mainly crude petroleum) for about 16 percent. Portugal imported about 60 million barrels of oil yearly during the late 1980s, but the share of crude petroleum varied between 8 and 20 percent of total imports depending on fluctuations in world oil prices.

Portugal's commodity trade is increasingly dominated by the EC (see table 9, Appendix). In 1990 the EC member countries purchased nearly 74 percent of Portugal's exports and supplied over 69 percent of its imports; in 1985, the year prior to Portugal's membership in the EC, the EC member countries purchased about 63 percent of Portugal's exports and supplied nearly 46 percent of Portugal's imports. Within the EC, the former West Germany, France, and Britain were Portugal's leading trading partners. But after the accession of both Iberian countries to the EC in 1986 (and the dismantling of trade restrictions between them), Spain suddenly emerged as a significant trading partner, taking over 13 percent of Portugal's exports in 1990 and providing 14.4 percent of the latter's imports. Thus, Spain ranked with West Germany as Portugal's premier national supplier in 1990, ahead of France, Britain, and Italy.

The relative position of the United States in Portugal's import trade declined sharply from nearly 10 percent of the total in 1985 to 3.9 percent in 1990. Because Portugal heavily imported grain, soybeans, and animal feedstuffs, its adoption of the CAP led to costly trade diversion from former, more efficient sources, mainly the United States, to higher-cost continental EC member countries. On the other hand, Portugal's full membership in the EC will permit its manufacturers to capture a larger share of exports to EC member countries at the expense of lower-cost exporters from Latin America and East Asia; similarly, Portuguese producers of quality wine are expected to gain market share at the expense of wine producers in Mediterranean countries that were not fully integrated into the EC. In both these cases, trade diversion will favor Portuguese entrepreneurs.

Portugal's trade with the previous Escudo Area (its former African colonies) has fallen sharply since the revolution. Still, a restructured Angola under a competent, non-Marxist regime could once more offer Portugal significant opportunities for two-way trade in the late 1990s. The share of Portuguese imports supplied by the Organization of the Petroleum Exporting Countries (OPEC), which amounted to over 17 percent in 1985 (the year before the collapse of world oil prices), shrank to below 7 percent in 1990.

The Balance of International Payments

The balance of payments reveals much about how the residents of a nation-state earn their livelihood by providing goods and services to foreigners in exchange for goods and services produced abroad. It may also reveal indirectly whether the country is a net creditor or net debtor in its dealings with the rest of the world. The Portuguese international balance is characterized by a protracted and large merchandise trade deficit that is largely offset (financed) by annual surpluses on invisibles, mainly emigrant worker remittances and tourism income. But because of its international debtor position (including a growing stock of private foreign investment in the country), Portugal annually remits substantial interest and dividend payments to foreigners. Portuguese traders rely predominantly on foreign carriers and insurance firms; as a result, the current account registers annual net payments (debits) for these services.

From 1974 to 1984, Portugal's current external deficits were financed by a combination of foreign reserve drawdowns and official external borrowing, mainly the latter. In the five-year period 1985–89, three years of current account surpluses (for 1985–87, totaling nearly US$2 billion) more than offset two years of current deficits (for 1988–89, totaling US$1.6 billion). Following Portugal's accession to the EC, large and growing inflows of private capital—direct investment, portfolio investment, and repatriation of flight capital—resulted in substantial accumulation of foreign reserves by the Bank of Portugal.

The 1989 balance of international payments was fairly representative of Portugal's position in the late 1980s. The merchandise trade deficit of US$5.1 billion was more than covered by the joint income from tourism (US$2.6 billion) and emigrant remittances (US$3.4 billion). The Portuguese paid exporters and importers

The beach at Nazaré
Courtesy Alan J. Savada

US$832 million (net) for the use of foreign carrier and insurance services and remitted US$800 million in net investment income of interest and dividends (US$1,323 million in payments and US$521 million in receipts). Although unilateral transfers (which do not give rise to claims) comprised mainly emigrant worker remittances, net public remittances of US$824 million in favor of Portugal, a recent component of the balance of payments, reflected mainly EC assistance to Portugal in support of economic restructuring.

The algebraic addition of the current account balance (– US$551 million) and the medium- and long-term capital account (US$2,560 million) netted a "basic balance" of around US$2 billion in 1989.

Tourism and Unilateral Transfers

Measured in terms of arrivals and foreign exchange receipts, Portuguese tourism has grown at a phenomenal rate since the early 1980s. Foreign arrivals, which averaged about 7.3 million in 1981–1982, expanded sharply each year thereafter, stabilized at between 16 and 17 million during 1987–89, and then increased to an estimated 18.4 million in 1990. Receipts from tourism rose from US$1.15 billion in 1980 to US$3.58 billion in 1990.

In 1990 unilateral transfers reached US$6.5 billion (22 percent of Portugal's current account receipts), of which 73 percent were private, mainly emigrant remittances. About three-fourths of the emigrant remittances originated in Western Europe (mainly France) and one-fifth in North America (mainly the United States). These private inflows not only contributed to the country's foreign exchange earnings, but also represented a significant component of Portuguese household savings.

Gross public transfers in favor of Portugal amounted to US$1,740 million in 1990, of which nearly half (US$837 million) represented structural funds from the EC in support of the country's economic and social modernization. The European Social Fund assisted in vocational and professional training; other funds participated in the Specific Plan for the Development of Portuguese Agriculture (Plano Económico para o Desenvolvimento da Agricultura Portuguesa—PEDAP) and the Specific Plan for the Development of Portuguese Industry (Plano Económico para o Desenvolvimento da Indústria Portuguesa—PEDIP). The Portuguese government was required to cofinance projects funded by these EC transfers. Although Portugal no longer was a member of EFTA, the latter continued to assist the former member country in its economic restructuring efforts. Finally, included in the category of official unilateral transfers were United States government military and economic grants that totaled some US$160 million annually for the use of the large United States Air Force base in the Azores.

Foreign Direct Investment

Foreign direct investment increased at an extraordinary pace after Portugal's accession to the EC. From a modest commitment of around US$166 million in 1986, the annual inflow of investment controlled and managed by foreigners rose sharply in the following years, reaching US$2.7 billion in 1991. At the end of that year, the accumulated stock of direct foreign investment exceeded US$8 billion, or eight times its value at the end of 1986.

From the perspective of multinational firms, Portugal is a strong export base to the emerging single market of 327 million high-income consumers, and since the mid-1980s the country has become especially competitive in attracting foreign investment. These attractions include political stability and a hospitable investment climate that includes EC investment subsidies, the lowest wage scale among the EC-12, and programs of economic deregulation and privatization, as well as robust national economic and export growth.

The participation of EC-based investors in the annual investment flow to Portugal increased from less than half of the total in 1985–86 to about 70 percent from 1987 to 1990, Britain being the principal country source. Interesting trends in the composition of this investment could be discerned. Britain was the leading country of origin throughout this period, but the United States share fell sharply from 18 percent of the total investment in 1985–86 to less than 3 percent in 1989–90. Within the recently enlarged EC, Spain emerged as a significant direct investor, increasing its share from only 3 percent of Portuguese new investment in 1985–1986 to over 13 percent in 1989–90. Brazilian investors, whose share was negligible in 1985–86, increased their participation to around 7 percent in 1989–90.

Manufacturing, the destination of just under half of foreign investment inflow in 1985–86, received only 27 percent of the total in 1988–89; by contrast, the services sector's share in total investment flow rose from 45 percent in 1985–86 to over 60 percent in 1988–89. Within that sector, banking and insurance increased their participation, although investment in wholesale and retail trade and in hotels and restaurants continued to be significant, reflecting foreign investor participation in Portugal's booming tourism industry. Several new investment projects in the automotive industry were being considered in 1991, including participation by Japanese and South Korean firms. None, however, approach in scale the Ford-Volkswagen commitment to organize an automotive complex at Sines. This joint venture capitalized at US$3.2 billion is to manufacture a new European minivan.

Portugal, unlike many other middle-income countries, is remarkably hospitable to foreign investment (foreign-owned enterprises were legally exempted from nationalization during 1975–76). The growing pace of privatization since 1988, however, gave rise to debate regarding the ultimate ownership and control of major state firms being divested. One school of thought anticipated that privatization would "de-Portugalize" vital sectors of the economy. To some degree, Prime Minister Cavaco Silva shared this anxiety: "At the same time, we shall have to foster economic groups in Portugal. These were destroyed at the time of the revolution with nationalization. We need them, as otherwise foreigners will come in and take over our enterprises and economic strategy will be determined from abroad. Thus we are supporting the new entrepreneurs in industry and agriculture."

Despite the formation of new Portuguese groups able to compete against foreign-based multinational companies, it is doubtful that these national firms are sufficient in number, risk capital, and managerial-technical know-how to absorb most of the large enterprises scheduled for divestiture.

Although the government has succeeded in limiting foreign participation in a number of key enterprises, including the withholding of a temporary ''golden share'' for the state, such limits on foreign direct investment are to become illegal in 1995, when Portugal's capital movement regulations will come fully into compliance with those of the rest of the EC members.

Consequently, the prospect of losing national control over large branches of the economy appears to be the inevitable price of securing Portugal's economic future and closing the income gap between the Portuguese and their more prosperous neighbors.

External Public Debt

Portugal's external public debt was on a steeply rising trend from 1976 onward, reaching nearly US$18.5 billion at the end of 1987, its peak dollar magnitude. After that year, early repayments of principal slightly reduced outstanding debt to slightly over US$18.4 billion in 1990. As the proceeds from privatization of nationalized enterprises are applied to debt reduction, Portugal's external public obligations will continue to diminish.

Debt-service indicators reveal much about the relative burden of Portugal's foreign indebtedness, as well as the capacity of the economy to service this debt (see table 10, Appendix). More relevant than the dollar value of the debt is the ratio of public external debt to GDP, which increased inexorably from 1980 to 1985 (from more than 36 percent to more than 80 percent, its highest level) and then abruptly fell to just under 29 percent in 1990. Total debt service (scheduled amortization and interest payments) as a share of current account credits (foreign exchange income from exporting goods and services, as well as from unilateral remittances) rose from over 15 percent in 1980 to 37 percent in 1985 and thereafter fell to 16.7 percent in 1990. Portugal's success in reducing its relative external debt-servicing burden by about half between 1985 and 1990 was largely the result of burgeoning export receipts, notably manufactured goods and tourism income, although growing emigrant worker remittances and transfers from the EC also played a role.

The interest/GDP ratio, which measures the net burden on the Portuguese economy, more than doubled from 3 percent in 1980 to 6.5 percent in 1985 before falling back to 2.9 percent in 1990. The external debt/reserves indicator, which compares Portugal's foreign/public obligations (mainly the stock of long- and medium-term debt) with its gross foreign assets (mainly liquid foreign exchange holdings of the Bank of Portugal and the Treasury, with gold valued at market prices) almost tripled between 1980 and 1985, when the country's external debt exceeded its official reserves by 67 percent. As a consequence of the rapid buildup of Portugal's

Amoreiras shopping and office complex in Lisbon Courtesy Alan J. Savada

official reserves from 1985 onward, the external debt/reserves indicator was reduced to just over 72 percent in 1990. This massive accumulation of foreign assets at the disposal of official institutions reflects not only Portugal's export drive, but also its success in attracting direct investments from its EC partners.

* * *

The Organisation for Economic Co-operation and Development annual economic surveys give an authoritative and readily available exposition of the country's economy with a strong policy orientation. The quarterly *Country Report: Portugal* and the annual *Country Profile: Portugal* from the Economist Intelligence Unit (EIU) provide current economic coverage, and Mark Hudson's *Portugal to 1993: Investing in a European Future,* also published by EIU, is particularly useful for analysis of Portugal's economy in the context of that country's accession to the EC. For additional current information on Portugal's private and public sector economic activities, special supplements of the *Economist* and *Financial Times,* both published in London, offer well-written coverage for the nonspecialist. From time to time, *Euromoney* publishes special reports on up-to-date banking and financial developments in Portugal. The Bank of Portugal's annual reports provide detailed information, including copious statistical tables, on the Portuguese economy.

Valentina Xavier Pintado's *Structure and Growth of the Portuguese Economy,* published by the European Free Trade Association, is the definitive study of the economy during the early Salazar period. Eric N. Baklanoff's *The Economic Transformation of Spain and Portugal* is a comparative analysis of accelerating economic growth in the two Iberian countries in response to the new, more open, market-oriented economic policies initiated in 1959 by the Franco and Salazar regimes.

Among the more useful books on the postrevolutionary period in English are Rodney J. Morrison's *Portugal: Revolutionary Change in an Open Economy;* the World Bank's *Portugal: Current and Prospective Trends,* a report based on the findings of a mission to Portugal in 1978; and *Portugal: Ancient Country, Young Democracy,* edited by Kenneth Maxwell and Michael H. Haltzel. This work includes three chapters on the economy.

Two comparative technical studies that illuminate Portugal's integration with the European Community are Juergen B. Donges, *The Second Enlargement of the European Community* and *European Integration and the Iberian Economies,* edited by George N. Yannopolous. (For further information and complete citations, see Bibliography.)

Chapter 4. Government and Politics

Newspaper vendor

ON APRIL 25, 1974, the Portuguese armed forces overthrew the ruling corporative government in a virtually bloodless coup d'état. The coup ended a dictatorial regime established by António de Oliveira Salazar in the late 1920s and early 1930s, and carried on by his successor, Marcello José das Neves Caetano, after 1968. What began, however, as a simple attempt by the Armed Forces Movement (Movimento das Forças Armadas—MFA) to replace the government in power and change its policies quickly became not only a political event of historic proportions, but also a full-scale social revolution.

The Revolution of 1974, as it came to be known, soon involved hundreds of thousands of Portuguese who took to the streets. The highly organized Portuguese Communist Party (Partido Comunista Português—PCP), emerging from exile and the underground, soon joined forces with the MFA. Many far-left groups also participated in the upheaval, as did the Socialist Party (Partido Socialista—PS). Many members of the country's middle class joined the process, organizing in a matter of months political parties not permitted under the old regime.

On the social side, the events that began in the spring of 1974 drew on the deep frustrations of a society and people emerging from half a century of dictatorship, isolation, and backwardness. Children rebelled against their parents, enlisted men against officers, employees against employers, workers against factory owners, and tenant farmers against absentee landlords.

There were, in short, two revolutions in Portugal: one was a process of political change that grew from a coup d'état that aimed only at changing the governmental structure at the top into a movement that touched every political relationship; the other was a profound social transformation that seemed bent on toppling all existing social relationships.

Portugal's opening to democracy attracted worldwide attention and was closely scrutinized. Portugal was, after all, not a remote Third World state, but part of Western Europe. It belonged to the European Free Trade Association (EFTA—see Glossary) and was a founding member of the North Atlantic Treaty Organization (NATO). A full-scale revolution on European soil and the possibility of a strong communist party in power made the United States and West European countries uneasy.

Eventually, however, the Portuguese revolution played itself out, and moderate forces came to direct the country's affairs. Elections for the Constituent Assembly in 1975 gave mainstream democratic political parties most of the body's seats and allowed the fashioning of the constitution of 1976. That constitution established parliamentary democracy while preserving many of the revolution's radical achievements and pledging a transition to socialism.

Constitutional amendments in 1982 strengthened the powers of the parliament, the Assembly of the Republic, and the prime minister, weakened those of the president, and placed the military under civilian control. Further amendments to the constitution in 1989 erased much of the document's ideological commitment to socialism and permitted the privatization of many of the economic assets nationalized in 1974 and 1975.

Seven national elections between 1976 and 1991 consolidated the place of the new system of democratic government, often called the Second Republic. In addition to the PCP and the PS, two other parties emerged as significant political forces: the Party of the Social Democratic Center (Partido do Centro Democrático Social—CDS), a right-wing Christian democratic party, and the Social Democrat Party (Partido Social Democrata—PSD), a center-right group. Until the national election of 1987, when the PSD won a majority in the Assembly of the Republic, the parties to the right of the PCP had usually formed coalition governments. None of these governments, however, was strong enough to serve out a four-year legislative period until the PSD government did so in the 1987–91 period. Under the forceful and able leadership of Aníbal Cavaco Silva as prime minister, the single-party PSD cabinet was able to meet the challenges posed by Portugal's membership in the European Community (EC—see Glossary). Cavaco Silva led his party to a second majority in the October 1991 parliamentary elections and formed another PSD government, an indication perhaps that the new democracy was taking root.

The country's first president elected according to the terms of the constitution also contributed significantly to the establishment of parliamentary democracy. President António dos Santos Ramalho Eanes (1976–86), although of military background, abided by the new constitution and submitted to amendments that reduced his powers and returned the military to the barracks. These actions served the fledgling democracy perhaps even more than his extinguishing the coup of November 1975, the last attempt of the revolutionary left to seize political control. Mário Alberto Nobre Lopez Soares, the leader of the PS, succeeded Eanes in 1986 and became the country's first civilian president in five decades. Soares was an effective and popular president and easily won a second five-year term in January 1991.

At the beginning of the 1990s, Portugal's democracy was only a decade and a half old, but the transition to democracy seemed to have been highly successful. Although the country had many social and economic problems to solve, the economy had improved noticeably and political stability had been achieved. A free press served the public, a marked contrast to the censorship of the Salazar regime. These developments were testaments that Portugal had at last found a place in the community of Western democratic nations, a remarkable transition from the long dictatorship and the subsequent periods of revolutionary upheaval and government weakness and instability.

The Revolution of 1974 and the Transition to Democracy

Portugal's experience with democracy before the Revolution of 1974 had not been particularly successful. Its First Republic lasted only sixteen years, from 1910 to 1926 (see The First Republic, ch. 1). Under the republic, parliamentary institutions worked poorly and were soon discredited. Corruption and economic mismanagement were widespread. When a military coup d'état ended the republic in 1926, few lamented its passing.

The Salazar-Caetano Era

The republic was replaced by a military dictatorship that promised order, authority, and discipline. The military regime abolished political parties, took steps against the small but vocal Marxist groups, and did away with republican institutions. In 1928 it invited University of Coimbra professor António de Oliveira Salazar to serve as minister of finance. In 1932 he became prime minister. That year marked the beginning of his regime, the New State (Estado Novo; see The New State, ch. 1).

Under Salazar (1932–68), Portugal became, at least formally, a corporative state. The new constitution of 1933 embodied the corporatist theory, under which government was to be formed of economic entities organized according to their function, rather than by individual representation. Employers were to form one group, labor another, and they and other groups were to deal with one another through their representative organizations.

In reality, however, Salazar headed an autocratic dictatorship with the help of an efficient secret police. Strict censorship was introduced, the politically suspect were monitored, and the regime's opponents were jailed, sent into exile, and occasionally killed.

Portugal drifted and floundered under this repressive regime for several decades. Economic conditions improved slightly in the 1950s, when Salazar instituted the first of two five-year economic plans. These plans stimulated some growth, and living standards began to rise.

The 1960s, however, were crisis years for Portugal. Guerrilla movements emerged in the Portuguese African colonies of Angola, Mozambique, and Guinea-Bissau (formerly Portuguese Guinea) that aimed at liberating those territories from "the last colonial empire." Fighting three guerrilla movements for more than a decade proved to be enormously draining for a small, poor country in terms of labor and financial resources. At the same time, social changes brought about by urbanization, emigration, the growth of the working class, and the emergence of a sizeable middle class put new pressures on the political system to liberalize. Instead, Salazar increased repression, and the regime became even more rigid and ossified.

When Salazar was incapacitated in an accident in 1968, the Council of State, a high-level advisory body created by the constitution of 1933, chose Marcello Caetano (1968–74) to succeed him. Caetano, though a Salazar protégé, tried to modernize and liberalize the old Salazar system. He was opposed, however, by a group widely referred to as "the bunker," the old Salazaristas. These included the country's president, Admiral Américo Tomás, the senior officers of the armed forces, and the heads of some of the country's largest financial groups. The bunker was powerful enough that any fundamental change would certainly have led to Caetano's immediate overthrow.

As Caetano promised reform but fell into indecision, the sense began to grow among all groups—the armed forces, the opposition, and liberals within the regime—that only a revolution could produce the changes that Portugal sorely needed. Contributing to this feeling were a number of growing tensions on the political and social scene.

The continuing economic drain caused by the military campaigns in Africa was exacerbated by the first great oil "shock" of 1973. Politically, the desire for democracy, or at least a greater opening up of the political system, was increasing. Social tensions mounted, as well, because of the slow pace of change and the absence of opportunities for advancement.

The decisive ingredient in these tensions was dissension within the military itself, long a bulwark of the regime. Younger military academy graduates resented a program introduced by Caetano whereby university graduates who completed a brief training program could be commissioned at the same rank as academy graduates. Caetano had begun the program because it was becoming increasingly difficult to recruit new officers as casualties from the African wars mounted (see The Military Takeover of 1974, ch. 5).

Spínola and Revolution

A key catalytic event in the process toward revolution was the publication in 1973 General António de Spínola's book, *Portugal and the Future,* which criticized the conduct of the war and offered a far-ranging program for Portugal's recovery. The general's work sent shock waves through the political establishment in Lisbon. As the first major and public challenge to the regime by a high-ranking figure from within the system, Spínola's experience in the African campaigns gave his opinions added weight. The book was widely seen—a correct assessment as it turned out—as the opening salvo in Spínola's ambitious campaign to become president.

On April 25, 1974, a group of younger officers belonging to an underground organization, the Armed Forces Movement (Movimento das Forças Armadas—MFA), overthrew the Caetano regime, and Spínola emerged as at least the titular head of the new government. The coup succeeded in hours with virtually no bloodshed. Caetano and other high-ranking officials of the old regime were arrested and exiled, many to Brazil. The military seized control of all important installations.

Spínola regarded the military's action as a simple military coup d'état aimed at reorganizing the political structure with himself as the head, a *renovação* (renovation) in his words. Within days, however, it became clear that the coup had released long pent-up frustrations when thousands, and then tens of thousands, of Portuguese poured into the streets celebrating the downfall of the regime and demanding further change. The coercive apparatus of the dictatorship—secret police, Republican Guard, official party, censorship—was overwhelmed and abolished. Workers began taking over shops from owners, peasants seized private lands, low-level employees took over hospitals from doctors and administrators, and government offices were occupied by workers who sacked the old management and demanded a thorough housecleaning.

Very early on, the demonstrations began to be manipulated by organized political elements, principally the PCP and other groups farther to the left. Radical labor and peasant leaders emerged from the underground where they had been operating for many years. Soares, the leader of the Socialist Party (Partido Socialista—PS) and Álvaro Cunhal, head of the Portuguese Communist Party (Partido Comunista Português—PCP) returned from exile to Portugal within days of the revolt and received heroes' welcomes.

Who actually ruled Portugal during this revolutionary period was not always clear, and various bodies vied for dominance. Spínola became the first interim president of the new regime in May 1974, and he chose the first of six provisional governments that were to govern the country until two years later when the first constitutional government was formed. Headed by a prime minister, the moderate civilian Adelino da Palma Carlos, the government consisted of the moderate Popular Democratic Party (Partido Popular Democrata—PPD), the PS, the PCP, five independents, and one military officers.

Beneath this formal structure, several other groups wielded considerable power. In the first weeks of the revolution, a key group was the Junta of National Salvation, composed entirely of high-ranking, politically moderate military officers. Working alongside it was a seven-member coordinating committee made up of politically radical junior officers who had managed the coup. By the end of May 1974, these two bodies worked together with other members in the Council of State, the nation's highest governing body.

Gradually, however, the MFA emerged as the most powerful single group in Portugal as it overruled Spínola in several major decisions. Members of the MFA formed the Continental Operations Command (Comando Operacional do Continente—COPCON) composed of 5,000 elite troops with Major (later Brigadier General) Otelo Saraiva de Carvalho as its commander. Known universally by his unusual first name Otelo, Carvalho had directed the April 25 coup. Because the regular police had withdrawn from the public sector during the time of revolutionary turmoil and the military was somewhat divided, COPCON became the most important force for order in the country and was firmly under the control of radical left-wing officers.

Spínola formed a second provisional government in mid-July with army Colonel (later General) Vasco Gonçalves as prime minister and eight military officers, along with members of the PS, PCP, and PPD. Spínola chose Gonçalves because he was a moderate, but he was to move increasingly to the left as he headed four provisional governments between July 1974 and September 1975. Spínola's position further weakened when he was obliged to consent to the independence of Portugal's African colonies, rather than achieving the federal solution he had outlined in his book. Guinea-Bissau gained independence in early September, and talks were underway on the liberation of the other colonies. Spínola attempted

Street demonstration during the Revolution of 1974
Courtesy Embassy of Portugal, Washington

to seize full power in late September but was blocked by COP-CON and resigned from office. His replacement was the moderate General Francisco de Costa Gomes. Gonçalves formed a third provisional government with heavy MFA membership, nine military officers in all, and members of the PS, PCP, and PPD.

In the next year, Portuguese politics moved steadily leftward. The PCP was highly successful in placing its members in many national and local political and administrative offices, and it was consolidating its hold on the country's labor unions. The MFA came ever more under the control of its radical wing, and some of its members came under the influence of the PCP. In addition, smaller, more radical left-wing groups joined with the PCP in staging huge demonstrations that brought about the increasing adoption of leftist policies, including nationalizations of private companies.

An attempted coup by Spínola in early March 1975 failed, and he fled the country. In response to this attack from the right, radical elements of the military abolished the Junta of National Salvation and formed the Council of the Revolution as the country's most powerful governing body. The council was made responsible to a 240-member radical military parliament, the Assembly of the Armed Forces. A fourth provisional government was formed, more radical than its predecessor, and was headed by Gonçalves, with eight military officers and members of the PS, PCP, PPD, and Portuguese Democratic Movement (Movimento Democrático Português—MDP), a party close to the PCP.

The new government began a wave of nationalizations of banks and large businesses (see Nationalization, ch. 3). Because the banks were often holding companies, the government came after a time to own almost all the country's newspapers, insurance companies, hotels, construction companies and many other kinds of businesses, so that its share of the country's gross national product (GNP— see Glossary) amounted to 70 percent.

The Transition to Civilian Rule

Elections were held on April 25, 1975, for the Constituent Assembly that was to draft a constitution. The PS won nearly 38 percent the vote, and the PPD took 26.4 percent. The PCP, which opposed the elections because its leadership expected to do poorly, won less than 13 percent of the vote. A democratic right-wing party, the Party of the Social Democratic Center (Partido do Centro Democrático Social—CDS), came in fourth with less than 8 percent (see table 11, Appendix). Despite the fact that the elections took place in a period of revolutionary ferment, most Portuguese voted for middle-class parties committed to pluralistic democracy.

Many Portuguese regarded the elections as a sign that democracy was being effectively established. In addition, most members of the military welcomed the beginning of a transition to civilian democracy. Some elements of the MFA, however, had opposed the elections, agreeing to them only after working out an agreement with political parties that the MFA's policies would be carried out regardless of election results.

Following the elections came the "hot summer" of 1975 when the revolution made itself felt in the countryside. Landless agricultural laborers in the south seized the large farms on which they worked. Many estates in the Alentejo were confiscated—over 1 million hectares in all—and transformed into collective farms (see Land Tenure and Agrarian Reform, ch. 3). In the north, where most farms were small and owned by those who worked them, such actions did not occur. The north's small farmers, conservative property-owners, violently repulsed the attempts of radical elements and the PCP to collectivize their land. Some farmers formed right-wing organizations in defense of private landownership, a reversal of the region's early welcoming of the revolution.

Other revolutionary actions were met with hostility, as well. In mid-July, the PS and the PPD withdrew from the fourth provisional government to protest antidemocratic actions by radical military and leftist political forces. The PS newspaper *República* had been closed by radical workers, causing a storm of protest both domestically and abroad. The PS and other democratic parties were also faced with a potentially lethal threat to the new freedom posed by the PCP's open contempt for parliamentary democracy and its dominance in Portugal's main trade union, Intersindical, or as it came to be known in 1977, the General Confederation of Portuguese Workers-National Intersindical (Confederação Geral dos Trabalhadores Portugueses-Intersindical Nacional—CGTP–IN).

The United States and many West European countries expressed considerable alarm at the prospect of a Marxist-Leninist takeover in a NATO country. United States Secretary of State Henry Kissinger told PS leader Soares that he would probably be the "Kerensky [the Russian social-democratic leader whose short-lived rule was the prelude to a Bolshevik takeover] of Portugal." The result of these concerns was an influx of foreign financial aid into Portugal to shore up groups committed to pluralist parliamentary democracy.

By the time of the "hot summer" of 1975, several currents could be seen within the MFA. A moderate group, the Group of Nine, issued a manifesto in August that advocated nonaligned socialism along the lines of Scandinavian social democracy. Another group published a manifesto that criticized both the Group of Nine and those who had drawn close to the PCP and singled out Prime Minister Gonçalves for his links to the Communists. These differences of opinion signaled the end of the fifth provisional government, in power only a month, under Gonçalves in early September. Gonçalves was subsequently expelled from the Council of the Revolution as this body became more moderate. The sixth provisional government was formed, headed by Admiral José Baptista Pinheiro de Azevedo; it included the leader of the Group of Nine and members of the PS, the PPD, and PCP. This government, which was to remain in power until July 1976, when the first constitutional government was formed, was pledged to adhere to the policies advocated by MFA moderates.

Evolving political stability did not reflect the country as a whole, which was on the verge of anarchy. Even the command structure of the military broke down. Political parties to the right of the PCP became more confident and increasingly fought for order, as did many in the military. The granting of independence to Mozambique in September 1975, to East Timor in October, and to Angola in November meant that the colonial wars had ended. The attainment of peace, the main aim of the military during all these months of political upheaval, was thus achieved, and the military could begin the transition to civilian rule. The polling results of the April 1975 constituent assembly elections legitimized the popular support given to the parties that could manage and would welcome this transition.

An attempted coup by radical military units in November 1975 marked the last serious leftist effort to seize power. The leftists were blocked, however, on November 25 when Colonel António dos Santos Ramalho Eanes declared a state of emergency. The revolutionary units were quickly surrounded and forced to surrender; about 200 extreme leftists were arrested and COPCON was abolished. The glamour of revolutionary goals had faded somewhat, and people returned to their jobs and daily routines after eighteen months of political and social turmoil. A degree of compromise was reached among competing political visions of how the new state should be organized, and the constitution of 1976 was proclaimed on April 2, 1976. Several weeks later, on April 25, elections for the new parliament, the Assembly of the Republic, were held.

These elections could be said to be the definitive end of a period of revolution. Moderate democratic parties received most of the vote. Revolutionary achievements were not discarded, however. The constitution pledged the country to realize socialism. Furthermore, the constitution declared the extensive nationalizations and land seizures of 1975 irreversible. The military supported these commitments through a pact with the main political parties; the pact guaranteed the military guardian rights over the new democracy for four more years.

Consolidation of Democracy

The PS won the first elections for the new parliament, the Assembly of the Republic. The PS took 36.7 percent of the vote, compared with 25.2 percent for the PDP, 16.7 percent for the CDS, and 15.2 percent for the PCP. Elections for the presidency were held in June and won easily by General Eanes, who enjoyed the backing of parties to the right of the communists, the PS, the PPD, and the CDS.

Although the PS did not have a majority in the Assembly of the Republic, Eanes allowed it to form the first constitutional government with Soares as prime minister. The PS governed from July 23, 1976, to January 30, 1978. A second government, formed from a coalition with the CDS, lasted from January to August of 1978 and was also led by Soares. The PS governments faced enormous economic and social problems, including runaway inflation, high unemployment, falling wages, and an enormous influx of Portuguese

*António dos Santos Ramalho
Eanes, president, 1976–86*

*Aníbal Cavaco Silva,
prime minister, 1985–
Courtesy Embassy of
Portugal, Washington*

settlers from Africa. The government's failure to fix the economy,
even after adopting a painful austerity program imposed by the
International Monetary Fund (IMF—see Glossary), ultimately
forced the PS to relinquish power. The party could be judged successful, however: it had governed Portugal democratically for two
years and helped thereby to consolidate the new political system.
After the collapse of the PS–CDS coalition government in July 1978,
President Eanes formed a number of caretaker governments in the
hope that they would rule until the parliamentary elections mandated by the constitution could be held in 1980. There were, therefore, three short-lived governments appointed by President Eanes.
These governments were led by Prime Minister Alfred Nobre da
Costa from August 28 to November 21, 1978; Carlos Mota Pinto
from November 21, 1978, to July 31, 1979; and Maria de Lourdes
Pintasilgo (Portugal's first woman prime minister) from July 31,
1979, to January 3, 1980.

The weakness of these governments and the failure of the PS
and the PPD, now renamed the Social Democrat Party (Partido

177

Social Democrata—PSD), to form a coalition government forced President Eanes to call for interim elections to be held in December 1979. Francisco Sá Carneiro, the dynamic leader of the PSD and a fierce personal rival of Soares, put together a coalition of his own PSD, the CDS, the Popular Monarchist Party (Partido Popular Monárquico—PPM), and another small party to form the Democratic Alliance (Aliança Democrática—AD). The AD downplayed its intentions to revise the constitution to reverse the nationalizations and land seizures of the mid-1970s and advocated a moderate economic policy. The coalition won 45.2 percent of the vote in the elections, or 128 seats, for a majority of 3 in the 250-seat assembly. The PS, which had also formed an electoral coalition with several small left-wing groups, suffered a drubbing and won only 27.4 percent, a large drop compared with 1976 results. The PCP, in coalition with another left-wing party, gained slightly.

Sá Carneiro became prime minister in January 1980, and the tenor of parliamentary politics moved to the right as the government attempted to undo some of the revolution's radical reforms. The powers conferred on the presidency by the constitution of 1976 enabled President Eanes to block the AD's centrist economic policies, however. For this reason, the AD concentrated on winning enough seats in the October 1980 elections to reach the two-thirds majority necessary to effect constitutional change and on electing someone other than Eanes in the presidential elections of December 1980.

Portuguese voters approved of the movement to the right. In the parliamentary elections, the AD coalition increased the number of its seats to 134, the PS held steady at 74 seats, and the PCP lost 6 seats for a total of 41. The AD's win was not complete, however, because President Eanes was easily reelected in December. In contrast to the election of 1976, when Eanes was supported by the PS and parties to its right, he was backed in 1980 by the PS, the PCP, and other left-wing parties. Voters admired Eanes for his integrity and obvious devotion to democracy. His election, however, made constitutional change less certain because the AD did not have by itself the required two-thirds majority. The AD also suffered a serious loss when its dynamic leader, Sá Carneiro, died in a plane crash just two days before the presidential election. His successor was Franciso Pinto Balsemão, the founder and editor of the *Expresso* newspaper.

The AD coalition remained in power until mid-1983, forming two governments with Balsemão as prime minister. In combination with the PS, which also desired fundamental changes in the political system, the AD was able to revise the constitution. Amendments were passed that enhanced the power of the prime minister and the Assembly of the Republic at the expense of the president and the military (see Constitutional Development, this ch.). The revised constitution was promulgated in September 1982.

Although the AD government had achieved its main objective of amending the constitution, the country's economic problems worsened, and the coalition gradually lost popular support. Balsemão also tired of the constant political skirmishing needed to hold the AD together and resigned in December 1982. Unable to choose a successor, the AD broke apart. Parliamentary elections in April 1983 gave the PS a stunning victory that increased its parliamentary seats to 101. After long negotiations, the PS joined with the PSD to form a governing coalition, the Central Bloc (Bloco Central), with Soares as prime minister.

The Central Bloc government was fragile from its beginning and lasted only two years. Faced with serious and worsening economic problems, the government had to adopt an unpopular austerity policy. Administrative and personality difficulties made relations within the government tense and resulted in bitter parliamentary maneuvers. Overshadowing these difficulties was the upcoming presidential election in early 1986. Soares made clear his ambition to succeed Eanes, who, according to the constitution, was not allowed to seek a third consecutive term. A split within the PSD over its presidential candidate ended the coalition government in June 1985.

In new assembly elections held in October 1985, the PS, blamed by the public for the country's severe economic problems, such as a 10 percent fall in wages since 1983, suffered serious losses and lost almost half its seats in the Assembly of the Republic. The PCP's electoral coalition lost six seats; the PSD won thirteen more seats because of new leadership; and the CDS lost almost a third of its seats. The big winner was a party formed by supporters of President Eanes, the Party of Democratic Renovation (Partido Renovador Democrático—PRD), which, although only months old, won nearly 18 percent of the vote and forty-five seats. The party's victory stemmed from the high regard Portuguese voters had for President Eanes.

No party emerged from the October 1985 elections with anything even close to an absolute majority. Hence, the 1985–87 period was unstable politically. The new head of the PSD, economist Aníbal Cavaco Silva, as prime minister headed a minority PSD government that managed to survive for only seventeen months. Its success was attributed partly to support from the PRD, which as a young party wished to establish itself, although it was a motion

179

of censure presented by this party in the spring of 1987 that eventually brought the government down. Cavaco Silva also benefited from the internal dissension of other parties.

The presidential election of 1986 did not yield a winner in the first round. The candidate of the CDS and the PSD, Diogo Freitas do Amaral, won 46.3 percent of the vote compared with 25.4 percent for Mário Soares. Freitas do Amaral, the candidate of a united right, profited from the left's mounting of three candidates. In the two-candidate runoff election in mid-February, Soares won with 51.3 percent of the vote, getting the support of most left-wing voters. The PCP supported him as the lesser of two evils, even though Soares repeatedly reminded voters that he, perhaps more than anyone else, had prevented the Communists from coming to power in the mid-1970s.

Cavaco Silva came to have full control of his party, the PSD. As prime minister, he governed boldly and pushed, through his influence in the parliament, for a liberalization of the economy. He was fortunate in that external economic trends and the infusion of funds from the European Community (EC—see Glossary) after Portugal became a member in 1986 enlivened the country's economy and began to bring an unaccustomed prosperity to Portuguese wage earners. Confident therefore that his party could win in parliamentary elections, Cavaco Silva maneuvered his political opponents into passing a vote of censure against his government in April 1987. Instead of asking for a new government composed of a variety of parties on the left, President Soares called for elections in July.

Cavaco Silva had judged the political situation correctly. The PSD won just over 50 percent of the vote, which gave it an absolute majority in the parliament, the first single-party majority since the restoration of democracy in 1974. The strong mandate enabled Cavaco Silva to put forward a more clearly defined program and perhaps to govern more effectively than his predecessors. The emergence of a single-party government supported by a parliamentary majority was for many observers the coming of age of Portuguese democracy.

The Governmental System

Portugal made remarkable political progress after 1974. It replaced the authoritarian-corporatist regime of Salazar, and, as of the early 1990s, the country appeared to have successfully made the transition to democracy. Although political and governmental problems remained, the government was popularly elected, it functioned according to the constitution, and, since the mid-1980s, had done so with notable stability. The successful transition to democracy in the Iberian Peninsula since the mid-1970s (in Spain, as well as in Portugal) may be thought of as one of the most significant political transformations of the late twentieth century.

Constitutional Development

Portugal is governed under the constitution of 1976 whose preliminary drafting was largely completed in 1975, then finished and officially promulgated in early 1976. At the time the constitution was being drafted, a democratic outcome was still uncertain because the country was in the midst of a revolution. Even after a leftist coup had been put down in November 1975, it was not known if the armed forces would respect the assembly and allow work on the constitution to go forward. The MFA and leftist groups pressured and cajoled the assembly, and there was much discussion of establishing a revolutionary and socialist system of government. Moreover, not all of the assembly's members were committed to parliamentary democracy. The membership was intensely partisan, with some 60 percent of the seats occupied by the left.

After great struggle, the Constituent Assembly eventually adopted a constitution that provided for a democratic, parliamentary system with political parties, elections, a parliament, and a prime minister. The document also established an independent judiciary and listed a number of human rights. Noteworthy features of the constitution include its ideological content, its provision for the role of the military, and its dual presidential-parliamentary system.

The constitution was a highly charged ideological document that included numerous references to socialism, the rights of workers, and the desirability of a socialist economy. It severely restricted private investment and business activity. Many of these articles were advanced by PCP representatives in the Constituent Assembly, but they were also advocated by members of the PS, who at that time, for electoral reasons, were seeking to be as revolutionary as the far left. The resulting document proclaimed that the object of the republic was "to ensure the transition to socialism." The constitution also urged the state to "socialize the means of production and abolish the exploitation of man by man," phrases that echoed Marx's *Communist Manifesto*. Workers' Committees were given the right to supervise the management of enterprises and to have their representatives elected to the boards of state-owned firms. The government, among many admonitions along the same vein, was to "direct its work toward the socialization of medicine and the medico-pharmaceutical sectors."

181

The constitution gave the military great political power through the role given to the MFA-controlled Council of the Revolution that, in effect, made the MFA a separate and almost co-equal branch of government. The council was to be an advisory body to the president (who was at first likely to come from the military itself) and would function as a sort of constitutional court to ensure that the laws passed by parliament were in accord with the MFA's desires and did not undermine the achievements of the revolution. The council was also to serve as a high-level decision-making body for the armed forces themselves. The council was a concession to the MFA for allowing the Constituent Assembly to sit and promulgate a new "basic law." Some members of the Portuguese left, especially the PCP, supported the council in the hope that they would continue to enjoy MFA support even if they lost ground with the electorate.

The final innovative feature of the constitution was its provision for a system of government that was both presidential and parliamentarian. The Constituent Assembly favored two centers of power in order to avoid both the dangers of an excessively strong executive, as was the case during the Salazar period, and the weaknesses of parliamentary instability, as was the case in the First Republic.

The constitution was controversial from the start. It was widely seen in political circles as a compromise document because all participants in its drafting had been able to incorporate in it provisions they found vital. The constitution's parliamentary sections had the support of the PS, the PSD, and the CDS; its socialistic content had the support of the PCP and its allies and the PS.

Even before the constitution became law, politicians had agreed to change some provisions after the five-year period in which changes were prohibited had elapsed. Objections to the document centered on its ideological content, its economic restrictions, and its recognition of a military role in the governance of the country. The CDS, the party furthest to the right among the groups that had participated in the document's drafting, refused to ratify it. The CDS did agree to abide by the constitution in the interim, however.

By the early 1980s, the political climate was ripe for constitutional reform. The center-right coalition AD, formed by the PSD, the CDS, and the monarchist party, the PPM, was in power; the PS had been voted out of office, and the PCP was politically isolated. The first amendments, enacted in 1982, dealt with the constitution's political arrangements. Although many of the economic provisions of the constitution had been not been implemented and were, in effect, being ignored, there were not yet enough votes to reach the required two-thirds majority needed to amend them.

The 1982 amendments were enacted through the combined votes of the AD and the PS. This combination of center-right and center-left political forces managed to end the military's control of Portuguese politics (see The Armed Forces in Political Life after 1974, ch. 5). It abolished the Council of the Revolution, controlled by the military, and replaced it with two consultative bodies. One of these, the Higher Council of National Defense, was limited to commenting on military matters. The other, the Council of State, was broadly representative of the entire country and did not have the power to prevent government and parliamentary actions by declaring them unconstitutional. Another amendment created a Constitutional Court to review the constitutionality of legislation. Because ten of its thirteen judges were chosen by the Assembly of the Republic, the court was under parliamentary control. Another important change reduced the president's power by restricting presidential ability to dismiss the government, dissolve parliament, or veto legislation.

Despite these amendments, centrists and conservatives continued to criticize the constitution as too ideological and economically restrictive. Hence, the constitution was amended again in 1989. Many economic restrictions were removed and much ideological language eliminated, while governmental structures remained unchanged. The most important change enabled the state to privatize much of the property and many of the enterprises nationalized during the mid-1970s.

Further amendments were to become possible in 1994. Political scientists speculated that the electoral system might be amended so that Portuguese living abroad could vote in presidential elections, a change that had long been sought. Another change could be the introduction of the concept of the "constructive vote of no confidence" used in Germany to help shore up minority governments. This parliamentary provision would permit a government to remain in place despite a vote of no confidence if the parliament could not form an alternative government and would prevent purely negative majorities from destroying a government. As of the early 1990s, a Portuguese government that received a vote of no confidence had to resign.

The Presidency

Although Portugal's government includes a parliament, an assembly, and a cabinet needing parliamentary support, its president has considerable power. As noted above, this dual system was a response to the Portugal's experiences with parliamentary instability and dictatorship. Yet, the extent of the president's power, even after the 1982 revision of the constitution, was not always clear. As a result, at times the relationships among the main institutions of the Portuguese system remained somewhat ambiguous.

The president is elected by majority vote in nationwide balloting. The term of office is five years, and no president may serve more than two consecutive terms. Real power is vested in the office of the president, who is not merely a symbol of national unity, but rather the chief of state. In times of national crisis, presidents can make or unmake governments, and even in situations when, for example, the government is weak and no party has a majority, they can exercise considerable influence behind the scenes.

According to the terms of the 1989 revised edition of the constitution, the president's powers and duties include acting as supreme commander of the armed forces, promulgating laws, declaring a state of siege, granting pardons, submitting legislation to the Constitutional Court for approval, making many high appointments, and, when needed, removing high officials from their posts. The president also calls elections, convenes special sessions of the Assembly of the Republic, dissolves this body in accordance with law, and appoints the prime minister.

The 1982 amendments to the constitution reduced the powers of the presidency somewhat, mainly by specifying the periods in which presidents may not dissolve the assembly (during the first six months after the assembly's election, in the last six months of a president's term, and during a state of siege or an emergency) and stipulating when they may dismiss a government ("only when this becomes necessary to secure the regular functioning of the democratic institutions"). The presidential veto power was reduced in that a simple majority in the assembly can override presidential vetoes. The power of pocket veto was also abolished. According to the 1982 amendments, the president must either accept legislation or reject it.

The presidency is intended for a national figure of great prestige and ideally one above partisan politics. As of the early 1990s, Portugal had had only two presidents since the constitution was promulgated in 1976. General Eanes was elected in 1976 and easily reelected to a second term in 1980. In 1986 PS leader Soares was elected to the presidency, but only in the runoff election after he had gained the support of the PCP and the PSD. In January 1991, he easily won reelection for a second term.

These two men were genuinely popular presidents because of their statesmanlike qualities and their obvious devotion to their country's welfare. General Eanes was widely regarded as the man who made possible Portugal's transition to centrist democracy after the tumult of the revolution. He was politically moderate and a conciliator who remained apart from the country's contending factions. In Portugal's democratic transition, Soares was also seen as a heroic figure who had fought tenaciously, first against the Salazar regime, enduring both imprisonment and exile, and later against Communist rule. He was also the country's first civilian president since the First Republic.

The Council of State

The Council of State, which in the 1982 constitutional reform replaced the Council of the Revolution, functions as a high-level advisory body to the president. Its members consist of the president of the Assembly of the Republic, the prime minister, the president of the Constitutional Court, the ombudsman, the chairpersons of the regional governments, former presidents, five citizens appointed by the president, and five persons elected by the Assembly of the Republic.

The council is a broadly consultative group with deep roots in Portuguese history. It is a kind of throwback to an earlier Portuguese concept of corporative, regional, or functional representation. However, it has no executive power and in recent times has been called into its advisory capacity only rarely. As a result, membership on it has come to be mainly honorary.

The Prime Minister

The prime minister of Portugal heads the government and manages the nation's affairs on a daily basis. The prime minister chooses or approves cabinet ministers and directs or coordinates their actions. The office thus differs from that in Britain, where the prime minister is the first among equals. Moreover, the entire cabinet bears responsibility for its actions, not the prime minister alone. The prime minister also directs the operations of the armed forces, although the president is formally the commander in chief. In other matters as well, the prime minister is autonomous, and the president has no right to direct the prime minister's policies.

Unlike the president, the prime minister is elected indirectly. As in other parliamentary systems, the prime minister is the leader of the largest party in the parliament or the head of a coalition of parties. The prime minister's term may last for up to four years, through an entire legislative period, after which time new elections are held. However, the prime minister may call earlier elections. The prime minister may ask for a vote of confidence from the parliament, but he can also be ousted by a vote of no confidence or through a leadership change in his own party. If a prime minister proves incompetent, loses support, or fails to provide needed national direction, the president may also request that a new government be formed.

In the ten years following the Revolution of 1974, Portugal was governed by nearly a dozen weak and short-lived governments; the number of prime ministers was not large, however, because all but two of them headed more than one cabinet. After mid-1985, the political system attained a greater stability when Aníbal Cavaco Silva, head of the Social Democrat Party (Partido Social-Democrata—PSD), formed first a minority government and then a majority government that lasted the entire 1987–91 legislative period. After his party won 50.4 percent of the vote in the 1991 national elections, Cavaco Silva formed another government that enjoyed an absolute parliamentary majority.

The Council of Ministers

The Council of Ministers, or cabinet, is the state's highest executive institution. The council consists of the prime minister and fifteen to eighteen cabinet ministers. Most ministers come from the parliament, but they are not required to do so. In coalition cabinets, the majority of ministers usually belongs to the coalition's largest party, that of the prime minister, and the remaining ministers come from other coalition parties. Once in the cabinet, a member of parliament has to relinquish, at least temporarily, his or her seat in that body.

The Council of Ministers has both administrative and policy-making functions, is responsible for national security and defense affairs, and is in charge of the day-to-day implementation of government policy. In addition, Portugal's cabinet has extensive legislative powers by virtue of its power to pass decree-laws within areas of its responsibility. It can also be granted the right by the Assembly of the Republic to pass legislation in areas of responsibility usually reserved to parliament, its "relatively reserved legislative powers." Because getting a bill through the assembly was often a slow process, the Council of Ministers often made use of this right. The council is responsible both individually and collectively for its actions, first to the prime minister and ultimately to the parliament.

In Portugal, the minister with the greatest power is the minister of finance, who prepares the budget and oversees the finances of the other ministries. Ministers are assisted by politically appointed secretaries of state, who vacate their positions when their ministers leave the council. As allowed by Article 203 of the 1989 revised

Assembly of the Republic, Lisbon
Courtesy Andrea Matles Savada

constitution, a number of ministers sometimes meet together and form what the constitution terms "councils of specialized ministers" to work on matters of mutual concern. They can call on their secretaries of state and civil servants for assistance and can submit the results of their collaboration to the entire cabinet for review.

Additional bodies were later created to assist individual ministers on the council as a whole. In 1984 the Office of Techno-Legislative Support, under the minister of justice, was formed to assist the council in drafting legislation. A number of superior councils assist ministers with studies and planning. Examples of this kind of body are the Superior Council of Finance and the National Board of Education. In addition to advising ministers, these bodies meet with groups affected by government decisions.

The Assembly of the Republic

According to the Portuguese constitution, the country's unicameral parliament, the Assembly of the Republic, "is the representative assembly of all Portuguese citizens." The constitution names the assembly as one of the country's organs of supreme authority and, in Article 114 of the 1989 revised constitution, charges it to exercise its powers both separately and interdependently with the president, the government, and the courts.

The assembly's power derives from its power to dismiss a government through a vote of no confidence, to impeach the president, to change the country's laws, and to amend the constitution. In addition to these key powers, the constitution grants to the Assembly of the Republic extensive legislative powers and substantial control over the budget, the right to authorize the government to raise taxes and grant loans, the power to ratify treaties and other kinds of international agreements, and the duty to approve or reject decisions by the president of the republic to declare war and make peace. The assembly also appoints many members of important state institutions, such as ten of the thirteen members of the Constitutional Court and seven of the sixteen members of the Higher Council of the Bench.

The constitution requires the assembly to quickly review and approve an incoming government's program. Parliamentary rules allow the assembly to call for committees of inquiry to examine the government's actions. Political opposition represented in the assembly has the power to review the cabinet's actions, even though it is unlikely that the actions can be reversed. For example, as few as ten members can request that the assembly ratify the government's decree-laws not belonging to the cabinet's exclusive jurisdiction. As little as one-fifth of the assembly can call for a motion of censure, although an absolute majority of the assembly is required to sustain the censure. Party groups can also call for interpellations that require debates about specific government policies.

The assembly consisted at first of 250 members, but the constitutional reforms of 1989 reduced its number to between 230 and 235. Members are elected by popular vote for legislative terms of four years from the country's constituencies (eighteen in mainland Portugal, one each for the autonomous regions of the Azores (Açores) and Madeira, one for Portuguese living in Western Europe, and one for those living in the rest of the world). The number of voters registered in a constituency determines the number of its members in the assembly. Constituencies vary greatly in size. As of the early 1990s, as many as three dozen representatives came from the Lisbon district and as few as three from some inland districts. The autonomous regions of the Azores and Madeira each sent five members to the assembly.

According to the constitution, members of the assembly represent the entire country, not the constituency from which they are elected. This directive was reinforced in practice by the strong role of political parties in regard to members of the assembly. As of the early 1990s, party leadership, for example, determined in which areas candidates were to run for office, thus often weakening members' ties to their constituencies. Moreover, members of the assembly were expected to vote with their party and to work within parliamentary groups based on party membership. Party discipline was strong, and insubordinate members could be coerced through a variety of means. A further obstacle to members' independence was that their bills first had to be submitted to the parliamentary groups, and it was these group leaders who set the assembly's agenda. The leader of the assembly, its president, was selected from the group leaders.

Assembly sessions are scheduled to run from mid-October to mid-June, but often extend beyond this period because of uncompleted business. When the body is not in session, it is represented by its Standing Committee, headed by the president of the assembly and composed of assembly members chosen to reflect the larger body's political composition. The committee monitors the president and the government and can call for meetings of the entire assembly if necessary.

Much of the assembly's work is done in committees, both permanent and ad hoc. Committee membership is to reflect the assembly party makeup, and members are usually not allowed to serve on more than two committees. The committees examine legislative proposals, most of which come from the government rather than from the assembly itself after a first reading in the assembly. Appropriate witnesses and expert testimony can be called; for certain types of legislation, labor legislation for example, concerned parties have to be heard. Once a committee approves a bill, the bill can receive a second reading and a plenary vote.

The Portuguese parliament did not enjoy much prestige initially. Its efficacy was impeded by the absence of adequate resources and staff and the lack of an efficient infrastructure of committees and subcommittees. This institutional inadequacy buttressed the traditional lack of respect the Portuguese felt for their governing institutions. To the public, the assembly personified democracy's defects in that it was inefficient, quarrelsome, splintered, and patronage-dominated. Its members were frequently seen as putting partisan interests ahead of the interests of the nation or of using their parliamentary positions to enhance their private careers and fortunes. In newspaper editorials and cartoons, parliament members were often portrayed as buffoonish, silly, and irrelevant. Polls in 1978 and 1984 found that the Portuguese saw parliament as less important than the president, the prime minister, or the cabinet. It was thus not surprising that at times Portuguese democracy seemed insufficiently rooted. Yet, democracy had survived the unstable period after the revolution, and, despite all its problems, many

Portuguese had come to see the Assembly of the Republic as indispensable to its preservation. In addition, reforms of the parliament's organization and practices, as well as increased numbers of skilled and experienced staffers, had improved the body's efficiency.

The Judiciary

The constitution provides for the Constitutional Court; the Supreme Court of Justice and the Supreme Administrative Court, both of which have subordinate courts; and a variety of special courts, including a military court system. It states that the courts are the "organs of supreme authority competent to administer justice in the name of the people." The courts are also designated as "independent and subject only to the law."

The Constitutional Court, called into existence by the constitutional reform of 1982, judges whether legislative acts are legal and constitutional. Among other duties, this court also ascertains the physical ability of the president to carry out presidential functions and examines international agreements for their constitutionality. Ten of its thirteen members are chosen by the Assembly of the Republic.

The Supreme Court of Justice is designated the "highest court of law," but "without prejudice to the jurisdiction of the Constitutional Court," and heads the court system that deals with civil and criminal cases. The courts of first instance (the first courts to try a case) are the municipal and district courts; the courts of second instance are, as a rule, courts of appeal. As of the early 1990s, there were four of these latter courts. The Supreme Court of Justice may serve as a court of first instance in some cases and as an appeals court in others.

The Supreme Court of Administration examines the fiscal and administrative conduct of government institutions. It is not concerned with the state's political decisions or legislation. One section of this court deals with administrative disputes; below it are three courts of first instance. Another section deals with tax disputes and is supported by courts of first and second instance. In addition to these courts, there is a Court of Audit situated in the Ministry of Finance.

Overseeing the nominations, training, promotions, transfers, and professional conduct of Portugal's judges are the Higher Council of the Bench and the Superior Council of the Administrative and Fiscal Courts. These bodies have the right to discipline judges whose conduct does not comply with the law. Also looking after the rights of the citizens is the ombudsman, elected by the Assembly of the

Republic for a four-year term. In the early 1990s, this official received some 3,000 complaints a year from Portuguese who felt they had been improperly dealt with by state institutions.

The Portuguese legal and judicial system is based on Roman civil law and was heavily influenced by the French system. It differs from the United States or British legal systems in that a complete body of law is found in the codes. As a result, judicial reasoning is deductive, and prior cases or precedent play little role. A judge is therefore seen mainly as a civil servant whose role is to discover and apply the appropriate law from the codes, not to interpret it or to apply new sociological findings. Hence, judges enjoy less prestige than in a system based on common law. In addition, law is seen as more fixed and immutable than in the United States, although over time it does change. The historically authoritarian nature of Portugal's system of government is often attributed to this centralized and hierarchical legal system.

Portugal's legal system is considered relatively fair and impartial. During the Salazar regime, the courts were loyal servants of the New State, and high officials of the regime were all but immune from judicial proceedings. After the Revolution of 1974, Salazar-appointed judges were largely removed in favor of revolutionary ones, and certain groups—such as workers and peasants— were often favored over owners and employers before the law. With time, however, the courts have come to function with greater impartiality. Most criticism centers on the fact that the courts are slow and overburdened. Long periods of time are often required for the legal system to deal with even routine matters, nor have the courts adequately kept pace with new judicial issues, such as drugs and white-collar crime.

Civil Service

According to Article 266 of the revised constitution, public administrative authorities shall ''seek to promote the public interest, while observing those rights and interests of citizens that are protected by law.'' Furthermore, the next article states that the structure of public administration shall be such as to avoid bureaucracy, to bring the state's services close to the people, and to involve the people in decision making. Citizens are entitled to be informed of proceedings in which they are directly concerned and of decisions affecting them.

These provisions were a reaction to Portuguese administrative traditions and to the abuses and favoritism of the Salazar era. As of the early 1990s, however, opinions remained divided about whether the Portuguese state was less ''bureaucratic'' than it had been in the past. The 1970s saw a tremendous increase in the number of persons employed by central and local governments (from 205,000 in 1968 to 550,000 in 1986) and the issuance of many regulations that slowed public administration. To counter these trends, numerous reforms were enacted in the 1980s to streamline government services and make public employees more responsive to the public's needs. For example, civil servants were encouraged to see themselves as servants of the public rather than as wielders of state power. Moreover, many trivial but time-consuming and otherwise onerous bureaucratic regulations were revoked. An example of this kind of reform was that photocopies rather than original documents could be used when dealing with government offices. Portugal's entry into the EC was also forcing a modernization of the public sector.

Portugal's public employees are classified as either public functionaries, those employed by the national government, or as administrative functionaries, those employed by local authorities. In 1986 national government employees accounted for 83 percent of government employees. Some 70 percent of these government workers were employed by the Ministry of Education and Culture and the Ministry of Health. As part of a concerted effort to reduce Portugal's traditional centralization of government, Lisbon's share of public employees of all kinds was reduced from 52.7 percent in 1978 to 44 percent in 1986.

The civil service's cumbersome and unfair classification and pay structures were also reformed during the 1980s. The pay of public employees came to be taxed more than it had been in the past. Career structures were simplified. Care was taken, however, that no public employee receive less pay than under the old system.

The recruitment of new public employees is also newly regulated. Candidates vie for state positions in public competitions. Juries select candidates in a way that guarantees fairness. Public employees are also allowed to be members of the main Portuguese labor unions.

Local Government

Portugal has long been a centralized political system not only in terms of its legal system, but also in terms of its system of public administration. The pattern, like the legal system, derives from Roman law and the French Napoleonic Code. The result was that Portugal's central authorities kept most powers for themselves and administered the country from Lisbon. Local government remained underdeveloped and passive.

The framers of the constitution of 1976 sought to change this pattern of centralization. Article 238 of the 1989 revised constitution states that "local authorities on the mainland shall be the parishes, municipal authorities and the administrative regions." A plan for dividing Portugal into seven administrative regions (five based on the country's major river basins, and one each for the Porto and Lisbon metropolitan areas) had been worked out in the mid-1970s, but in the early 1990s its implementation had not yet been effected. Fear of officials in the capital that they would lose power to local authorities was seen as a principal reason for this delay.

Article 291 of the revised constitution of 1989 states that until the administrative regions have been created, the highest level of subnational government will be the mainland's eighteen districts, administrative divisions established in the nineteenth century. In the early 1990s, these eighteen districts (each bearing the name of its capital) constituted the layer of government between the national government and local government. Portugal is not a federal state, and the districts have no legislative powers. District officials conduct elections, maintain public order, and exercise what the Portuguese term "administrative tutelage" by monitoring the performance of local government. Each district is directed by a civil governor, who is a political appointee.

The districts do not function as administrative bodies. As a result, most of the national government's activities are carried out by the ministries within territorial divisions that they establish and that do not necessarily correspond with those of the districts. The district governor is not seen as occupying a higher position than ministerial officials.

Because the administrative regions envisioned in the constitution had not been established as of the early 1990s, Portugal's local government at that time consisted of 305 municipalities, further subdivided into about 4,000 parishes. Despite its name, a parish has no ecclesiastical functions but merely provides social assistance and maintains voter registration lists. An elected parish assembly meets four times a year and chooses the parish board, which serves as the parish's government. The board draws up the parish's budget, executes the parish assembly's laws, and manages its public business. The size of these bodies is determined by the population of the parish.

Municipalities, like parishes, are classified as urban or rural, except for those of Lisbon and Porto, which are classified as metropolitan areas. A municipality is governed by a municipal assembly, half of whose members are elected every four years and half of whom are the presidents of parish boards operating within the municipality. A municipal assembly meets five times a year, and its members are unpaid. A municipality's executive body is the municipal chamber. Its members (aldermen) are elected, serve year-round, and are paid. The chamber is headed by a president (mayor). The president of a municipal chamber is the candidate for that body who received the most votes. Each chamber has a council, composed of representatives from a variety of organizations, which serves as a consultative body. The size of these municipal bodies is determined by the number of registered voters within a municipality.

The many tasks managed by a municipality are carried out both by city employees and private firms considered part of the municipal government. Funds to pay for these tasks come both from the national government and local sources (taxes, licensing fees, etc). The constitution stipulates that these local authorities should be financially independent, and plans exist to establish by law a system of local finance that will arrange the ''fair apportionment'' of public funds between the state and local authorities. As of the early 1990s, however, over 90 percent of the funds used by local government were still national in origin. In addition, the national government was obliged to see that these funds were spent properly, thereby reducing even further the independence of local authorities.

Autonomous Regions and Macau

The archipelagoes of the Azores and Madeira had long enjoyed a substantial degree of administrative autonomy when in 1976 the new constitution established them as autonomous political regions. According to the constitution, political autonomy was granted in response to the islands' geographical, economic, social, and cultural characteristics and because of ''the historic aspirations of the peoples of the islands to autonomy.'' This autonomy, however, ''shall in no way affect the [Portuguese] State's full sovereignty and shall be exercised within the limits of the Constitution.''

The constitution grants the autonomous regions a number of powers, among them the power to legislate in areas relating specifically to them, execute laws, tax, supervise local public institutions, and participate in drafting international agreements that affect them. This last provision has meant that Azorean officials have participated in talks between the United States and Portugal about military bases located on their islands.

The national government is represented by the minister of the republic, who functions in much the same manner as the president of the republic does on the mainland. The minister has veto powers similar to those of the president. If the autonomous regions' governing organs have acted contrary to the dictates of the constitution, they may be dissolved by the president of the republic.

Each autonomous region has a legislative assembly elected for four-year terms. The d'Hondt method (see Glossary) is used to determine voting results. A president heads a regional government composed of regional secretaries, which reflects the party composition of the regional assembly. This government is politically responsible to the regional assembly in the same manner that the national government is responsible to the Assembly of the Republic.

Among other powers, the regional assembly has the right to initiate legislation, review the regional government's budget, and vote motions of censure. A regional government has powers similar to those of the national government, and its members direct a number of regional secretariats that correspond to the mainland's ministries. Local government in the autonomous regions corresponds to the mainland's municipalities and parishes.

Macau consists of a peninsula attached to the Chinese mainland and two islands with a total area of about seventeen square kilometers. In 1987 its population is estimated at 435,000 persons. Portuguese explorers first reached Macau in the early sixteenth century; it became a Portuguese colony in 1557. According to an agreement in 1987 between Portugal and China, Macau is to become a "special administrative region" of China on January 20, 1999. Even after this date, however, Macau will be allowed to maintain its capitalist economy, and Portuguese will remain its official language. Until 1999 Macau will remain a Special Territory of Portugal. Although the territory's highest executive official is a governor appointed by the president of Portugal, Macau enjoys a substantial degree of autonomy and has its own legislative assembly.

The Electoral System

The constitution states that the people exercise political power through universal, equal, direct, secret, and periodic elections. All citizens over the age of eighteen have the right to vote, and those over the age of twenty-one have the right to hold public office, under conditions of equality and freedom. Portuguese citizens are obliged to register to vote, but voting itself is voluntary. Freedom of association is guaranteed and is defined to include the right to establish or join political parties and "through them to work democratically to give form to the will of the people and to organize political power."

Elections for the president's term of five years in Portugal's semi-presidential system are by popular vote. If a candidate fails to receive an absolute majority on the first ballot, a runoff election between the two leading candidates is to be held within two weeks.

Elections for the four-year legislative terms of the Assembly of the Republic are by proportional representation in each constituency. Portugal uses the d'Hondt method of proportional representation, which is based on the highest average method and favors large parties by awarding them a greater percentage of assembly seats than the percentage of votes they won. Small parties are protected in that there is no minimum percentage of votes they must receive to gain a seat in the assembly. Nonetheless, unless these parties are members of a coalition, they rarely win a seat in the assembly. The d'Hondt method was adopted because it leads to stronger, more stable governments in countries that are deeply divided and have multiple parties.

Municipal elections, which serve as a barometer of public opinion on the national government, are held every four years. In contrast to national elections, this schedule is maintained because local governments do not fall. The national parties participate in these elections.

Political Dynamics

In the early 1990s, Portuguese politics operated at several different levels. The constitution and the laws constituted the first level. This formal structure of government often appears rigid, legalistic, and impenetrable, especially to outsiders. Yet, these legal and constitutional structures are more obvious and more easily understood than the other levels of the Portuguese system of government.

The second level consists of political parties and interest groups. Because of its legalistic tradition, a strict separation exists in Portugal between the formal governmental system and the sphere of political parties and interest groups. Portuguese tend to respect their formal system of government but to denigrate political parties and interest groups. As Portuguese democracy flourished through the 1980s, however, political parties and interest groups gained greater acceptance as an integral part of the system of government.

Unlike these first two levels, the third level of Portuguese politics is largely invisible and is the most difficult for outsiders to penetrate and comprehend. This level consists of the informal connections, family relationships, interpersonal ties, kinships, and patronage networks that are so much the heart of the Portuguese political system. Seldom spoken of or described by the Portuguese, these relationships enable the Portuguese system to function and to cut through vast layers of red tape.

Many of the informal networks that had long steered Portuguese affairs were severely disrupted by the Revolution of 1974 when many families and extended clans lost their property and their positions. However, many of these networks were rebuilt in subsequent years, and others were formed by the forging of new political and economic relationships. Knowledge of this third level of Portuguese politics is crucial for a full understanding of the formal and the informal dynamics within the Portuguese political system.

Political Parties

As Portugal became democratic after 1974, it also developed a political party system with a full spectrum of parties that ranged from the far left to the far right. During the Salazar-Caetano regime, only one party was legal, the National Union (União Nacional—UN), later renamed the National Popular Action (Acção Nacional Popular—ANP). The UN/ANP was dissolved in the first weeks of the revolution, and a great variety of new parties soon replaced it.

Some political parties emerged very quickly because they already existed in preliminary form. Several factions of the old UN/ANP, for example, became separate political parties after the revolution. The socialists and, to a far greater extent, the Communists already had underground groups operating in Portugal, as well as organizations in exile. Finally, some opposition elements had formed "study groups" that served as the basis of later political parties.

The party system increased in importance during the Second Republic. Large, strong parties were fostered under the d'Hondt method of proportional representation, and parties soon began to receive state subsidies. The parties' strength was also bolstered by their exclusive right to nominate political candidates and by the strict party discipline they enforced on successful candidates once they entered parliament. By the beginning of the early 1990s, only four parties regularly won seats in the parliament, and two were so much stronger than the others that Portugal seemed on the way to an essentially two-party system.

Far Left

Far-left groups, most importantly the Portuguese Democratic

Movement (Movimento Democrático Português—MDP), had considerable influence in the early part of the revolution. Consisting mostly of students and intellectuals, these groups were augmented by leftists from all over the world who flocked to Portugal to witness and participate in the revolution. They often engaged in guerrilla tactics, street demonstrations, and takeovers of private lands and industries. On their own, these groups could mount major demonstrations; in alliance with the PCP, they could be even more formidable. Since the heady revolutionary days of the mid-1970s, however, most of these groups have been absorbed into the larger parties or dissolved. As of the beginning of 1990s, some far-left groups were still active at the universities and in intellectual circles, but they were seen as a fringe phenomenon and lacked their former disruptive capacity.

Portuguese Communist Party

The main party on the revolutionary left in Portugal was for decades the Portuguese Communist Party (Partido Comunista Português—PCP). The PCP had a long history of defiance to the Salazar dictatorship, and many of the party's leaders had spent long years in jail or in exile. Party members who remained in Portugal worked underground where they formed associations and organized the labor union Intersindical. The party was strongly Stalinist and Moscow-oriented.

Returning from exile in 1974, the PCP's leaders, many of whom were reputed to be capable and formidable politicians, tried to seize power by means of a coup, allying themselves with revolutionary elements in the Armed Forces Movement (Movimento das Forças Armadas—MFA). The party came close to seizing power in 1975 but failed because moderate elements within the armed forces and the political parties to the right of it were committed to Western democracy. Extensive financial aid from Western countries to these parties also contributed to the PCP's ultimate defeat.

The PCP, along with its far-left allies, got 17 percent of the vote in the first democratic election in Portugal in 1975, and for several elections after that it held its position at approximately 12 to 19 percent of the vote. But during the 1980s, as Portugal moved away from the radical politics of the mid-1970s and began to prosper economically, the PCP's popularity declined to less than 10 percent of the vote. The party remained strong in the trade unions, but younger members of the party challenged the old leadership and questioned the party's hard-line Stalinist positions. Some of these young challengers were expelled from the party. The collapse of communism in Europe, the aging of the party's leadership (the party had been headed by Álvaro Cunhal since 1941) and of its membership, and the party's poor showing in elections indicate that the party either will have to transform itself fundamentally or fade away as a political force.

Socialist Party

The history of the Socialist Party (Partido Socialista—PS) in Portugal dates back to the late nineteenth century. Like the PCP, it was persecuted and forced into exile by Salazar. The party was reestablished in 1973 in the Federal Republic of Germany (West Germany) under the leadership of Mário Soares, who had opposed the regime as a young man and had been imprisoned for his political activities. Soares returned to Portugal a few days after the coup of April 25, 1974, and the PS began to function openly as a political party. It had both a moderate and a militant wing, but its militancy was tempered by the articulate and politically shrewd Soares.

The PS, as one of the two largest parties in Portugal, has often formed governments. During the revolutionary situation in 1974–75, the socialists were looked on as the most viable moderate opposition to the PCP. The PS therefore received considerable foreign support, as well as domestic votes, that it might not otherwise have had. It regularly received about 28 to 35 percent of the vote; it was in power from 1976 to 1978 and in a governing coalition with the PSD from 1983 to 1985.

In power the PS followed a moderate, centrist program. As the Portuguese electorate became more conservative in the 1980s, however, the party lost support. In the 1985 election, it got only 20.8 percent of the vote, although this percentage improved slightly in the 1987 national elections. The party won the 1989 municipal elections, but despite an impressive improvement in the 1991 national election when it polled 29.3 percent of the vote, it still lagged far behind the PSD. Persistent leadership problems dating from when Soares left the party in 1986 when he was elected president and inept campaigns were seen as causes of the party's secondary position in Portuguese politics. At times the disputes between the moderate and Marxist factions were renewed, but the party as a whole had moved far enough to the right that in the 1991 national election the PS had difficulty distinguishing itself from the PSD on most major issues.

Social Democrat Party

The Social Democrat Party (Partido Social Democrata—PSD)

emerged as the somewhat open and tolerated opposition under Caetano in the early 1970s. For a time, the PSD, then known as the Popular Democratic Party (Partido Popular Democrata—PPD), adopted the reformist political doctrines popular during the revolutionary period of the mid-1970s. It was soon overtaken, however, by the PS as the main opposition party, and it moved toward the democratic center. The radical constitution of 1976 was drafted and promulgated with its help, but even then the PSD was committed to its revision.

The PSD's fortunes generally improved as revolutionary fervor waned. In the earliest postrevolutionary elections, the PSD got about 24 to 27 percent of the vote, second to the PS. It had scored well in the conservative north of Portugal but not in the revolutionary south. As the party began to occupy the broad center of the political spectrum under the dynamic leadership of Francisco Sá Carneiro, the PSD's electoral support grew. In 1978 the PSD formed an electoral coalition, the Democratic Alliance (Aliança Democrática—AD), with two other parties and came to power in early 1980 with Sá Carneiro as prime minister. After the formation of this government, the PSD remained in government throughout the 1980s and into the first half of the 1990s, either as part of a coalition, in a minority single-party cabinet, or as a majority single-party government.

The AD won the parliamentary election of October 1980, but the coalition's forward movement slowed somewhat after the death of Sá Carneiro in a plane crash in December 1980. His successor, *Expresso* founder and editor Francisco Pinto Balsemão, lacked Sá Carneiro's forcefulness and charisma. The party formed an electoral coalition, the Central Bloc, with the PS in 1983 and was in government until 1985 when the coalition ended. For two years, the PSD formed a minority government with its new leader, Aníbal Cavaco Silva, as prime minister. In the 1987 national elections, the PSD won the Second Republic's first absolute parliamentary majority, a feat the party repeated in the 1991 elections. By consistently favoring free-market policies, the PSD benefited from Portugal's improved economy after the country joined the EC in 1986 and the electorate returned to a more conservative position after the radical politics of the mid-1970s.

Party of the Social Democratic Center

The Party of the Social Democratic Center (Partido do Centro Democrático Social—CDS) is a Christian democratic party to the right of the political spectrum. Although not officially a religious party, the CDS is mainly linked to conservative Portuguese Catholicism and most of its officials and followers are Roman Catholic. Unlike some other Christian democratic parties, the conservative CDS does not advocate liberation theology (see Glossary). The party was founded in 1975 by Diogo Freitas do Amaral, a respected politician and a professor of administrative law.

The CDS won 15.9 percent of the vote in the 1976 elections and for a time formed a government with the PS. It increased its power when it formed an electoral coalition with the PSD in 1979 and was in power until the coalition ended in 1983. Since then the party has lost much of its electoral support, gaining only a little more than 4 percent of the vote in the 1987 and 1991 parliamentary elections. The strength of the PSD at the polls meant that the CDS was no longer needed to form center-right governments. A decline of the PSD seems the only opportunity for the CDS to return to power, either with the PSD or with the PS.

Far Right

As of the beginning of the 1990s, Portugal had not had a strong far-right party since the fall of the Salazar-Caetano regime. Most of those associated with the old regime were driven into exile during the revolution, and all far-right parties were declared illegal. Some of the prohibitions against right-wing political activities still remained law, although in the 1980s many of those associated with the former regime had returned to the country and a handful had reentered politics. Rather than establishing new right-wing parties, conservatives and supporters of the old regime were most likely to be active politically through the PSD or the CDS.

Popular Monarchist Party

The Popular Monarchist Party (Partido Popular Monárquico— PPM) favors the restoration of the Bragança royal family, overthrown in 1910. Their program is complicated, however, by the existence of several competing Bragança pretenders to the throne. The PPM stands for a constitutional and limited monarchy similar to the one in Spain. This would mean that the monarch is a ceremonial chief of state, not a ruling head of government. The PPM has argued that a monarchy would help unify the government, promote stability, and give the country a single, if mainly symbolic, head. In addition, the PPM campaigned for ecological concerns. Only once, in the 1987 elections for the EC, did the PPM win even 3 percent of the vote. Generally it won less than 1 percent. In the late 1970s and early 1980s, however, the PPM was

was part of the AD governing coalition, which consisted mainly of the CDS and the PSD.

Other Parties

Portugal has a number of other, largely personalistic parties that rally around a single leading personality rather than an issue or program. Most of these are small parties, frequently rising and falling quickly, and they command little electoral strength. These personalistic parties are often used as bargaining chips in the larger political arena, where their modest support might be traded for a cabinet post or other position. An exception to some of these rules is the Party of Democratic Renovation (Partido Renovador Democrático—PRD), made up of supporters of President Eanes. In the national elections of 1985, the PRD received 17.9 percent of the vote and seemed poised to emerge as a major electoral contender. In the national elections of 1987, however, it got just under 5 percent of the vote. After Eanes himself withdrew from politics, the party faded away, winning only 0.6 percent of the vote in the 1991 elections.

Interest Groups

Despite the flourishing of democracy since 1974, interest groups are not a significant force in Portugal. Portuguese politics are pluralist but to a lesser degree than in many other countries, especially when compared with the United States. Whereas the United States had over 50,000 interest groups functioning in Washington alone as of the early 1990s, the number functioning in Portugal was probably less than 100.

Armed Forces

The armed forces in Portugal trace their origins to the armies and military orders of medieval times. The orders were often autonomous from the state, and, because they were formed during the reconquest, may have predated it. Hence, the armed forces came to be thought of—and thought of themselves—as a separate unit in society, independent of any civil authority and perhaps above it. Even at the beginning of the 1990s, the military still had to some extent this sense of aloofness and of ideals of a higher order.

Up until the 1980s, the military had been the ultimate arbiter of Portuguese national politics. In the nineteenth century, the armed forces participated in chaotic, man-on-horseback politics. Military *cum* civilian factions "rotated" (*rotativismo*) in and out of power with frequent regularity. The armed forces helped usher in the

Portuguese Republic in 1910 and ended it in 1926. The military brought Salazar to power and served as an indispensable prop of his dictatorship.

It was the armed forces that overthrew Caetano in 1974, and the MFA that launched the revolution. The MFA took pains to retain special powers by creating the Council of the Revolution, which guaranteed the armed forces the power to prohibit legislation that they saw as harmful to the revolution's democratic achievements. The military agreed, however, that these powers were to be of limited duration.

During the 1980s, the political and social roles of the armed forces diminished. The 1982 constitutional amendments reduced the military's political power by abolishing the Council of the Revolution, thereby ending the military's guardianship over Portuguese politics. The National Defense Law of 1982 put the military completely under civilian control. In addition, the armed forces were significantly reduced in size and budget. On the other hand, Portuguese officers became better educated, more technologically sophisticated, and more professional.

By the beginning of the 1990s, the Portuguese armed forces had a social role similar to that of armed forces in other West European countries. Only extreme events could possibly pull Portugal's soldiers back into politics, although like any other interest group they did lobby to protect their interests, benefits, budget, and position in society.

Roman Catholic Church

Like the armed forces, the Roman Catholic Church in Portugal also declined in influence during the 1980s. The church, along with the military, had been one of *the* historical corporate units in society, predating the state and then existing parallel to it. As a result, Portugal was historically a Roman Catholic nation. Roman Catholicism not only was the sole religion of the country, but also permeated the culture, the legal system, the society, and the polity. Salazar derived many of his corporatist beliefs from the papal encyclicals, and during his long rule the church served as an indispensable pillar of the regime.

In recent decades, however, as society has become more secularized, the church has come to play a lesser role in people's lives. During the 1974–76 period, the church helped turn the population away from the appeals of communism and radicalism, but since those tumultuous years the church has been quiescent politically. The church has, however, expressed itself on some issues, such as the legalization of abortion, on which it feels morally obliged to take a public stance. Polls of Portuguese show that the church's ranking among main interest groups has fallen from second- or third-most influential to seventh- or eighth-most influential.

Economic Elites

The "oligarchy" was the third of the historical triumvirate of power in Portugal (armed forces, church, and oligarchy) to be in decline. Many of the old oligarchical families trace their origins to the Reconquest. They acquired their land, position, and titles, and eventually peasants and cattle, as the Reconquest drove the Moors farther south, opening up new territories for settlement.

This oligarchy, armed with titles of nobility granted it by the royal family in return for loyalty, dominated Portuguese politics for centuries. But over time, its character changed. In the south of Portugal, the Alentejo, the landowning class became increasingly absentee landlords, leaving managers in charge of its estates and moving to Lisbon. In the north, where smallholdings predominated, many members of the oligarchy became impoverished—or went into businesses like wine making. During the reign of Salazar, members of the elite went into banking, insurance, construction, and similar fields in which they could establish oligopolies and monopolies based on their close ties with the government.

After the Revolution of 1974, this economic elite was stripped of power. Its properties were confiscated, many from the elite were jailed or sent into exile, and the group lost all political power. In addition, members of the elite were barred from participating in politics or from forming political movements of their own because of laws forbidding far-right political activity.

As of the early 1990s, most of the exiles had been permitted to return to Portugal, and those who had spent time in jail were freed. Some of the elite managed to regain their power by taking advantage of the economy's need for financial expertise, but the elite as a whole did not regain its old financial position. Its political influence remained limited, as well, and only one member of the old Salazar regime had been elected to parliament.

Organized Labor

Portuguese trade unionism has a history of militancy and radicalism. Its roots go back to the late nineteenth century when modern industry first appeared. The unions grew during the period of the First Republic, 1910–26, when they enjoyed freedom to organize. It was in this period that Marxist, Bolshevik, Trotskyite, anarchist, and syndicalist ideas were discussed and disseminated. Although the labor movement was small, a reflection of the low level of Portuguese industrialization, it was active and vocal.

During the Salazar-Caetano era, militant unions were abolished, and the labor movement was forcibly subordinated to corporatist controls. Many labor leaders were jailed or sent into exile. Some cooperated with the new corporative system; others organized a militant, Communist-controlled underground labor organization. With time this union, Intersindical, was well enough established that the government actually dealt with it almost as if it were a legal bargaining agent.

During the Revolution of 1974, Intersindical, or as it came to be known in 1977, the General Confederation of Portuguese Workers-National Intersindical (Confederação Geral dos Trabalhadores Portugueses-Intersindical Nacional—CGTP-IN), was at last able to function as a legal labor organization, and it expanded rapidly. Controlled by the Communists, the CGTP-IN was closely associated with the PCP's bid for power and for a time was the only union permitted to function. Soon, however, it faced opposition from the Socialist labor organization, the General Union of Workers (União Geral dos Trabalhadores—UGT). For a time, the Communist labor group was overwhelmingly dominant, but during the 1980s the UGT grew in size, especially in the service sector, and by the end of the decade its overall membership was about half that of the CGTP-IN. Many other small unions were active at the beginning of the 1990s, most notably those representing highly specialized professions such as airline pilots. There was also a Christian democratic trade union movement.

After 1974 organized labor emerged as a powerful force in Portuguese politics, although its influence waned somewhat after the revolutionary period. Union membership was not high, and as of the early 1990s only about 30 percent of the work force was unionized. The Communist-led unions were not able to block the constitutional amendments of 1982 and 1989, which reduced the radical legacy of the revolution. Moreover, some unions backed away from the intense ideological unionism of the 1970s in favor of more limited and practical objectives.

Middle Class

Portugal had long been an essentially two-class society consisting of elites and peasants between which existed a small class of artisans, soldiers, and tradespeople. With the acceleration of industrialization and economic development after the 1950s, this middle class began to grow. As it came to prefer democracy and a more open West European society, it provided the strongest opposition to the Salazar-Caetano regime. As a result, the middle class participated strongly in the Revolution of 1974 and the political maneuvering that followed. In the following decade, after the old elites were shunted aside by the revolution and labor organizations lost power, the middle class emerged as Portugal's most important class.

At the beginning of the 1990s, the middle class constituted some 25 to 30 percent of the population. The most important Portuguese institutions were dominated by the middle class: the military officer corps, the Roman Catholic Church, political parties, public administration, the universities, and commerce and industry.

The middle class remained divided on many social and political issues, however. For example, political leadership in Portugal was solidly middle class and spanned all parties from the far left to the far right. The success of the PSD under Cavaco Silva both in parliament and in the election of 1987 was perhaps an indication, however, that Portugal's new socially significant middle class was developing a degree of social cohesion.

The commercial segment of the middle class defended its interests through the PSD and the CDS and also through some large representative organizations. The leading organizations of this type were the Portuguese Industrial Association (Associação Industrial Portuguesa—AIP), founded in 1860, the much larger Confederation of Portuguese Industry (Confederação da Indústria Portuguesa—CIP), founded in 1974, and the Portuguese Confederation of Commerce (Confederação do Comércio Português—CCP), founded in 1977. These organizations, and others like them, met with important labor groups and with government officials and lobbied behind the scenes to better the conditions under which Portugal's new middle class had to work.

Students and Intellectuals

Students and intellectuals in Portugal had long been influential out of proportion to their numbers. This influence was a consequence of higher education's exclusivity. The small percentage of the population who passed the difficult university entrance exams was widely respected, and Portugal's lower classes looked up to educated persons as their intellectual and political mentors.

Intellectuals and students were among the leading advocates of a republic in 1910. Although hostile to the republic, Salazar was also an intellectual and recruited so many of his fellow university colleagues into his administration that it was sometimes called a ''regime of professors.'' Much of the opposition to Salazar and Caetano, however, was made up of intellectuals and students who formed the "study groups" that served as the nuclei for what later became political parties. Intellectuals and students were very active in the Revolution of 1974, and, as of the beginning of the 1990s, many intellectuals served in high positions in government and the political parties.

Universities in Portugal were traditionally heavily politicized, especially during the revolutionary upheavals of the 1970s. Socialist, Communist, and other far-left groups competed for dominance on the campuses (mainly at the historical universities in Lisbon and Coimbra) and in publishing houses, newspapers, and study centers where intellectuals congregated.

Rising enrollment pressures, the competition of new regional universities and technical institutes, and the desire to find good jobs in the more affluent Portugal of the 1980s sapped the students' enthusiasm for political action. Many preferred to finish their courses and degrees and secure a rewarding professional position rather than to engage in constant political activity. As a result, Portugal's institutions of higher learning became calmer politically; they also became better, more serious universities.

Peasants

Peasants were long the neglected and forgotten people of Portuguese politics. Although the largest group numerically, they were the weakest politically. Nonparticipation was encouraged by Salazar's strategy of keeping the peasants illiterate and apathetic.

The peasants comprised a variety of groups. A basic distinction exists between the conservative peasants of the north who own their small plots of land and the peasants of the south who have no land, live under conditions of tenancy, and have been receptive to the appeals of radical political groups. The PCP, for example, had quietly organized southern peasants under its banner even during the Salazar era. During and after the Revolution of 1974, the south, especially the Alentejo, was a hotbed of land seizures, radical political action, and strong voting preferences for the PCP.

Since the revolution, however, both the PS and the PSD have made electoral inroads into what were PCP strongholds in the south. The rural areas were once again to some degree de-politicized, although the countryside would never return to the quiescence of decades past, despite the large numbers of farmers and agrarian laborers who migrated to urban areas or went abroad.

Political Events since 1987

The parliamentary election of July 1987 was a milestone in the consolidation of Portuguese democracy: for the first time in the

Second Republic, it gave a single party, the PSD, an absolute majority in the Assembly of the Republic and permitted the formation of a strong single-party government. The party's leader, Aníbal Cavaco Silva, ran an efficient campaign that stressed the PSD's competence and pragmatism and avoided the ideological arguments common to Portuguese politics. The party won a comfortable majority of 148 seats in the assembly when 50.2 percent of the voters, a stunning increase over the 29.9 percent who voted for it in the 1985 elections, decided Portugal needed to continue the PSD's program of reducing the government's role in the economy. Most of the PSD's increased share of the votes came from the virtual collapse of the PRD and the severe losses of the CDS. The PS improved significantly its performance compared to 1985, whereas the PCP continued its decline toward political marginality.

An improving economy contributed to the PSD victory, but also essential to its success was the party's leader since 1985, Aníbal Cavaco Silva. He captured the imagination of many Portuguese, who saw him as a welcome alternative to traditional Portuguese politicians. Cavaco Silva differed from Portugal's narrow governing elite in many respects. He was not from Lisbon but came from a lower-middle class southern family. He was not a lawyer but an economist who had earned his doctorate from the University of York in Britain and subsequently had taught economics in Lisbon. Although for a time minister of finance in the early 1980s, he did not favor political games and intrigues but publically disdained these aspects of party politics. Observers frequently characterized Cavaco Silva as somewhat aloof and arrogant, more interested in competence than connections. Through hard work and intelligence, he was able to thwart even powerful members of his own party who resisted reform and modernization. These qualities won Cavaco Silva the votes of many younger people and members of the middle class.

Supported by a majority in parliament, Cavaco Silva's government, in which he served as prime minister, aimed at a liberalization of the Portuguese economy. A principal goal was to further revise the constitution by removing much of its ideological language. The two-thirds majority this undertaking required was achieved with help from the PS. Another goal was a reform of the constitution's provisions relating to the dismissal of employees; these provisions were so strict that firings were very difficult. Some relaxation of labor law was achieved but not nearly that which had been envisaged. A general strike in early 1988 and a judgment from the Constitutional Court that the government's proposals were unconstitutional prevented radical reform in this area (see Wages and

*Mário Soares,
president,
1986–
Courtesy Embassy of
Portugal, Washington*

the Distribution of Income, Ch. 3). The Cavaco Silva government had much more success in privatizing land and businesses nationalized in 1975 (see Land Tenure and Agrarian Reform, ch, 3; Industrial Organization, ch. 3). By the end of 1991, many of the largest companies seized by the state had been returned in whole or in part to the private sector, and further privatizations were scheduled.

A presidential election was held in January 1991, at the end of Mário Soares's five-year term. Faced with only token opposition, Soares won reelection easily, taking 70 percent of the vote. Such was the expectation of his victory that the PSD did not even field a candidate. Despite his reputation as a highly partisan leader of the PS and the narrowness of his victory in 1986, Soares had quickly become a very popular president. In general, he and Cavaco Silva got along well with one another as they carried out the duties of their respective offices. Soares interfered only rarely in the working of the cabinet and legislature, and when confronted with difficult political issues he called upon the Constitutional Court for a decision. He instituted a practice of informal town meetings throughout Portugal where he learned of the concerns of the average citizen. An articulate speaker, he was later able to voice these concerns himself and plead publicly for the betterment of social conditions. Soares also represented his country ably abroad.

Parliamentary elections were held in October 1991 after the Cavaco Silva government had completed the four-year legislative term, the first government to do so in the Second Republic. Although the PSD was expected to win a majority, few expected it to better its results of 1987. It did so, however, by a tiny margin and once again achieved an absolute parliamentary majority. An economy that had performed better than the EC average, thanks in part to the billions of dollars the organization had transferred to Portugal since 1986, helped Cavaco Silva achieve his second triumph, but his own popularity also played a role. He conducted a highly effective campaign centered on his capabilities as prime minister. Assurances from Cavaco Silva that he would not serve in a PSD government that did not have a clear majority probably caused many voters to favor his party. As in 1987, the PSD did well in all parts of the country. It failed to come in first in only one district, compared to three in 1987, an indication that the old regional cleavages were disappearing as the country modernized and became more prosperous.

The PSD's main opponent in the 1991 election was the PS, which polled 29.3 percent of the vote, a significant improvement over the results of 1987 and 1985. The PS's success, despite a poorly run campaign and long-standing leadership problems since Soares had relinquished his role, indicated that Portugal was perhaps moving toward an essentially two-party system. Although the PS trailed the PSD badly in this election, it had won the local elections of 1989. The PS and the PSD seemed to be the only parties in Portugal able to increase their votes. They had also come to resemble one another so closely that their differences on main issues had become marginal.

The PRD, which had scored such a success in the 1985 elections, failed to win a single seat. The PCP received only 8.8 percent of the votes cast, a result that showed the party to be in a steady and steep decline. It remained tied to old orthodoxies, approving the reactionary coup in Moscow in August 1991, for example. The CDS won 4.4 percent of the votes for five seats in parliament. It did not seem likely to be politically significant in the future, except perhaps as a coalition partner with one of the two largest parties.

The Media

During the long Salazar regime, the media operated under strict authoritarian control. The press was heavily censored, radio and television were government-controlled, and writers who violated the regime's guidelines were subject to severe sanctions. Even the lists of books requested by readers from the National Library in Lisbon were reviewed by secret police officials. Foreign magazines were similarly inspected before being put on the newsstands; sometimes whole stories were blotted out. The controls and censorship were stifling and led to a pervasive and boring conformity in the media.

Under Caetano the rules were relaxed somewhat. Some novelists and essayists were able to publish critical and controversial works without punishment. The press occasionally spoke out indirectly, providing long analyses of elections in Chile or West Germany, for example, that everyone understood to be a commentary on the absence of free elections in Portugal. Only the weekly newspaper *Expresso* was strong enough to test the regime's tolerance with virtually every issue.

After the coup of April 25, 1974, the mass communications media underwent a radical transformation. One of the first acts of the revolutionary government was to abolish censorship. But as the revolution veered to the left, some portions of the media were seized by opponents of the views they expressed. Two of the most celebrated cases involved the closing of the Socialist Party newspaper *República* and the Roman Catholic Church's Rádio Renascença.

Government involvement in the media greatly increased when the banks were nationalized. Because most banks owned at least one newspaper, the state found itself the owner of many newspapers. With time, however, the government divested itself of these properties. By the beginning of the 1990s, no newspapers in Portugal were government owned, and the country had a completely free press. Although the state still operated radio and television broadcasting systems, the constitution states that they are to provide equal access to political parties, in or out of power. Large interest groups are also to have access to the state-owned electronic media.

At the beginning of the 1990s, about thirty newspapers were published daily in Portugal. They ranged from excellent newspapers like *Público*, an independent, and the historic *Diário de Notícias*, a newspaper of record, to sensationalistic crowd-pleasers such as *Correio da Manhã*. *Público*, founded in 1990, had sections dealing with both Lisbon and Porto and provided perhaps the most national news. Two excellent weekly newspapers filled the place taken in the United States by *Time* and *Newsweek*: *Expresso*, which had fought bravely for press freedom before the revolution, and *O Independente*, founded in 1988, which included pages enlivened by wicked satires of public figures. In addition to these publications, Portugal had a variety of specialized magazines.

In 1975 all commercial broadcasting facilities except those belonging to the Roman Catholic Church were nationalized. As of the beginning of the 1990s, however, hundreds of private radio stations were in operation, in addition to the large Roman Catholic radio system Rádio Renascença. The state broadcasting system was named Radiodifusão Portuguesa (RDP). Television service was furnished by the state system, Radiotelevisão Portuguesa (RTP), which broadcast on two channels. At the beginning of the 1990s, however, plans were being made to establish privately owned television in Portugal.

Portugal's film industry is very small. It produces mainly short films and documentaries for local television. Few full-length films are made in Portugal, and those that are have not found a market abroad. However, a few Portuguese directors, the veteran Manoel de Oliveira and Paolo Rocha, for example, are highly esteemed by film cognoscenti the world over.

Book publishing is more prosperous, within the limits of the local market. Portugal has more than fifty publishing houses. They publish books by Portuguese authors but also do a major business in translations of foreign authors. During the mid-1970s, works by Marx, Lenin, Rosa Luxemburg, and other writers on the left dominated the bestseller lists. In the period since then, Portuguese readers have turned to a greater diversity of authors. The country's relatively high illiteracy rate of about 15 percent and the fact that most Portuguese read little make for a small market. As a result, books are expensive, and printings of even bestselling books are usually limited to 2,000 to 3,000 copies.

Foreign Relations

The Revolution of 1974 did not merely transform Portugal's domestic politics; it led to a transformation of its foreign relations, as well. For centuries Portugal's foreign relations were directed away from Europe, first down the South Atlantic and to Africa, then to Brazil and the Orient. Lisbon's relations with Europe were limited to an alliance dating from 1386 with Britain, another Atlantic country, that was intended to protect it from Spain and any other European power that might threaten Portugal's independence and its vast empire. Over the centuries, much of this empire was lost. Preserving what remained of this empire, the country's African colonies and a few other small entities, became the core of Portuguese foreign policy in the nineteenth and twentieth centuries. Moreover, the Portuguese saw themselves as a people with an "Atlantic vocation" rather than as an integral part of Europe.

Postwar developments for a time buttressed the traditional attitude that Portugal's true concerns and interests lay in the South Atlantic and beyond and away from Europe. Portugal became a founding member of the North Atlantic Treaty Organization

(NATO) not for what its army could do in Central Europe but for the importance of the Azores as a site for military bases. Other than permitting the United States access to these islands, Portugal's contribution to the alliance was negligible.

The wave of anticolonialism that swept through the Third World after World War II sparked rebellion in Portugal's African colonies. Lisbon's great efforts to quell these struggles for independence intensified the metropole's traditional interest in Africa. In the end, however, Portugal was not strong enough to put down the wars of independence. In fact, the great expenditure of manpower and revenue in the African wars was the main cause of the Revolution of 1974. The revolution brought to power members of the military who were determined to end the fighting, and within a matter of eighteen months Portugal's empire was gone.

Shorn of its colonies, Portugal was forced to concede that its future lay in Europe, a revolutionary change in the country's view of its place in the world. It became a member of the EC in 1986 and enjoyed the benefits and endured the change that this membership entailed. Portugal's most important foreign relationship, its relationship with the United States, changed only in degree, not in kind. In other respects, however, Portugal began a whole new era in its foreign policy.

Africa

During the 1960s and early 1970s, Portugal waged three colonial wars simultaneously on the African continent (see The Role of the Armed Forces in Africa, ch. 5). These campaigns hurt the economy, drained morale, and gradually became politically unpopular. The end of the wars in Africa brought independence to the colonies almost immediately. The manner in which independence was granted, however, and the results that were produced proved to be highly controversial.

In his unsettling book, *Portugal and the Future,* General António de Spínola had proposed stopping the wars, finding a peaceful resolution, and granting independence to the colonies. But he wanted to maintain good relations with the colonies and to link them with Portugal and possibly Brazil through a Portuguese-speaking Lusitanian confederation of nations that would resemble the British Commonwealth. This proposal was rejected by the radical and more impatient members of the Armed Forces Movement (Movimento das Forças Armadas—MFA).

In Guinea-Bissau, after brief negotiations and a cease-fire, Portugal granted independence to its former colony and turned power over to the Marxist African Party for the Independence of Guinea and Cape Verde (Partido Africano pela Independência de Guiné e Cabo Verde—PAIGC). Cape Verde also became independent but did not become part of Guinea-Bissau. In the much larger territory of Mozambique, Portugal turned over the reins of government to the Front for the Liberation of Mozambique (Frente de Libertação de Moçambique—FRELIMO), another Marxist-Leninist guerrilla group. And in Angola, Portugal's most valuable African colony, power was given to the similarly Marxist-Leninist Popular Movement for the Liberation of Angola (Movimento Popular de Libertação de Angola—MPLA) which, among the three factions fighting for independence, was the only one allied with the Soviet Union. The smaller colony of São Tomé and Príncipe also became independent.

The haste with which independence was granted and the simple turning of power over to the very Marxist-Leninist elements Portugal had been fighting, without any further guarantees, had a number of serious consequences. Hundreds of thousands of Portuguese settlers were stranded, many of whom had lived in the colonies for generations. They lost their homes, land, and positions. Most of them returned to Portugal, where many lived in squalid conditions and added to the country's unemployment problems. Their departure left the African colonies without the teachers, educators, managers, and other trained personnel needed to make a successful transition to independence. Plagued by continuing civil wars and violence, political conditions and living standards in the newly independent states deteriorated.

Portugal's relations with these former colonies long remained strained, for they felt they had been abandoned by the mother country. With time, however, relations improved, trade resumed, Portuguese educators and technicians were welcomed back, and new ties among the Portuguese-speaking nations began to be forged. Portugal served as a useful intermediary in arranging agreements to reduce conflicts in Angola and Mozambique. In 1984, for example, Portugal sponsored the Nkomati Accords between Mozambique and South Africa by which the two latter countries agreed to stop supporting guerrilla groups in each other's territory. The three countries later agreed to manage the giant Cahora Bassa hydroelectric power plant for the benefit of all. Although Portugal will no longer play a large role in Africa, its special relationship with the continent's Lusophone (Portuguese-speaking) countries make it likely that it will play a role of some importance.

Western Europe

At the beginning of the 1990s, Portugal's relations with Western

214

Europe were closer than ever before. Historically, Portugal had remained aloof from Europe, its main link to the continent being a long-standing alliance with Britain. In 1949 Portugal became a founding member of NATO, in 1955 it joined the United Nations (UN), in 1960 it became a part of the European Free Trade Association (EFTA), and the following year joined the Organisation for Economic Co-operation and Development (OECD—see Glossary). Portugal signed a free-trade agreement with the European Economic Community (EEC—see Glossary) in 1972 and gained admittance to the Council of Europe (see Glossary) in 1976. In 1988 Portugal became a member of the Western European Union (WEU—see Glossary).

Portugal's application to the EC in 1977 marked a major change in its relationship with Europe. After years of negotiations, it was granted admission on January 1, 1986. Becoming part of the EC affected not only the country's economy but also government and society (see Foreign Economic Relations, ch. 3). As the poorest member of the EC, Portugal would receive large grants from the EC bodies to bring the country's infrastructure, living conditions, and education up to the level of the community's other members. The formation of the EC's single market in 1993 would be another step toward Portugal's integration into Europe.

As a result of these and many other international ties, traditional issues of whether Portugal would be First, Second, or Third World, socialist or capitalist, European or South Atlanticist were no longer issues at the beginning of the 1990s. Portugal had become part of the community of Western, European, democratic states. Nevertheless, Portuguese worry at times whether their country's identity may be lost in this larger community and whether its industry and commerce will be able to compete in the large tariff-free single market. Although it has prospered since it joined the EC in 1986, the real economic challenges will come in the 1990s.

EC membership has meant that Portugal has close voluntary relations with Spain for the first time in its history. Until then Portugal had maintained a wary distance from its large neighbor, although once, against its will, it had actually been a part of Spain for sixty years (1580–1640). For the most part, however, Portugal has looked to its alliance with Britain for support in remaining independent. Although the Portuguese no longer believe that Spain poses a military threat, they are concerned that the stronger Spanish economy could gradually absorb them.

After the revolution, relations between the two countries were tense at times. As a means of tempering disputes, a treaty of 1977 set up a Luso-Iberian Council to promote cooperation. In addition, the countries' prime ministers have held occasional summit meetings since 1983. The most serious disagreements have centered on the access of Spain's modern fishing fleet to Portuguese waters. Spain won on this issue but made some economic concessions to Portugal in return.

Some of the tensions between Portugal and Spain during the 1980s had a military origin, however. When Spain joined NATO in 1982, the Portuguese feared that an Iberian Command would be created with the result that Portuguese forces would come under the control of Madrid. Portuguese objections to this proposal ended when Spain was included under the Supreme Allied Commander Europe (SACEUR). Portugal kept its long-standing role under NATO's Supreme Allied Commander Atlantic (SACLANT) (see Portugal and NATO, ch. 5).

Portuguese ties with Britain, also an Atlantic power, date from the signing in 1386 of the Treaty of Windsor, the longest-lasting alliance in the Western world. The two countries had long secured mutual benefits from this treaty. Portugal sought British protection against Spain and later France; Britain saw Portugal as its point of access on the European continent when other avenues were closed. This was the case at times during the Napoleonic period and during World War II when Britain was allowed to use the Azores for military purposes. Also binding the countries together was substantial British investment over the centuries, most notably in Portugal's wine and port industries.

Portugal traditionally has maintained good relations with France, mainly to balance Spain's power. Portugal also has strong feelings of affinity with France, and French intellectual trends have had a steady following in Lisbon. French influence is seen in the Portuguese legal system and administrative system. Until recently, when it was displaced by English, French was the second language of educated Portuguese. Many working-class Portuguese also have links with France. During the 1950s and 1960s, some three-quarters of a million Portuguese emigrated to that country in search of work.

United States

The United States and Portugal traditionally have considered each other friends and allies. These sentiments were reinforced by the large number of Portuguese immigrants to the United States and the growing economic and political importance of this Portuguese community. Since 1943, when the United States built the Lajes Air Base on Terceira Island in the Azores, American interests in Portugal have been mainly strategic and military. In return for the use of this vitally important base, the United States gave military aid to Portugal. Portugal also benefited from the European Recovery Program (ERP), more commonly known as the Marshall Plan. During the 1960s and early 1970s, however, relations between the two countries were sometimes strained because the United States took an anticolonial stand with regard to Portuguese Africa.

United States officials were not worried initially by the Revolution of 1974. They assumed that General Spínola, a military man and a conservative, would maintain control. As the revolution moved sharply to the left, however, and it appeared possible the PCP might come to power, United States officials became uneasy. Frank Carlucci, the United States ambassador in Lisbon, directed a campaign to aid democratic groups. The United States and its NATO allies provided assistance to the Socialists and Socialist trade unions because they were viewed as the best alternative to a Communist takeover. The United States also sought to rally the moderate elements within the military and in Portugal generally. The campaign paid off as Portugal remained democratic.

United States assistance, presence, and involvement remained high during the late 1970s. But as Portuguese politics came to resemble those of other West European nations during the 1980s, United States assistance declined. In 1983 the base agreement was renegotiated, but Portuguese officials were subsequently disappointed by a reduction in American military aid. As part of the base agreement, the Luso-American Development Foundation was created to promote economic and cultural ties between the two countries. The next base negotiations, scheduled for the early 1990s, are certain to be onerous as the two countries each seek to realize their respective aims. The United States will continue to have a keen interest in the Lajes Air Base, the only such base available, while Portugal, less dependent on the United States as it becomes integrated into Europe, will have a strong hand at the negotiating table (see Bilateral Military Relations with Other Countries, Ch. 5).

Other Countries and Areas

At the beginning of the 1990s, Portugal still retained a special interest in its former colony Brazil, although the Portuguese continued to occasionally look down on Brazilians as ''people from the tropics,'' just as Brazilians had their own jokes about the Portuguese. Relations between the two countries were shaped by Brazil's much greater size and more powerful economy. For this reason, Brazilian investment in Portugal in the 1970s and 1980s was considerably greater than Portuguese investment in Brazil.

Brazilian *telenovelas* (soap operas) also dominated Portuguese television, leading to additional resentments. In general, however, relations between the two countries are good, although as of the early 1990s, any "special" relationship was now largely historical, cultural, and nostalgic, rather than a reflection of concrete interests.

Portugal also seeks to maintain good relations with North African and Middle Eastern countries, in part because of geography and in part because Portugal depends entirely on imported oil. Its "tilt" toward the Islamic countries sometimes produced strains in United States-Portuguese relations, particularly when the Middle East was in turmoil and the United States wished to use its bases in the Azores in pursuit of its own Middle Eastern policies.

East Timor, Portugal's former colony on the eastern half of the island of Timor in Indonesia, remained a concern for Lisbon in the early 1990s. Portuguese settlers first came to the island in 1520, but it was not until the second half of the nineteenth century that Portugal had control of the territory. In 1975 war broke out between rival groups striving for independence from Portugal. Late in the year, Indonesian troops invaded to stop the fighting, and in 1976 East Timor was declared part of Indonesia. As of the early 1990s, continuing resistance on the part of Timorese guerrillas against Indonesian rule had claimed the lives of as many as 100,000 people.

As of the early 1990s, the UN continued to regard Portugal as the administering authority in East Timor. Portuguese officials, for their part, believed that their country had a moral obligation to remain involved in the affairs of its former colony. Through a variety of diplomatic moves, Lisbon attempted to move the Indonesian government to arrange a settlement that could bring peace and even independence to East Timor. Indonesia refused to loosen its hold on the territory because it feared such an action might embolden other areas restive under its control, such as West Irian, to seek independence.

* * *

During the Salazar era, the authoritarian nature of the regime made it difficult to carry out serious, scholarly research; in the immediate aftermath of the Revolution of 1974, some of the research was partisan and ideological. More recently, a wealth of scholarship has begun to emerge.

The Salazar era is covered in António de Figueiredo's *Portugal: Fifty Years of Dictatorship;* Hugh Kay's *Salazar and Modern Portugal;*

and Howard J. Wiarda's *Corporatism and Development.* Richard Alan Hodgson Robinson's *Contemporary Portugal* and Tom Gallagher's *Portugal: A Twentieth Century Interpretation* are thoughtful and analytical introductions to Portuguese affairs. Especially valuable are the edited volume by Lawrence S. Graham and Harry M. Makler, *Contemporary Portugal,* and that by Graham and Douglas L. Wheeler, *In Search of Modern Portugal,* incorporating papers from the meetings of the Conference Group on Modern Portugal.

The revolutionary period of the mid-1970s is covered well in Kenneth Maxwell's articles in *Foreign Affairs* and the *New York Review of Books,* and in Douglas Porch's *The Portuguese Armed Forces and the Revolution.* A more specialized account is Nancy Bermeo's *The Revolution Within the Revolution.*

Albert P. Blaustein and Gisbert H. Flanz's *Constitution of the Countries of the World* provides a text and commentary on the constitutional changes of the post-Salazar period. Good treatments of political events and of the main forces involved are in Thomas C. Bruneau's *Politics and Nationhood,* Bruneau and Alex Macleod's *Politics in Contemporary Portugal,* Walter C. Opello's *Portugal's Political Development,* and *Portugal in the 1980s,* edited by Kenneth Maxwell. A skeptical view of Portuguese developments is provided in Howard J. Wiarda's *The Transition to Democracy in Spain and Portugal;* a more hopeful perspective by the same author is *Politics in Iberia.* (For further information and complete citations, see Bibliography.)

Chapter 5. National Security

Afonso Henriques, patron of the Portuguese Armed Forces, at the Battle of Ourique in 1139

IN THE SEVENTEEN YEARS following the Revolution of 1974 that restored democratic rule to Portugal, the armed forces underwent striking changes. The counterinsurgency warfare of 1961–74 in Angola, Mozambique, and Portuguese Guinea (present-day Guinea-Bissau) brought an expansion of the personnel strength of the armed forces to 250,000. By early 1992, however, military forces were down to about 61,000. The army, reduced to scarcely 20 percent of its peak strength, suffered by far the greatest cut.

The drastic contraction of the armed forces was accompanied by a redefinition of the nation's security policies. Until 1974, the resources of all three services were dedicated to suppressing the independence movements of the African territories. Although Portugal was one of the original members of the North Atlantic Treaty Organization (NATO), its principal contribution was in the form of strategic facilities, notably the United States base in the Azores (Açores), which was viewed as indispensable for reinforcing the alliance in the event of conflict with the Soviet and Warsaw Pact forces. Portugal did maintain two army divisions at home, one committed to NATO and the other to the defense of the Iberian Peninsula under the terms of a long-standing treaty with Spain, the Iberian Pact (also known as Treaty of Friendship and Nonaggression). Both divisions were staffed far below their authorized strengths.

After the restoration of elective government in 1976, Portugal adopted a more active role with respect to NATO. Determined to offer more than basing facilities, it committed itself to maintain a modern army unit, the First Composite Brigade, for potential deployment in northeastern Italy under NATO command. A Special Forces Brigade and a number of thinly staffed and under-equipped infantry and artillery regiments were responsible for the defense of continental Portugal and the Azores and Madeira archipelagoes. The navy and air force were reorganized to emphasize defense against potential maritime threat in the waters within the Portugal-Madeira-Azores triangle (also known as the strategic triangle).

The equipment of the three services was, however, approaching obsolescence, and they were ill-prepared to handle the new defense obligations. Portugal depended on assistance from the United States and other NATO allies for its major weaponry, but the rate of delivery fell short of essential requirements. Nonetheless, the United States had supplied maritime reconnaissance aircraft and had agreed to furnish F–16 interceptor aircraft, air defense missile systems, and a variety of helicopters, including combat helicopters needed by the First Composite Brigade. Germany had provided three new frigates, giving the Portuguese Navy a limited but up-to-date antisubmarine capability.

The military-led revolution of April 1974 dismantled the repressive system established by António de Oliveira Salazar and maintained by his successor, Marcello José das Neves Caetano. For two years after the 1974 coup, the armed forces were the dominant element in the political system, although the military leadership itself was torn into bitterly competing factions. Under the constitution of 1976, a politico-military body—the Council of the Revolution—retained review powers over the actions of the civilian government. This transition stage ended in 1982 when the constitution was amended to subordinate the military to the elective political forces. The National Defense Law, passed in the same year, limited the mission of the armed forces to defense of the country against external threat, contrary to the traditional view of senior officers that the armed forces were also responsible for safeguarding the nation's internal security and the stability of its institutions. Although the military remained involved in defense policy matters, its weight in civilian political affairs had declined with the reduction in the size of the armed forces and the shrinking military threat in Europe.

Historical Background

The military has played a major role in the development of Portugal throughout the country's history. During the Middle Ages, the armed forces drove the Moors out of the country and resisted Spanish attempts to end Portugal's newly won independence. During the Renaissance, Portuguese navigators and explorers established settlements and trade routes around the world, and the armed forces played an important role in establishing and maintaining the greatest empire then known (see Maritime Expansion, ch. 1).

The glories of conquest and riches of trade were short-lived. A military disaster took place when King Sebastião led his poorly prepared army to defeat against the Moors in Morocco in 1578. Portugal was left leaderless without a legitimate heir, and the country soon came under the rule of Philip II of Spain, who had a valid claim to the throne. Although Spain did not actually occupy Portugal, it involved Portugal in its numerous dynastic and religious wars. As a result, Portugal lost most of its navy when it joined the Spanish Armada against Portugal's former ally, England. Portugal also lost much of its empire in the Far East to the Dutch (see Imperial Decline, ch. 1).

After Portugal threw off Spanish domination in 1640, it created a permanent army of 4,000 cavalrymen and 20,000 infantrymen, based on a conscription system covering all able-bodied men. Portugal renewed its alliance with England and was subsequently drawn into many European wars in the seventeenth and eighteenth centuries. Portugal was occupied by Napoleon's troops in 1807. British forces came to Portugal's aid, driving the French out of the country and then, using Portugal as a base of operations, out of Spain in 1813. During the middle and late nineteenth century, the army was instrumental in the exploration and effective occupation of Angola and Mozambique.

A military revolt ended the Portuguese monarchy in 1910. Portugal attempted to maintain neutrality during World War I but was drawn into the conflict both in Europe and in Africa and fought on the side of the Allies. After Germany declared war on Portugal in March 1916, some 200,000 men were conscripted. An expeditionary force of two divisions saw service in France, sustaining heavy casualties at the Battle of Lys in April 1918. Other troops clashed with the German East African colonial army in Mozambique.

The First Republic (1910–26) had a precarious existence marked by a rapid turnover of governments, coup attempts, and plots. Eventually, in 1926, the mounting social disorder and discontent over the civilian governments' interference in military matters precipitated an unopposed military takeover. Disagreement among the military factions over the goals of their intervention brought only further instability. By 1928, however, a new military-civilian cabinet was in place under a nonpartisan president, General Óscar Fragoso Carmona. The civilian minister of finance, António de Oliveira Salazar, became the most powerful figure in the government. In 1932, Salazar was appointed prime minister, bringing the military dictatorship to an end.

The Military in the Salazar Era

The new prime minister was able to counteract anti-Salazar sentiment in the military by publicly flattering the armed forces and by exempting them at first from ruthless cuts in government spending. Although the backward state of the army's weaponry had by 1935 become acute, Salazar refused to address the need for modernization until the army reduced its overstaffing. In 1936, he appointed himself minister of war and in the following year introduced a major reorganization, including the pensioning of many senior officers to clear the way for younger, more dynamic officers. Officer pay remained low; marriages had to be approved, and officers were pressured to choose wives from the wealthier classes so they would have an alternative source of income. The effect was to perpetuate familial links between the higher military and the economic elites.

Salazar also formed several paramilitary organizations to offset the army's monopoly of armed strength. The most notable of these was the Portuguese Legion. Its members were the most loyal partisans of Salazar's regime, the New State (Estado Novo). At its peak, the legion had 20,000 personnel trained and commanded by active or retired army officers. It was subject to military control when called upon to cooperate with the regular armed forces. Although not formally abolished until 1974, it was never more than a militia at the service of the regime and presented no threat to the power of the orthodox military establishment.

Fearing that the success of the Spanish republican forces during the Spanish Civil War would lead to communist domination of the Iberian Peninsula, Salazar gave material and diplomatic aid to Francisco Franco's nationalist forces while maintaining a formal neutrality. A special volunteer force of 18,000 led by regular army officers was recruited to fight as part of Franco's army. When the civil war ended in 1939, Portugal and Spain negotiated the Treaty of Friendship and Nonaggression (Iberian Pact). The pact committed the two countries to defend the Iberian Peninsula against any power that attacked either country and helped to ensure Iberian neutrality during World War II.

The Azores were considered to be of prime strategic importance in the war. The Allies feared a possible German move to occupy the islands and needed their naval and air bases to combat Nazi submarine attacks against Allied shipping and to support transatlantic air links. In 1943, mindful of German defeats and Portugal's treaties with Britain, Salazar acceded to Britain's request for facilities in the Azores. Later, the United States was also permitted to establish bases in the islands. Portugal recognized the American need for transit facilities to support its continued military presence in Western Europe after the war, and it authorized continued use of the Lajes Air Base in the Azores until the arrangement was formalized in the bilateral Defense Agreement of 1951 (see Bilateral Military Relations with Other Countries, this ch.).

Portugal became one of the twelve charter members of NATO in 1949. Although the organization's collective security provisions did not apply to Portugal's overseas possessions, membership in NATO enabled the armed forces to acquire sophisticated weaponry and training from the United States and other NATO member countries. However, Portugal's colonial policies after fighting began in Africa in 1961 formed an obstacle to its full participation in the NATO system.

The Role of the Armed Forces in Africa

The Portuguese presence in Africa dates from the sixteenth century when fuel and water stations were established for ships enroute to the spice market of Goa. Portugal neglected these outposts for a time after the pepper trade declined. British and German colonial ambitions after 1885, however, led the Portuguese to undertake a series of military campaigns to control the interior of Angola, Mozambique, and Portuguese Guinea. The effort to subdue the African colonies was a slow process that was not completed until 1915. The costly campaigns were pursued by the Lisbon authorities to maintain prestige and to keep the oversized military establishment gainfully occupied.

Salazar strongly rejected pressures from the European powers to decolonize after World War II. He was grimly determined to maintain Portugal's overseas empire. Salazar's successor in 1968, Marcello Caetano, continued the struggle against the African independence movements in spite of its drain on resources and manpower.

Angola

The first uprising against Portuguese rule in Africa occurred in Angola in March 1961, when primitively armed Bakongo tribal nationalists in the extreme north of the province attacked several coffee plantations, massacring white Portuguese owners and their families, as well as black African workers who refused to cooperate. Bloody retribution followed at the hands of local whites and blacks who had suffered at the hands of the insurgents. The revenge killings abated only in May 1961, when 10,000 troops arrived to reinforce the 6,000 white soldiers and a similar number of locally conscripted Africans already in Angola. Under the leadership of Holden Roberto, the insurgents found sanctuary across Angola's northern and northeastern borders in the Democratic Republic of the Congo (present-day Zaire). Roberto's group eventually became the National Front for the Liberation of Angola (Frente Nacional de Libertação de Angola—FNLA), one of the three major anti-Portuguese guerrilla forces. Portuguese units, relying heavily on aerial bombardment and strafing attacks, managed to stabilize the military situation in the north. They brought large segments of the population into *aldeamentos* (controlled villages), similar to the strategic hamlets used during the Vietnam conflict.

227

The intermittent warfare dragged on into the mid-1960s, and as many as 70,000 troops (40,000 of them European) were involved in the Angolan conflict. By 1966, two rival insurgent groups gradually superseded the FNLA. One was the Popular Movement for the Liberation of Angola (Movimento Popular de Libertação de Angola—MPLA), a communist-oriented group supported militarily by the Soviet Union and other communist countries. The other was the National Union for the Total Independence of Angola (União Nacional para a Independência Total de Angola—UNITA), based among the Ovimbundu in the south.

From the mid-1960s until the April 1974 coup, Portuguese government forces were generally in control. Insurgency continued, however, as long as the guerrilla movements could obtain sanctuary in neighboring states. The long years of conflict increasingly damaged the morale of both the military and a large segment of the Portuguese people. A few months after the revolutionary government came to power in Lisbon in 1974, it began negotiations with the Angolan factions. Full independence was granted on November 11, 1975. Portugal officially announced its losses in Angola as 1,526 killed in action and 1,465 noncombat deaths. Other sources estimated a much higher mortality figure.

Portuguese Guinea

In Portuguese Guinea (present-day Guinea-Bissau), the struggle against Portuguese rule began officially in January 1963, although there had been earlier acts of sabotage by members of the African Party for the Independence of Guinea and Cape Verde (Partido Africano pela Independência de Guiné e Cabo Verde—PAIGC). PAIGC was a Marxist movement guided by the Maoist concept of achieving revolution through the rural peasantry. By 1968 PAIGC claimed control of nearly 70 percent of the territory and half the population of the province, the Portuguese being confined largely to the towns and major villages of the coastal area. Under a vigorous new governor, General António de Spínola, regular forces numbering 33,000 (about half Africans) were supplemented by local armed militia based in strategic villages. PAIGC nevertheless kept up its pressure by guerrilla raids mounted from neighboring Senegal and the Republic of Guinea. The military situation was already deteriorating in 1973 when Soviet surface-to-air missiles (SAMs) were introduced and a number of Portuguese planes were shot down. Portuguese pilots became reluctant to fly, and as a result Portugal had to curtail the air attacks that had been highly effective against guerrilla operations.

After Spínola returned to Lisbon in 1973, military morale eroded because the soldiers felt that they were fighting an unwinnable war in a territory of little value. A few months later, the revolutionary government that had recently come to power in Portugal began negotiations for withdrawing Portuguese troops from the province. Portugal recognized Guinea-Bissau as an independent state in September 1974. Portuguese losses in Portuguese Guinea were reported to be 1,656 killed in action and 696 noncombat deaths.

Mozambique

The insurgency in Mozambique began in the extreme northern areas of the province in 1964 and was led by guerrilla forces of the Front for the Liberation of Mozambique (Frente de Libertação de Moçambique—FRELIMO). FRELIMO was well armed by various communist countries, and its fighters were trained by the Chinese. At the time of the outbreak of hostilities, Portugal had about 16,000 troops in the province, all deployed in the north where the FRELIMO attacks were concentrated. For several years, Portuguese forces were able to prevent the guerrillas from moving southward. They could not end the warfare, however, because the guerrillas had a sanctuary to which they could retreat and a constant source of arms. Eventually the guerrillas were able to skirt the Portuguese strength in the north and mount incursions into the relatively unprotected center.

Of the 60,000 government troops ultimately involved in Mozambique, 35,000 were black Africans, 10,000 were white Africans, and the remaining 15,000 were from Portugal. This relatively large force faced approximately 8,000 insurgents. Despite this numerical superiority, the Portuguese government was unable to counter the guerrillas' tactics, which included ambushes, selective terrorism, and severing road and rail links. By September 1975, when the former province became independent as the People's Republic of Mozambique, Portuguese losses were officially reported as 1,606 killed in action and 724 noncombat deaths.

Role of the Military in Portuguese Political Life

Throughout the nineteenth century, the Portuguese military played a prominent role in national life. Although the army was itself divided ideologically, it often acted as a liberal influence among the political groupings striving for power. During the events leading up to the revolution of 1910, the military remained on the sidelines, lending strong backing neither to the monarchy nor to the republican politicians. When the revolt broke out, loyalist units were of little help to the monarchy because of the republican sympathies of junior officers and sergeants.

During the highly unstable First Republic (1910–26), military power seekers frequently dominated the political scene. The army itself became severely factionalized as a result of its involvement in domestic political disputes. The junior officers who carried out the coup of May 28, 1926, were united in little more than their disdain for the civilian politicians. Their actions were also inspired by the government's failure to deal with their grievances over pay, equipment, discipline, and professional status. Political turmoil continued unabated; a countercoup in 1927 was put down with much bloodshed and harsh punishment of the troops involved. Salazar, then a civilian university professor, was appointed minister of finance by the military government and given sweeping powers to curb loose spending policies.

Although military dissent surfaced several times after Salazar's elevation to prime minister in 1932, he was able to keep rebellious officers under control without depriving the many officers with liberal convictions of their careers. Nevertheless, political reliability rather than professional competence was likely to determine the rate of promotion. Disillusioned senior officers entered hopeless presidential contests against the official candidates, who were also high military figures. In 1958, a previously solid supporter of the regime, General Humberto Delgado, defied Salazar by running against the official candidate, Admiral Américo Tomás. Delgado was easily defeated, but he received a quarter of the vote, considered a credible showing. In 1961 Salazar's unyielding colonial policy touched off a major conspiracy in the senior ranks of the military. Salazar succeeded, however, in rallying the army and paramilitary forces loyal to him to bring about a rapid collapse of the coup attempt. Dissent within the military did not vanish, however, and the regime remained wary. In 1965, for example, it felt sufficiently threatened by the presence of Delgado in neighboring Spain that its intelligence agents assassinated him.

The Military Takeover of 1974

As the inconclusive colonial wars of the 1960s and early 1970s dragged on, support for them turned to indifference at home. Separated from home and family during repeated twenty-four-month tours of duty, military professionals felt increasingly estranged and demoralized. White officers, especially those commanding black troops, were often hostile to the white settlers over their treatment of blacks and in many cases were sympathetic to black aspirations for freedom. The mounting antiwar sentiment in Portugal was reflected in a growing rate of desertion and failures of conscripts to report for duty. Evasion of combat by unenthusiastic conscripts and university graduates commissioned as junior officers (*milicianos*) became increasingly common. Many of the *milicianos* formed a radical element that agitated against Portugal's involvement in overseas wars.

Traditionally, the officer corps had been the preserve of younger sons of wealthy families and sons of officers who could afford the tuition charged by the Military Academy. Military careers were sought by wealthy candidates more for prestige than reward because pay was relatively poor compared with that of other professions. The low salaries of senior officers, however, were often augmented by remunerative sinecures as corporation board members. Extended periods of leave to work in the private sector were not unusual.

In 1958 the Military Academy, failing to attract sufficient numbers of cadets needed for the army, ended its tuition requirements, and henceforth the student body was dominated by sons of shopkeepers, smallholders, and lower-level provincial bureaucrats who could not have afforded a university education earlier. This new class of cadets expected that after graduation they would enter the peaceful garrison life at home or in the colonies that the Portuguese army had known for generations. Instead, they were thrown directly into the colonial wars and eventually became the disgruntled captains who instigated the revolution.

A number of events in the 1960s and 1970s helped to coalesce revolutionary sentiment in the military. One such event was the loss of Portuguese Goa. In 1961 the Portuguese enclave of Goa on the coast of India was threatened by an Indian invasion force of some 30,000. The 3,000 Portuguese troops in Goa were badly equipped and unprepared to put up more than token resistance. In spite of Salazar's insistence that the colony should be defended, it was quickly overrun. Salazar punished the army for its failure to make a stand by ordering a number of dismissals and other penalties. The army, in turn, blamed the Goan debacle on Salazar and resented the punishments that they felt humiliated the entire officer corps.

Further undermining the loyalty of career officers was Decree Law 353-73, issued by the government of Prime Minister Marcello Caetano. The decree law stated that nonregular officers, in most cases *milicianos* commissioned after a short army course, would be permitted to convert to a regular commission at their conscript rank and to receive the same consideration for promotion as those who had graduated from the Military Academy. Career officers felt that the decree undermined their status in the army, as well as in society.

231

The growing dissatisfaction, based largely among junior career officers, led to the formation in 1973 of the Captains' Movement. This ad hoc committee of career officers—mostly captains—initially banded together to give voice to their professional grievances. In a short time, the captains found that their grievances were shared by career officers of the navy and the air force, as well as noncareer officers of all services. The Captains' Movement became the Armed Forces Movement (Movimento das Forças Armadas—MFA) and emerged in November 1973 as a full-blown dissident group whose clandestine membership ranged across the political spectrum. In addition to the question of professional status, officers were discontented over their low pay and long postings abroad under harsh conditions. They were also disturbed over the lack of modern equipment to match the arms furnished to the African insurgents by the Soviet Union, the East European countries, and China. The United States and several other NATO countries had imposed an embargo on the shipment of arms to Portugal that might be employed against the African liberation movements.

Dissatisfaction among senior officers with the government's conduct of the colonial wars was centered in two groups. The right wing was associated with General Kaúlza de Arriaga, the former commander in chief in Mozambique, who conspired to seize power to enforce a military solution to the wars in Africa. More moderate officers, such as Chief of Staff General Francisco de Costa Gomes and General Spínola, who had been named deputy chief of staff, favored negotiation with the liberation movements. Spínola's influential book, *Portugal and the Future,* advocating a loose confederation with the African colonies because military victory was impossible, hardened the resolve of the increasingly radical MFA plotters.

In March 1974, when Spínola and Costa Gomes failed to appear at a public ceremony in which they were to endorse existing policy in Africa, Caetano fired both of them. A premature coup attempt followed Spínola's dismissal, but loyal troops turned back a column marching on Lisbon. No shots were fired, but many officers were arrested or transferred. Five weeks later, on April 25, 1974, the main group of MFA conspirators deposed the Caetano government without resistance by the loyalist forces. The chief architect of the meticulously planned coup was the leftist Major (later Brigadier General) Otelo Saraiva de Carvalho.

The MFA quickly appointed a board of seven officers—the Junta of National Salvation—with General Spínola at its head to govern the country according to the MFA program. Assuming power for the first time in almost fifty years, the military pledged that authority would be transferred to a new government when constitutional institutions freely chosen by the people had been established.

Friction developed almost immediately between the then-anonymous leadership of the MFA and President Spínola's junta over the issue of the pace and direction of decolonization. The MFA favored immediate dissolution of the links with the colonies and withdrawal of Portuguese forces, whereas Spínola favored a gradual solution leading to limited autonomy within a Portuguese federation. Most conscript officers and men were anxious to abandon the struggle in Africa and return home. Although Spínola had wide popular appeal, his position was shaky because he was viewed as insufficiently committed to the revolution by radicals controlling the MFA. A powerful weapon in the hands of the MFA was an elite military organization—Continental Operations Command (Comando Operacional do Continente—COPCON)—with Carvalho at its head. Formed in July 1974 of paratroopers, marines, and army commandos, its mission was to control rising political and labor violence at a time when the police were reluctant to appear on the streets to enforce the law.

In September 1974, after his rightist supporters attempted without success to dislodge the left-wing inner circle of the MFA from control, Spínola resigned the presidency. The leftist climate within the military strengthened as the MFA continued to shift radical officers into key positions while sidelining those considered to lack revolutionary zeal. Nevertheless, when officers were able to express their choice by ballot, support for the left wing seemed weak, and many officers were eager to return to the barracks.

After conservative military units backing Spínola mounted an abortive countercoup in March 1975, Spínola and other officers were forced to flee to Spain by helicopter. The MFA moved rapidly to consolidate its control, setting up a Council of the Revolution that consisted of the leading MFA officers. The council had the power to control the presidency and a veto over the legislative process.

Elections held for the Constituent Assembly in April 1975 showed the Communist and ultra-left parties to be in the minority. The MFA continued to advance revolutionary plans but became increasingly factionalized in the mounting political turbulence. The angry reaction to takeovers of the pro-Socialist opposition newspaper and of the Roman Catholic radio station by ultra-leftists, together with attacks against Communists by conservative northern peasants, attested to a shift in the tide against radical elements.

Discipline began to break down within the armed forces under the anarchic conditions prevailing in the late summer and fall of

1975. Moderates, still a majority among the officers, gradually improved their position. A left-wing coup attempt by air force paratroopers and various Lisbon army detachments was decisively put down by a well-organized countercoup on November 25, 1975. COPCON was dissolved, Carvalho and 200 other radical officers were arrested, and others were purged from the armed forces. With the moderate element of the MFA firmly in charge, the military formally agreed to hand power back to the civilians after a new constitution was drawn up.

The Armed Forces in Political Life after 1975

The Council of the Revolution relinquished legislative power to the national parliament elected in April 1976, and two months later executive power was handed over to General António dos Santos Ramalho Eanes upon his election as president. Eanes had served briefly as army chief of staff, and it was widely felt that having a military man as president would reduce the likelihood of renewed military involvement in politics. Eanes would only agree to become president if he were also made chief of staff of the armed forces. Thus Eanes served as both president and chief of staff until 1981, when the two positions were separated. In 1982 Eanes was deprived of exclusive power to select the chiefs of staff, who subsequently were appointed by the president acting upon a formal proposal of the government. Eanes was reelected for a second presidential term, but in early 1986 he was succeeded by the former prime minister, Mário Alberto Nobre Lopes Soares, who thus became the first nonmilitary head of state in sixty years.

Under Article 273 of the constitution of 1976, the armed forces had the "historic mission of guaranteeing the conditions permitting the pluralist and peaceful transition . . . towards democracy and socialism." Nevertheless, under Article 275, the armed forces were to be strictly nonpartisan and were not to use their arms or their ranks to "influence or impede the selection of a particular democratic path." The Council of the Revolution was retained. Its membership consisted of the president, the chief and deputy chief of staff and the three service chiefs, the prime minister if a military person, and fourteen MFA officers. The council advised the president on the selection of a prime minister and had veto power over pending legislation, as well as decision-making power over military regulations and appointments. The MFA leaders declared that they had no desire to retain these powers permanently but only until the democratic system was fully established.

The continued existence of the Council of the Revolution became a political issue when the council frustrated the government

Portuguese marines practicing an assault landing
Portuguese infantry during an air assault exercise
Courtesy Embassy of Portugal, Washington

235

by vetoing a number of laws, including those dealing with military reform and the denationalization of banks and industry. In 1982 a center-right coalition government that had run on a platform of constitutional change was eventually able to force through amendments that dissolved the Council of the Revolution and removed the residual military powers over the elected civilian government. The council was replaced by the Higher Council of National Defense, whose powers are only advisory and are limited to questions of national defense and the organization, functioning, and discipline of the armed forces. It also confirmed officer promotions to general rank. The revised Article 273 of the constitution restricted the mission of the armed forces to "safeguarding national independence, the integrity of the territory, and the freedom and security of the population against any external aggression or threat, while respecting democratic institutions." In justifying these changes, the minister of defense explained that the government "deemed it inadvisable to provide legal pretexts which might one day be invoked to justify appeals for the intervention of the military in resolving internal political problems by means alien to democracy and the Constitution."

The subordination of Portugal's military to the civilian authorities was codified by the National Defense Law of 1982. It was passed in November of that year by the Assembly of the Republic over the objections of President Eanes who feared that the armed forces would be politicized by allowing the minister of defense to choose the chief of staff and the heads of the three services.

In spite of the measures taken in 1982 to divest the military of its remaining political powers, the military retained for a time considerable weight in matters of security. It also continued to feel a measure of responsibility for maintaining internal stability. In 1982 for example, the Association of the 25th of April, a club dominated by left-wing former members of the MFA, was founded to "fight for the preservation of the ideas" of the revolution of April 25, 1974.

By the early 1990s, however, under a determined prime minister and a strong minister of defense, the political influence of the military had waned. The National Defense Law of 1991 further strengthened civilian control. The law increased the power of the chief of staff and made him directly responsible to the minister of defense. Senior officers regarded as troublemakers or too active politically had been eased aside, and Portugal's military leadership differed little from that of other West European nations.

Strategic Concepts Underlying the Portuguese Defense Posture

Historically, Portugal has had two essential security objectives: the protection of its colonial empire and the maintenance of its status as a distinctive national entity on the Iberian Peninsula. The nation's geographic position—a band of territory on the Atlantic coast, isolated from the main powers of Europe—has always been central to its strategic thinking. Portugal has never been strong enough to defend itself without assistance, but it had a long tradition of resistance to the presence of foreign troops on its soil. Accordingly, it has followed a policy of aligning itself with the leading naval power of the time. Its alliance with Britain, first established by the 1386 Treaty of Windsor, was periodically reaffirmed until the twentieth century. After World War II and the creation of NATO, a close relationship with the United States came to be regarded as essential to preserving the country's overseas possessions. The nation's territorial integrity has not been even remotely threatened since the Napoleonic period, nor have immediate concerns of national security been the most compelling factors in military planning or the decision to join NATO. Rather, the country's participation in NATO until the mid-1970s was primarily aimed at winning political and military support for its colonial policies in Africa.

Portugal made only a marginal contribution to NATO during the Salazar and Caetano eras, and its involvement in Africa alienated it from the other members of the alliance. However, the prevailing Portuguese attitude after 1974 was favorable to greater Portuguese activity in NATO and the defense of the West, based on recognition of the dangers represented by the Soviet Union and the Warsaw Pact. Public opinion polls in Portugal reflected a decidedly pro-Atlantic, pro-NATO sentiment, especially when compared with that of other countries in NATO's southern tier, such as Spain and Greece. The events of 1974–75, when Portuguese Communists gained control of important functions of the state and deeply infiltrated the military, solidified the majority perception that the nation's interests lay in association with the West European community and NATO. The upheavals of 1974–75, together with Moscow's role in supporting the African liberation movements, inclined the Portuguese military leaders to regard the Soviet Union as a hostile power against which the country must constantly remain vigilant.

In geostrategic terms, the country is perceived as a narrow strip along the Atlantic flank of the Iberian Peninsula that, together with the archipelagoes of Madeira and the Azores, forms the Portuguese "strategic triangle." It occupies an intermediate position between the Atlantic and Mediterranean areas and between Europe and Africa. The strategic triangle is crossed by important sea and air lines of communication, linking North America and the east coast of South America to Europe, southern Africa to Europe, and the Mediterranean lands to Northern Europe. In the event of an East-West confrontation, the defense of these waters would be imperative for reinforcing the European southern flank. The Portuguese territories and waters would also be critical to control over the Straits of Gibraltar. The Lajes Air Base in the Azores, in addition to its advanced position for air resupply, is ideal for surveillance of the Atlantic and the conduct of antisubmarine warfare. As stated by United States Secretary of State George Shultz in 1984: "The Azores base is pivotal if the United States is to react effectively to military challenges in Europe or to threats to Western security outside NATO."

The military doctrine incorporated in the Portuguese strategic concept emphasizes the role of air and naval components to protect communications linking the Azores, Madeira, and the Portuguese mainland. This task has always necessitated the employment of naval vessels equipped for antisubmarine warfare and the use of the "angles" of the strategic triangle as bases for maritime patrol and interceptor aircraft. Another part of Portuguese strategic thinking stresses the growing ability of the North African countries—Morocco, Algeria, and Libya—to engage in modern military operations. Regional or religious conflicts in the area or the establishment of Soviet basing privileges would affect NATO's lines of communications and Portugal's responsibilities. Lisbon's efforts to foster good relations with the North African countries, especially Morocco, have as one objective, therefore, the reduction of such risks.

Recognizing that with the withdrawal of Soviet forces from Central Europe and the dismantling of the Warsaw Pact the military threat to Europe had subsided, the Portuguese political leadership became increasingly reluctant to assume financial and personnel commitments needed to carry out NATO missions. As of early 1993, defense strategy was clearly at a transitional stage. According to official statements, the armed forces would continue to be scaled down in areas of secondary importance, while efforts would be made to continue modernization and to achieve high operational efficiency in designated areas, notably air defense, naval patrols, and rapid reinforcement capability at any point of the national territory. The break-up of the Warsaw Pact has not, according to the official view, caused all threats to disappear. There is no guarantee that regional crises, low-intensity conflicts, and religious fundamentalism will not destabilize nations and entire regions. Prime Minister Aníbal Cavaco Silva pointed out in May 1990 that the NATO alliance had served peace for more than forty years over a vast territory. It would be rash, he said, for the West to disarm unilaterally and hurriedly and for the existing balance in Europe to be jeopardized. Similarly, Portugal was reluctant to assign security responsibilities to the European Community (EC—see Glossary) that would diminish the standing of NATO as the primary instrument of collective self-defense.

During the period in late 1990 leading up to the Persian Gulf conflict, Portuguese political leaders supported the United Nations (UN) resolution and expressed strong solidarity with the country's allies. In addition to quickly approving transit facilities in the Azores and on the mainland, Portugal provided medical assistance teams and a transport plane for evacuating refugees. A cargo vessel is assigned to support the movement of British forces to the Persian Gulf, and Portuguese vessels joined NATO standby forces in the Mediterranean. However, the government announced that Portugal would not contribute ships or troop units to take a direct part in the conflict, a decision reportedly received with discontent by senior military officers.

The Armed Forces

The three services of the Portuguese armed forces had a combined personnel strength of about 61,000 in 1992: about 33,000 in the army, 15,000 in the navy, and 13,000 in the air force. The president of the republic is commander in chief of the armed forces, while the senior military officer is the chief of staff of the armed forces. The president's formal powers include the right to declare war and appoint the chiefs of staff from names proposed by the government in power. The president chairs the Higher Council of National Defense, whose members are the prime minister, the minister of defense and other cabinet ministers; the chief of staff of the armed forces; the three service chiefs of staff; and the presidents of the regional governments of the Azores and Madeira (see fig. 10).

Prior to the passage of the National Defense Law of 1982, the military controlled the passage of laws affecting the armed forces, established budgetary and procurement policies, and had the power to veto international agreements involving national defense. The 1982 law was intended to make the military subordinate to civilian political authority, functioning through the minister of defense, in defense policy matters. Successive governments were reluctant to

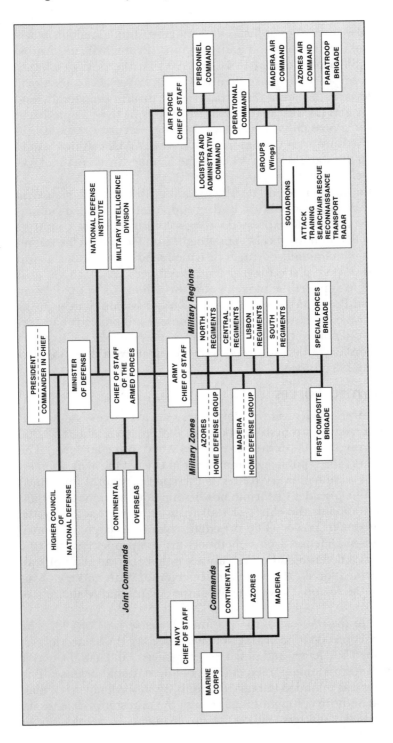

Figure 10. Organization of the Armed Forces, 1992

antagonize the military establishment by depriving it of its former powers, and initially the chiefs of staff retained practical control over budgets, strategic options, and procurement matters. By the early 1990s, however, civilian authority incorporated in the 1982 law was being more rigorously applied.

Army

The army's personnel strength was estimated at about 33,000 as of late 1991. About 75 percent of army personnel were conscripts serving a twelve-month period of service, and 10 percent were officers of both career and conscript status. The army was organized into four military regions (North with headquarters at Porto, Central with headquarters at Coimbra, South with headquarters at Évora, and Lisbon) and two military zones (Madeira with headquarters at Funchal and Azores with headquarters at Ponta Delgada (see fig. 11).

The size of the army had been drastically reduced since 1974, when it consisted of 211,000 soldiers of all ranks, the bulk of whom were committed to the fighting in Africa. During the colonial wars, elements of two divisions remained in metropolitan Portugal; one of these was earmarked for assignment to NATO's Central Region along the Rhine River, and the other was assigned to peninsular defense in the framework of the 1939 Iberian Pact. Both divisions were below 50 percent strength and were equipped with outmoded weapons.

Major revisions in the army structure have occurred since the withdrawal of troops from the colonies in 1974. Most of the army is organized along regimental lines. By 1992, it included fifteen infantry regiments, six artillery regiments, three cavalry regiments, two engineering regiments, one commando regiment, a signals regiment, and a military police regiment. The infantry regiments normally consist of a headquarters battalion, an infantry battalion, and a training battalion. New recruits are immediately assigned to one of the regiments, where they receive their basic training. The infantry regiments bear the names of communities within the military region where they are located. Forces in the Azores and Madeira are designated as Home Defense Groups, each consisting of two infantry battalions, one artillery battalion with antiaircraft and coastal guns, and support units.

The army's two most important units are the Special Forces Brigade and the First Composite Brigade committed to NATO. Unlike other army formations, which are subordinate to regional military commanders in the areas where they are located, these two units are directly subordinate to the army chief of staff. For

Figure 11. Major Military Installations, 1992

purposes of logistics and administration, however, the First Composite Brigade is under the commander of the Central military region.

The Special Forces Brigade, located in the Lisbon area, is composed of 2,000 men organized into two special forces battalions, one infantry battalion, and a logistics battalion. However, some units are only earmarked for service with the brigade and are still carried within the regimental structure.

The organization of the First Composite Brigade was begun in 1976 to replace the division previously committed to NATO. The brigade is located at Santa Margarida, 120 kilometers northeast of Lisbon, and maintained at 90 percent of its authorized strength of 5,200. Designed to conduct delaying and defensive operations, the brigade would come under Allied Land Forces Southern Europe (AFSOUTH) in periods of crisis or war. It has taken part in NATO exercises in northeastern Italy. Its constituent units are one mechanized infantry battalion with M–113 armored personnel carriers, two motorized infantry battalions, one armored battalion equipped with M–48A5 tanks, a field artillery battalion equipped with 155mm self-propelled howitzers, an armored reconnaissance unit, and engineering and signal companies.

Beginning in 1987, the army acted to improve the combat potential of the First Composite Brigade, particularly in overcoming its weaknesses in antitank weaponry and low-level air defense. The First Composite Brigade would face problems of transport and supply if deployed in Italy at a distance of 2,500 kilometers from its logistics base. Most of the brigade would be airlifted to its assigned position, with the heavy equipment to follow by sealift. Portugal does not have sufficient transport aircraft available to move the unit quickly, nor are there plans to position equipment in Italy in advance of the troops.

Newly enlisted army personnel are generally assigned to a unit from their own region of the country, where they also receive their basic training. After about six months of service, enlisted men who meet educational and other requirements can apply to the sergeants' school for training as noncommissioned officers (NCOs). Senior NCOs can qualify for commissions after attending the Higher Military Institute.

Discharged personnel are assigned to the reserves. Conscripts are carried on the reserve rolls until the age of thirty-five. There is no annual training period, although the call-up system is tested from time to time.

Young men aspiring for an army career can, after completing high school, compete for places at the Military Academy located near Lisbon; it had an enrollment of about 500 in 1991. Subsequent training of officers is conducted in the specialized schools of the various branches of the service. Advanced officer training, corresponding to the Command and General Staff School and the Army War College of the United States Army, is carried out at the Institute for Higher Military Studies in Lisbon. The highest level of professional education, corresponding to the United States National Defense University, is the National Defense Institute.

The students, senior officers of the military, high civil servants, and leading figures in the private sector, devote half a day for one year to the program. The army also operates prestigious military academies at the high-school level, primarily for the children of career officers and NCOs but open to children of civilian families on a restricted basis. Most of the students continue on to university and a civilian career after graduation.

The basic infantry weapon of the Portuguese army is the Heckler and Koch 7.62mm G–3 rifle manufactured domestically under a German license. Armored units are equipped with M–48A5 tanks and M–113 armored personnel carriers from the United States, supplemented by wheeled armored vehicles from a variety of sources. The principal antitank weapons are TOW (tube-launched, optically tracked, wire-guided) and Milan wire-guided missiles. In addition to a few self-propelled howitzers assigned to the First Composite Brigade, the army has an inventory of towed field guns and coastal artillery. The effort to modernize the NATO-earmarked First Composite Brigade has priority on resources, which means that units with home defense missions are equipped with obsolete weapons. Any substantial improvement is dependent on assistance from the United States, which has not supplied aid on the scale needed. It is possible that additional armored equipment, modern artillery, and antitank and air defense weapons will become available after deactivation by the United States Army under the 1990 Treaty on Conventional Forces in Europe, although Portugal faces competing demands by other NATO countries (see table 12, Appendix).

Navy

Portugal has a strong maritime tradition dating from the fourteenth and fifteenth centuries, when explorers inspired by Prince Henry the Navigator reached Madeira, the Azores, and the west coast of Africa, rounded the Cape of Good Hope, and sailed on to establish the sea route to India (see Maritime Expansion, ch.1). Although traditionally the service with the greatest prestige, the navy declined during the nineteenth and twentieth centuries. For a period in the 1950s, this trend was reversed when modern frigates, corvettes, minesweepers, and patrol vessels are acquired through military assistance from the United States. After the Revolution of 1974, the number of operational fighting vessels declined by more than half, from forty to seventeen.

During the colonial wars, the navy was active in efforts to interdict guerrilla movements on rivers, lakes, and coastal waters of Africa. After the withdrawal of the armed forces from Africa, the navy's emphasis shifted to home waters, where its missions have been defined as protecting the sea lanes between the mainland and the islands of the Azores and Madeira, cooperating with the other services in the defense of Portuguese territory, patrolling the 200-mile Exclusive Economic Zone (EEZ) off Portugal's coast, and meeting Portugal's NATO responsibilities in the Iberian Atlantic Command (IBERLANT) zone of operations (see Portugal and NATO, this ch.).

The chief of the naval staff (an admiral) is supported by the vice chief of naval staff (a vice admiral), the continental naval commander (also a vice admiral), the Azores naval commander (a rear admiral), the Madeira naval commander (a captain), and the Marine Corps commandant (a captain). The main naval base is at Alfeite near Lisbon, as is the Naval Academy. The continental naval command is at Portimão on the south coast. The commanders in the Azores and Madeira exercise the concurrent role of NATO island commander.

Between the end of the colonial wars in 1974 and 1992, the navy's personnel strength decreased from 19,400 to 15,300. As of 1992, about 5,000 of the navy's personnel were conscripts serving for sixteen months. Standards of performance and motivation of career NCO personnel are reported to have been affected by the decline. Many NCOs, trained at considerable expense by the navy, departed for private-sector employment. Lack of advancement, wage levels not commensurate with the skills involved, and the diminishing prestige of naval careers are said to be contributing factors. As a result of the flight of technicians, previous training and fitness standards could not be maintained.

The principal combat vessels of the Portuguese navy are four frigates and three submarines of French construction and ten small frigates (sometimes classified as corvettes) built in Spain and Germany. The French frigates and submarines were commissioned in the late 1960s, and the corvettes were commissioned between 1970 and 1975, although they were later modernized by the addition of new communications and electronics gear. The navy also operates a number of coastal patrol and auxiliary vessels (see table 13, Appendix). Three modern MEKO–200 frigates were commissioned in 1991. These ships, built in Germany and financed with the help of seven NATO members, were, at 3,200 tons, much larger than any other vessels in the existing fleet. They were to be armed with torpedoes, Harpoon surface-to-surface missiles, the Sea Sparrow SAM, and advanced sonar and fire-control systems. They would also accommodate two helicopters for antisubmarine operations.

Even with the addition of the MEKO frigates, Portugal has only a limited capability to carry out its IBERLANT responsibilities. The main potential threats are submarines that might interdict the Atlantic sea lanes and mines that could force the closure of ports. The navy's antisubmarine warfare capability, although improving, is still deemed deficient, particularly in view of the lack of air reconnaissance. The lack of minesweepers to operate in the Portugal-Madeira-Azores triangle is a further shortcoming in view of the strategic importance of this zone for European shipping. The navy has plans to replace its submarines and to purchase ocean-going patrol vessels and minesweepers, but it is not clear how they would be financed.

The Marine Corps consists of 2,500 men, of whom approximately half are conscripts. They are organized into two infantry battalions and one naval police battalion. The marines are trained for small amphibious operations and shore patrol duties. In addition to light arms, their equipment includes wheeled armored vehicles, mortars, and landing craft.

Air Force

Although the Portuguese air force did not become an independent service branch until 1952, it has existed since 1912. Portuguese pilots flew missions in World War I, and Portuguese aircraft are involved in the Spanish Civil War. The air force played a major role in the colonial wars, attacking guerrilla raiding parties, supporting ground troops, and performing reconnaissance, transport, and medical evacuation missions. During this period, its strength increased from about 12,500 in 1962 to a peak of 21,000 in 1973. After the Revolution of 1974 and the withdrawal from Africa, air force strength shrank as low as 8,000, but it was at a level of 10,300 in 1992. This total included 3,000 conscripts whose service obligation is sixteen months, as well as 2,200 airborne troops who were scheduled to be shifted to army command. The air force's sixteen squadrons operate from seven principal bases, including six in continental Portugal and Lajes in the Azores. One battalion of the airborne brigade is at the Monsanto Air Base, one battalion is at Aveiro, and the unit's training center is at Tancos.

The air force has a reputation as a well-trained, dynamically led, and disciplined service. Its aircraft maintenance and overhaul facilities at Alverca are considered to be excellent. Nevertheless, it has not had a clearly defined mission since the end of the African wars, and its capabilities are limited by the lack of up-to-date combat aircraft. With the exception of ten Alpha Jets obtained from France and Germany in the early 1990s, the air force is largely

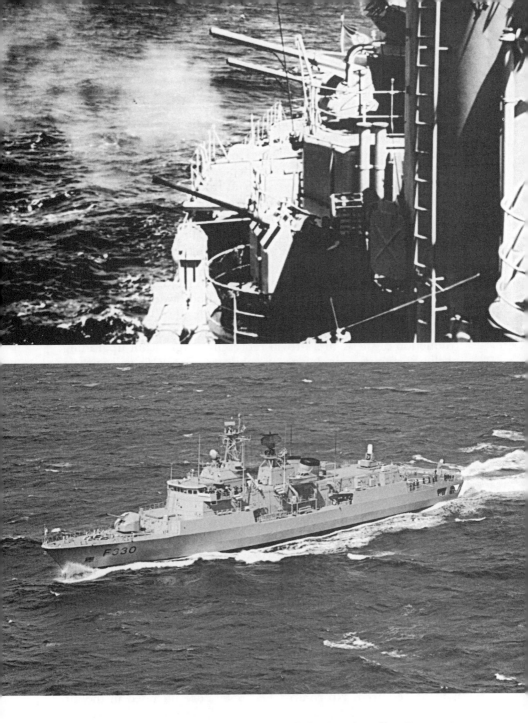

A Portuguese Navy frigate of the João Belo class in a live-fire exercise
A Portuguese Navy frigate of the Vasco da Gama class
Courtesy Embassy of Portugal, Washington

dependent on the transfer of obsolete aircraft from surplus stocks of other NATO members.

The backbone of the air forces is composed of two squadrons of A-7P Corsairs received under the United States military assistance program between 1982 and 1985 (see table 14, Appendix). The air force had previously been dependent on Fiat G-91s in the attack role. Deliveries of these aircraft from the German air force began in 1965-66 as partial reimbursement for German use of the Beja Air Base for training purposes. Portugal has no planes designed primarily for air defense, but both the A-7Ps and the Fiat G-91s are equipped with Sidewinder air-to-air missiles, providing them with the means to perform a secondary air defense role.

A result of the 1989 review of the Lajes Air Base agreement is the delivery of seventeen F-16A fighters and three F-16Bs (training versions) from the United States beginning in 1994. Although these are earlier models of the highly regarded F-16 series, the introduction of these aircraft will represent a significant upgrading of the Portuguese air defense capabilities. The F16s will operate from Monte Real Air Base and from two forward bases in Madeira and the Azores. As part of the same agreement, Portugal is scheduled to receive a battery of Hawk SAMs and associated radar to boost its air defenses.

In 1988 the air force acquired six Lockheed P-3B Orion maritime reconnaissance aircraft that had previously been in service in the Australian air force. After modernization in Portugal by the addition of newer radar and navigation systems, acoustic sensors, and armaments, the aircraft entered service in 1990. Operating from Montijo Air Base, the aircraft provide the air force with a patrol capability against submarines within the sea space linking Portugal with the Azores and Madeira. For reasons of economy, however, few patrol missions have been flown.

The air force also has in its inventory C-130H Hercules transport aircraft intended to provide partial airlift for the First Composite Brigade earmarked for NATO, as well as Spanish-built CASA C-212 Aviocar light transports, some of which are fitted for additional maritime surveillance, weather reconnaissance, and survey missions. Two of the C-130s are scheduled to be stretched to increase their load capacities, and an additional stretched C-130 is to be acquired. No combat helicopters are included in the air force inventory of aging French-built Alouettes and Pumas, the survivors of a considerable fleet of helicopters used during the wars in Africa. Under the 1989 Azores review, the United States is committed to supply fifty-seven combat, antisubmarine, and transport helicopters.

A major component of the air force modernization plan is the introduction of an air command and control system for the planning, tasking, and execution of air operations, including coordination with ground and naval forces. The system will be linked to the Spanish, French, and NATO air defense systems. Although NATO approved a large share of the funding, a reassessment is underway in light of the dramatic changes in the European security situation.

The Air Force Academy, a four-year institution, is located at Sintra near Lisbon. Elementary pilot training for cadets is conducted on Aerospatiale Epsilons, eighteen of which were acquired from France in 1989 for assembly in Portugal. Jet basic training follows on Cessna T–37Cs and advanced training on Alpha Jets or Northrop T–38A Talons. Additional officer training, carried out at the Air College, consists of a basic command course for lieutenants, a command and staff course for captains, and the air war course for colonels.

The air force faces major problems arising from career dissatisfaction among its highly trained personnel. Pilots are requesting permission for transfer to the reserves, indefinite leave, or permanent discharge. As of the early 1990s, the pilot shortfall was estimated at about 30 percent. The principal reasons are economic. Even with flight pay, officers earn much less than commercial pilots. Air force pilots also complain that they do not have sufficient opportunity to develop and hone their skills. Annual flying times for pilots and crews are reportedly well below the NATO-recommended minima owing to budgetary and fuel restrictions and the shortage of serviceable aircraft.

Conditions of Service

The armed forces entered a period of transition in the early 1990s that was the source of considerable uncertainty and turmoil among professional personnel. The severe cutbacks in the size of the military establishment, particularly the army, and the unsettled status of the military role and missions had a demoralizing effect. Career prospects seemed increasingly circumscribed, and the government's budgetary measures made the armed services seem unattractive in comparison with the opportunities in civilian life. The promotion possibilities were limited by the excessive number of officer personnel. As of 1988, the army's personnel strength had been reduced to only 20 percent of its strength in 1974. Yet during the same period, the officer complement had fallen by little more than half. The air force and the navy experienced more moderate reductions in staffing between 1974 and 1988. Naval officer strength had declined slightly, but the number of air force officers had actually increased.

The armed forces had formerly been admired as the defenders of democracy for their role in the toppling of the Salazar-Caetano regime in 1974. Military officers sensed that their profession had since suffered a decline in social status and prestige and that they were regarded by the public as superfluous. The historic left-wing and right-wing factions from the 1974–76 period were still distinguishable in the officer corps, although younger officers who had entered the service since the end of the colonial wars represented a separate and growing category. The upsurge of discontent against the government's perceived indifference to career military personnel was common to all elements, however.

The armed services are forbidden by law from forming unions to express their demands. This prohibition has been skirted by the formation of sergeants' "movements" and periodic large dinner gatherings among the officers. NCOs have also staged mild demonstrations to draw attention to their grievances. NCO advisory commissions have been established by the government, but these have proven to be ineffective because the officers representing the military establishment have no authority to negotiate over the issues raised. The NCOs have sought the elimination of promotions outside the normal sequence, reduction in the maximum time served at each grade, greater access to officer training courses, improvement in salary scales, and earlier retirement. Although sergeants could attain officer rank after attending the Higher Military Institute, few could hope to be promoted beyond captain because of insufficient vacancies at the major level. Naval NCOs have sought more training opportunities and the establishment of new specialties. The sergeants have called for an updating of the Code of Military Justice and Military Disciplinary Regulations, including the right of assembly and association.

In addition to the general feeling that salary levels do not correspond to the demands and risks associated with the military profession, officers feel that special benefits they previously enjoyed are being curtailed, including extra tax exemptions, subsidized gasoline, and overtime pay. Prices for food at military commissaries are no longer significantly below prices in civilian outlets. The officers have sought a lowering of age limits on active duty at the upper ranks as a means of increasing opportunities for advancement.

The length of compulsory military service was a subject of contention in the early 1990s, and the outcome is likely to have a pronounced effect on the future status of the career service and

Jet fighters of the Portuguese Air Force
Portuguese Air Force personnel manning a control tower
Courtesy Embassy of Portugal, Washington

on the effectiveness of the armed forces. The army service obligation, which had been twenty-four months at the end of the colonial wars in 1974, had been reduced to sixteen months by 1984 and to twelve months in 1990. Conscripts in the air force and navy served for sixteen months. In 1989, of 80,000 young men eligible for military service, 60,000 are deemed physically fit, although only 45,000 were actually inducted. In 1990 the number of inductees was lowered to 35,000. Those considered first for exemptions from service, in order of priority, are married men, heads of households, and only sons.

Conscientious objector status is recognized, although under the law, those granted exemption from active service are required to perform civil defense duties. Over 4 percent of those on enrollment lists file applications as conscientious objectors. Few young people acknowledge the need for military service, viewing it as a waste of time during a prime period of their lives. The youth branches of the main political parties are among those groups advocating a shorter period of military service.

One plan for reducing the period of conscription to four months is under discussion in the early 1990s. Under the plan, 20,000 conscripts would be in the service at any single time, 10,000 would be undergoing a two-month period of accelerated training, and 10,000 would be serving in their units. A safety clause would permit the minister of defense to extend the period of service to eight months for the army and twelve months for the navy and air force if the needs of the services were not being adequately met. The government plan called for the introduction of two new recruitment systems: one for volunteers, who would serve a minimum of eight months, and another for contract enlistments, which might be as long as eight years, to attract specialists in such fields as telecommunications, electronics, and computer technology. It was foreseen that the eight-month volunteers would be attracted by a higher wage (about US$200 a month) than conscripts and incentives in the form of preferences for academic study and careers in the police services.

This much discussed service plan is a further source of dissatisfaction for many in the officer corps who feel that the four-month term of service, the shortest of any country in Europe, would lead to a military establishment that is more costly to maintain and only marginally effective. Although the total number inducted each year would increase, the time allowed for training is regarded as insufficient to teach more than basic infantry skills and would seriously degrade unit performance. Doubts have been expressed over the adequacy of the wages and incentives offered to retain a permanent cadre of skilled NCOs and specialists.

Although women have the legal right to volunteer for military duty and the armed forces are under obligation to accept them, it was only in the late 1980s that a few women with special qualifications, such as doctors, lawyers, and engineers, were taken into the officer corps. Several women were also enrolled at the Air Force Academy to train as pilots. No women were serving in the enlisted ranks. As of 1991, fewer than 100 women served in the armed services, fewer than any other country of NATO.

Uniforms, Ranks, and Insignia

The official grade structure of the Portuguese armed forces shows nine officer ranks for the army and the air force and nine for the navy (see fig. 12). The rank of general is not subdivided as in the United States Armed Forces. Officers of the highest rank, that of general, wear three stars, except for the chief of staff of the armed forces and the three service chiefs of staff, who wear four stars. The rank of *marechal* (fleet admiral in the navy) is honorary and, as of early 1993, is held by only two persons, both retired army generals. The army and air force each have nine enlisted ranks; the navy uses only seven (see fig. 13). Officer ranks are displayed by peak decorations on the headgear and chin cords. The peaked caps of all three services also bear the Portuguese coat of arms.

On the pale gray full-dress uniform of the army, rank designations are displayed in the form of gorget patches for general officers and cuff bars for other officers. On the olive green service uniform, usually worn with shirt and tie, shoulder board insignia denote officer ranks. Shoulder boards or sleeve chevrons are worn by enlisted personnel and warrant officers. The highest NCO rank of first sergeant is denoted by four upward-pointing chevrons.

Army fatigue uniforms are olive green, and combat uniforms are of camouflage material. The standard headgear for enlisted personnel is a brown beret bearing the national colors of red and green. Armored troops are distinguished by black berets, and paratroops wear green berets. Special forces wear distinctive camouflage uniforms with red berets.

The air force uniform is light blue with a peaked cap as standard headgear for both officers and NCOs and berets for other ranks. All ranks wear garrison caps with nondress uniforms. Stars and sleeve rings denoting ranks are worn on the sleeve cuffs of officer uniforms. Rank chevrons similar to those of the army are worn on the shoulder by enlisted personnel.

PORTUGUESE RANK	ALFERES	TENENTE	CAPITÃO	MAJOR	TENENTE-CORONEL	CORONEL	NO RANK	BRIGADEIRO	GENERAL	GENERAL *
ARMY	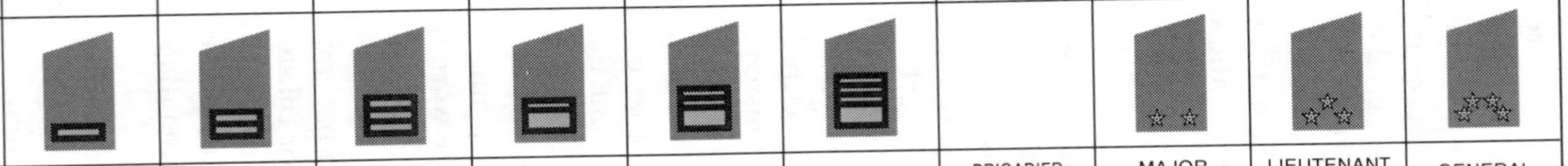									
U.S. RANK TITLE	2D LIEUTENANT	1ST LIEUTENANT	CAPTAIN	MAJOR	LIEUTENANT COLONEL	COLONEL	BRIGADIER GENERAL	MAJOR GENERAL	LIEUTENANT GENERAL	GENERAL
PORTUGUESE RANK	ALFERES	TENENTE	CAPITÃO	MAJOR	TENENTE-CORONEL	CORONEL	NO RANK	BRIGADEIRO	GENERAL	GENERAL *
AIR FORCE	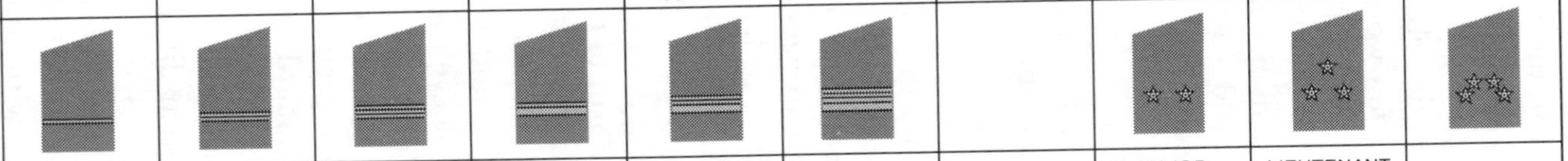									
U.S. RANK TITLE	2D LIEUTENANT	1ST LIEUTENANT	CAPTAIN	MAJOR	LIEUTENANT COLONEL	COLONEL	BRIGADIER GENERAL	MAJOR GENERAL	LIEUTENANT GENERAL	GENERAL
PORTUGUESE RANK	GUARDA-MARINHA	SEGUNDO-TENENTE	PRIMEIRO-TENENTE	CAPITÃO-TENENTE	CAPITÃO-DE-FRAGATA	CAPITÃO-DE-MAR-E-GUERRA	NO RANK	CONTRA-ALMIRANTE	VICE-ALMIRANTE	ALMIRANTE *
NAVY										
U.S. RANK TITLE	ENSIGN	LIEUTENANT JUNIOR GRADE	LIEUTENANT	LIEUTENANT COMMANDER	COMMANDER	CAPTAIN	REAR ADMIRAL LOWER HALF	REAR ADMIRAL UPPER HALF	VICE ADMIRAL	ADMIRAL

* Serves as chief of staff of respective service branch or of armed forces as a whole.

Figure 12. Officer Ranks and Insignia, 1992

Figure 13. Enlisted Ranks and Insignia, 1992

PORTUGUESE RANK	SOLDADO RECRUTA	SOLDADO	SEGUNDO-CABO	PRIMEIRO-CABO	SEGUNDO-FURRIEL	FURRIEL	SEGUNDO-SARGENTO	PRIMEIRO-SARGENTO	SARGENTO-AJUDANTE	SARGENTO-CHEFE	SARGENTO-MOR
ARMY	NO INSIGNIA	NO INSIGNIA									
U.S. RANK TITLE	BASIC PRIVATE	PRIVATE	PRIVATE 1ST CLASS	CORPORAL/SPECIALIST		SERGEANT		STAFF SERGEANT	SERGEANT 1ST CLASS	MASTER SERGEANT / FIRST SERGEANT	SERGEANT MAJOR / COMMAND SERGEANT MAJOR

PORTUGUESE RANK	SOLDADO RECRUTA	SOLDADO	SEGUNDO-CABO	PRIMEIRO-CABO	SEGUNDO-FURRIEL	FURRIEL	SEGUNDO-SARGENTO	PRIMEIRO-SARGENTO	SARGENTO-AJUDANTE	SARGENTO-CHEFE	SARGENTO-MOR
AIR FORCE	NO INSIGNIA	NO INSIGNIA									
U.S. RANK TITLE	AIRMAN BASIC	AIRMAN	AIRMAN 1ST CLASS	SENIOR AIRMAN	SERGEANT		STAFF SERGEANT	TECHNICAL SERGEANT	MASTER SERGEANT	SENIOR MASTER SERGEANT	CHIEF MASTER SERGEANT

PORTUGUESE RANK	SEGUNDO-GRUMETE	PRIMEIRO-GRUMETE	MARINHEIRO	CABO		SUB-SARGENTO	SEGUNDO-SARGENTO	PRIMEIRO-SARGENTO	SARGENTO-AJUDANTE	SARGENTO-CHEFE	SARGENTO-MOR
NAVY	NO INSIGNIA	NO INSIGNIA									
U.S. RANK TITLE	SEAMAN RECRUIT	SEAMAN APPRENTICE	SEAMAN	PETTY OFFICER 3rd CLASS		PETTY OFFICER 2nd CLASS		PETTY OFFICER 1st CLASS	CHIEF PETTY OFFICER	SENIOR CHIEF PETTY OFFICER	MASTER CHIEF PETTY OFFICER

Navy personnel wear either blue wool or white cotton uniforms for shore or sea duty. In either case, pullover blouses are standard. Navy enlisted men's headgear is similar to those of other European navies—round caps with the name of the ship sewn on the headband. Peaked caps, bearing the state arms and designating rank by peak decoration, are worn by officers and petty officers. Marines wear dark blue berets. Ranks displayed on uniforms consist of sleeve rings for officers and rank chevrons for NCOs. As in the other services, warrant officers' ranks are denoted by a combination of chevrons and the coat of arms.

Defense Expenditures

The Portuguese defense budget was 197.5 billion escudos (US$1.25 billion) in 1989, 219.1 billion escudos (US$1.54 billion) in 1990, and 206.8 billion escudos (US$1.73 billion) in 1991 (for value of the escudo—see Glossary). Over the period 1978–89, the defense budget increased by an average of 1.9 percent annually in real terms. According to a survey by the United States Arms Control and Disarmament Agency (ACDA), which applied certain adjustments to the official figures for defense, Portuguese military expenditures rose in real terms from US$1.189 billion in 1979 to US$1.457 billion in 1989 (both amounts in constant 1989 dollars).

Portugal's defense outlays are the lowest in NATO with the exception of Luxembourg (Iceland has no military forces). In terms of defense expenditures per capita, Portugal was the lowest in NATO (US$141 in 1989) with the exception of Turkey. However, in terms of the share of gross national product (GNP—see Glossary) allotted to defense, most NATO countries spent less than Portugal. Portugal's expenditures on its military establishment had risen from 4.5 percent of GNP in 1960 to 8.3 percent of GNP during the course of the colonial wars. In the 1980s, defense expenditures averaged 3.43 percent of GNP. Defense outlays, which had constituted 26.7 percent of the national budget in 1960, rose to nearly 46 percent of the budget during the peak of the overseas wars in 1971. By 1977 defense expenditures had declined to 10 percent of central government expenditures, and they remained below 10 percent throughout the 1980s.

In 1988 expenditures were allocated among the services on the following basis: army, 36.9 percent; navy, 30.6 percent; air force, 22.3 percent; and general staff, 10.1 percent. The largest expenditure category was personnel (64.5 percent), among the highest in NATO and exceeded only by Belgium and Luxembourg. The principal cause was the fact that the rapid decline in total staff was not matched by a decline in the officer roster. Moreover, pension payments to demobilized personnel were a significant cost factor. Of the service branches, the army was burdened with the highest outlay for personnel, amounting to 80 percent of its budget. This outlay was attributable in part to the large number of officers on active duty in excess of the army's requirements. By comparison, 60 percent of the navy's budget was absorbed by personnel expenses. Portugal's outlays on major equipment items as a share of the defense budget (13.4 percent) were among the lowest in NATO, as well.

Portugal and NATO

Portugal was one of the founding members of NATO in 1949. For more than two decades, Portugal's material contribution to the alliance was marginal. Its armed forces were preoccupied with the fighting in Africa, and its efforts to maintain a colonial empire alienated it from the other members of the alliance. Nevertheless, its contribution in the form of strategically located bases and other military facilities was substantial. Major air bases and ports on the Portuguese mainland were deemed vital for rapid reinforcement and sea resupply of NATO forces on the continent. Control of Madeira was considered crucial for keeping the North Atlantic routes to the Straits of Gibraltar open for allied operations. The Azores provided essential refueling facilities for the rapid deployment of forces to Central Europe, the Mediterranean and the Middle East, as well as a key base for antisubmarine tracking and naval surveillance.

In the immediate postrevolutionary period when leftist ideology was in the ascendancy in the military, the question of Portugal's continued active participation in the alliance came into question. In 1975 Portuguese representatives absented themselves from highly classified NATO discussions. By 1980, however, Portugal had returned to full participation, rejoining NATO's Nuclear Planning Group and again taking part in NATO exercises. The establishment of a pro-Western democratic government, followed by the accession of Portugal to the European Community (EC) in 1986, inspired renewed interest in an active role in the alliance. The desire to provide the armed forces with a meaningful military mission after the African operations ended and to divert them from further involvement in civilian politics were additional factors in Portugal's willingness to undertake fresh NATO commitments. Portugal accordingly accepted the obligation to equip the First Composite Brigade to be at the disposal of the Supreme Allied Commander Europe (SACEUR) and agreed to increase its surveillance and control over a large sector of the eastern Atlantic by acquiring modern frigates and reconnaissance aircraft.

The Iberian Atlantic Command (IBERLANT), a major subordinate command under the Supreme Allied Commander Atlantic (SACLANT) located at Norfolk, Virginia, has its headquarters at Oeiras, near Lisbon. Since 1982 the IBERLANT commander has been Portuguese, a vice admiral with a staff of about sixty-five officers and 200 enlisted personnel mainly from Portugal, the United States, and Britain. IBERLANT encompasses the area extending from the northern border of Portugal southward to the Tropic of Cancer and approximately 1,150 kilometers seaward from the Straits of Gibraltar. Madeira is within IBERLANT's area, as are the Azores after transfer from NATO's Western Atlantic Command (WESTLANT) to meet Portuguese concerns.

The IBERLANT commander has no permanently assigned combat forces in peacetime. The IBERLANT staff carries out planning and conducts exercises to ensure the headquarters' readiness to assume command and logistic support of forces that would be assigned in a period of tension or war. In addition to the administrative facilities and underground command post at Oeiras, IBERLANT has extensive communications links with SACLANT at Norfolk and other command posts. Other NATO facilities in Portugal include ammunition and fuel depots and strategic reserves at Lisbon and a reserve airport at Ovar near Porto. NATO also occupies a portion of the Montijo Air Base for the same purpose and has fuel storage areas and access to the air base in the Azores. The Portuguese navy participates in exercises with other NATO fleets, particularly those involving protection of resupply convoys in the IBERLANT area.

When Spain became a member of NATO in 1982, Portugal is concerned that a reorganization of the NATO command structure might follow. Portuguese misgivings focused on the possibility that an integrated Iberian command would be formed under a Spanish commander and that Spain might be entrusted with security tasks within the area of Portuguese territories for which the Portuguese armed forces were not yet fully equipped. After Spain's decision in 1986 to remain outside NATO's integrated military structure, however, the issue of assignment of commands and missions in the Iberian Peninsula and adjacent sea areas became dormant.

Bilateral Military Relations with Other Countries

Since World War II, Portugal has maintained a significant level of defense cooperation with several NATO countries, but its military relations with the United States have been of paramount importance. The United States was granted facilities at Lajes Air Base on Terceira Island in the Azores in 1944. Under a 1951 bilateral defense agreement and subsequent technical agreements, the United States has continued to enjoy access to this base. Lajes has been an important refueling stop for military transport aircraft and a base for tanker aircraft to refuel fighter aircraft shuttling between the United States and Europe and the Middle East. It has also been a base for American antisubmarine aircraft that patrolled a large sector of the sealanes linking the United States Sixth Fleet in the Mediterranean with its supply depots on the east coast of the United States. As of 1992, the United States had about 1,200 air force personnel in the Azores.

The use of the Lajes Air Base for non-NATO purposes required prior clearance by Portugal. When Israel was subjected to a surprise attack by Egypt and Syria in October 1973, the Lajes Air Base was used to support the emergency transport of military supplies to Israel. Portugal was the only NATO country to grant the United States the use of its facilities during the 1973 crisis. When UN forces were deployed in 1990 in response to the Iraqi occupation of Kuwait, Portugal gave early and comprehensive approval to use Lajes and mainland bases for aerial refueling and moving United States aircraft and equipment to Saudi Arabia.

The 1951 Azores agreement was extended in late 1983 to permit the United States to have continued use of Lajes for seven years until February 1991. As of 1993, no firm settlement had been reached to extend the agreement. As part of the 1983 understandings, the United States pledged its best efforts to bring its military aid up to an annual level of US$125 million. Assistance totaling US$90 million was provided in fiscal year (FY) 1984 and US$105 million in FY 1985 but, owing to Congressional reductions in the administration's requests, was lower in subsequent years. Estimated military assistance obligations in FY 1990 were US$84.6 million. Disappointment expressed by the Portuguese prime minister with the level of military aid under the 1983 agreement led to consultations in 1988. As a result, the United States agreed to supply additional weaponry to help Portugal bring its NATO-committed forces to a more active posture. Portugal's air defense capabilities were also to be strengthened by introducing interceptor aircraft and modernizing the A–7 squadrons. Among the additional items of equipment the United States committed itself to supply were twenty F–16 fighter aircraft, fifty-seven helicopters of various types, a battery of Hawk SAMs, air defense radar, vehicles, ammunition, and a hydrographic vessel. The previous delivery of P–3 maritime patrol aircraft and the United States contribution to the MEKO frigate program were aimed at augmenting Portugal's antisubmarine warfare capability in the Atlantic.

The United States has also provided training assistance valued at about US$2.5 million annually. This aid enabled more than 500 Portuguese personnel to receive professional military education each year, as well as training in the effective use and maintenance of weapons systems being delivered under the aid program.

The Federal Republic of Germany (West Germany) has also been a substantial supplier of arms to Portugal, transferring excess Fiat G-91 aircraft, M-48A5 tanks, trucks, and other vehicles. In 1986 West Germany announced that about US$200 million would be earmarked for the construction of the three MEKO-200 frigates. The West German air force maintains eighteen Alpha Jets at Beja Air Base for advanced training of its personnel under an agreement dating from 1960. Both the United States and Germany use the aircraft repair and overhaul facilities at Alverca under contract with the Portuguese air force. Several other NATO countries have contributed modestly to meet Portugal's military needs, including components for the MEKO frigates. France operates a missile-tracking station on Ilha das Flores in the Azores. In partial compensation, France provided Epsilon training aircraft to the Portuguese air force in 1989.

According to data compiled by the ACDA, the value of arms transfers to Portugal amounted to US$370 million between 1984 and 1988. Of this total, US$210 million originated in the United States, US$30 million in West Germany, and US$20 million in France. The remaining US$100 million came from a variety of suppliers.

Domestic Defense Production

Portugal has had a small defense industry since the eighteenth century, consisting originally of a naval arsenal, a gunpowder plant, a cannon foundry, and an arms factory. Beginning in the mid-nineteenth century, the military's food, supplies, and, later, fuels were provided by a government agency, the Manutenção Militar. At the beginning of the twentieth century, a factory for supplying military uniforms and equipment was established. During the 1960s, the defense industry expanded to meet the specialized requirements of the antiguerrilla operations in Africa. However, since the end of the fighting in 1974 and the subsequent scaling back of the armed forces, production capabilities have exceeded the country's needs. A modest level of sales abroad have helped the Ministry of Defense keep production lines open for artillery, mortar, and small arms ammunition.

Under Portuguese law, private companies are not permitted to engage in research, planning, testing, manufacturing or overhaul of equipment exclusively intended for military purposes. These laws have been interpreted to restrict to government-owned enterprises the production of bombs, missiles, torpedoes, mines, hand grenades, propellant powders, and other explosives. The construction of combat aircraft, helicopters, and warships is also limited to nationally owned companies, although component manufacture could be subcontracted to private firms.

In addition to Manutenção Militar, the principal government enterprises include Oficinas Gerais de Fardamento e Equipamento (OGFE) for production of uniforms and equipment; Oficinas Gerais de Material de Engenharia (OGME) for the overhaul of military vehicles; and Oficinas Gerais de Material Aeronautico (OGMA) for maintenance and repair of all aircraft, avionics, engines, communications, and radar equipment of the Portuguese Air Force. OGMA also has maintenance contracts for United States air force and navy equipment and to supply parts and components to several European aircraft manufacturers. The main ordnance factory is Industrias Nacionais de Defesa E.P. (INDEP), a producer of 60mm and 81mm mortars, artillery and mortar munitions, small arms ammunition, machine guns, and, under a German license, the Heckler and Koch 7.62mm G–3 rifle used by the Portuguese army. Arsenal do Alfeite near the Lisbon naval base has facilities for building patrol craft, auxiliary ships, and corvettes, but all of its larger modern vessels have been constructed abroad, and its activities are confined to maintenance and overhaul. Bravia, a private company, produces a range of wheeled armored personnel carriers, reconnaissance vehicles, and military trucks.

According to the ACDA, Portugal's arms exports reached a peak of US$220 million in 1986, falling off to US$40 million in 1989. In the latter year, arms exports accounted for only 0.3 percent of total Portuguese exports. In 1989 the minister of defense said that the defense industry, employing 3,000 to 4,000 people, faced contraction because fewer countries were in the market for arms.

Public Order and Internal Security

Following the end of the long authoritarian regime in Portugal in April 1974, the system of internal security is reorganized. The Public Security Police (Polícia de Segurança Pública—PSP) and the National Republican Guard (Guarda Nacional Republicana—GNR), viewed as having been active supporters of the regime, were put temporarily under military command. As of 1990, internal security is the responsibility of the Ministry of Justice and the Ministry of Internal Administration (formerly the Ministry of Interior). The forces of security were ctotrolled by, and fully responsible to, the government.

The revolutionary turmoil of 1974 to 1976 imposed a severe challenge to the maintenance of law and order. In addition to occasional violence by leftist and rightist groups, the emergence of separatist activity in the Azores and Madeira posed threats to the territorial integrity of Portugal. After constitutional government was established in 1976, political violence abated. Between 1980 and 1986, however, an ultra left-wing terrorist group, Popular Forces of the 25th of April (Forças Populares do 25 Abril—FP–25), its name referring to the coup d'état of April 25, 1974, conducted a campaign of bombing, assassinations, and bank robberies (see Terrorist Groups, this ch.).

The Police System

Although the main duties of the police had always been the prevention, detection, and investigation of crime and the maintenance of public order, their involvement under successive governments in suppressing political and labor organizations left a reservoir of fear and mistrust among the Portuguese people. The authority of the police, which was identified with the old regime, was seriously compromised by the Revolution of 1974. During the months after the revolution, there was a sharp rise in crime and disorder owing to the virtual disappearance of social and moral constraints imposed by tradition and reinforced by the authoritarian regime. Until the civilian police forces, disarmed after the revolution, could be reorganized and retrained to operate in Portugal's new political environment, armed forces security units assumed responsibility for internal security. By 1976, control of the police apparatus was returned to civilian authorities in the Ministry of Internal Administration.

Article 272 of the constitution of 1976, as revised in 1982, emphasizes the responsibility of the police to defend the democratic process and to ensure that they act within the law and do not exceed their authority. In carrying out their mission of preventing crimes, including crimes against the security of the state, the police are enjoined to observe the rights, freedoms, and safeguards of citizens. The constitution stipulates that each of the forces of security are to have a single organization for the entire national territory.

National Republican Guard

The GNR was formed in 1913 as a heavily armed paramilitary constabulary organized up to battalion strength. It was intended as a check against the military and was first employed to confront monarchist-inspired revolts within the ranks of the armed forces. Although its essential mission was one of maintaining order in the countryside, the GNR's activities were subsequently extended to those of helping the urban police to control demonstrations and quell labor unrest.

In 1990 the GNR numbered approximately 19,000 officers and men and was equipped with Commando armored cars and twelve Alouette II helicopters transferred from the German army. The guard is organized into battalions stationed in the major cities and companies and sections in district capitals and smaller communities. Highway patrols are conducted by a separate Traffic Brigade and by rural units of the GNR.

Reserve and career officers from all branches of the armed forces can be seconded to tours of duty in the GNR on a voluntary basis. Reservists who are university graduates can apply to continue as GNR officers upon completion of their military obligations.

Public Security Police

The PSP is a paramilitary police force under the jurisdiction the Ministry of Internal Administration. Its basic mission is the protection of property and public security in urban areas. Before its reorganization in 1953, the urban police had been under the control of provincial governors. During the colonial wars, security police assault units were dispatched to Africa, where they participated in combat operations against guerrilla forces. The PSP was reorganized and retrained in 1975, and its heavy equipment was turned over to the army.

PSP detachments operate from divisional headquarters in Lisbon and from the eighteen districts of continental Portugal, which are divided into North, South, and Central zones. There are also headquarters for Madeira and the Azores and sectional headquarters in smaller towns. Greater Lisbon and greater Porto have separate commands. A specialized traffic service shares highway patrol responsibilities with the GNR Traffic Brigade. A special group, the Intervention Police, has mobile sections poised for deployment anywhere in the country. Criminal investigation and data gathering are centralized under the General Anti-Crime Directorate, which employs 1,500 specialized officers and investigators. As of 1990, the PSP had a complement of 17,000 individuals. Staff are drawn from among former service personnel. Since the early 1970s, women have also been recruited for plainclothes investigations and traffic control assignments.

In 1989, a demonstration by some 1,000 police personnel outside the Ministry of Internal Administration took a violent turn.
The police had tried to form a union, but the government rejected
the idea on grounds that the police, as a military organization, were
prohibited by the National Defense Law of 1982 from having a
union. The police maintained that they needed a union to improve
working conditions that were marked by long hours and low pay.
In the late 1980s, for example, an ordinary patrol officer earned
the equivalent of only US$390 a month.

Other Police Forces

In 1990 the Fiscal Guard (Guarda Fiscal; also known as Treasury Police), a border control force, numbered 8,500 and was
charged with customs inspections and the collection of import duties.
In addition, the force investigates smuggling, tax evasion, and illegal
financial transactions, particularly those involving import-export
businesses and currency exchange. Most of its uniformed and plainclothes police are stationed at frontier crossing points, ports, and
terminals of entry. Their monitoring of entries and departures by
foreigners also produces a flow of information needed by internal
security agencies. The Maritime Police has functions similar to a
coast guard service. The Judicial Police, responsible to the minister
of justice, acts in conjunction with the court system in investigating crimes, particularly those involving subversion and terrorism,
and preparing cases for prosecution.

Intelligence Services

The existence in Portugal of an intelligence apparatus for political surveillance and control is as old as the modern state and dates
at least from the sixteenth century. Under Salazar, however, a secret
police organization of extensive and pervasive influence became
a formidable component of his authoritarian regime. The secret
police, called the International Police for the Defense of the State
(Polícia Internacional e de Defesa do Estado—PIDE), although under jurisdiction of the Ministry of Justice, was in fact controlled
directly by Salazar. Under revisions of the law after 1954, PIDE
officers were entitled to act as inquiring magistrates empowered to detain for trial persons suspected of crimes against the state.
Suspects were routinely arrested without warrants and often held
for months without specific charges brought against them and
without access to legal assistance. Disappearance and torture were
commonplace.

Agents of PIDE carried out covert operations within communist
organizations, the government-run labor unions, the armed forces,

the universities, and the Portuguese emigré communities abroad. During the 1960s and 1970s, PIDE directed its efforts to suppressing opposition to the war effort in the African colonies, particularly on university campuses, and to tracking down antiregime terrorists responsible for bombing military and strategic installations.

Although PIDE was renamed the General Security Directorate (Direcção Geral de Segurança—DGS) by Marcello Caetano's government, it retained its old image. The abhorrence felt for it was so strong that it was abolished in Portugal the day after the Caetano regime was toppled. Abuses by the security apparatus were subsequently reported in detail in the Portuguese press, causing even more revulsion among the public. Outrage over the prolonged detention and torture of suspected terrorists and opposition politicians resulted in the arrest of PIDE–DGS agents and investigations of past operations of the organization.

The lingering specter of PIDE and DGS as pillars of the authoritarian regime in the memory of the Portuguese people delayed the establishment of a new civilian intelligence agency for more than a decade. Following an Armenian terrorist attack on the Embassy of Turkey in 1983, the assassination of a Palestine Liberation Organization representative at a Socialist International conference the same year, and a number of domestic terrorist attacks, the Portuguese government became convinced of the need for a new intelligence agency. After the passage of authorizing legislation in late 1984, the Intelligence System of the Republic of Portugal (Sistema de Informações da República Portuguesa—SIRP) was established in 1986. SIRP was intended to be the parent body for three separate intelligence services: the Security Intelligence Service (Serviço de Informações e Segurança—SIS), the Military Intelligence Service (Serviço de Informações Militares—SIM), and the Defense Strategic Intelligence Service (Serviço de Informações Estratégicas de Defesa—SIED). SIS, under the minister of internal administration, was given the mission of gathering intelligence to ensure internal security and to prevent sabotage, terrorism, espionage, and acts that could alter or destroy the constitutionally established state of law. SIM was intended to replace the Military Intelligence Division of the armed forces, but the transition had not been effected as of 1993. Military intelligence continued to be the responsibility of the chief of staff of the armed forces. Its authority was limited to gathering intelligence needed to carry out the missions of the armed forces and to guarantee military security, although some strategic intelligence collection abroad was reportedly also conducted.

Under the 1984 legislation, SIED, reporting directly to the prime minister, was to be responsible for producing intelligence needed to safeguard the independence and external security of the Portuguese state. The government decided to defer the creation of SIED, however, asserting that the limited financial resources available should be dedicated to developing an effective internal security organization rather than an agency focusing on external security. Thus, SIS was the only arm of the intelligence apparatus operating as contemplated in the 1984 legislation. SIS functions under considerable handicaps, employing only about eighty persons as of 1990. Its sole office is in Lisbon, although branches are planned for Porto, Ponta Delgada, and Funchal. SIS agents are not authorized to make searches or arrests, to intercept correspondence or tap telephones, or to intervene in normal criminal cases. Although no SIS agents are known to have been exposed to violence, they are entitled to hazardous duty pay at about 30 percent above normal civil service scales.

The 1984 security law prohibited the employment of former PIDE agents in any Portuguese intelligence function. Accordingly, SIS was launched with few adequately qualified individuals. In spite of a public recruiting drive, analysts estimated that it would be some years before Portugal could boast of a domestic intelligence service staffed with fully seasoned personnel.

In light of the history of violations of civil rights by PIDE, several bodies were formed to monitor the activities of the Portuguese intelligence community. The Council to Oversee the Intelligence Services, composed of three deputies elected by the Assembly of the Republic, is mandated to review the actions of the intelligence services and report its findings annually to the Assembly of the Republic. The Commission to Control Data, made up of three judges, monitors the intelligence data center to protect individuals against any collection of data violating their rights under the Constitution. The Superior Intelligence Council, a twelve-member interministerial body, advises the prime minister and coordinated intelligence matters.

Terrorist Groups

Since the transition to democratic rule was completed in 1976, the country has been relatively free from subversive or terrorist activity threatening the maintenance of constitutional authority. The only significant terrorist group, the Popular Forces of the 25th of April (Forças Populares do 25 Abril—FP-25), carried out a number of attacks between 1980 and 1986, but at no time did it pose a major threat to the security of the state. Effective counterterrorism measures and the absence of public support sharply curtailed the ability of FP-25 to sustain its campaign of violent operations against the Portuguese government and Western and NATO missions in Portugal.

FP-25 claimed to be a workers' organization dedicated to a struggle against exploitation, misery, and repression. Its stated goals were to defeat "imperialism," to lead a "workers' assault on bourgeois power," and to achieve the violent overthrow of the Portuguese government. The FP-25 also bitterly opposed the United States and NATO. No evidence of direct ties to other European terrorist groups existed, although Portuguese authorities asserted that some financial support had come from Libya. Between 1980 and 1984, most FP-25 actions involved assassinations, bombings, and bank robberies. Beginning in 1984, the group focused its attacks on United States and NATO targets. Mortars were fired at the compound of the Embassy of the United States, at NATO's IBERLANT headquarters, and at NATO ships anchored in Lisbon harbor. Bombs destroyed a number of cars owned by West German air force personnel. FP-25's ability to wage its terrorist campaign was curtailed by the arrest of a large number of its adherents in June 1984, including Otelo Saraiva de Carvalho, who had become a popular hero in Portugal after playing a key role in the Revolution of 1974 (see The Military Takeover of 1974, this ch.). Other obscure radical groups claimed responsibility for subsequent minor bombing attacks, but such acts of terrorism abated in 1987. As of 1993, Carvalho was free on a conditional basis, and the issue of a general amnesty for members of FP-25 had aroused wide public interest.

Separatist independence movements have long existed in the Azores and Madeira archipelagoes. The main group, the Azorean Liberation Front, has been responsible for many demonstrations but has not been associated with clandestine activities and violence. A newer group, the Azorean Nationalist Movement, is regarded as illegal because Portuguese law prohibits any association advocating the independence of the Azores. The existing system of autonomy recognized by the constitution of 1976 and subsequent legislation have endowed the regional governments with considerable rights and greatly reduced the appeal of the separatist movements.

Judicial System

Restrictions on freedom of assembly and of the press, on the rights of association and of public protest, and on the right to strike were removed with the promulgation of the new constitution in April

1976. The constitutionally mandated Council of Social Communication, whose members are elected by the Assembly of the Republic, act as a watchdog to protect freedom of speech and access to the media. The council publicizes abuses, makes recommendations to the Assembly of the Republic, and has enforcement powers; however, it has never been required to exercise such powers. There are two restrictions on civil liberties. "Fascist" organizations are prohibited by law. In addition, persons can be prosecuted for "insulting" civil or military authorities if such an "insult" is intended to undermine the rule of law. Several prosecutions have resulted under these provisions.

The constitution of 1976 drastically altered the role of the police to protect civil rights. It gives guidelines for criminal investigation and treatment of suspects. The constitution specifies that no person can be held without trial or imprisoned without a definite sentence. Individuals cannot be deprived of citizenship for political reasons. The principle of habeas corpus is restated and is applied without exception to both civilian criminal courts and military tribunals. A petition for a writ of habeas corpus is to be answered by a judge within eight days. Torture and inhumane detention are made illegal. Confessions obtained under duress and any material obtained by illegal means are declared inadmissible as evidence in criminal proceedings. The privacy of personal correspondence and telephone communication is also guaranteed in the constitution, and forcible entry into homes and searches without a judicial warrant are forbidden.

Criminal Law Procedure

The Portuguese criminal justice system is organized on a national basis. The Ministry of Justice has control over the court system, the office of the attorney general, the Judicial Police, and prisons. The office of the attorney general has a hierarchy parallel to that of the judiciary. Its representatives prosecute cases in each of Portugal's judicial districts and their subdivisions. An assistant deputy attorney general prosecutes cases before the municipal court at the local level or municipality. At the district level, above the municipality, the deputy attorney general represents the state before the district court, which houses a panel of one to three judges to determine guilt or innocence and decide the sentence.

Portugal has four judicial regions, each with an appeals court having appellate jurisdiction over cases tried in the district or lower courts in its area. The districts are Lisbon, with 66 courts; Porto, with 110 courts; Coimbra, with 80 courts; and Évora, with 60 courts. Appeals are allowed only on the basis of judicial error in the original proceedings. Cases tried in a district court are automatically reviewed after sentencing by the appeals court of the region. The Ministry of Justice reviews all cases and can intervene to initiate a formal appeal. Because the appeals process is often lengthy, bail is frequently allowed the accused during the proceeding, except in cases involving homicide, serious assault, or grand larceny, or when it is likely that the accused will flee.

Persons apprehended while committing a crime are typically held in preventive detention and are usually not considered eligible for conditional liberty. Persons not caught in the commission of a crime are usually given conditional liberty on submission of a bail bond or article of value. An individual taken into custody may not be held for more than forty-eight hours without being brought before a prosecuting magistrate who reviews the case and determines whether the accused person should be held in preventive detention or released on bail. Preventive detention is limited to a maximum of four months for each crime. Because of the cumbersome and backlogged judicial system and vacant judgeships, however, detention beyond four months is not unusual for major crimes, such as murder or armed robbery. For this reason, judges are required to give priority to cases of those in preventive detention.

Persons unable to afford an attorney have one appointed by the court. Detainees are given access to their lawyers while awaiting trial. The indictments are made available to the accused and their attorneys, and charges can be answered in briefs by the defense attorneys. Presiding judges can dismiss a case on the basis of a defense attorney's brief or continue the trial at their own discretion.

A clear procedural distinction exists between arrest and trial. A panel of three judges (which do not include the prosecuting judge) presides over cases that go to trial. A ministerial delegate assists the judges in reviewing the evidence. At the request of the accused, a jury can be used in trials for major crimes. Provision for a jury system is a particularly significant innovation of the constitution.

The constitution reaffirms the basic guarantee of a fair trial and stipulates that trials are to be public except when they could offend the dignity of the victim, as in cases involving sexual abuse of children. To avoid the malpractices of the authoritarian Salazar-Caetano regime, when agents of the secret police exercised the power of magistrates, strict judicial supervision over indictments and trial procedure is provided. An ombudsman, elected to serve a four-year term by the Assembly of the Republic, is Portugal's chief civil and human rights officer. The ombudsman receives about

3,500 complaints annually; the majority involve alleged maladministration by the bureaucracy.

Before the Salazar-Caetano era ended in 1974, persons accused of offenses defined as crimes against the state could be legally detained for periods ranging from six months to three years without being charged. Suspects convicted of crimes against the state could be held in prison for renewable three-year terms, which could result in life imprisonment. Those considered less dangerous were exiled to an overseas territory or were obliged to post large bonds as guarantees of acceptable conduct in the future. Acts and conspiracies of military or civilians against the government were severely prosecuted. Advocating or acting in favor of African liberation movements was considered to be a political offense. Conspiring to participate in antigovernment demonstrations or strikes, inciting others to strike, or taking part in violence associated with a strike were punishable under similar laws. Membership in the Portuguese Communist Party (Partido Comunista Português— PCP) or in any group dedicated to the violent overthrow of the government was prohibited.

After the revolution, specific laws against the PCP, which had been harshly suppressed and forced to operate clandestinely from 1926 to 1974, were voided, allowing the party to participate openly in Portugal's political life. In spite of the ban on ''fascist'' organizations, some small extreme right-wing groups function without interference. The only other remaining restriction on political activity bars simultaneous membership in more than one party.

Although Portugal holds no political prisoners, some of the radical leftist opponents of the regime have claimed that prosecutions for participating in terrorist organizations are politically motivated. Among these is the 1987 prosecution of sixty-four persons sentenced to prison because they were members of FP–25; the most notable of those sentenced was Carvalho, one of the leaders of the Revolution of 1974 (see Terrorist Groups, this ch.). According to the United States Department of State's human rights reports, there appears to be substantial evidence for the criminal charges brought in these cases, and Carvalho's conviction was upheld after appeal to the Portuguese Supreme Court of Justice.

Incidence of Crime

In general, the Portuguese are law-abiding people who respect the virtues of honesty. In addition, social discontent has been kept low by emigration, which served traditionally as a release for social pressures in both rural and urban areas. Decolonization in Africa, however, brought over 500,000 unemployed refugees to Portugal, some of whom became involved in crime. Some other young adults and discharged soldiers, unemployed and unable to emigrate, turned to crime. Nevertheless, statistics on the commission of crime between 1984 and 1988 showed an actual reduction in most categories. Drug offenses, however, increased from 1,154 to 1,782. Portugal is an important transshipment point for narcotics because of its geographic position near the North African coast and on the air routes between South America and Western Europe. Indigenous drug use and production are not, however, considered to be major problems.

Violent crimes, though not unknown in Portugal, are rare. Murders are generally crimes of passion and only infrequently associated with robbery. Premeditated homicide is punishable by a prison sentence of from sixteen to twenty years, although mitigating circumstances often lead to reduced terms. In 1988, out of a total of 513 homicide arrests, 205 were for negligent homicide; 331 of the arrested received prison terms.

Larceny is by far the most common form of crime. In 1988 over 41,000 thefts of all kinds were recorded. They included 12,800 thefts under aggravated circumstances, 4,000 armed or violent thefts, 7,400 cases of breaking and entering, and 5,300 automobile thefts. In 1988 nearly 4,000 cases of fraud and more than 17,000 cases involving bad checks were reported, although few of the latter resulted in court trials. There were 121 rapes and 165 other sexual offenses. A total of 10,800 persons were tried for crimes against the person, although only 73 of these were classified as serious attacks.

Penal System

The Portuguese penal system is under the control of the minister of justice. Portugal had thirty-nine civilian prisons and three military prisons as of 1988. The civilian prisons included twelve central prisons, twenty-four regional prisons, and three special institutions. Their total capacity was 7,633, and the actual population as of December 31, 1987, was 8,361. Of this total, 6,964 were adult males, 475 were adult females, and 922 were youths under the age of twenty-one. There were 186 military prisoners. The prison population had remained fairly stable between 1984 and 1988. By far the largest institutions were the central prisons, which had a total capacity of 4,870. The regional prison capacity was 1,758; the special prison, 706; and the military prisons, 299. Seven reformatories held 457 male youths, and 211 female juveniles were detained at three institutions. The remainder were assigned to observation and social action centers at Lisbon, Porto, and Coimbra.

The average time served in prisons by adult males is about six months. The incarceration ratio in 1990 is 83 per 100,000 population, comparable to the ratios in neighboring Spain and France but only one-fifth that of the United States.

The type of prison regime to which an offender is sentenced is designated by the district punishment court upon conviction. Youthful offenders are given opportunities to learn trades. The mastery of a trade while in prison and good behavior are considered in reducing time spent in prison. Individuals convicted three times of the same crime are considered a danger to society and are not usually eligible for parole. Unlike other prisoners, who might be allowed to do farm work, they could be kept to a strict prison regime. All prisoners earn money for their work while in prison, and work is considered a necessary part of the rehabilitation process.

Occasional complaints of individual mistreatment by police and prison authorities are investigated by the ombudsman. In 1985 a number of FP–25 prisoners engaged in periodic hunger strikes and other protests against prison conditions. A stricter regime was imposed on those remaining after ten FP–25 members accused of common crimes escaped from Lisbon's main penitentiary. The United States Department of State's human rights reports assert that no independent evidence has appeared confirming the inadequacy of prison conditions.

* * *

Among various studies analyzing Portugal's national security objectives, a particularly incisive treatment is "Portuguese Defense Policy," by Alvaro Vasconcelos. Appraising the armed forces' modernization program since the early 1980s, Vasconcelos also discusses Portugal's changing goals during several phases of its membership in the NATO alliance. *Portuguese Defense and Foreign Policy since Democratization,* edited by Kenneth Maxwell, contains a number of valuable essays on Portugal's defense policy. A full account of the involvement of the Portuguese armed forces in the political events of 1974–75 can be found in Douglas Porch's *The Portuguese Armed Forces and the Revolution.* Richard Alan Hodgson Robinson's *Contemporary Portugal* addresses the relationship between the political and military leadership during the Salazar and Caetano eras and through the revolution. Works by Tom Gallagher and Thomas C. Bruneau add observations on the interaction between the military and civilian politicians into the 1980s. The Portuguese justice system and the status of civil rights are briefly surveyed in the United States Department of State's annual *Country Reports on Human Rights Practices.*

Data on the size, organization, and armaments of the Portuguese armed forces can be found in *The Military Balance, 1992-93,* published by the International Institute for Strategic Studies in London, supplemented by information in *Jane's Fighting Ships, DMS Market Intelligence Reports,* and occasional reports in the Portuguese press. *Jane's NATO Handbook, 1990-91* contains additional information on the Portuguese defense establishment and on Portuguese links to NATO and IBERLANT. (For further information and complete citations, see Bibliography.)

Appendix

Table 1. Metric Conversion Coefficients and Factors

When you know	Multiply by	To find
Millimeters	0.04	inches
Centimeters	0.39	inches
Meters	3.3	feet
Kilometers	0.62	miles
Hectares (10,000 m²)	2.47	acres
Square kilometers	0.39	square miles
Cubic meters	35.3	cubic feet
Liters	0.26	gallons
Kilograms	2.2	pounds
Metric tons	0.98	long tons
....	1.1	short tons
....	2,204	pounds
Degrees Celsius	1.8 and add 32	degrees Fahrenheit
(Centigrade)		

Table 2. Population, Selected Years, 1801–1992 [1]
(in thousands)

Year	Population	Year	Population
1801	3,115	1950	8,510
1864	4,287	1960	8,889
1878	4,669	1970	8,663
1900	5,447	1981	9,776
1920	6,080	1989 [2]	10,337
1930	6,802	1992 [2]	10,448
1940	7,755		

[1] Includes the population of the Azores and Madeira.
[2] Estimate.

Table 3. *Estimated Population by District and Autonomous Region, December 1989*
(in thousands)

Administrative Division	Population
Districts	
Aveiro	674.4
Beja	173.2
Braga	784.8
Bragança	182.8
Castelo Branco	218.7
Coimbra	446.7
Évora	171.5
Faro	344.9
Guarda	191.8
Leiria	436.5
Lisbon	2,130.6
Portalegre	134.9
Porto	1,695.1
Santarém	459.0
Setúbal	817.9
Viana do Castelo	266.9
Vila Real	259.8
Viseu	419.4
Autonomous regions	
Azores	253.1
Madeira	275.0
TOTAL	10,337.0

Source: Based on information from Portugal, Instituto Nacional de Estatística, *Estatísticas Demográficas: Continente, Açores, e Madeira, 1989,* Lisbon, 1990, 34.

Table 4. *Selected Economic Indicators, 1960–73 and 1981–90*
(in average annual percentage changes)

	1960–73	1981–90
Gross domestic product (GDP)	6.9	2.7
Industrial production	9.0	4.8
Private consumption	6.5	2.7
Employment	– 0.5	1.4
Labor productivity *	7.4	1.3
Investment productivity	28.6	10.1
Inflation	4.0	17.9

* GDP growth rate/employment growth.

Source: Based on information from European Community, Commission, Directorate-General for Economic and Financial Affairs, *European Economy,* No. 46, Brussels, December 1990, 126, Table 1; and Organisation for Economic Co-operation and Development, *Economic Surveys: Portugal, 1991–1992,* Statistical Annex, Paris, 1992, 112.

Table 5. *Government Transactions, 1973, 1984, and 1990*
(as a percentage of GDP) [1]

	1973	1984	1990
Current account			
Revenues			
Direct taxes and social insurance contributions	10.3	17.7	20.0
Indirect taxes	10.8	15.2	15.2
Other	1.6	1.7	4.0
Total revenues	22.7	34.6	39.2
Expenditures			
Goods and services	13.2	14.4	16.2
Subsidies	1.0	7.6	1.5
Current transfers	4.8	13.6	13.4
Interest paid	0.4	7.1	8.2
Other	0.1	—	0.9
Total expenditures	19.5	42.7	40.2
Capital account			
Revenues	n.a.	0.3	1.3
Expenditures			
Investment	2.3	2.6	3.7
Capital transfers	0.9	1.6	2.0
Total expenditures	3.2	4.2	5.7
Overall balance [2]	n.a.	− 12.0	− 5.4
Lending capacity (+) or borrowing requirement(−)	1.4	− 13.4	− 6.3

—means negligible.
n.a.—not available.
[1] GDP—gross domestic product.
[2] Includes financial transactions and other adjustments.

Source: Based on information from Organisation for Economic Co-operation and Development, *Economic Survey: Portugal, 1981,* Paris, 1981, 23, Table 11; Organisation for Economic Co-operation and Development, *Economic Survey: Portugal, 1988–89,* Paris, 1989, 44, Table 15; and Organisation for Economic Co-operation and Development, *Economic Survey: Portugal, 1991–1992,* Paris, 1992, 55, Table 13.

Table 6. Composition of Labor Force by Sector, 1960,
1973, and 1990

Sector	1960 Thousands	1960 Percentage	1973 Thousands	1973 Percentage	1990 Thousands	1990 Percentage
Agriculture, forestry, and fishing	1,363	43.6	812	27.8	847	17.8
Industry, including construction ...	897	28.7	1,042	35.6	1,655	34.8
Services	866	27.7	1,072	36.6	2,254	47.4
TOTAL *	3,126	100.0	2,925	100.0	4,756	100.0

* Figures may not add to totals because of rounding.

Source: Based on information from Portugal, Secretaria-General da Assembleia Nacional, *III Plano de Fomento para 1968-1973,* Lisbon, 1967, 321; Portugal, Presidencia do Conselho, *IV Plano de Fomento, 1974-1979,* I, Lisbon, 1973, 75-76, Tables VII and XV; and Organisation for Economic Co-operation and Development, *Economic Outlook: Historical Statistics, 1960-1990,* Paris, 1992, 40-41.

Table 7. Grain Crop Yields of Selected European Countries, 1990
(in kilograms per hectare)

Crop	Portugal	Greece	Spain	West Germany	France
Cereals	1,731	2,769	2,488	5,790	6,205
Wheat	1,502	1,758	2,373	6,615	6,487
Rice	4,598	6,250	6,397	0	5,737
Barley	1,171	1,739	2,160	5,432	6,499
Corn	2,462	8,763	6,399	6,789	5,808

Source: Based on information from United Nations Food and Agriculture Organization, *Yearbook: Production, 1990,* 44, Rome, 1991, 67-80, Tables 15, 16, 17, 19, and 20.

Table 8. Collective Production Units by District, 1979

Districts	Number of Units	Total Area of Units *	Average Area per Unit *
Évora	165	392,000	2,376
Beja	80	284,258	3,553
Setúbal	78	92,000	1,179
Portalegre	61	257,000	4,213
Santarém	51	43,957	862
Lisbon, Castelo Branco, and Faro	14	11,062	790
PORTUGAL	449	1,080,277	2,406

* In hectares.

Source: Based on information from International Labour Organisation, *Employment and Basic Needs in Portugal,* Geneva, 1979, 142, Table 71.

Table 9. Foreign Trade by Country, 1985 and 1990
(in percentages)

Country	1985	1990
Exports, f.o.b. [1]		
European Community		
Britain	14.6	12.1
West Germany	13.7	16.7
France	12.7	15.5
Spain	4.1	13.3
Italy	3.9	4.0
Other	13.5	12.1
Total European Community [2]	62.5	73.7
United States	9.2	4.8
Previous Escudo Area [3]	3.9	3.4
OPEC [4]	2.5	0.6
Other	21.9	17.5
Total exports	100.0	100.0
Imports, c.i.f. [5]		
European Community		
West Germany	11.5	14.3
France	8.0	11.5
Britain	7.5	7.5
Spain	7.4	14.4
Italy	5.2	10.0
Other	6.3	11.4
Total European Community	45.9	69.1
United States	9.7	3.9
Previous Escudo Area	1.2	0.4
OPEC	17.3	6.8
Other	25.9	19.8
Total imports	100.0	100.0

[1] f.o.b.—free on board.
[2] Including figures for Spain, not yet a member.
[3] Former Portuguese colonies in Africa.
[4] Organization of the Petroleum Exporting Countries.
[5] c.i.f.—cost, insurance, and freight.

Source: Based on information from Bank of Portugal, *Report of the Directors and Economic and Financial Survey for the Year 1990,* Statistical Appendix, Lisbon, 1991, Tables 2.2.1 and 2.2.2.

Table 10. External Public Debt and Debt-Service Indicators, Selected Years, 1980-90

	1980	1982	1985	1987	1990
External debt (in millions of United States dollars)	8,978	13,464	16,682	18,464	18,434
External debt as a percentage of reserves [1]	56.3	110.5	167.2	116.6	72.2
External debt as a percentage of GDP [2]	36.3	58.8	80.4	50.3	28.9
Debt service (interest and amortization) as a percentage of current account credits ...	15.2	27.0	37.0	30.6	16.7
Interest payments as a percentage of GDP	3.0	5.6	6.5	3.3	2.9 [3]

[1] Reserves consist of gross foreign assets of the Bank of Portugal and the Treasury, with gold valued at market prices.
[2] GDP—gross domestic product.
[3] 1989.

Source: Based on information from Bank of Portugal, *Annual Report*, Lisbon, various years.

Table 11. Parliamentary Election Results, 1975-91

	1975		1976		1979		1980	
Party	Seats	Percentage of Votes	Seats	Percentage of Votes	Seats	Percentage of Votes	Seats	Percentage of Votes
PS [1]	115	37.9	107	35.0	74	27.4	74	27.8
PSD [2] ..	80	26.4	73	24.0	128	45.2	134	47.5
CDS [3] ..	16	7.6	42	15.9	— [4]	— [4]	— [4]	— [4]
PCP [5] ..	30	12.5	40	14.6	47	18.8	41	16.9
PRD [6] ..	— [7]	— [7]	— [7]	— [7]	— [7]	— [7]	— [7]	— [7]

	1983		1985		1987		1991	
Party	Seats	Percentage of Votes	Seats	Percentage of Votes	Seats	Percentage of Votes	Seats	Percentage of Votes
PS	101	36.3	57	20.8	60	22.3	72	29.3
PSD	75	27.0	88	29.9	148	50.2	135	50.4
CDS ...	30	12.4	22	10.0	4	4.4	5	4.4
PCP ...	44	18.2	38	15.5	31	12.2	17	8.8
PRD ...	— [7]	— [7]	45	17.9	7	4.9	0	0.6

[1] Partido Socialista (Socialist Party). The PS was in an electoral coalition, the Republican and Socialist Front (Frente Republicana e Socialista—FRS), with several smaller parties for the 1980 election.
[2] Partido Social Democrata (Social Democrat Party).
[3] Partido do Centro Democrático Social (Party of the Social Democratic Center).
[4] The PSD, the CDS, and two smaller parties formed an electoral coalition, the Democratic Alliance (Aliança Democrática—AD), for the 1979 and 1980 elections.
[5] Partido Comunista Português (Portuguese Communist Party). The PCP formed electoral coalitions with other leftist groups for parliamentary elections beginning in 1979: the United People's Alliance (Aliança Povo Unido—APU) for the 1980, 1983, and 1985 elections; and the Democratic Unitary Coalition (Coligação Democrático Unitário—CDU) for the 1987 and 1991 elections.
[6] Partido Renovador Democrático (Party of Democratic Renovation).
[7] The PRD was not established until 1985.

Table 12. *Major Army Equipment, 1992*

Type and Description	Country of Origin	In Inventory
Tanks		
M–47	United States	43
M–48A5	-do-	86
Armored vehicles		
M–113 personnel carriers	-do-	172
Chaimite V–200	Portugal	79
Saladin reconnaissance vehicles	Britain	8
Ferret Mk 4 scout cars	-do-	30
AML 60 armored cars	France	40
Self-propelled artillery		
155mm M–109A2 howitzers	United States	6
Towed artillery		
105mm M–101	-do-	54
105mm M–56 pack	-do-	24
5.5-inch medium guns (140mm)	Britain	24
155mm M–114 howitzers	United States	40
Coastal artillery		
150mm, 152mm, and 234mm	Britain and other	27
Mortars		
107mm M–30	United States	58
120mm	Finland	100
Antitank weapons		
90mm and 106mm recoilless rifles	United States	240
TOW missiles	-do-	48
SS–11 wire-guided missiles	France	31
Milan wire-guided missiles	-do-	45
Air defense weapons		
20mm M–163A1 Vulcan self-propelled	United States	34
20mm Rh-202	Germany	30
40mm L–60 Bofors	Sweden	322
Blowpipe surface-to-air missiles	Britain	12
Chaparral surface-to-air missiles	United States	5

Source: Based on information from *The Military Balance, 1992–1993,* London, 1992, 55; and *Jane's NATO Handbook, 1990–91,* Coulsdon, Surrey, United Kingdom, 1990, 461.

Table 13. Major Naval Equipment, 1992

Type and Description	Country of Origin	In Inventory
Frigates		
Vasco da Gama class (MEKO–200)	Germany	3
João Belo class	France	4
Baptista de Andrade class	Spain	4
João Continho class	Germany and Spain	6
Submarines		
Albacora (Daphné) class	France	3
Coastal patrol vessels		
São Roque class (converted		
minesweepers)	Portugal	2
Cacine class (large)	-do-	10
Dom Aleixo class	-do-	2
Albatroz class	-do-	6
Amphibious vessels		
Bombarda class LCT (landing craft,		
tank)	-do-	3
LDM–400 class LCM (landing craft,		
mechanized)	-do-	6
LDM–100 class LCM	-do-	3

Source: Based on information from *Jane's Fighting Ships, 1992–93,* London, 1992, 473–80.

Table 14. Major Air Force Equipment, 1992

Type and Description	Country of Origin	In Inventory
Fighter-ground attack		
A–7P Corsair (including six		
training versions)	United States	38
Alpha Jet	France and Germany	10
Fiat G–91	Italy	29
Maritime reconnaissance		
P–3P Orion	United States	6
Transport		
C–130H Hercules	-do-	6
CASA C–212 Aviocar	Spain	26
Falcon 20	France	3
Falcon 50	-do-	3
Liaison		
Reims-Cessna FTB–337G	-do-	12
Training		
Epsilon TB–30	-do-	18
Cessna T–37C	United States	23
Lockheed T–33A	-do-	7
Northrop T–38 Talon	-do-	12
RF–10 Aérospatiale	France	2
Helicopters		
SA–330 Puma	-do-	10
SA–316 Alouette III	-do-	35

Source: Based on information from *The Military Balance, 1992–93,* London, 1992, 56.

284

Bibliography

Chapter 1

Abshire, David M., and Michael Samuels (eds.). *Portuguese Africa: A Handbook.* New York: Praeger, 1969.

Boxer, Charles R. *Four Centuries of Portuguese Expansion: A Succinct Survey.* Berkeley: University of California Press, 1969.

_____. *Portuguese Society in the Tropics: The Municipal Councils of Goa, Bahia, and Luanda, 1510–1800.* Madison: University of Wisconsin Press, 1965.

Bradford, Sarah. *Portugal.* New York: Walker, 1973.

Chilcote, Ronald H. *Portuguese Africa.* Englewood Cliffs, New Jersey: Prentice-Hall, 1967.

Duffy, James. *Portuguese Africa.* Cambridge: Harvard University Press, 1968.

Figueiredo, António de. *Portugal: Fifty Years of Dictatorship.* New York: Holmes and Meier, 1975.

Gallagher, Tom. *Portugal: A Twentieth-Century Interpretation.* Manchester: Manchester University Press, 1983.

Isaacman, Allen F. *Mozambique: The Africanization of a European Institution: The Zambesi Prazos, 1750–1902.* Madison: University of Wisconsin Press, 1972.

Kay, Hugh. *Salazar and Modern Portugal.* New York: Hawthorn Books, 1970.

Livermore, H.V. *A New History of Portugal.* Cambridge: Cambridge University Press, 1969.

Marques, A.H. de Oliveira. *Daily Life in Portugal in the Late Middle Ages.* Madison: University of Wisconsin Press, 1971.

_____. *History of Portugal.* (2 vols.) New York: Columbia University Press, 1972.

Nowell, Charles. *Portugal.* Englewood Cliffs, New Jersey: Prentice-Hall, 1973.

Opello, Walter C., Jr. *Portugal: From Monarchy to Pluralist Democracy.* Boulder, Colorado: Westview Press, 1991.

Payne, Stanley G. *A History of Spain and Portugal.* (2 vols.) Madison: University of Wisconsin Press, 1973.

Porch, Douglas. *The Portuguese Armed Forces and the Revolution.* London: Croom Helm, 1977.

Raby, Dawn Linda. *Fascism and Resistance in Portugal: Communists, Liberals, and Military Dissidents in the Opposition to Salazar, 1941–1974.* Manchester: Manchester University Press, 1988.

Robinson, Richard Alan Hodgson. *Contemporary Portugal: A History.* London: George Allen and Unwin, 1979.

Stanislawski, Dan. *The Individuality of Portugal: A Study of Historical-Political Geography.* Austin: University of Texas Press, 1959.

Wheeler, Douglas L. *Republican Portugal: A Political History, 1910–1926.* Madison: University of Wisconsin Press, 1978.

Wiarda, Howard J. *Corporatism and Development: The Portuguese Experience.* Amherst: University of Massachusetts Press, 1977.

Chapter 2

Baklanoff, Eric N. *The Economic Transformation of Spain and Portugal.* New York: Praeger, 1978.

Barata, Oscar Soares. *Natalidade e política social em Portugal.* Lisbon: Universidade Tecnica de Lisboa, Instituto Superior de Ciências Sociais e Políticas, 1985.

Bentley, Jeffrey W. *Today There Is No Misery: The Ethnography of Farming in Northwest Portugal.* Tucson: University of Arizona Press, 1992.

Bermeo, Nancy. *The Revolution Within the Revolution: Workers' Control in Rural Portugal.* Princeton: Princeton University Press, 1986.

Brettell, Caroline. *Men Who Migrate, Women Who Wait.* Princeton: Princeton University Press, 1986.

———. *We Have Already Cried Many Tears: Portuguese Women and Migration.* Cambridge, Massachusetts: Schenkman, 1982.

Brøgger, Jan. *Nazaré: Women and Men in a Prebureacratic Portuguese Fishing Village.* Fort Worth, Texas: Harcourt Brace Javanovich, 1992.

Bruce, Neil. *Portugal: The Last Empire.* New York: Wiley, 1975.

Bruneau, Thomas C. "Church and State in Portugal: Crises of Cross and Sword," *Journal of Church and State,* 18, No. 3, Autumn 1976, 463–90.

Bruneau, Thomas C., and Alex Macleod. *Politics in Contemporary Portugal: Parties and the Consolidation of Democracy.* Boulder, Colorado: Lynne Rienner, 1986.

Bruneau, Thomas C., Victor M.P. Da Rosa, and Alex Macleod. *Portugal in Development: Emigration, Industrialization, and the European Community.* Ottawa: University of Ottawa Press, 1984.

Chilcote, Ronald. *Portuguese Africa.* Englewood Cliffs, New Jersey: Prentice-Hall, 1967.

Cole, Sally. *Women of the Praia: Work and Lives in a Portuguese Coastal Community.* Princeton: Princeton University Press, 1991.

Cutileiro, José. *A Portuguese Rural Society.* Oxford: Clarendon Press, 1971.

Da Costa, Alfredo Bruto. "Some Factors of Impoverishment in a Mediterranean Country: The Case of Portugal." Pages 176–91 in Paul-Marc Henry (ed.), *Poverty, Progress and Development*. London: Kegan Paul International-UNESCO, 1991.

Eisfeld, Rainer. "Portugal and Western Europe." Pages 29–62 in Kenneth Maxwell (ed.), *Portugal in the 1980s: Dilemmas of Democratic Consolidation*. (Contributions in Political Science, No. 138.) New York: Greenwood Press, 1986.

Gallagher, Tom. *Portugal: A Twentieth-Century Interpretation*. Manchester: Manchester University Press, 1983.

Graham, Lawrence S., and Harry M. Makler (eds.) *Contemporary Portugal: The Revolution and Its Antecedents*. Austin: University of Texas Press, 1979.

Graham, Lawrence S., and Douglas L. Wheeler (eds.). *In Search of Modern Portugal: The Revolution and Its Consequences*. Madison: University of Wisconsin Press, 1983.

Grande Enciclopédia Portuguesa e Brasileira, 9. Lisbon: Enciclopédia, 1987.

Kaplan, Marion. *The Portuguese: The Land and Its People*. New York: Viking Press, 1991.

Kurian, George, and Joaquim Ferreira Gomes. "Portugal." Pages 1021–27 in George Thomas Kurian (ed.), *World Education Encyclopedia*, 2. New York: Facts on File, 1988.

Livi Bacci, Massimo. *A Century of Portuguese Fertility*. Princeton: Princeton University Press, 1971.

Makler, Harry M. "A Case Study of the Portuguese Business Elite, 1964–1966." Pages 228–41 in Raymond S. Sayers (ed.), *Portugal and Brazil in Transition*. Minneapolis: University of Minnesota Press, 1968.

––––––. *A "Elite" industrial portuguesa*. Lisbon: Instituto Gulbenkian de Ciência, 1969.

Martins, Maria Belmira. *Sociedades e grupos em Portugal*. Lisbon: Editorial Estampa, 1973.

Maxwell, Kenneth (ed.). *Portugal in the 1980s: Dilemmas of Democratic Consolidation*. (Contributions in Political Science, No. 138.) New York: Greenwood Press, 1986.

––––––. *Portugal: Ten Years after the Revolution: Reports of Three Columbia-Gulbenkian Workshops*. New York: Research Institute on International Change, Columbia University, 1984.

Miranda, David J. "A População Universitária e a População Portuguesa," *Analise Social* [Lisbon], 7, Nos. 25 and 26, 1969, 158–65.

Nunes, Aderito Sedas. *Sociologia e ideologia do desenvolvimento: estúdios e ensaios*. Lisbon: Moreas, 1968.

287

O'Neill, Brian Juan. *Social Inequality in a Portuguese Hamlet: Land, Late Marriage, and Bastardy, 1870–1978.* Cambridge: Cambridge University Press, 1987.

Opello, Walter C., Jr. *Portugal: From Monarchy to Pluralist Democracy.* Boulder, Colorado: Westview Press, 1991.

————. *Portugal's Political Development: A Comparative Approach.* Boulder, Colorado: Westview Press, 1985.

Penniman, Howard (ed.). *Portugal at the Polls.* Durham, North Carolina: Duke University Press, 1992.

Pereira Neto, João Baptista Nunes, "Social Evolution in Portugal Since 1945." Pages 212–27 in Raymond S. Sayer (ed.), *Portugal and Brazil in Transition.* Minneapolis: University of Minnesota Press: 1968.

Portugal. *Constitution of the Portuguese Republic.* (Second Revision, 1989.) Lisbon: General Directorate of Mass Communication, 1991.

————. *Portugal.* Lisbon: General Directorate of Mass Communication, 1987.

————. Instituto Nacional de Estatística. *Annuário Estatístico: Continente, Açores e Madeira, 1988.* Lisbon: 1988.

————. Instituto Nacional de Estatística. *Estatísticas Demográficas: Continente, Açores, e Madeira, 1989.* Lisbon: 1990.

————. Instituto Nacional de Estatística. *Estatísticas Demográficas: Continente e Ilhas Adjacentes, 1972.* Lisbon: 1973.

Riegelhaupt, Joyce Firstenberg. "Festas and Padres: The Organization of Religious Action in a Portuguese Village," *American Anthropologist,* 75, No. 3, June 1973, 835–52.

————. "Saloio Women: An Analysis of Informal and Formal Political and Economic Roles of Portuguese Peasant Women," *Anthropological Quarterly,* 40, No. 3, July 1967, 109–26.

Robinson, Richard Alan Hodgson. *Contemporary Portugal: A History.* London: George Allen and Unwin, 1979.

Rostow, W.W. *The Stages of Economic Growth.* Cambridge: Cambridge University Press, 1960.

Sayer, Raymond S. (ed.). *Portugal and Brazil in Transition.* Minneapolis: University of Minnesota Press, 1968.

Sousa, Maria Reynolds de, and Dina Canço (eds.). *Portugal: Status of Women 1991.* Lisbon: Commission for Equality and Women's Rights, Prime Minister's Office, 1991.

Tuchman, Barbara. *The Proud Tower.* New York: Macmillan, 1966.

United Nations. Department of International Economic and Social Affairs. *World Population Policies,* 3. (Population Studies, 102/Add. 2.) New York: 1990.

United States. Department of State. *Background Notes: Portugal.* Washington: GPO, 1990.

Valente, M.O. "Portugal." Pages 564–68 in T. Neville Postlethwaite (ed.), *The Encyclopedia of Comparative and National Systems of Education.* Oxford: Pergamon Press, 1988.

————. "Portugal." Pages 4006–11 in Torsten Husen and T. Neville Postlethwaite (eds.), *The International Encyclopedia of Education: Research and Studies,* 7. Oxford: Pergamon Press, 1985.

Wiarda, Howard J. *Corporatism and Development: The Portuguese Experience.* Amherst: University of Massachusetts Press, 1977.

————. *The Iberian-Latin American Connection.* Washington: The American Enterprise Institute for Public Policy Research, 1986.

————. *The Transition to Democracy in Spain and Portugal.* Washington: The American Enterprise Institute for Public Policy Research, 1989.

World Bank. *World Development Report, 1988.* New York: Oxford University Press, 1988.

Chapter 3

Amaral, João Ferreirado, Diogo de Lucena, and António Sampaio Mello. *The Portuguese Economy Towards 1992: Proceedings of a Conference Sponsored by Junta Nacional de Investigação Científica e Tecnológica and Banco de Portugal.* Boston: Kluwer Academic, 1992.

Baklanoff, Eric N. "Changing Systems: The Portuguese Revolution and the Public Enterprise Sector," *Comparative Economic Studies,* 26, No. 2–3, Summer–Fall 1984, 63–75.

————. *The Economic Transformation of Spain and Portugal.* New York: Praeger, 1978.

————. "Spain and Portugal in the European Community: An Economic Perspective," *AEI Foreign Policy and Defense Review,* 6, No. 2, 1986, 36–45.

Bank of Portugal. *Annual Report.* Lisbon: 1991.

————. *Economic Indicators, 1975–1980.* Lisbon: 1981.

————. *Economic Indicators, 1978–1983.* Lisbon: 1984.

————. *Economic Indicators, 1981–1986.* Lisbon: 1987.

————. "Empresas públicas nao financieras," *Boletim Trimestral* [Lisbon], 4, No. 3, September 1982, 33–45.

————. *Report of the Board of Governors, 1989.* Lisbon: 1990.

————. *Report of the Board of Governors, 1990.* Lisbon: 1991.

————. *Report of the Directors and Economic and Financial Survey for the Year 1990,* Statistical Appendix. Lisbon: 1991.

Barreto, José. "Portugal: Industrial Relations under Democracy."

Pages 445–81 in Anthony Ferner and Richard Hyman (eds.), *Industrial Relations in the New Europe*. Oxford: Basil Blackwell, 1992.

Bermeo, Nancy. "The Politics of Public Enterprise in Portugal, Spain, and Greece." Pages 137–62 in Ezra N. Suleiman and John Waterbury (eds.), *The Political Economy of Public Sector Reform and Privatization*. Boulder, Colorado: Westview Press, 1990.

Bruneau, Thomas C., Victor M.P. Da Rosa, and Alex Macleod. *Portugal in Development: Emigration, Industrialization, and the European Community*. Ottawa: University of Ottawa Press, 1984.

Corkill, David. "Menos estado, melhor estado: Portugal's Privatisation." *Journal of the Association for Contemporary Iberian Studies* [London], 4, No. 1, Spring, 1991, 41–47.

Craynon, John R. "The Mineral Industry in Portugal." Pages 715–25, in *Minerals Yearbook, 1986*, 3. (Area Reports: International.) Washington: GPO, 1988.

Donges, Juergen B. *Foreign Investment in Portugal*. Reprinted from Segunda Conferência International sobre Economia Portuguesa, 1979. Lisbon: 1980.

Donges, Juergen B., et al. *The Second Enlargement of the European Community: Adjustment Requirements and Challenges for Policy Reform*. Tübingen, Germany: J.C.B. Mohr, 1982.

European Community. Commission. Directorate-General for Economic and Financial Affairs. *European Economy*. (No. 46.) Brussels: December 1990.

Harsgor, Michael. *Portugal in Revolution*. (Washington Papers, No. 32.) Beverly Hills, California: Sage, 1976.

Hudson, Mark. *Portugal to 1993: Investing in a European Future*. (Special Report, No. 1157.) London: Economist Intelligence Unit, 1989.

International Labor Organisation. *Employment and Basic Needs in Portugal*. Geneva: 1979.

Kay, Hugh. *Salazar and Modern Portugal*. New York: Hawthorne Books, 1970.

Lewis, Paul H. "Salazar's Ministerial Elite, 1932–1968," *Journal of Politics*, 40, No. 3, August 1978, 622–47.

Macedo, Jorge Bragda de, and Simon Serfaty (eds.). *Portugal since the Revolution: Economic and Political Perspectives*. Boulder, Colorado: Westview Press, 1981.

Makler, Harry M. *A "Elite" industrial portuguesa*. Lisbon: Instituto Gulbenkian de Ciência, 1969.

————. "The Portuguese Industrial Elite." Pages 147–65 in Lawrence S. Graham and Harry M. Makler (eds.), *Contemporary Portugal: The Revolution and Its Antecedents*. Austin: University of Texas Press, 1979.

Marques, Miguel A. "Why Is Portugal an Attractive Location for Investment?" *Business America,* May 20, 1991, 10-13.

Martins, Maria Belmira. *Sociedades e grupos em Portugal.* Lisbon: Editorial Estampa, 1973.

Martins, Maria Belmira, and José Chaves Rosa. *O grupo estado: Análise e listagem completa das sociedades do sector público empresarial.* Lisbon: Editora SOJOURNAL, 1979.

Maxwell, Kenneth, and Michael H. Haltzel (eds.). *Portugal: Ancient Country, Young Democracy.* Washington: The Wilson Center Press, 1990.

Morrison, Rodney J. *Portugal: Revolutionary Change in an Open Economy.* Boston: Auburn House, 1981.

Organisation for Economic Co-operation and Development. *Economic Outlook: Historical Statistics, 1960-1990.* Paris: 1992.

––––––. *Economic Survey: Portugal, 1981.* Paris: 1981.

––––––. *Economic Survey: Portugal, 1988-89.* Paris: 1989.

––––––. *Economic Survey: Portugal, 1991-1992.* Paris: 1992.

––––––. *Economic Survey: Portugal, 1991-1992,* Statistical Annex. Paris: 1992.

Palha, Ana Maria de Castro. *The Banking and Financial System in Portugal.* (Discussion paper, No. 3/1.) Lisbon: Banco de Portugal, April 1983.

Pattee, Richard. *Portugal and the Portuguese World.* Milwaukee, Wisconsin: Bruce, 1957.

Pearson, Scott R., et al. *Portuguese Agriculture in Transition.* Ithaca, New York: Cornell University Press, 1987.

Pintado, Valentina Xavier. *Structure and Growth of the Portuguese Economy.* Geneva: European Free Trade Association, 1964.

Portugal. *III Plano de Fomento para 1968-1973.* Lisbon: Secretaria General da Assembléia Nacional, 1967.

––––––. Ministry of Finance. *Estratégia de progresso controlado,* 1. Lisbon: 1987.

––––––. Ministry of Finance. Agency for Financial Analysis of the State and Public Enterprises (GAFEEP). *O financiamento de sector público.* Lisbon: n.d.

––––––. Ministry of Industry and Energy. *O sector empresarial do estado na indústria e energia: Análise e propostas de atuação.* Lisbon: 1984.

––––––. Presidência do Conselho. *IV Plano de Fomento, 1974-1979,* 1. Lisbon: Imprensa Nacional, 1973.

"Portugal's Free Trade Ties in Europe Give New Thrust to Portugal's Growth," *IMF Survey,* 3, No. 4, April 22, 1974, 119-21.

Raby, Dawn Linda. "Portugal." Pages 357-72 in Joan Campbell and John P. Windmuller (eds.), *European Labor Unions.* Westport, Connecticut: Greenwood Press, 1992.

Sanders, Thomas G. *Portuguese Migrants—International and Domestic.* (Universities Field Staff International, UFSI Reports, No. 18.) Indianapolis: 1986.

Schmitt, Hans O. *Economic Stabilization and Growth in Portugal.* (Occasional Paper, No. 2.) Washington: International Monetary Fund, April 1981.

Smith, T. Lynn. "The Social Relationship of Man to the Land in Portugal," *Revue Internationale de Sociologie* [Paris], 2, No. 2, December 1965, 1-30.

Spínola, António de. *Portugal and the Future.* Johannesburg: Perskor, 1974.

Stoleroff, Alan D. "Between Corporatism and Class Struggle: The Portuguese Labour Movement and the Cavaco Silva Governments," *West European Politics* [London], 15, No. 4, October 1992, 118-50.

Tovias, Alfred. *Foreign Economic Relations of the European Community: The Impact of Spain and Portugal.* Boulder, Colorado: Lynne Rienner, 1990.

United Nations. Food and Agriculture Organization. *Yearbook: Production, 1990,* 44. Rome: 1991.

Veiga, António Jorge da Motta. *Draft of the Third Development Plan for 1968-1973.* Lisbon: National Information Service, June 1967.

World Bank. *Portugal: Current and Prospective Economic Trends.* Washington: 1978.

Yannopolous, George N. (ed.). *European Integration and the Iberian Economies.* New York: St. Martin's Press, 1989.

(Various issues of the following publications also were used in the preparation of this chapter: *Economist* [London]; Economist Intelligence Unit, *Country Profile: Portugal* [London]; Economist Intelligence Unit, *Country Report: Portugal* [London]; *Financial Times* [London].)

Chapter 4

Agee, Warren Kendall, and Nelson Traquima. *A Frustrated Fourth Estate: Portugal's Post-Revolutionary Mass Media.* Columbia: Association for Education in Journalism and Mass Communication, College of Journalism, University of South Carolina, 1984.

"Aníbal Cavaco Silva." Pages 123-27 in *Current Biography Yearbook, 1991.* Bronx, New York: H. W. Wilson, 1991.

Barreto, José. "Portugal: Industrial Relations under Democracy." Pages 445-81 in Anthony Ferner and Richard Hyman (eds.),

Industrial Relations in the New Europe. Oxford: Basil Blackwell, 1992.

Bermeo, Nancy. "Redemocratization and Transition Elections: A Comparison of Spain and Portugal," *Comparative Politics,* 19, No. 2, January 1987, 213–31.

_____. *The Revolution Within the Revolution: Workers' Control in Rural Portugal.* Princeton: Princeton University Press, 1986.

Blaustein, Albert P., and Gisbert H. Flanz (eds.). *Constitutions of the Countries of the World.* New York: Oceana, 1991.

Bruce, Neil. *Portugal: The Last Empire.* New York: Wiley, 1975.

Bruneau, Thomas C. "Church and State in Portugal: Crises of Cross and Sword," *Journal of Church and State,* 18, No. 3, Autumn 1976, 463–90.

_____. *Politics and Nationhood: Post-Revolutionary Portugal.* New York: Praeger, 1984.

Bruneau, Thomas C., and Mário Bacalhau. *Os portuguêses e a política quatro anos depois do 25 de abril.* Lisbon: Editorial Meseta, 1978.

Bruneau, Thomas C., and Alex Macleod. *Politics in Contemporary Portugal: Parties and the Consolidation of Democracy.* Boulder, Colorado: Lynne Rienner, 1986.

Bruneau, Thomas C., Victor M.P. Da Rosa, and Alex Macleod (eds.). *Portugal in Development: Emigration, Industrialization, and the European Community.* Ottawa: University of Ottawa Press, 1984.

Calder, Carlos. "An Orange Sweep: The Portuguese General Election of 1991," *West European Politics* [London], 15, No. 2, April 1992, 167–70.

Corkill, David. "Portugal's Political Transformation: The Election of July 1987," *Parliamentary Affairs* [Oxford], 41, No. 2, April 1988, 247–57.

_____. "The Portuguese Presidential Election of 13 January 1991," *West European Politics* [London], 14, No. 4, October 1991, 185–92.

Cruz, M. Braga da, and Miguel Lobo Antunes. "Revolutionary Transition and Problems of Parliamentary Institutionalization: The Case of the Portuguese National Assembly." Pages 154–83 in Ulrike Liebert and Maruizio Cotta (eds.), *Parliament and Democratic Consolidation in Southern Europe: Greece, Italy, Portugal, Spain and Turkey.* London: Pinter, 1990.

Cunha, Carlos A. *The Portuguese Communist Party's Strategy for Power, 1921–1986.* New York: Garland, 1992.

Cutileiro, José. *A Portuguese Rural Society.* Oxford: Clarendon Press, 1971.

Eisfeld, Rainer. "Political and Economic Problems of Portugal's

Accession to the EC," *Assuntos Europeus* [Lisbon], 1982, 345–81.

Ferreira, Hugo Gil, and Michael W. Marshall (eds.). *Portugal's Revolution: Ten Years On.* Cambridge: Cambridge University Press, 1986.

Figueiredo, António de. *Portugal: Fifty Years of Dictatorship.* New York: Holmes and Meier, 1975.

Gallagher, Tom. "Goodbye to Revolution: The Portuguese Election of July 1987," *West European Politics* [London], 11, No. 1, January 1988, 140–45.

_____. *Portugal: A Twentieth Century Interpretation.* Manchester: Manchester University Press, 1983.

_____. "Portugal's Bid for Democracy: The Role of the Socialist Party," *West European Politics* [London], 2, No. 2, May 1979, 198–217.

_____. "The Portuguese Communist Party." Pages 45–65 in Bogdan Szajkowski (ed.), *Marxist Local Governments in Western Europe and Japan.* Boulder, Colorado: Lynne Rienner, 1985.

_____. "Twice Choosing the Unexpected: the Portuguese Elections of 1985 and 1986," *West European Politics* [London], 9, No. 4, October 1986, 233–37.

Gaspar, Carlos. "Portuguese Communism since 1976: Limited Decline," *Problems of Communism*, 39, No. 1, January–February 1990, 45–63.

Gladdish, Ken. "Portugal: An Open Verdict." Pages 104–25 in Geoffrey Pridham (ed.), *Securing Democracy: Political Parties and Democratic Consolidation in Southern Europe.* London: Routledge, 1990.

Graham, Lawrence S. *Portugal: The Decline and Collapse of an Authoritarian Order.* Beverly Hills, California: Sage, 1975.

Graham, Lawrence S., and Harry M. Makler (eds.). *Contemporary Portugal: The Revolution and Its Antecedents.* Austin: University of Texas Press, 1979.

Graham, Lawrence S., and Douglas L. Wheeler (eds.). *In Search of Modern Portugal: The Revolution and Its Consequences,* Madison: University of Wisconsin Press, 1983.

Gunther, Richard. "Spain and Portugal." Pages 214–64 in Gerald A. Dorfman and Peter J. Duignan (eds.), *Politics in Western Europe.* (2d ed.) Stanford, California: Hoover Institution Press, 1991.

Harvey, Robert. *Portugal: Birth of a Democracy.* London: Macmillan, 1978.

Kay, Hugh. *Salazar and Modern Portugal.* New York: Hawthorn Books, 1970.

Macleod, Alex. "Portrait of a Model Ally: The Portuguese Communist Party and the International Communist Movement, 1968-1983," *Studies in Comparative Communism,* 17, No. 1, Spring 1984, 31-52.

MacDonald, Scott B. *European Destiny, Atlantic Transformations: Portuguese Foreign Policy under the Second Republic, 1974-1992.* New Brunswick, New Jersey: Transaction, 1993.

Maxwell, Kenneth. "The Hidden Revolution in Portugal," *New York Review of Books,* 22, No. 6, April 17, 1975, 29-35.

_____. "Portugal under Pressure," *New York Review of Books,* 22, No. 9, May 29, 1975, 20-30.

_____. "The Thorns of the Portuguese Revolution," *Foreign Affairs,* 54, No. 2, January 1976, 250-70.

Maxwell, Kenneth (ed.). *Portugal in the 1980s: Dilemmas of Democratic Consolidation.* (Contributions in Political Science, No. 138.) New York: Greenwood Press, 1986.

_____. *Portugal: Ten Years after the Revolution: Reports of Three Columbia-Gulbenkian Workshops.* New York: Research Institute on International Change, Columbia University Press, 1984.

Maxwell, Kenneth, and Michael H. Haltzel (eds.). *Portugal: Ancient Country, Young Democracy.* Washington: The Wilson Center Press, 1990.

Maxwell, Kenneth, and Scott C. Monje (eds.). *Portugal: The Constitution and the Consolidation of Democracy, 1976-1989.* (Camões Center Special Report, No. 2.) New York: Camões Center, 1990.

Opello, Walter C., Jr. "Local Government and Political Culture in a Portuguese Rural County," *Comparative Politics,* 13, No. 3, April 1981, 271-89.

_____. "The New Parliament in Portugal," *Legislative Studies Quarterly,* 3, No. 2, May 1978, 309-34.

_____. *Portugal: From Monarchy to Pluralist Democracy.* Boulder, Colorado: Westview Press, 1991.

_____. "Portugal's Parliament: An Organizational Analysis of Legislative Performance," *Legislative Studies Quarterly,* 11, No. 3, August 1986, 291-319.

_____. *Portugal's Political Development: A Comparative Approach.* Boulder, Colorado: Westview Press, 1985.

_____. "The Second Portuguese Republic: Politico-Administrative Decentralization since April 25, 1974," *Iberian Studies* [Keele, Staffordshire, United Kingdom], 7, No. 1, Spring 1978, 43-48.

Pimlott, Ben. "Portugal—Two Battles in the War of the Constitution," *West European Politics* [London], 4, No. 3, October 1981, 286-96.

Porch, Douglas. *The Portuguese Armed Forces and the Revolution.* London: Croom Helm, 1977.

Raby, Dawn Linda. "Portugal." Pages 357–72 in Joan Campbell (ed.), *European Labor Unions.* Westport, Conneticut: Greenwood Press, 1992.

Robinson, Richard Alan Hodgson. *Contemporary Portugal: A History.* London: George Allen and Unwin, 1979.

Smith, Diana. *Portugal and the Challenge of 1992.* (Camões Center Special Report, No. 1.) New York: Camões Center, 1990.

Spínola, António de. *Portugal and the Future.* Johannesburg: Perskor, 1974.

Stoleroff, Alan D. "Between Corporatism and Class Struggle: The Portuguese Labour Movement and the Cavaco Silva Governments," *West European Politics* [London], 15, No. 4, October 1992, 118–50.

Wiarda, Howard J. *Corporatism and Development: The Portuguese Experience.* Amherst: University of Massachusetts Press, 1977.

_____. *Politics in Iberia: The Political Systems of Spain and Portugal.* New York: Harper Collins, 1993.

_____. *The Transition to Democracy in Spain and Portugal.* Washington: The American Enterprise Institute for Public Research, 1989.

Chapter 5

Barata, Filipe Themudo. "The Defense Industry of Portugal," *NATO's Sixteen Nations* [Brussels], (Special Issue, No. 2), 28, No. 6, 1983, 71–72, 74–75.

Bosgra, S.J., and Chr. van Krimpen. *Portugal and NATO.* Amsterdam: Angola Comité, 1972.

Brochado de Miranda, Jorge Manuel. "Air Operations in the Eastern Atlantic," *NATO's Sixteen Nations* [Brussels], 32, February–March 1987, 91–93.

Brochado de Miranda, Jorge Manuel. "Portugal." Pages 855–59 in Gregory R. Copley (ed.), *Defense and Foreign Affairs Handbook 1989.* Alexandria, Virginia: International Media, 1989.

Bruneau, Thomas C. *Politics and Nationhood: Post-Revolutionary Portugal.* New York: Praeger, 1984.

Carneiro, F. Sá. "Portugal and the North Atlantic Alliance," *Atlantic Community Quarterly,* 18, Winter 1980–81, 387–93.

Crollen, Luc. *Portugal, the United States, and NATO.* (Studies in International Relations Series.) Leuven, Belgium: Leuven University Press, 1973.

Darnton, John. "Lisbon Officers Club: Coup Makers or Breakers?" *New York Times,* February 18, 1984, A2.

Davis, Brian L. *NATO Forces: An Illustrated Reference to Their Organization and Insignia.* London: Blandford, 1988.

Defense and Foreign Affairs Handbook, 1989. (Ed., Gregory R. Copley.) Alexandria, Virginia: International Media, 1989.

Eisfeld, Rainer. "Revolutionäre und gegenrevolutionäre Bewegungen in Portugal seit 1974: Rolle und Entwicklung der Streitkräfte," *Politische Vierteljahresschrift* [Wiesbaden, Germany], 23, No. 2, July 1982, 153–77.

Gallagher, Tom. *Portugal: A Twentieth Century Interpretation.* Manchester: Manchester University Press, 1983.

Gaspar, Carlos."Portuguese Communism since 1976: Limited Decline," *Problems of Communism,* 39, No. 1, January–February 1990, 45–63.

Hammond, John L. "The Armed Forces Movement and the Portuguese Revolution: Two Steps Forward, One Step Back," *Journal of Political and Military Sociology,* 10, No. 1, Spring 1982, 71–101.

Jane's Fighting Ships, 1992–93. London: Jane's Information Group, 1992.

Jane's NATO Handbook, 1990–91. Coulsdon, Surrey, United Kingdom: Jane's Information Group, 1990.

Leitão, António Egidio de Sousa. "The Portuguese Navy," *Naval Forces* [Aldershot, Hampshire, United Kingdom], 4, No. 5, 1983, 24–29.

_____. "The Strategic Relevance of the Azores," *NATO's Sixteen Nations* [Brussels], 29, No. 1, April–May 1984.

Manwaring, Max G., and Alan Ned Sabrosky. "Iberia's Role in NATO's Future: Strategic Reserve, Reinforcement, and Redoubt," *Parameters,* 16, No. 1, Spring 1986, 48–54.

Maxwell, Kenneth (ed.). *Portuguese Defense and Foreign Policy since Democratization.* (Camões Center Special Report, No. 3.) New York: Camões Center, 1991.

Menual, Stewart. "The Geo-strategic Importance of the Iberian Peninsula," *Conflict Studies No. 133.* London: Institute for the Study of Conflict, 1981.

Midlane, Matthew. "The Spanish and Portuguese Defense Forces." Pages 126–56 in L.H. Gann (ed.), *The Defense of Western Europe.* Dover, Massachusetts: Auburn House, 1987.

_____. "Portugal." Pages 483–88 in John Keegan (ed.), *World Armies.* Detroit: Gale Research, 1983.

Miguel, Mario Firmino. "Army Support of the Southern Flank:

The First Composite Brigade," *NATO's Sixteen Nations* [Brussels], 33, October 1988, 67–68.

The Military Balance, 1990–1991. London: International Institute for Strategic Studies, 1990.

The Military Balance, 1991–1992. London: International Institute for Strategic Studies, 1991.

The Military Balance, 1992–1993. London: International Institute for Strategic Studies, 1992.

Milton, T.R. "Airpower in Iberia," *Air Force Magazine*, 69, No. 6, June 1986, 94–99.

The North Atlantic Treaty Organization: Facts and Figures. Brussels: NATO Information Service, 1989.

Pereira, Bernardo Futscher. "Portugal and Spain." Pages 63–87 in Kenneth Maxwell (ed.), *Portugal in the 1980s: Dilemmas of Democratic Consolidation.* (Constributions in Political Science, No. 138.) New York: Greenwood Press, 1986.

Platt, Alan. "NATO's Southern Flank: A Troubled Region." Pages 164–85 in Barry M. Blechman and Edward N. Luttwak (eds.), *Global Security: A Review of Strategic and Economic Issues.* Boulder, Colorado: Westview Press, 1987.

Porch, Douglas. *The Portuguese Armed Forces and the Revolution.* London: Croom Helm, 1977.

Portugal. Instituto National de Estatística. *Anuário Estatístico 1988: Continente, Açores e Madeira.* Lisbon: 1988.

"Portugal." Pages 318–20 in Thomas Kurian (ed.), *World Encyclopedia of Police Forces and Penal Systems.* New York: Facts on File, 1988.

"Portugal." Pages 344–50 in *Truppendienst Handbook: The Armies of the NATO Nations*, 3. Vienna: Herold, 1987.

"Portugal." In *DMS Market Intelligenge Reports.* Greenwich, Connecticut: Defense Market Services, 1989.

"Portuguese Air Force." Pages 385–88 in *International Air Forces and Military Aircraft Directory.* Stapleford Airfield, Essex, United Kingdom: Aviation Advisory Services, 1989.

Robinson, H. Leslie. "Portugal." Pages 613–16 in Richard F. Staar (ed.), *1989 Yearbook on International Communist Affairs.* Stanford, California: Hoover Institution Press, 1989.

Robinson, Richard Alan Hodgson. *Contemporary Portugal: A History.* London: George Allen and Unwin, 1979.

Santos, Alberto. *La Peninsula luso-iberique: Enjeu stratégique.* Paris: Fondation pour les études de défence nationale, 1980.

Sharpe, Richard (ed.). *Jane's Fighting Ships, 1992–93.* London: Jane's Information Group, 1992.

Silva, Tomás George Conceição. "Reorganization and Modernization of the Portuguese Air Force," *NATO's Sixteen Nations*
[Brussels], 36, No. 1, February 1991, 64–67.

Snyder, Jed C. *Defending the Fringe: NATO, the Mediterranean, and
the Persian Gulf.* (SAIS Papers in International Affairs, No. 11.)
Washington: Johns Hopkins Foreign Policy Institute, 1987.

Spínola, António de. *Portugal and the Future.* Johannesburg: Perskor, 1974.

Stenhouse, Mark, and Bruce George. "Portugal." Pages 40–43
in Bruce George (ed.), *Jane's NATO Handbook, 1989–90.* Coulsdon, Surrey, United Kingdom: Jane's Information Group, 1989.

Stenhouse, Mark. "Portugal." Pages 389–92 in Bruce George (ed.),
Jane's NATO Handbook, 1990–91. Coulsdon, Surrey, United
Kingdom: Jane's Information Group, 1990.

Thomas, Nigel. *NATO Armies Today.* London: Osprey, 1988.

United States. Arms Control and Disarmament Agency. *World Military Expenditures and Arms Transfers, 1989.* Washington: GPO,
1990.

_____. Department of Defense. *Terrorist Group Profiles.* Washing-
ton: GPO, 1988.

_____. Department of State. *Background Notes: Portugal.* Washing-
ton: GPO, 1990.

_____. Department of State. *Country Reports on Human Rights Prac-
tices for 1989.* (Report submitted to the United States Congress,
101st, 2d Session. House of Representatives, Committee on Foreign Affairs, and Senate, Committee on Foreign Relations.
Washington: GPO, 1990.

_____. Department of State. *Country Reports on Human Rights Prac-
tices for 1990.* Report submitted to the United States Congress,
102d, 1st Session, Senate, Committee on Foreign Relations, and
House of Representatives, Committee on Foreign Affairs.
Washington: GPO, 1991.

"Unsteady Course: Political Stability Being Attained by Inches,"
The Economist [London], 291, No. 7348, June 30, 1984, 7–10.

Vasconcelos, Alvaro. "Portugal and NATO," *NATO Review,* 34,
No. 2, April 1986, 8–14.

_____. "Portuguese Defense Policy: Internal Politics and Defence
Commitments." Pages 86–139 in John Chipman (ed.), *NATO's
Southern Allies: Internal and External Challenges.* London: Routledge,
1988.

Wigg, Richard. "Neighbors with Their Backs to Each Other."
NATO's Sixteen Nations [Brussels], (Special Issue, No. 2.), 28,
No. 6, 1983, 44–45, 48.

Williams, Louis A. "The Atlantic Connection—IBERLANT,"

NATO's Sixteen Nations [Brussels], (Special Issue, No. 2.), 28, No. 6, 1983, 30–31, 33–35, 38.

(Various issues of the following publications were also used in the preparation of this chapter: *DMS Market Intelligence Reports; Economist* [London]; Foreign Broadcast Information Service, *Daily Report: West Europe; Jane's Defence Weekly* [London]; *Jornal do Exército* [Lisbon]; *Keesing's Record of World Events; New York Times;* and *Washington Post.*)

Glossary

conto—See escudo.

Council of Europe—Founded in 1949 to foster parliamentary democracy, social and economic progress, and unity among its member states. Membership is limited to those European countries that respect the rule of law and the fundamental human rights and freedoms of all those living within their boundaries. As of 1993, its membership consisted of twenty-seven European countries.

d'Hondt method—Also known as the highest-average method of determining the allocation of seats to political parties after an election. It was devised by the Belgian Victor d'Hondt to be used in electoral systems based on proportional representation. In addition to Portugal, Austria, Belgium, Finland, and Switzerland have adopted the method. Under this procedure, voters do not choose a candidate but vote for a party, each of which has published a list of candidates. The party winning the most votes in a constituency is awarded the area's first seat, which goes to the candidate at the top of the winning party's list. The total vote of this party is then divided by two, and this amount is compared with the totals of other parties. The party with the greatest number of votes at this point receives the next seat to be awarded. Each time a party wins a seat, its total is divided by the number of seats it has won plus one. This process continues until all the seats in a constituency are awarded. The d'Hondt method slightly favors large parties. Because there is no minimum threshold for winning a seat, however, small parties can also elect representatives.

escudo—Basic Portuguese currency unit, consists of 100 centavos. 1,000 escudos are a conto. The exchange rate averaged 27.5 escudos = US$1 in 1975; 53.0 escudos = US$1 in 1980; 170.4 escudos = US$1 in 1985; 144.0 escudos = US$1 in 1988; 157.5 escudos = US$1 in 1989; 142.5 escudos = US$1 in 1990; 144.5 escudos = US$1 in 1991; and 135.0 escudos = US$1 in 1992.

European Community (EC—also commonly called the Community)—The EC comprises three communities: the European Coal and Steel Community (ECSC), the European Economic Community (EEC), and the European Atomic Energy Community (EURATOM). Each community is a legally distinct body, but since 1967 they have shared common governing institutions. The EC forms more than a framework for free trade and economic cooperation: the signatories to the treaties governing the communities have agreed in principle to integrate their economies and ultimately to form a political union. Belgium, France, Italy, Luxembourg, the Netherlands, and the Federal Republic of Germany (West Germany) are charter members of the EC. Britain, Denmark, and Ireland joined on January 1, 1973; Greece became a member on January 1, 1981; and Portugal and Spain entered on January 1, 1986.

European Currency Unit (ECU)—Instituted in 1979, the ECU is the unit of account of the EC (*q.v.*). The value of the ECU is determined by the value of a basket that includes the currencies of all EC member states. In establishing the value of the basket, each member's currency receives a share that reflects the relative strength and importance of the member's economy. On September 30, 1992, one ECU was equivalent to US$1.40.

European Economic Community (EEC)—See EC.

European Free Trade Association (EFTA)—Founded in 1961, EFTA aims at supporting free trade among its members and increasing the liberalization of trade on a global basis, but particularly within Western Europe. In 1993 the organization's member states were Austria, Finland, Iceland, Norway, Sweden, and Switzerland.

gross domestic product (GDP)—The total value of goods and services produced by the domestic economy during a given period, usually one year. Obtained by adding the value contributed by each sector of the economy in the form of profits, compensation to employees, and depreciation (consumption of capital). Most GDP usage in this book is based on GDP at factor cost. Real GDP is the value of GDP when inflation has been taken into account.

gross national product (GNP)—Obtained by adding GDP (*q.v.*) and the income received from abroad by residents less payments remitted abroad to nonresidents. GNP valued at market prices is used in this book. Real GNP is the value of GNP when inflation has been taken into account.

International Monetary Fund (IMF)—Established along with the World Bank (*q.v.*) in 1945, the IMF is a specialized agency affiliated with the United Nations (UN) that takes responsibility for stabilizing international exchange rates and payments. The main business of the IMF is the provision of loans to its members when they experience balance-of-payment difficulties. These loans often carry conditions that require substantial internal economic adjustments by the recipients.

liberation theology—An activist movement led by Roman Catholic clergy who trace their inspiration to Vatican Council II (1965), where some church procedures were liberalized, and the Second Latin American Bishops' Conference in Medellín (1968), which endorsed greater direct efforts to improve the lot of the poor. Advocates of liberation theology—sometimes referred to as "liberationists"—work mainly through Christian Base Communities (Comunidades Eclesiásticas de Base—CEBs). Members of CEBS meet in small groups to reflect on scripture and discuss its meaning in their lives. They are introduced to a radical interpretation of the Bible, one that employs Marxist terminology to analyze and condemn the wide disparities between the wealthy elite and the impoverished masses in most underdeveloped countries. This reflection often leads members to organize to improve their living standards through cooperatives and civic improvement projects.

Organisation for Economic Co-operation and Development (OECD)—Established in 1961 to replace the Organisation for European Economic Co-operation, the OECD is an international organization composed of the industrialized market economy countries (twenty-four full members as of 1993). It seeks to promote economic and social welfare in member countries, as well as in developing countries, by providing a forum in which to formulate and to coordinate policies.

rotativismo—The alternation of political factions at regular intervals with little or no change to the political system as a whole.

single market—The Single European Act of 1987 committed the EC *(q.v.)* to gradually reduce restrictions so that by the end of 1992 the EC would constitute a single market in which the free movement of goods, persons, and capital was guaranteed.

VAT—Value-added tax. A tax applied to the additional value created at a given stage of production and calculated as a percentage of the difference between the product value at that stage and the cost of all materials and services purchased as inputs. The VAT is the primary form of indirect taxation applied in the EEC *(q.v.)*, and it is the basis of each country's contribution to the community budget.

Western European Union (WEU)—Founded in 1948 to facilitate West European cooperation in economic, social, cultural, and defense matters. Reactivated in 1984 to concentrate on the defense and disarmament concerns of its nine members (Belgium, France, Germany, Italy, Luxembourg, the Netherlands, Portugal, Spain, and Britain), the WEU is headed by a council consisting of its members' ministers of foreign affairs and defense. The council meets twice a year; lower-level WEU entities meet with greater frequency.

World Bank—Informal name used to designate a group of four affiliated international institutions: the International Bank for Reconstruction and Development (IBRD), the International Development Association (IDA), the International Finance Corporation (IFC), and the Multilateral Investment Guarantee Agency (MIGA). The IBRD, established in 1945, has the primary purpose of providing loans to developing countries for productive projects. The IDA, a legally separate loan fund administered by the staff of the IBRD, was set up in 1960 to furnish credits to the poorest developing countries on much easier terms than those of conventional IBRD loans. The IFC, founded in 1956, supplements the activities of the IBRD through loans and assistance designed specifically to encourage the growth of productive private enterprises in less developed countries. The president and certain senior officers of the IBRD hold the same positions in the IFC. The four institutions are owned by the governments of the countries that subscribe their capital. To participate in the World Bank group, member states must first belong to the IMF (*q.v.*).

Index

abortion, xxxiv, 82, 99, 204
Abrilada revolt (1824), 44
Accão Nacional Popular (ANP). *See* National Popular Action
ACDA. *See* United States Arms Control and Disarmament Agency
AD. *See* Democratic Alliance
Afonsine Ordinances, 22
Afonso (duke of Bragança), 22, 23
Afonso II, 12; landownership under, 16; royal patrimony under, 16
Afonso III, 12, 13
Afonso IV, 18, 19
Afonso V, 22, 23; explorations under, 26; Moroccan campaigns of, 26
Afonso VI, 37
Afonso Henriques: background of, 9; becomes king, 10; land distribution by, 12; political organization under, 13–16; religious administration under, 14–15, 96; royal council of, 13; settler communities under, 12; social organization under, 13–16; territorial administration under, 14; territorial enlargement by, 10–12
afrancesados, 43
Africa, 213–14; armed forces in, xxv, 60, 227–34; decolonization of, xxvii, 233; emigration to, 78; exploration of coast of, 25–26; exploration of interior of, 48–49; partition of, 49; Portuguese living in, 78; returnees from, xxviii, 73, 75, 78–79, 95, 122, 136–37, 177
Africa, North: relations with, 218, 238
African campaigns, 171, 213–14, 230, 263; arms supplied for, 232; deaths in, 228, 229; military morale in, 229; opposition to, 230–31
African Party for the Independence of Guinea and Cape Verde (PAIGC), 213–14, 228
AFSOUTH. *See* Allied Land Forces Southern Europe
agrarian reform, 143–44, 174, 209
Agrarian Reform Law (1975), 143
Agrarian Reform Law (1988), 144
agricultural: development, 18, 40; estates, 91, 124, 184; labor, 16, 143; policy,

144; prices, 144; production, xxxii, 140, 142; zones, 140–41
Agricultural Institute, 104
agricultural products (*see also under individual crops*): Brazilian, 38; exports of, 156; grain, 141; tree crops, 70, 140, 141, 142
agriculture: decollectivization of, 116, 143–44, 209; in early history, 4, 5, 6, 7, 8, 16; employment in, xxxii, 134, 136, 137; expansion of, 38, 40, 120; export crops, 141; northern, 140–41; as percentage of gross domestic product, 120, 123, 139; productivity of, xxxii, 116, 140; suitability for, 70
AIP. *See* Portuguese Industrial Association
Air College, 249
air force, 238, 246–49; bases, 246; conscripts, 246, 252; downsizing of, 249; insignia, 253; matériel, 246–48; mission of, 246; modernization plan, 249; number of personnel, 239, 246; origins of, 246; pilot shortage in, 249; ranks, 253; reorganized, 223; in Spanish Civil War, 246; spending on, 256; training, 249; uniforms, 253; in World War I, 246
Air Force Academy, 249, 253
Alans, 6
Albuquerque, Afonso de, 31–32
Alcalar necropolis, 4
aldeamentos, 227
Alentejo, 10, 13, 16, 67–68; capture of, 10, 12; farmers in, 67, 91, 141; landowners in, 88, 204; topography of, 67, 140, 141
Alexander VI (pope), 32
Alfonso VI, 9
Alfonso VII, 9, 10
Alfonso VIII of Castile, 12
Alfonso XI, 19
Algarve, 7, 12, 67, 68; geography of, 69, 141; Muslim influence in, 7, 67; topography of, 140; tourism in, 67
Aliança Democráca (AD). *See* Democratic Alliance
Aliança Seguradora, 155

in, 206; modernization of, 192; professionalization of, 51; professors as employees of, 107; proliferation of jobs in, 122, 192; reform of, 192; selection for employment in, 192
civil war, 53
clergy: categories of, 15; disputes of, with nobility, 16; in early history, 15; land owned by, 16; privileges of, 15
climate, 4, 69; rainfall, 4
CNP. *See* Companhia Nacional de Petroquímica
coal, 149
coastline, 66
Cochin, 31; Jesuits in, 33
Code of Military Justice, 250
Coimbra, 10, 13; French sack of, 42; population of, 74
collectivization, xxvii, 91, 143, 174
Colonial Act of 1930, 59–60
colonies (*see also under individual colonies*): Asian, 32; development in, 58; establishment of, 67; as factor in economy, xxiv, 119; granted independence, xxvii, 124, 172, 213; investment in, 121; policies in, 226–27; relations with, 214; self-supporting, 59–60
colonies, African, 25–26, 48–49, 265; determination to retain, xxv; emigration to, 78; immigrants from, 95–96; independence gained by, xxvii, 78, 213; independence struggle in, 119; Portuguese living in, 78; returnees from, xxviii, 95
commerce, 150–52; employment in, 150; middle class in, 206; retail, 150
Commission for Equality and Women's Rights (*see also* Commission on the Status of Women), xxxv, 83
Commission on the Status of Women (*see also* Commission for Equality and Women's Rights), 83
Commission to Control Data, 266
Common Agricultural Policy (CAP), 115, 144
commoners: categories of, 16; in early history, 16
Common External Tariff, 115
communications, 152
Companhia de Seguros de Créditos (Cosec), 155
Companhia de Seguros Tranquilidade, 155

Companhia Nacional de Petroquímica (CNP), 147
Companhia União Fabril (CUF): nationalized, 125
concelhos. See settler communities
Concordat of 1940, 83, 98
Confederação de Indústria Portuguesa (CIP). *See* Confederation of Portuguese Industry
Confederação do Comércio Português (CCP). *See* Portuguese Confederation of Commerce
Confederação Geral dos Trabalhadores Portugueses-Intersindical Nacional (CGTP-IN). *See* General Confederation of Portuguese Workers-National Intersindical
Confederation of Portuguese Industry (CIP), 206
Conference of Samora, 10
Congo, 227
Congregationalists, 102
Congress of the Republic, 51
Constituent Assembly, xxvii, 47, 181; elections for, 168, 174, 233
Constitutional Charter, 45; nullified, 46
Constitutional Court, xxviii–xxix, 190, 208; appointments to, 188; created, 183
constitution of 1822, 44; reestablished, 46
constitution of 1838, 47
constitution of 1933, 56
constitution of 1976, xxvii, 181; amendments to, xxviii, 168, 178–79, 182–83, 208; armed forces under, 182, 224, 234–36; cabinet under, 186; church under, 98–99; civil rights under, 268; civil service under, 191; controversy over, 182; drafting committee for, 168; economy under, 128; education under, 105; equal rights for women under, 82; executive under, 182; judiciary under, 190–91; parliament under, 182; police under, 262; president under, xxvii, 182, 183–85; prime minister under, 185–86; promulgated, 176, 181; separation of church and state in, 96, 98–99; women under, 82, 83
construction, 147; growth of, 120; of housing, 110; as percentage of gross domestic product, 120, 121; to support tourism, 150
consumer groups, 129
consumption, 121; growth of, 122

Sines: industry in, 146, 161; port of, 152

SIRP. *See* Intelligence System of the Republic of Portugal

SIS. *See* Security Intelligence Service

Sistema de Informações da República Portuguesa (SIRP). *See* Intelligence System of the Republic of Portugal

Six-Year Plan for National Development (1959–64), 119

slaves, 16, 25; importation of, 38; trade in, 48

Soares, Mário Alberto Nobre Lopes, xxvi, 175; exiled, 199; popularity of, 209; as president, 168–69, 180, 234; as prime minister, xxix, 176, 179; qualities of, 184–85; return from exile, 171–72, 199

social classes, 85–94; changes in, 88, 94; divisions among, 65; in early history, 15; identification of, 92; impact of 1974 revolution on, 89–90; mobility among, 65, 85, 92, 120, 127; organization of, 85; perpetuation of, 86–88

Social Democrat Party (PSD) (*see also* Popular Democrat Party), xxix, xxxi, 168, 199–200, 206; origins of, 200; support for, 91, 186, 200, 208, 210

Socialist Party (PS), 167, 199; in elections, xxviii, 176, 178, 179, 210; leaders of, exiled, 199; origins of, 199; peasants in, 207; platform of, xxi, 199; in provisional governments, 174; in Revolution of 1974, xxvi, 171–72, 174; support for, 91, 199

social revolution, 21–22

social structure, 85–94

society: changes in, xxxiv–xxxv, 65, 167, 170; effect of European Community membership on, 133, 215

Society of Jesus. *See* Jesuits

Socotra Island, 31

Soult, Nicholas, 42

Sousa, Caetano de, 39

Sousa, Martim Afonso de, 32

Sousa, Tomé de, 32, 33

South Korea. *See* Korea, Republic of

Soviet Union, 237; matériel from, for African insurgents, 232

Spain: annexation of Portugal by, 35; fear of reannexation by, 37, 66, 215; investment from, 161; matériel from, 245, 248; as member of North Atlantic Treaty Organization, 216, 258; rela-

tions with, 215–16; tourists from, 150; trade with, 116, 157; war of, with France, 41

Spanish Civil War (1936–39), 59; aid to, 226; participation in, 226, 246

Special Forces Brigade, 223, 241–42; personnel of, 242

Specific Plan for the Development of Portuguese Agriculture (PEDAP), 160

Specific Plan for the Development of Portuguese Industry (PEDIP), 160

spices: cultivation of, 38; trade in, 23–24

Spínola, António de, xxvi, 61, 171–74; book by, 171, 213, 232; as governor of Portuguese Guinea, 228; as head of Junta of National Salvation, 232; objectives of, 124–25; as president, 124, 172; resignation of, 233

state enterprises: abolished, 41

state of emergency, 176

Straits of Gibraltar, 238, 257

strategic triangle (Portugal-Madeira-Azores triangle), 223, 237–38

students: political activities of, 198; political role of, 206–7

suffrage. *See* voting rights

sugar: as Brazilian export crop, 32

Sunda Islands: spice trade in, 31, 31

Superior Council of Finance, 187

Superior Council of the Administrative and Fiscal Courts, 190

Superior Intelligence Council, 266

Supreme Administrative Court, 190

Supreme Allied Commander Atlantic (SACLANT), 216, 258

Supreme Allied Commander Europe (SACEUR), 216

Supreme Court of Administration, 190

Supreme Court of Justice, 190

Swabians, 6; defeat of, 7; legacy of, 6

Switzerland: Portuguese guestworkers in, 79

Tabaqueira, 126

Tagus River, 4, 69, 140, 141, 142

Tanzania, 31

TAP. *See* Transportes Aéreos Portugueses

tariff system, 119

Tariq ibn Ziyad, 7

taxes: evasion of, 131; increase in revenue from, 132; local, 194; to pay for reforms, 104; under Spanish occupation,

Contributors

Eric N. Baklanoff is Research Professor of Economics Emeritus at the University of Alabama.

Walter C. Opello, Jr. is Chairman of Political Science at the State University of New York at Oswego.

Eric Solsten is Senior Research Specialist in West European Affairs, Federal Research Division, Library of Congress.

Jean R. Tartter is a retired Foreign Service Officer, who has written extensively on Western Europe for Country Study volumes.

Howard J. Wiarda is Professor of Political Science at the University of Massachusetts/Amherst.

Published Country Studies

(Area Handbook Series)

550-65	Afghanistan	550-87	Greece
550-98	Albania	550-78	Guatemala
550-44	Algeria	550-174	Guinea
550-59	Angola	550-82	Guyana and Belize
550-73	Argentina	550-151	Honduras
550-169	Australia	550-165	Hungary
550-176	Austria	550-21	India
550-175	Bangladesh	550-154	Indian Ocean
550-170	Belgium	550-39	Indonesia
550-66	Bolivia	550-68	Iran
550-20	Brazil	550-31	Iraq
550-168	Bulgaria	550-25	Israel
550-61	Burma	550-182	Italy
550-50	Cambodia	550-30	Japan
550-166	Cameroon	550-34	Jordan
550-159	Chad	550-56	Kenya
550-77	Chile	550-81	Korea, North
550-60	China	550-41	Korea, South
550-26	Colombia	550-58	Laos
550-33	Commonwealth Caribbean, Islands of the	550-24	Lebanon
550-91	Congo	550-38	Liberia
550-90	Costa Rica	550-85	Libya
550-69	Côte d'Ivoire (Ivory Coast)	550-172	Malawi
550-152	Cuba	550-45	Malaysia
550-22	Cyprus	550-161	Mauritania
550-158	Czechoslovakia	550-79	Mexico
550-36	Dominican Republic and Haiti	550-76	Mongolia
550-52	Ecuador	550-49	Morocco
550-43	Egypt	550-64	Mozambique
550-150	El Salvador	550-35	Nepal and Bhutan
550-28	Ethiopia	550-88	Nicaragua
550-167	Finland	550-157	Nigeria
550-155	Germany, East	550-94	Oceania
550-173	Germany, Fed. Rep. of	550-48	Pakistan
550-153	Ghana	550-46	Panama

329

550–156	Paraguay		550–53	Thailand
550–185	Persian Gulf States		550–89	Tunisia
550–42	Peru		550–80	Turkey
550–72	Philippines		550–74	Uganda
550–162	Poland		550–97	Uruguay
550–181	Portugal		550–71	Venezuela
550–160	Romania		550–32	Vietnam
550–37	Rwanda and Burundi		550–183	Yemens, The
550–51	Saudi Arabia		550–99	Yugoslavia
550–70	Senegal		550–67	Zaire
550–180	Sierra Leone		550–75	Zambia
550–184	Singapore		550–171	Zimbabwe
550–86	Somalia			
550–93	South Africa			
550–95	Soviet Union			
550–179	Spain			
550–96	Sri Lanka			
550–27	Sudan			
550–47	Syria			
550–62	Tanzania